RUDE, CRUDE, AND TATTOOED

Also by Jerry Scott and Jim Borgman

Zits: Sketchbook 1
Growth Spurt: Zits Sketchbook 2
Don't Roll Your Eyes at Me, Young Man!: Zits Sketchbook 3
Are We an "Us"?: Zits Sketchbook 4
Zits Unzipped: Zits Sketchbook 5
Busted!: Zits Sketchbook 6
Road Trip: Zits Sketchbook 7
Teenage Tales: Zits Sketchbook No. 8
Thrashed: Zits Sketchbook No. 9
Pimp My Lunch: Zits Sketchbook No. 10
Are We Out of the Driveway Yet? Zits Sketchbook No. 11

Treasuries
Humongous Zits
Big Honkin' Zits
Zits: Supersized
Random Zits
Crack of Noon

RUDE, CRUDE, AND TATTOOED

Zits Sketchbook 12

by Jerry Scott and Jim Borgman

Andrews McMeel
Publishing, LLC

Kansas City

Zits® is syndicated internationally by King Features Syndicate, Inc. For information, write King Features Syndicate, Inc., 300 West Fifty-Seventh Street, New York, New York 10019.

09 10 11 BBG 10 9 8 7 6 5 4 3 2

ISBN-13: 978-0-7407-6357-1
ISBN-10: 0-7407-6357-1

Library of Congress Control Number: 2006937455

Zits® may be viewed online at
www.kingfeatures.com.

www.andrewsmcmeel.com

To Lonnie, for dragging me kicking and screaming toward physical fitness.
— J.S.

To Rob and Lynne, battle-hardened veterans of the *Zits* years.
—J.B.

Zits

by JERRY SCOTT and JIM BORGMAN

WHAT CAN YOU TELL ME ABOUT THE TV IN YOUR BEDROOM, DAD?

THE PORTABLE?

WELL, WE HAD IT IN THE KITCHEN FOR YEARS, THEN WE MOVED IT IN HERE BECAUSE IT FITS ON THE SHELF FAIRLY WELL.

WHY "FAIRLY WELL"?

THE SIZE OF THE PICTURE TUBE MAKES IT STICK OUT OVER THE EDGE A LITTLE.

WHAT SIZE IS THE SCREEN?

I DUNNO... FIFTEEN INCHES?

IT'S FOURTEEN. WHY DOES IT HAVE ALL OF THOSE NUMBERED BUTTONS ON THE FRONT?

THAT'S HOW YOU CHANGE THE CHANNEL AND STUFF.

NOT WITH THE REMOTE?

THIS TV DIDN'T COME WITH A REMOTE.

GASP!

NO WAY!

NOW WE'LL CONTINUE OUR LOOK BACKWARD IN TIME WITH A PEEK AT MY DAD'S WARDROBE!

CLICK!

REMIND ME AGAIN WHY WE WANTED CHILDREN...

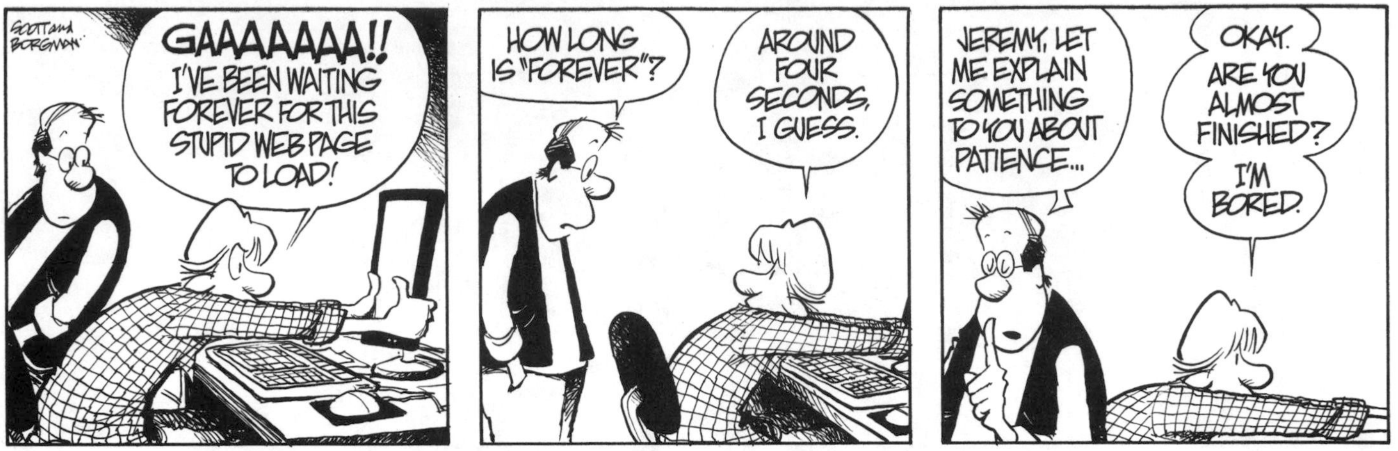
GAAAAAAA!!
I'VE BEEN WAITING FOREVER FOR THIS STUPID WEB PAGE TO LOAD!
HOW LONG IS "FOREVER"?
AROUND FOUR SECONDS, I GUESS.
JEREMY, LET ME EXPLAIN SOMETHING TO YOU ABOUT PATIENCE...
OKAY.
ARE YOU ALMOST FINISHED?
I'M BORED.

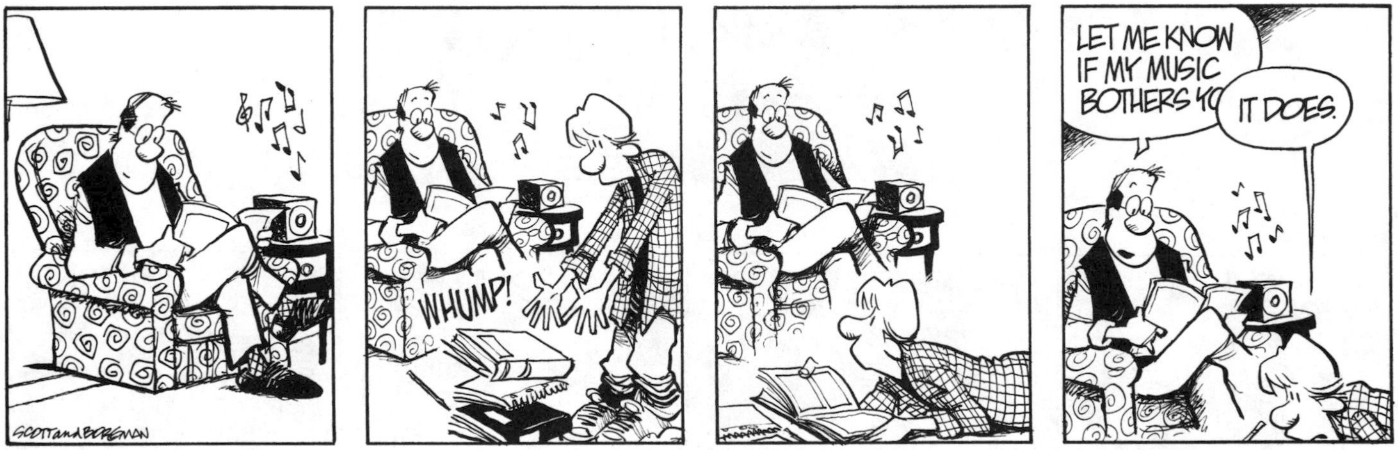
WHUMP!
LET ME KNOW IF MY MUSIC BOTHERS YO
IT DOES.

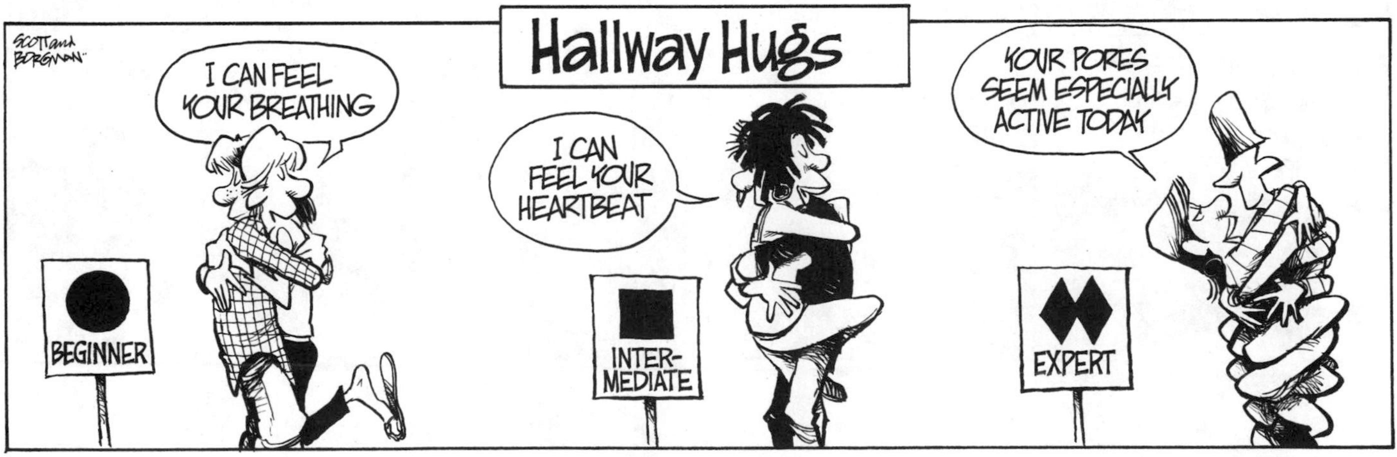
Hallway Hugs
I CAN FEEL YOUR BREATHING
BEGINNER
I CAN FEEL YOUR HEARTBEAT
INTER-
MEDIATE
YOUR PORES SEEM ESPECIALLY ACTIVE TODAY
EXPERT

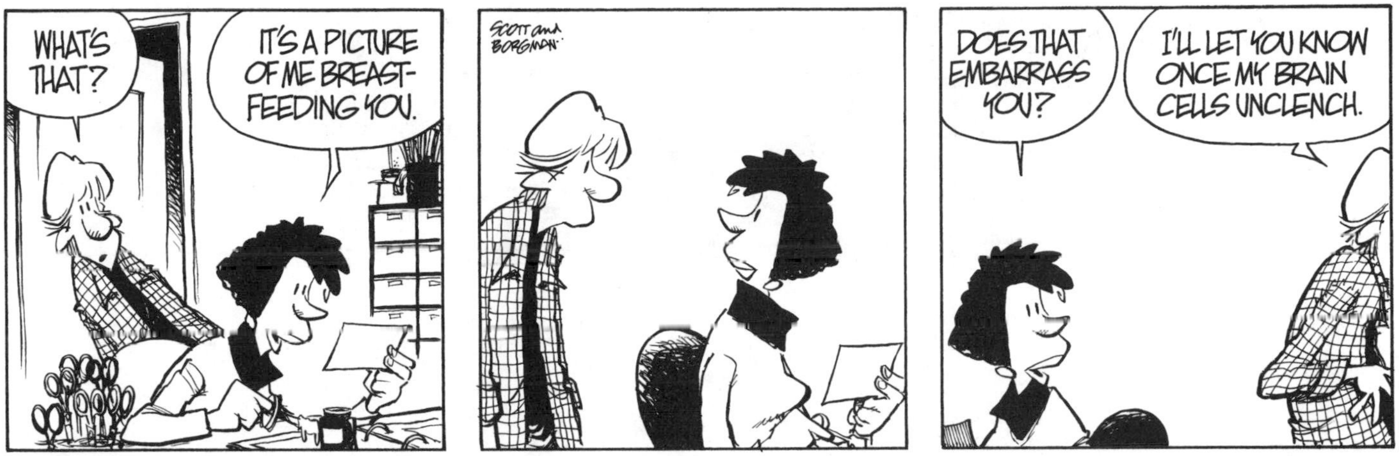
WHAT'S THAT?
IT'S A PICTURE OF ME BREAST-FEEDING YOU.
DOES THAT EMBARRASS YOU?
I'LL LET YOU KNOW ONCE MY BRAIN CELLS UNCLENCH.

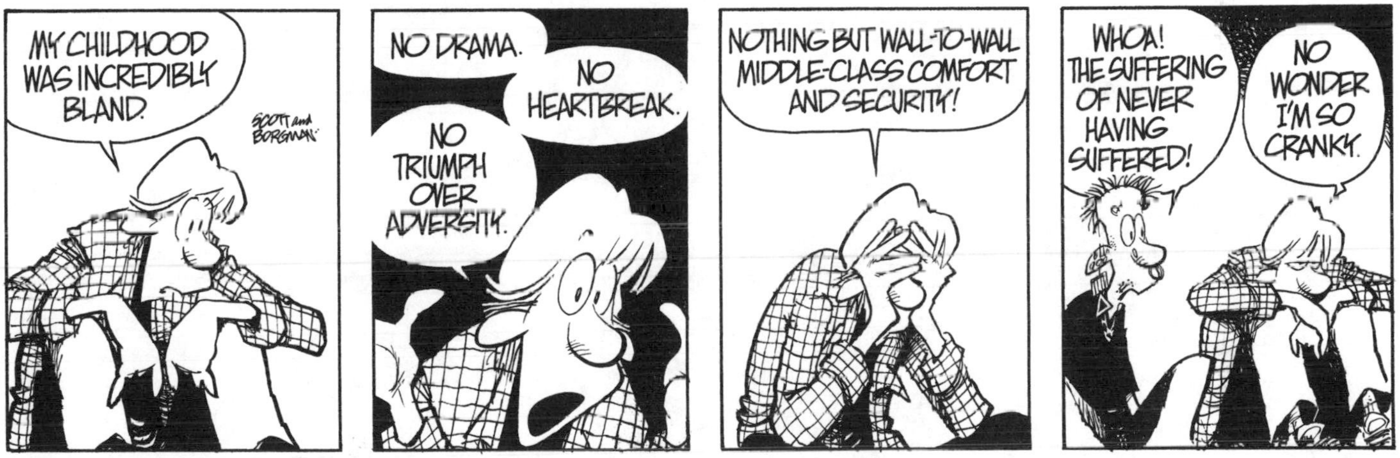
MY CHILDHOOD WAS INCREDIBLY BLAND.
NO DRAMA.
NO HEARTBREAK.
NO TRIUMPH OVER ADVERSITY.
NOTHING BUT WALL-TO-WALL MIDDLE-CLASS COMFORT AND SECURITY!
WHOA! THE SUFFERING OF NEVER HAVING SUFFERED!
NO WONDER I'M SO CRANKY.

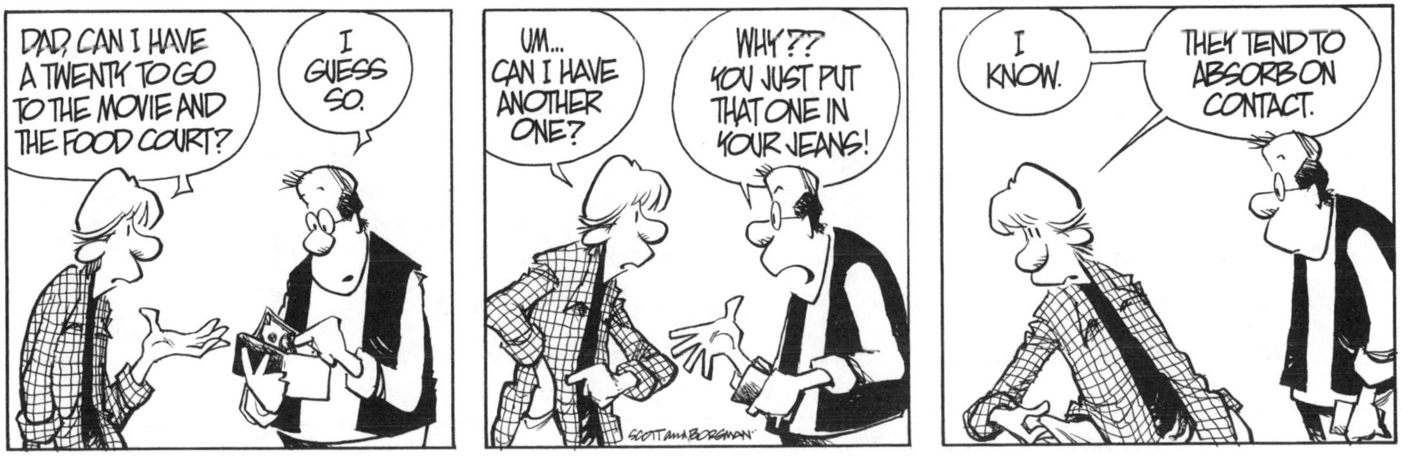
DAD, CAN I HAVE A TWENTY TO GO TO THE MOVIE AND THE FOOD COURT?
I GUESS SO.
UM... CAN I HAVE ANOTHER ONE?
WHY?? YOU JUST PUT THAT ONE IN YOUR JEANS!
I KNOW.
THEY TEND TO ABSORB ON CONTACT.

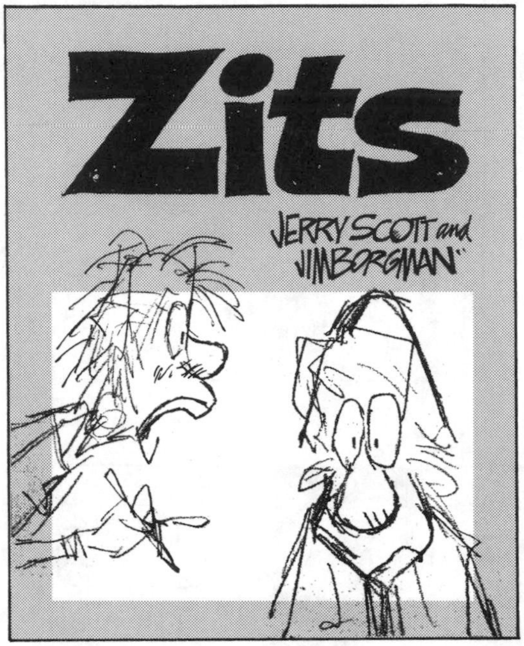
Zits
JERRY SCOTT and JIM BORGMAN

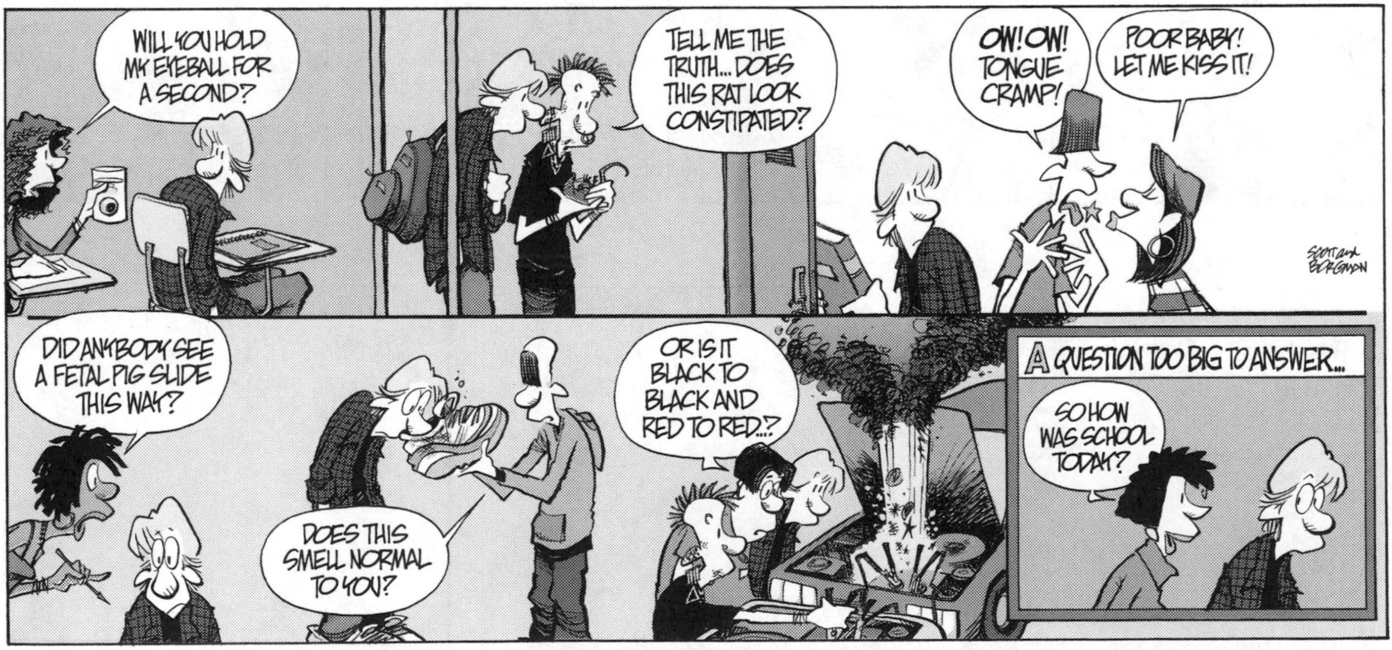
WILL YOU HOLD MY EYEBALL FOR A SECOND?
TELL ME THE TRUTH... DOES THIS RAT LOOK CONSTIPATED?
OW! OW! TONGUE CRAMP!
POOR BABY! LET ME KISS IT!
SCOTT and BORGMAN
DID ANYBODY SEE A FETAL PIG SLIDE THIS WAY?
DOES THIS SMELL NORMAL TO YOU?
OR IS IT BLACK TO BLACK AND RED TO RED...?
A QUESTION TOO BIG TO ANSWER...
SO HOW WAS SCHOOL TODAY?

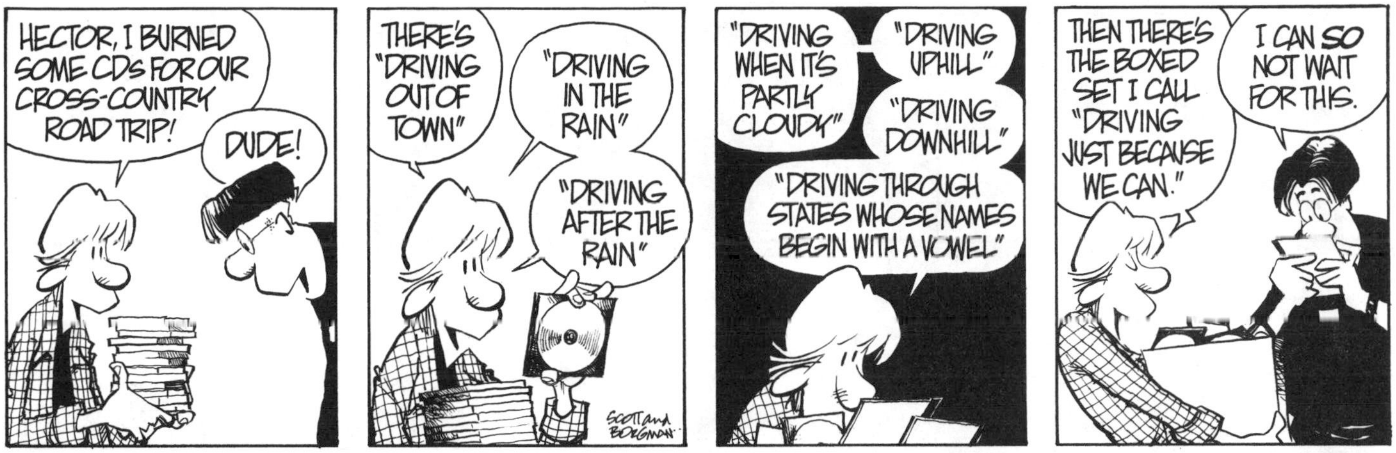
HECTOR, I BURNED SOME CDs FOR OUR CROSS-COUNTRY ROAD TRIP!
DUDE!
THERE'S "DRIVING OUT OF TOWN"
"DRIVING IN THE RAIN"
"DRIVING AFTER THE RAIN"
SCOTT and BORGMAN
"DRIVING WHEN IT'S PARTLY CLOUDY"
"DRIVING UPHILL"
"DRIVING DOWNHILL"
"DRIVING THROUGH STATES WHOSE NAMES BEGIN WITH A VOWEL"
THEN THERE'S THE BOXED SET I CALL "DRIVING JUST BECAUSE WE CAN."
I CAN SO NOT WAIT FOR THIS.

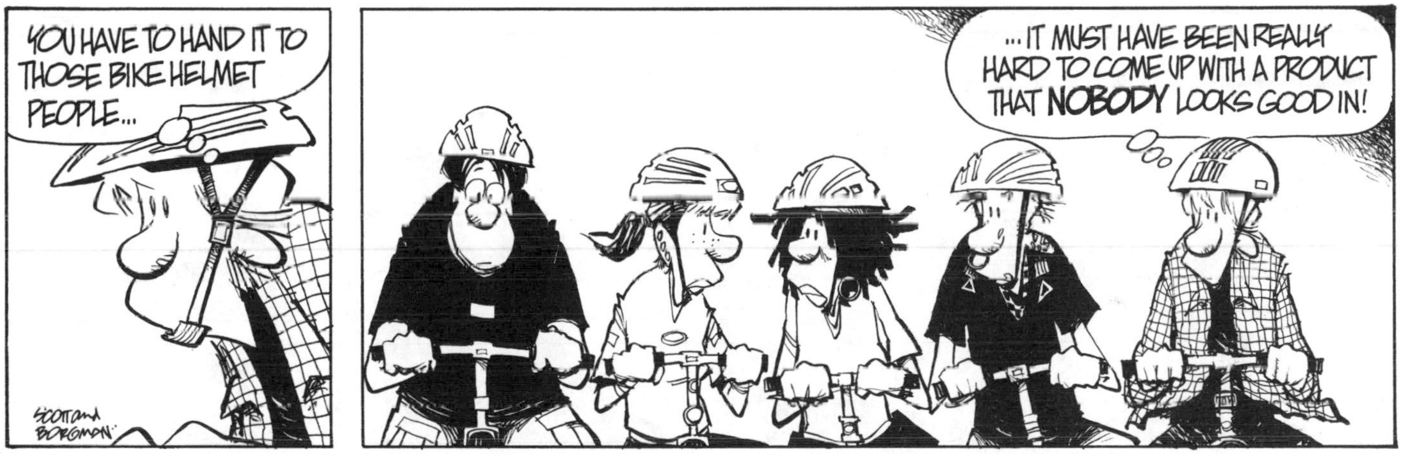
YOU HAVE TO HAND IT TO THOSE BIKE HELMET PEOPLE...
SCOTT and BORGMAN
...IT MUST HAVE BEEN REALLY HARD TO COME UP WITH A PRODUCT THAT NOBODY LOOKS GOOD IN!

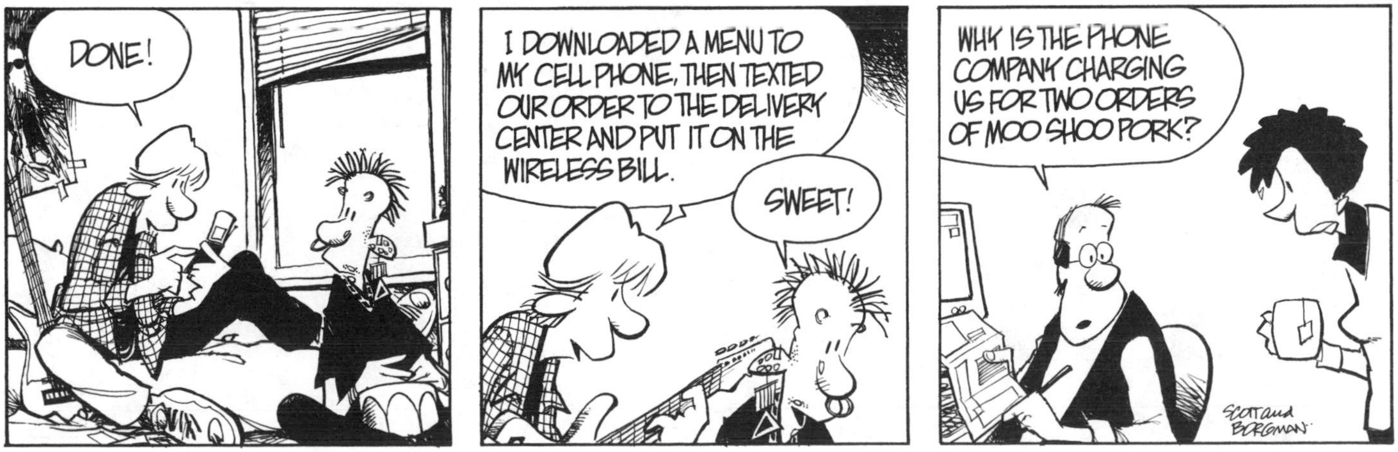
DONE!
I DOWNLOADED A MENU TO MY CELL PHONE, THEN TEXTED OUR ORDER TO THE DELIVERY CENTER AND PUT IT ON THE WIRELESS BILL.
SWEET!
WHY IS THE PHONE COMPANY CHARGING US FOR TWO ORDERS OF MOO SHOO PORK?
SCOTT and BORGMAN

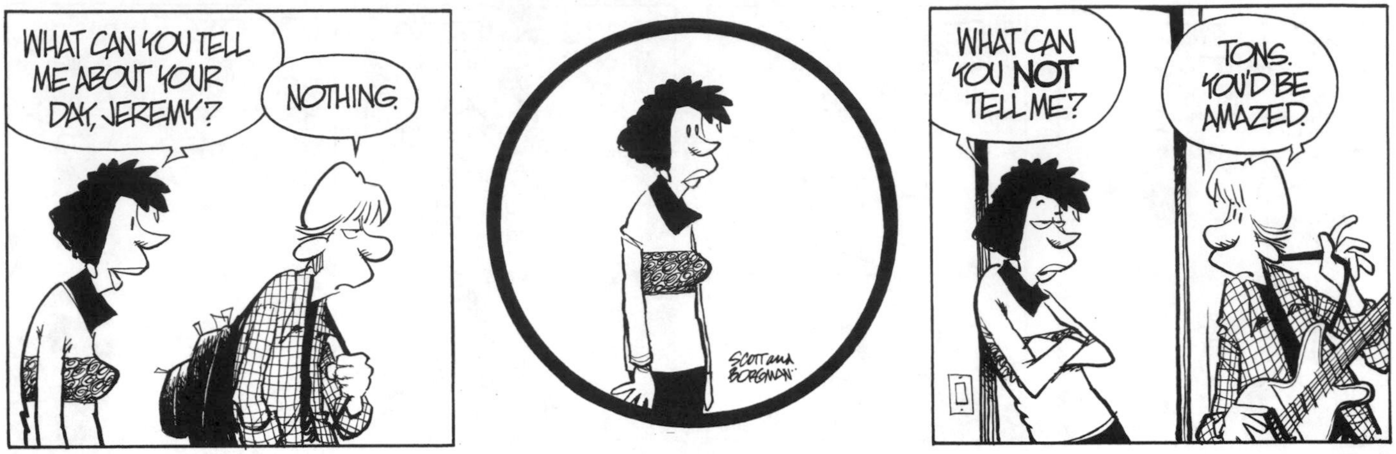
WHAT CAN YOU TELL ME ABOUT YOUR DAY, JEREMY?
NOTHING.
WHAT CAN YOU **NOT** TELL ME?
TONS. YOU'D BE AMAZED.

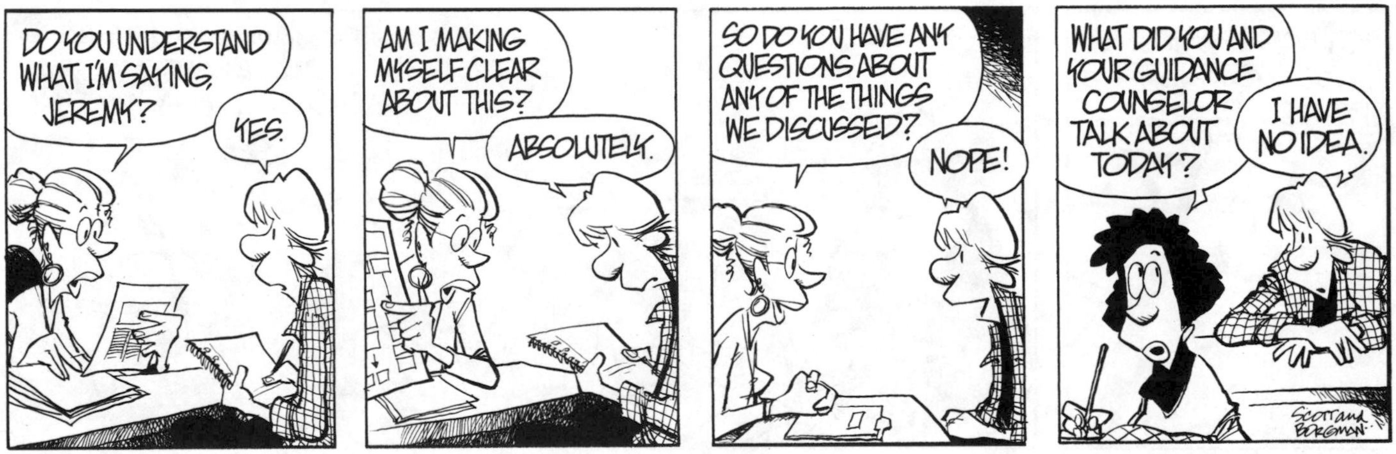
DO YOU UNDERSTAND WHAT I'M SAYING, JEREMY?
YES.
AM I MAKING MYSELF CLEAR ABOUT THIS?
ABSOLUTELY.
SO DO YOU HAVE ANY QUESTIONS ABOUT ANY OF THE THINGS WE DISCUSSED?
NOPE!
WHAT DID YOU AND YOUR GUIDANCE COUNSELOR TALK ABOUT TODAY?
I HAVE NO IDEA.

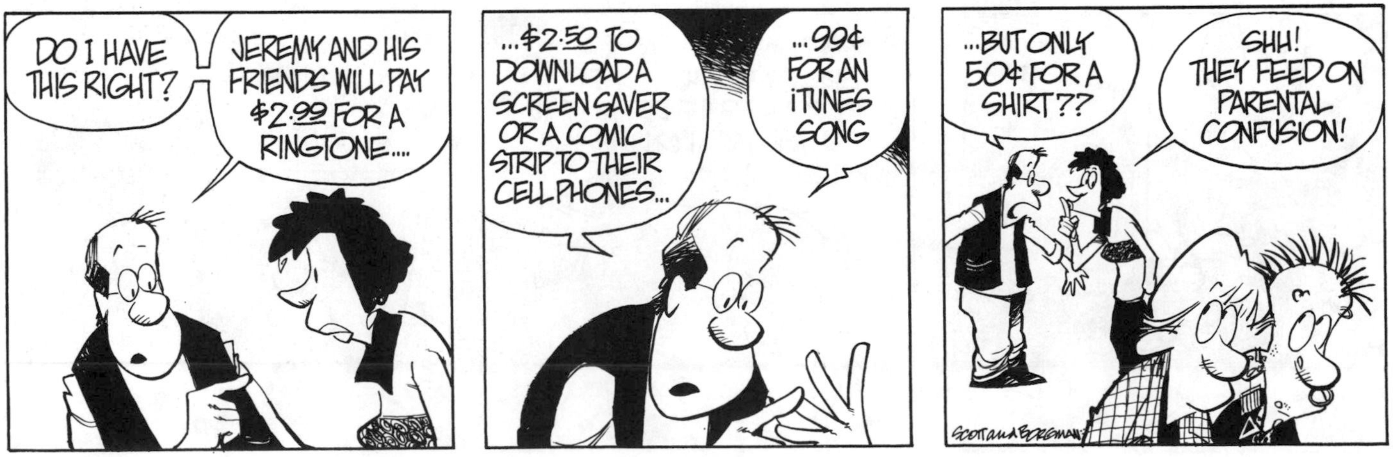
DO I HAVE THIS RIGHT?
JEREMY AND HIS FRIENDS WILL PAY $2.99 FOR A RINGTONE....
...$2.50 TO DOWNLOAD A SCREEN SAVER OR A COMIC STRIP TO THEIR CELL PHONES...
...99¢ FOR AN iTUNES SONG
...BUT ONLY 50¢ FOR A SHIRT??
SHH! THEY FEED ON PARENTAL CONFUSION!

Zits
JERRY SCOTT and JIM BORGMAN

AHHHHHHH!
JEREMY, YOU DIDN'T JUST TAKE YOUR SHIRT OUT OF THE DRYER AND LEAVE THE REST OF THE CLOTHES IN THERE, DID YOU?
NO.
YOU HUNG THEM ALL UP, LIKE I ASKED YOU TO?
YES!
REALLY??
THE TONE OF YOUR QUESTION IMPLIES A DEGREE OF SURPRISE WHICH I FIND INSULTING.

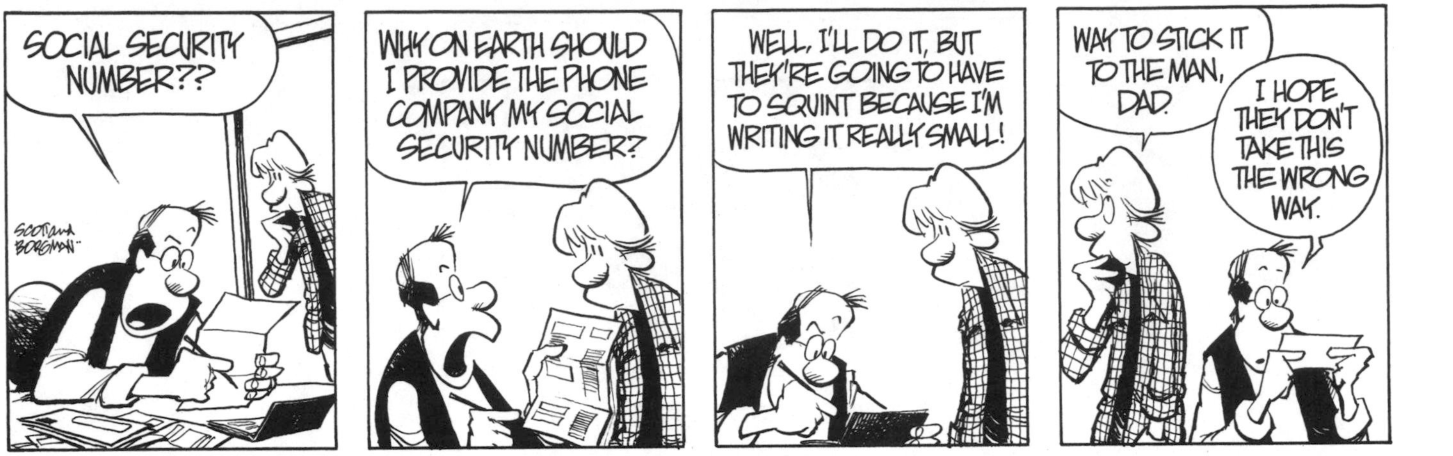
SOCIAL SECURITY NUMBER??
SCOTT AND BORGMAN
WHY ON EARTH SHOULD I PROVIDE THE PHONE COMPANY MY SOCIAL SECURITY NUMBER?
WELL, I'LL DO IT, BUT THEY'RE GOING TO HAVE TO SQUINT BECAUSE I'M WRITING IT REALLY SMALL!
WAY TO STICK IT TO THE MAN, DAD.
I HOPE THEY DON'T TAKE THIS THE WRONG WAY.

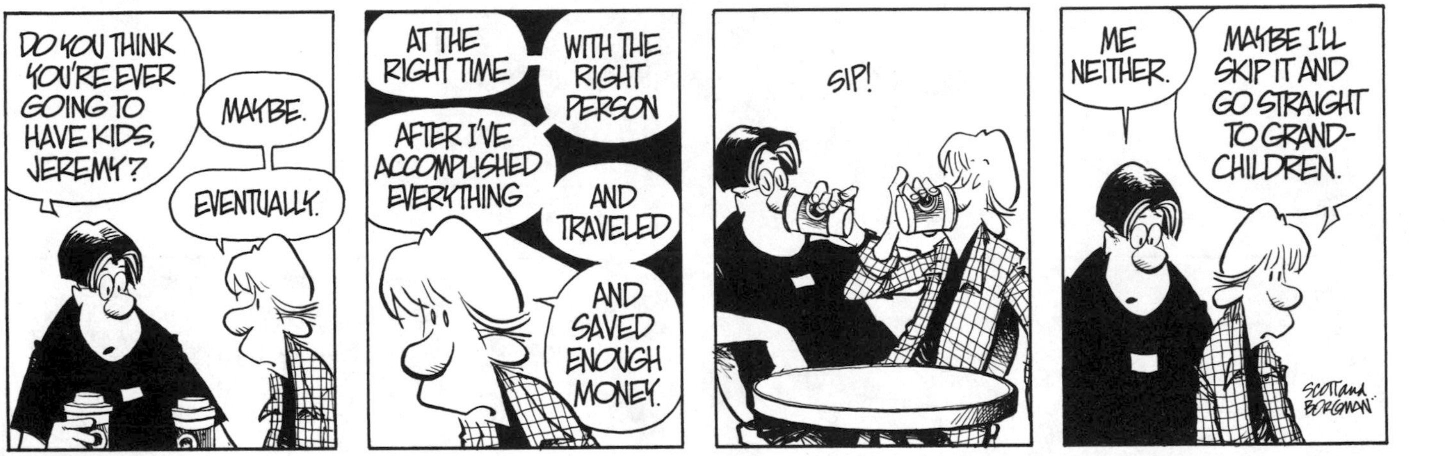
DO YOU THINK YOU'RE EVER GOING TO HAVE KIDS, JEREMY?
MAYBE.
EVENTUALLY.
AT THE RIGHT TIME
WITH THE RIGHT PERSON
AFTER I'VE ACCOMPLISHED EVERYTHING
AND TRAVELED
AND SAVED ENOUGH MONEY.
SIP!
ME NEITHER.
MAYBE I'LL SKIP IT AND GO STRAIGHT TO GRAND-CHILDREN.
SCOTT AND BORGMAN

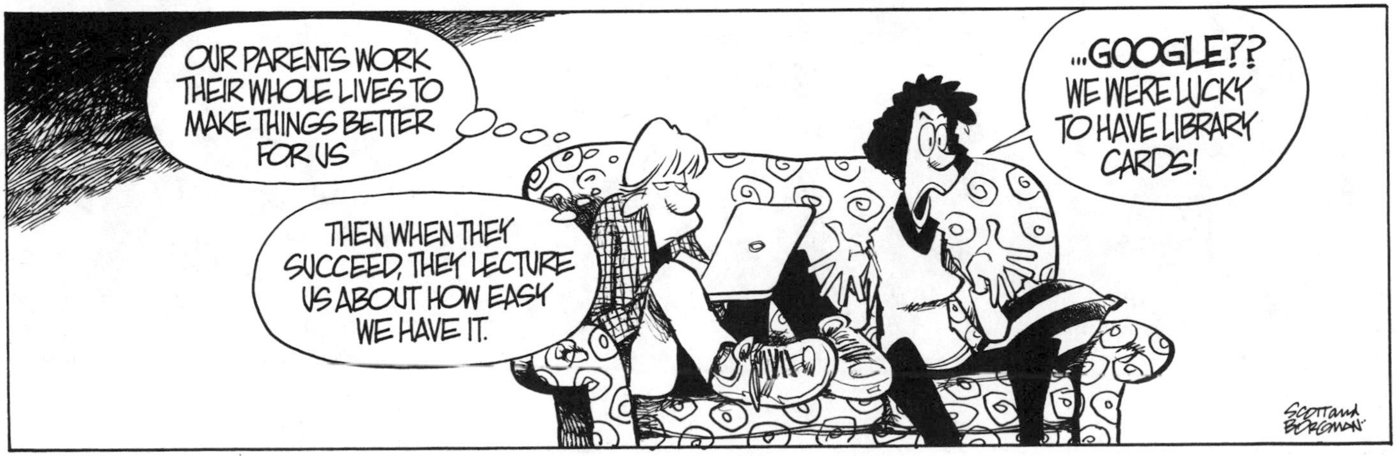
OUR PARENTS WORK THEIR WHOLE LIVES TO MAKE THINGS BETTER FOR US
THEN WHEN THEY SUCCEED, THEY LECTURE US ABOUT HOW EASY WE HAVE IT.
...GOOGLE?? WE WERE LUCKY TO HAVE LIBRARY CARDS!
SCOTT AND BORGMAN

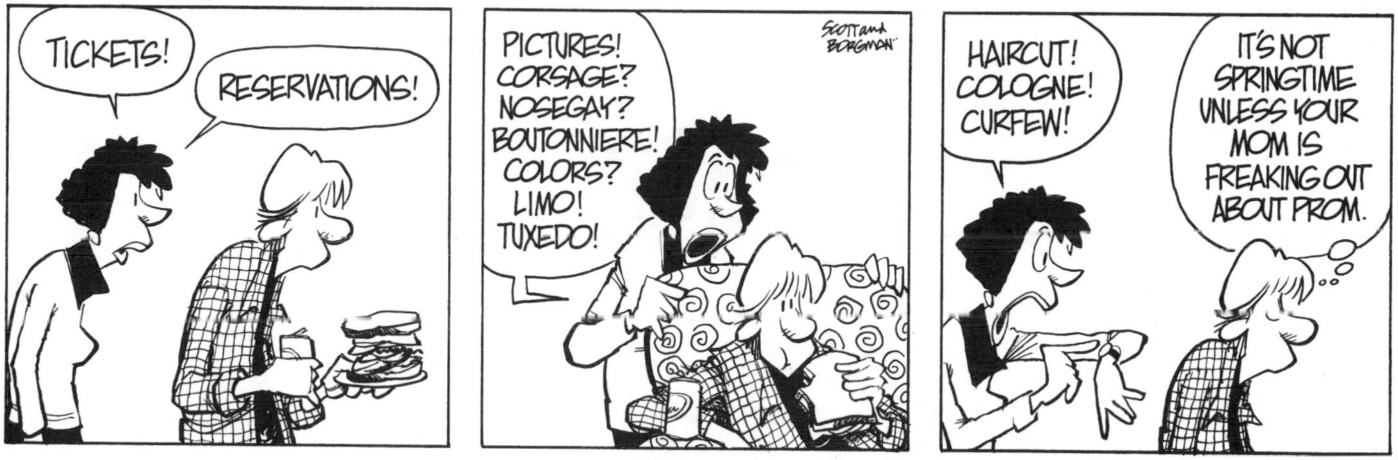
TICKETS!
RESERVATIONS!
PICTURES! CORSAGE? NOSEGAY? BOUTONNIERE! COLORS? LIMO! TUXEDO!
HAIRCUT! COLOGNE! CURFEW!
IT'S NOT SPRINGTIME UNLESS YOUR MOM IS FREAKING OUT ABOUT PROM.

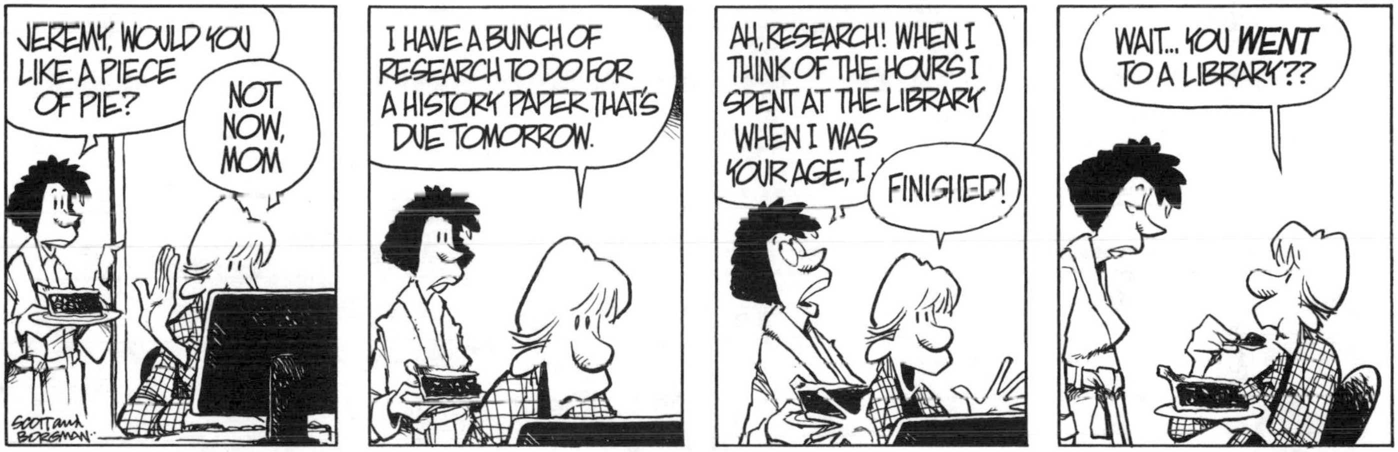
JEREMY, WOULD YOU LIKE A PIECE OF PIE?
NOT NOW, MOM
I HAVE A BUNCH OF RESEARCH TO DO FOR A HISTORY PAPER THAT'S DUE TOMORROW.
AH, RESEARCH! WHEN I THINK OF THE HOURS I SPENT AT THE LIBRARY WHEN I WAS YOUR AGE, I
FINISHED!
WAIT... YOU **WENT** TO A LIBRARY??

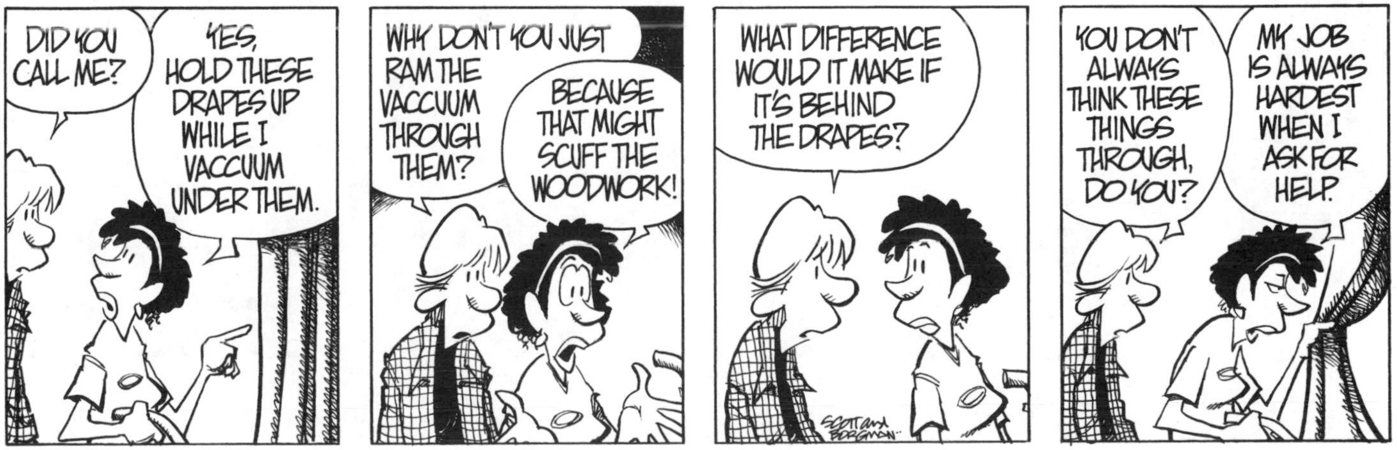
DID YOU CALL ME?
YES, HOLD THESE DRAPES UP WHILE I VACCUUM UNDER THEM.
WHY DON'T YOU JUST RAM THE VACCUUM THROUGH THEM?
BECAUSE THAT MIGHT SCUFF THE WOODWORK!
WHAT DIFFERENCE WOULD IT MAKE IF IT'S BEHIND THE DRAPES?
YOU DON'T ALWAYS THINK THESE THINGS THROUGH, DO YOU?
MY JOB IS ALWAYS HARDEST WHEN I ASK FOR HELP.

Zits
by JERRY SCOTT and
JIM BORGMAN

(SIGH)
IS SOMETHING BOTHERING YOU, BRITTANY?
TAYLOR SWIPED THIS WASABI iSKIN FROM HIS COUSIN AND GAVE IT TO ME BECAUSE IT MATCHED THE COLOR OF MY TOENAILS.
WOW.
I KNOW.
ILLEGAL POSSESSION OF iSTUFF... YOU MUST BE FREAKED!
MORE IMPORTANTLY, NOW I HAVE TO LEAVE MY TOE-NAILS THIS COLOR LIKE, 4-EVER!
SCOTT and BORGMAN

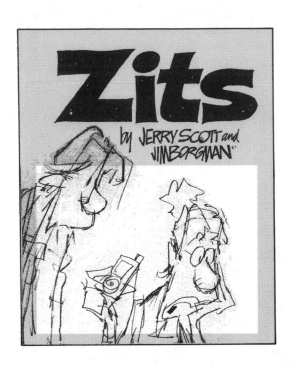

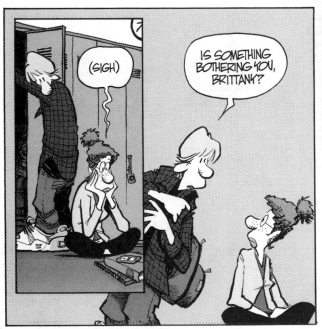

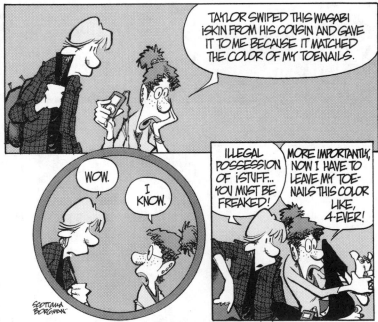

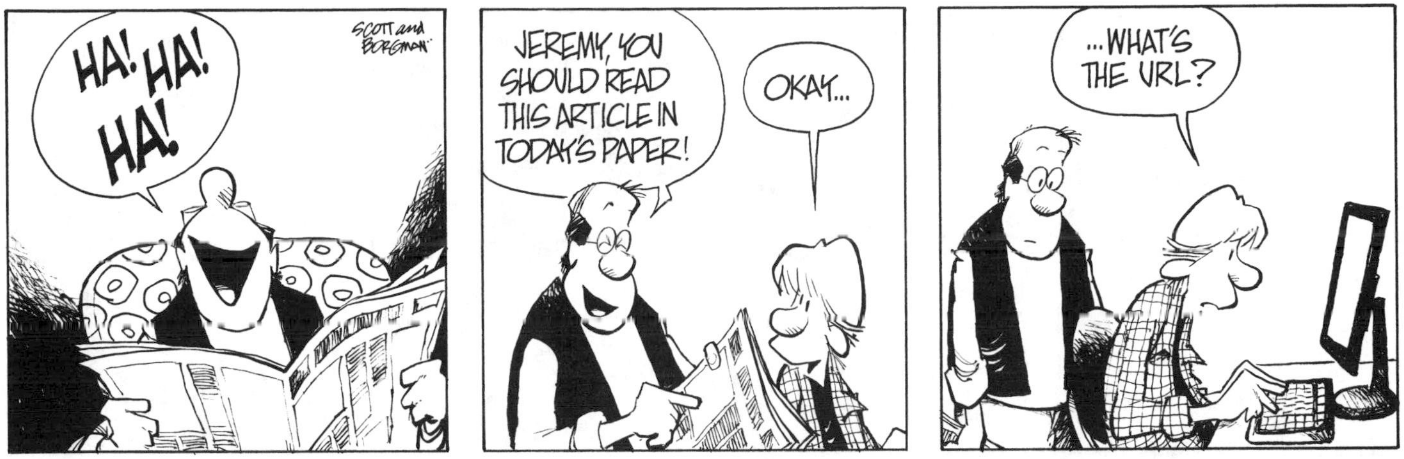
SCOTT and BORGMAN
HA! HA! HA!
JEREMY, YOU SHOULD READ THIS ARTICLE IN TODAY'S PAPER!
OKAY...
...WHAT'S THE URL?

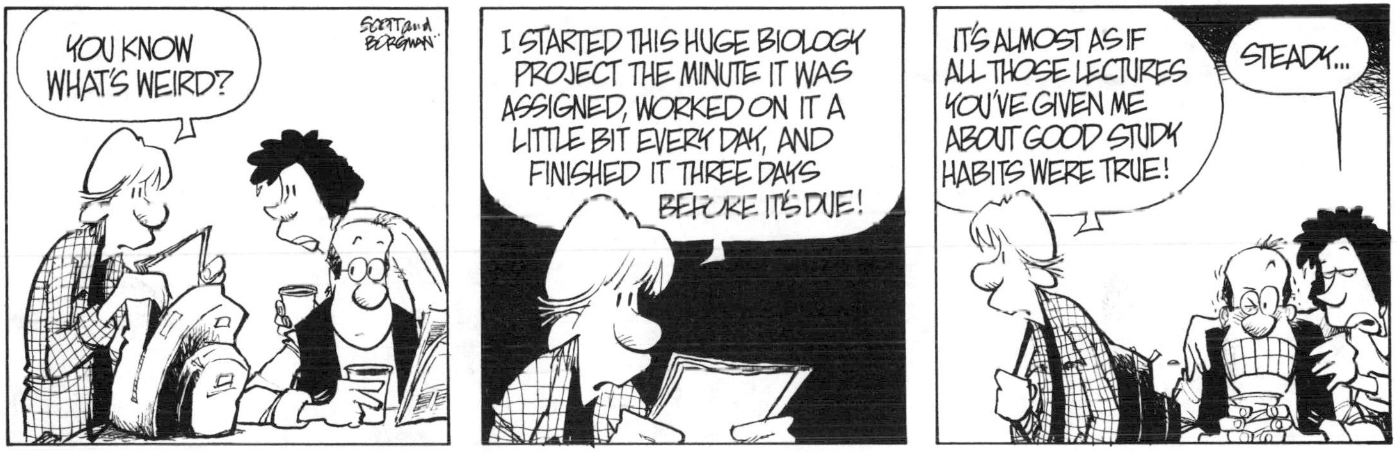
SCOTT and BORGMAN
YOU KNOW WHAT'S WEIRD?
I STARTED THIS HUGE BIOLOGY PROJECT THE MINUTE IT WAS ASSIGNED, WORKED ON IT A LITTLE BIT EVERY DAY, AND FINISHED IT THREE DAYS BEFORE IT'S DUE!
IT'S ALMOST AS IF ALL THOSE LECTURES YOU'VE GIVEN ME ABOUT GOOD STUDY HABITS WERE TRUE!
STEADY...

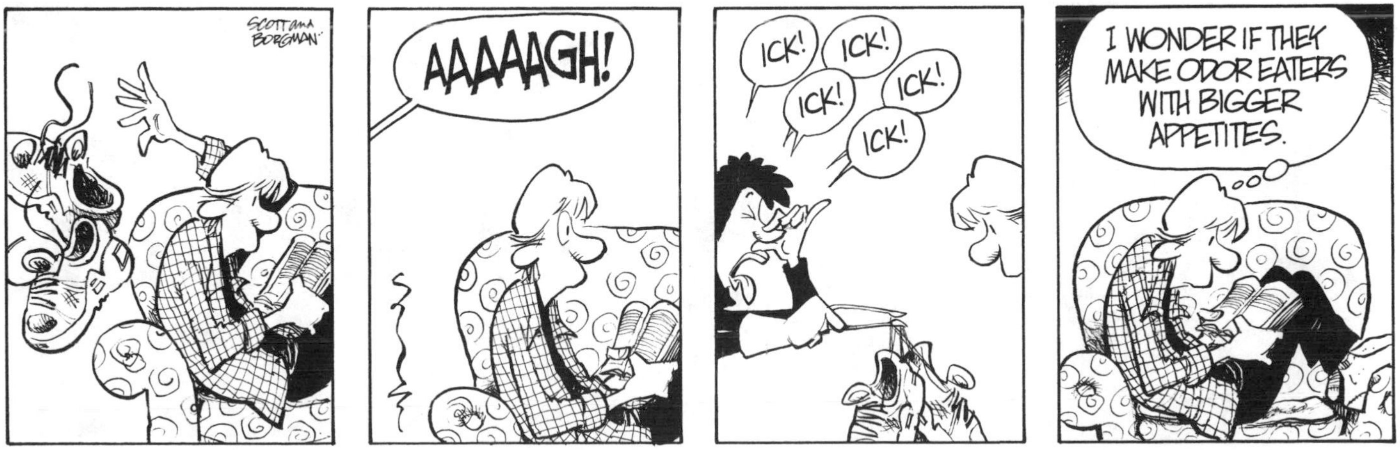
SCOTT and BORGMAN
AAAAAGH!
ICK!
ICK!
ICK!
ICK!
ICK!
I WONDER IF THEY MAKE ODOR EATERS WITH BIGGER APPETITES.

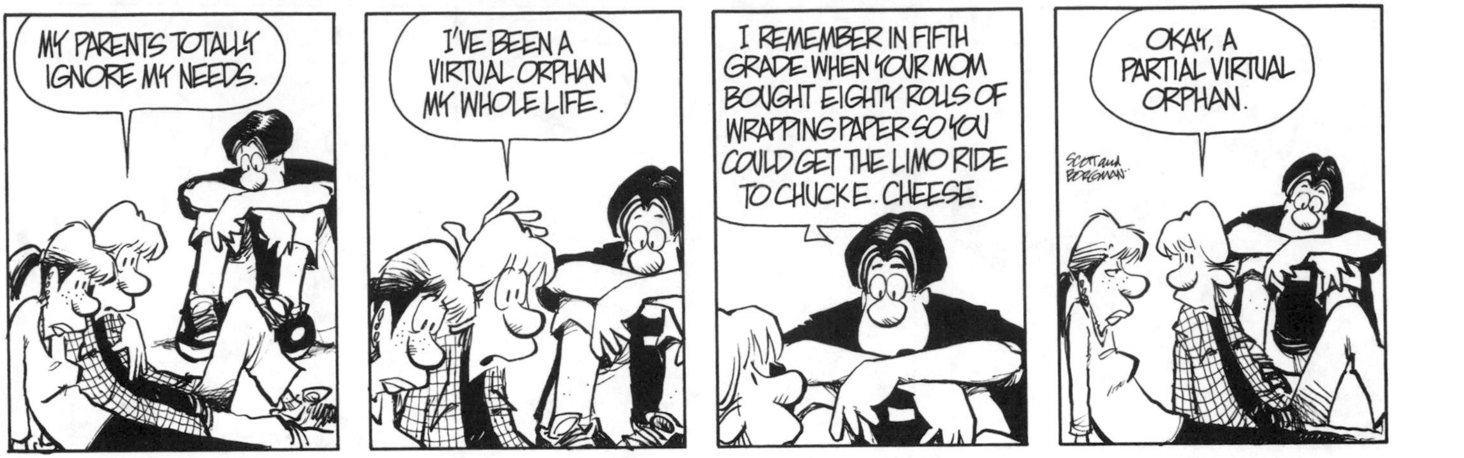
MY PARENTS TOTALLY IGNORE MY NEEDS.
I'VE BEEN A VIRTUAL ORPHAN MY WHOLE LIFE.
I REMEMBER IN FIFTH GRADE WHEN YOUR MOM BOUGHT EIGHTY ROLLS OF WRAPPING PAPER SO YOU COULD GET THE LIMO RIDE TO CHUCK E. CHEESE.
OKAY, A PARTIAL VIRTUAL ORPHAN.

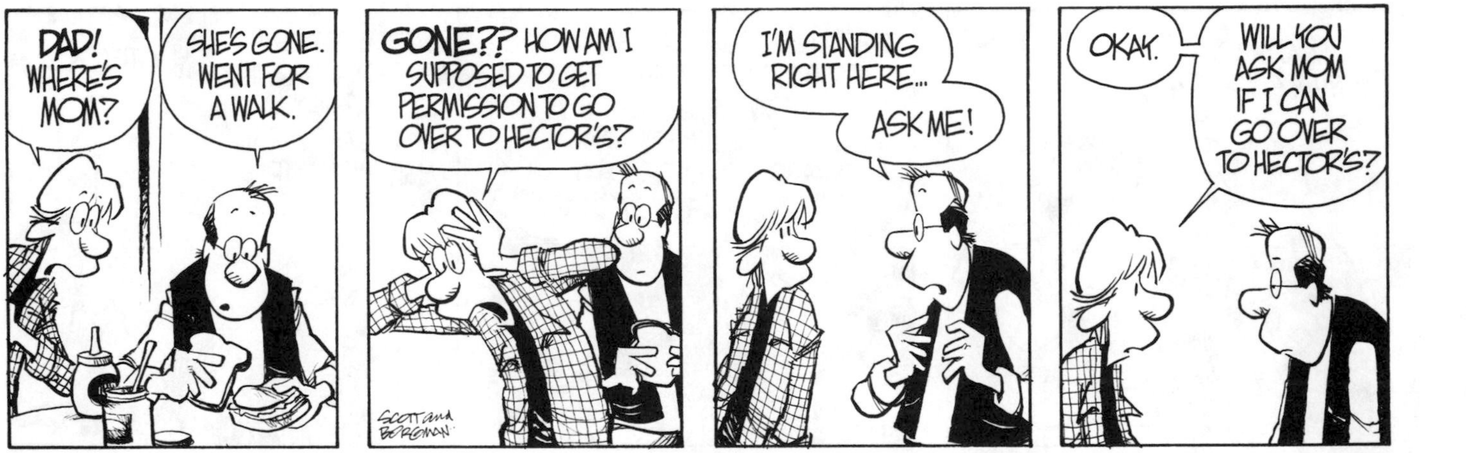
DAD! WHERE'S MOM?
SHE'S GONE. WENT FOR A WALK.
GONE?? HOW AM I SUPPOSED TO GET PERMISSION TO GO OVER TO HECTOR'S?
I'M STANDING RIGHT HERE...
ASK ME!
WILL YOU ASK MOM IF I CAN GO OVER TO HECTOR'S?
OKAY.

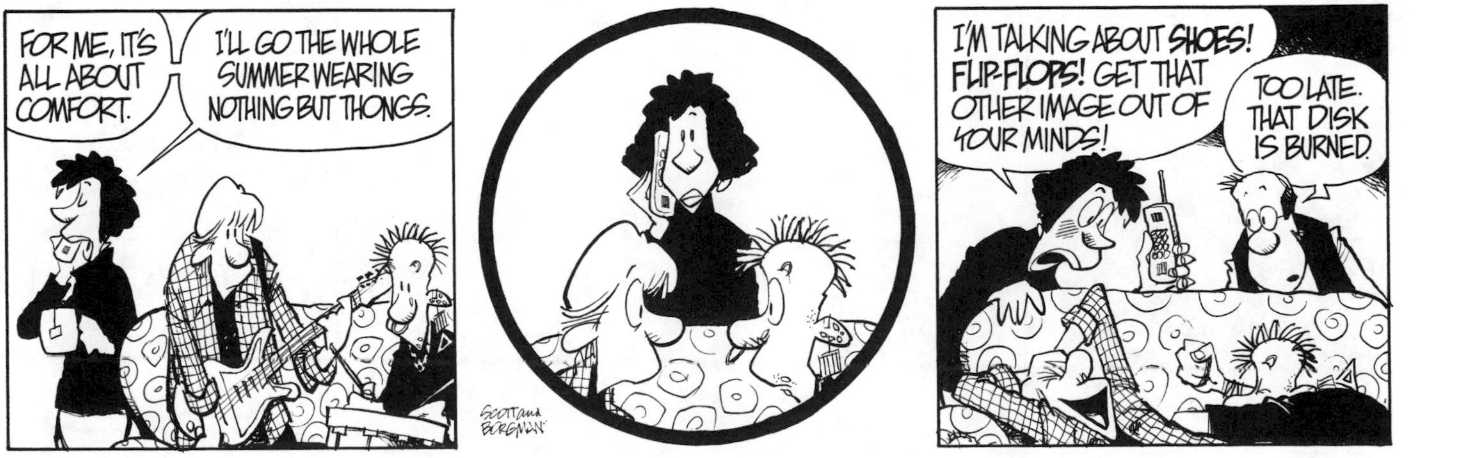
FOR ME, IT'S ALL ABOUT COMFORT.
I'LL GO THE WHOLE SUMMER WEARING NOTHING BUT THONGS.
I'M TALKING ABOUT SHOES! FLIP-FLOPS! GET THAT OTHER IMAGE OUT OF YOUR MINDS!
TOO LATE. THAT DISK IS BURNED.

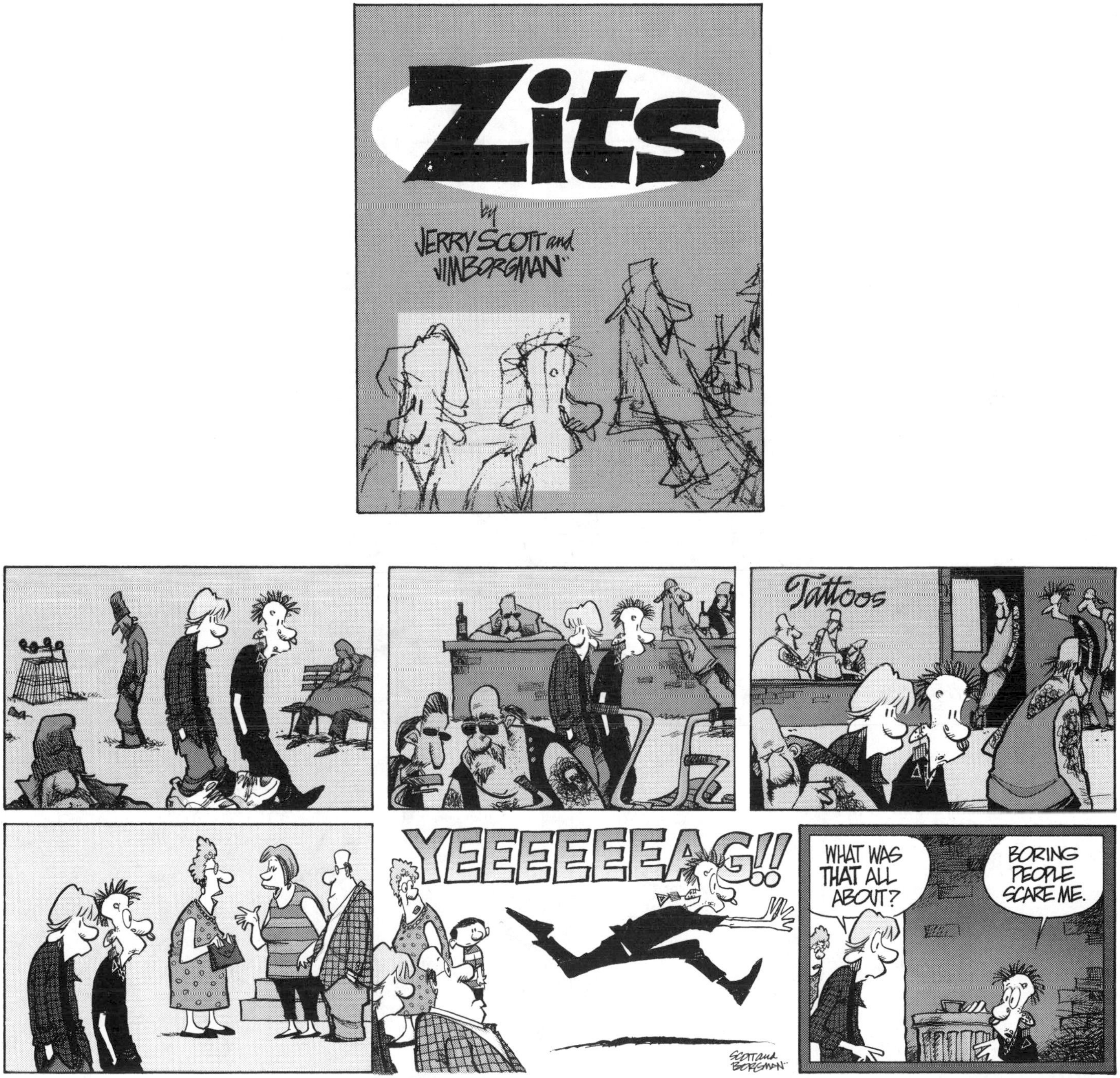
Zits
by
JERRY SCOTT and
JIM BORGMAN
Tattoos
YEEEEEEEAG!!
WHAT WAS THAT ALL ABOUT?
BORING PEOPLE SCARE ME.
SCOTT and BORGMAN

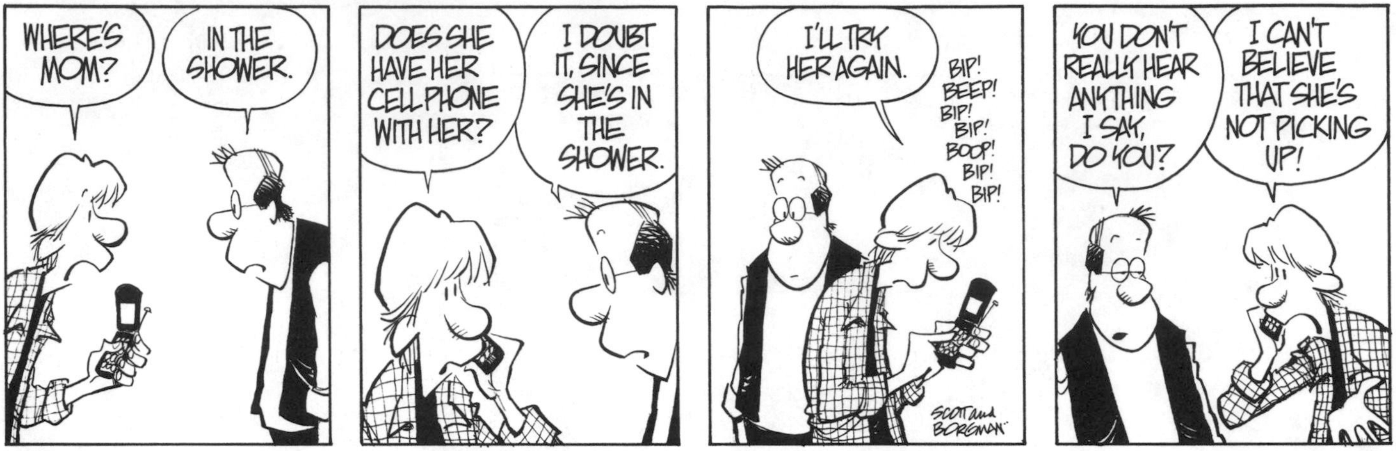
WHERE'S MOM?
IN THE SHOWER.
DOES SHE HAVE HER CELL PHONE WITH HER?
I DOUBT IT, SINCE SHE'S IN THE SHOWER.
I'LL TRY HER AGAIN.
BIP! BEEP! BIP! BIP! BOOP! BIP! BIP!
YOU DON'T REALLY HEAR ANYTHING I SAY, DO YOU?
I CAN'T BELIEVE THAT SHE'S NOT PICKING UP!
SCOTT and BORGMAN

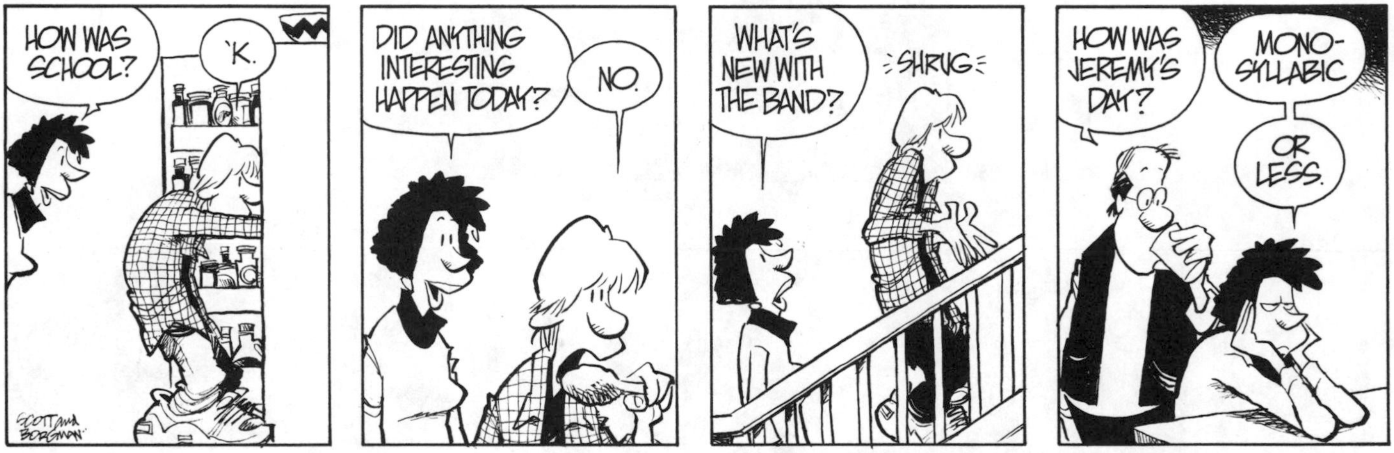
HOW WAS SCHOOL?
'K.
SCOTT and BORGMAN
DID ANYTHING INTERESTING HAPPEN TODAY?
NO.
WHAT'S NEW WITH THE BAND?
SHRUG
HOW WAS JEREMY'S DAY?
MONO-SYLLABIC
OR LESS.

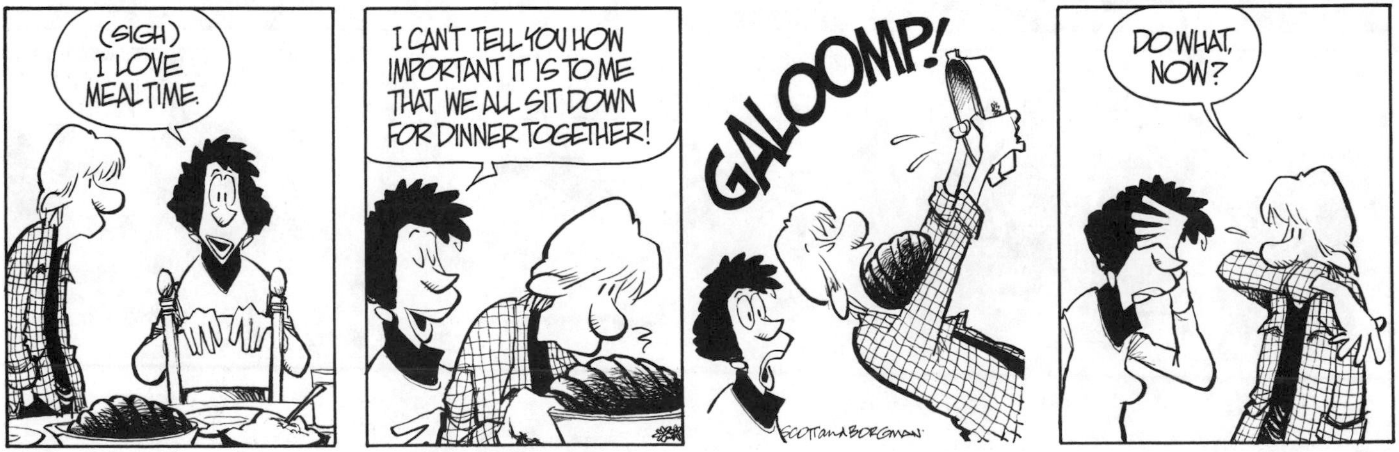
(SIGH) I LOVE MEALTIME.
I CAN'T TELL YOU HOW IMPORTANT IT IS TO ME THAT WE ALL SIT DOWN FOR DINNER TOGETHER!
GALOOMP!
SCOTT and BORGMAN
DO WHAT, NOW?

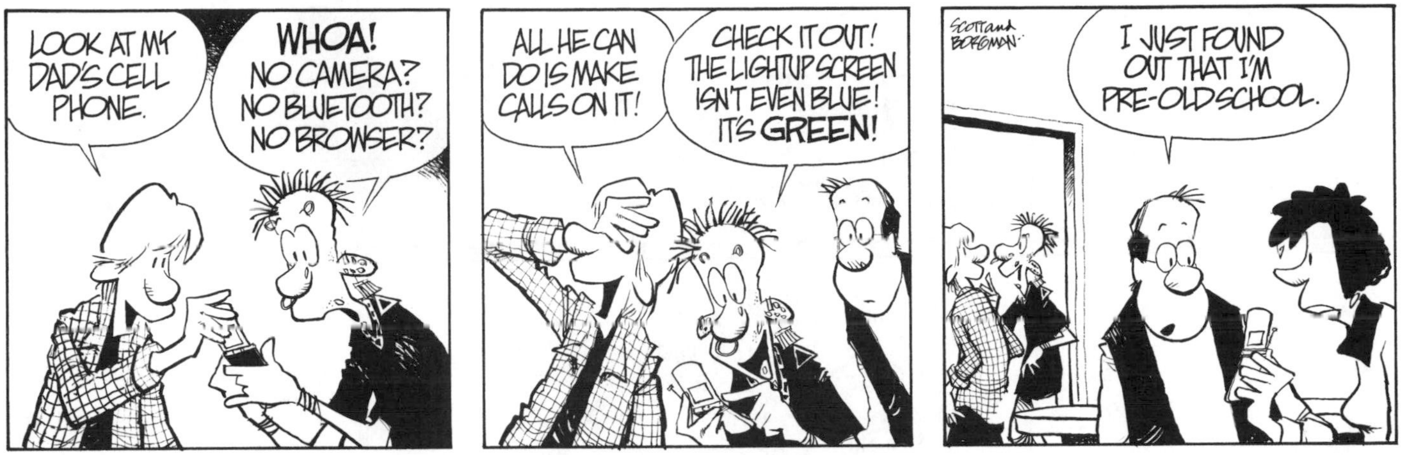
LOOK AT MY DAD'S CELL PHONE.
WHOA! NO CAMERA? NO BLUETOOTH? NO BROWSER?
ALL HE CAN DO IS MAKE CALLS ON IT!
CHECK IT OUT! THE LIGHTUP SCREEN ISN'T EVEN BLUE! IT'S GREEN!
SCOTT and BORGMAN
I JUST FOUND OUT THAT I'M PRE-OLDSCHOOL.

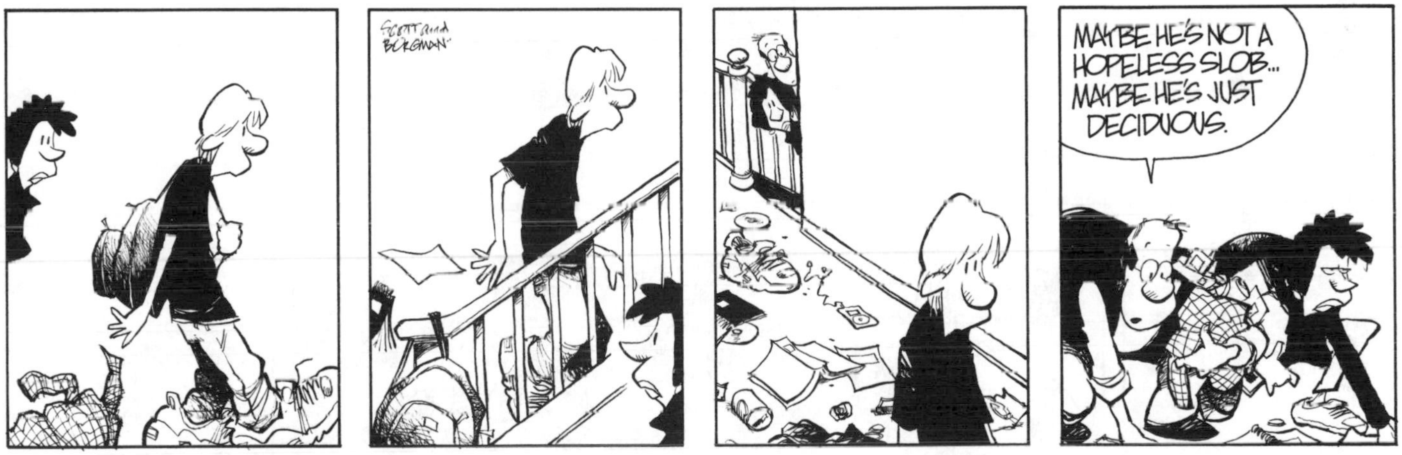
SCOTT and BORGMAN
MAYBE HE'S NOT A HOPELESS SLOB... MAYBE HE'S JUST DECIDUOUS.

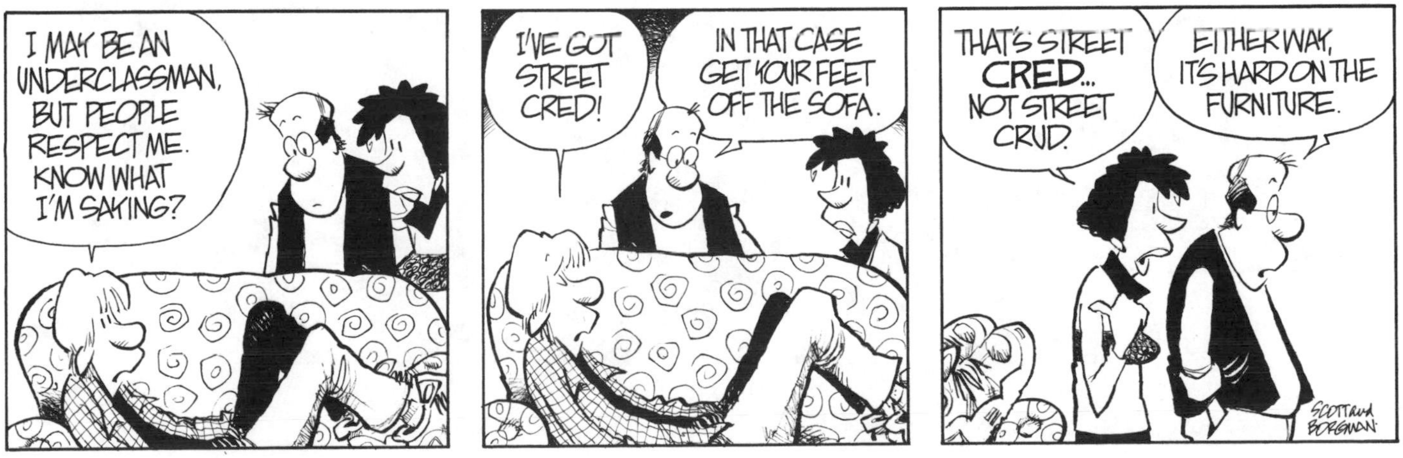
I MAY BE AN UNDERCLASSMAN, BUT PEOPLE RESPECT ME. KNOW WHAT I'M SAYING?
I'VE GOT STREET CRED!
IN THAT CASE GET YOUR FEET OFF THE SOFA.
THAT'S STREET CRED... NOT STREET CRUD.
EITHER WAY, IT'S HARD ON THE FURNITURE.
SCOTT and BORGMAN

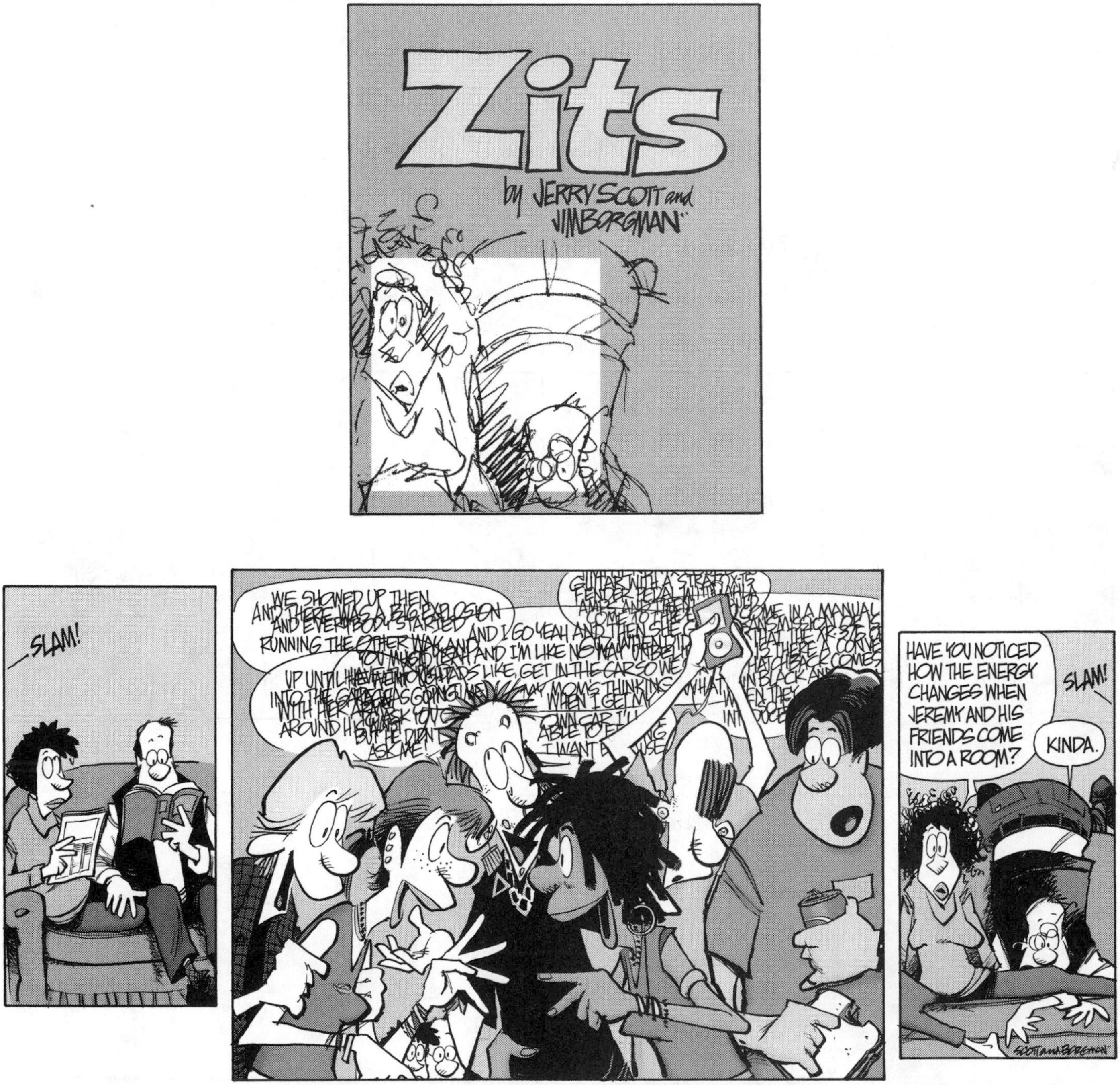
Zits
by JERRY SCOTT and JIM BORGMAN
SLAM!
HAVE YOU NOTICED HOW THE ENERGY CHANGES WHEN JEREMY AND HIS FRIENDS COME INTO A ROOM?
KINDA.
SLAM!

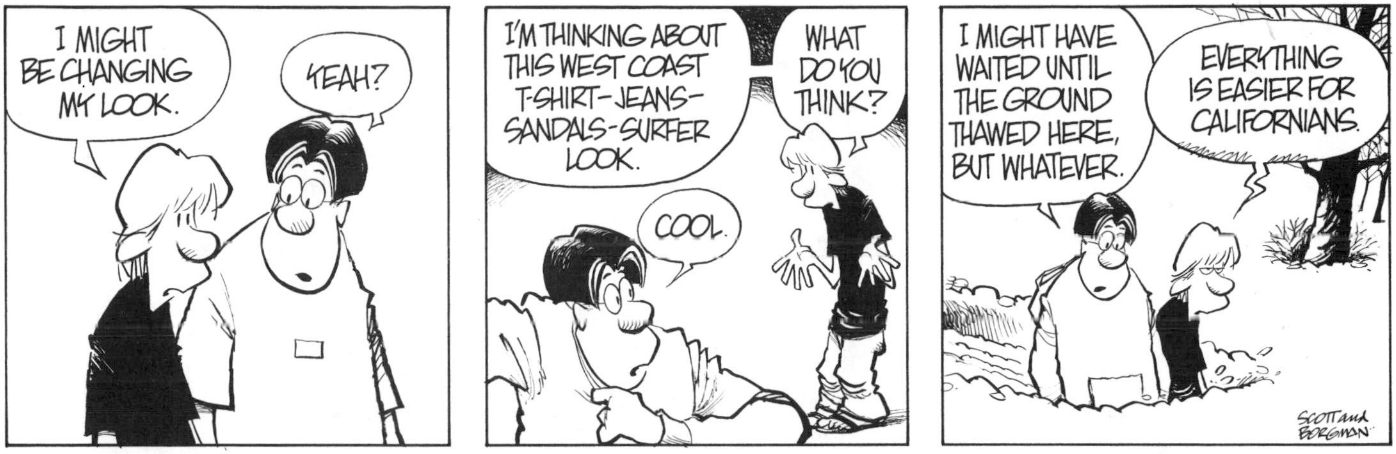
I MIGHT BE CHANGING MY LOOK.
YEAH?
I'M THINKING ABOUT THIS WEST COAST T-SHIRT-JEANS-SANDALS-SURFER LOOK.
WHAT DO YOU THINK?
COOL.
I MIGHT HAVE WAITED UNTIL THE GROUND THAWED HERE, BUT WHATEVER.
EVERYTHING IS EASIER FOR CALIFORNIANS.
SCOTT and BORGMAN

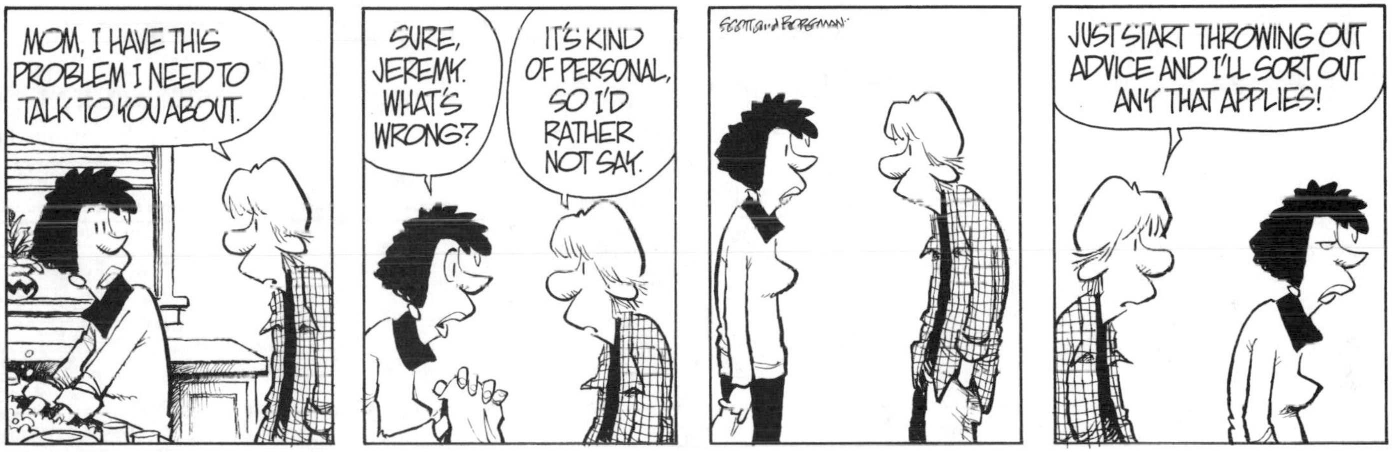
MOM, I HAVE THIS PROBLEM I NEED TO TALK TO YOU ABOUT.
SURE, JEREMY. WHAT'S WRONG?
IT'S KIND OF PERSONAL, SO I'D RATHER NOT SAY.
SCOTT and BORGMAN
JUST START THROWING OUT ADVICE AND I'LL SORT OUT ANY THAT APPLIES!

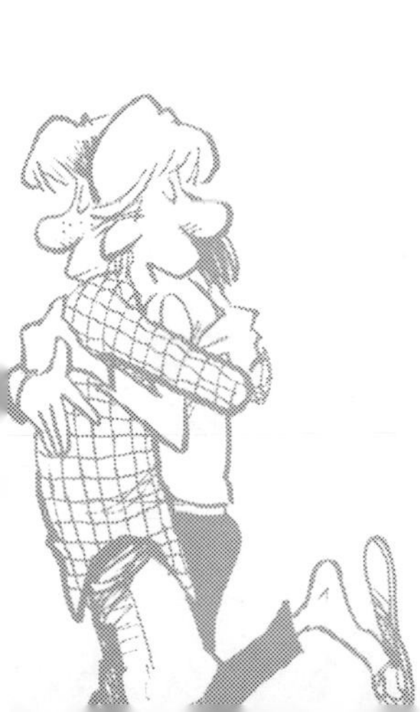

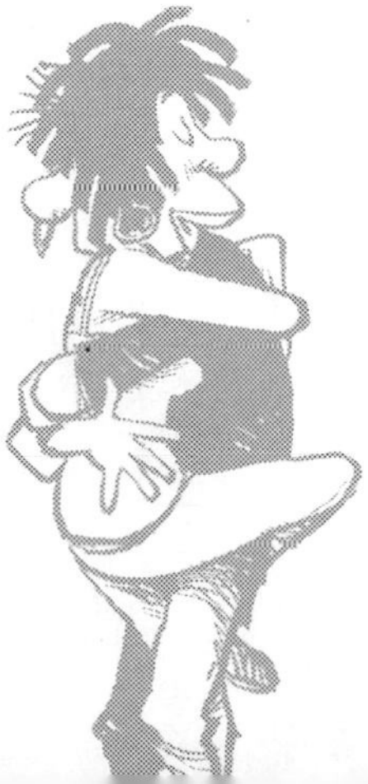

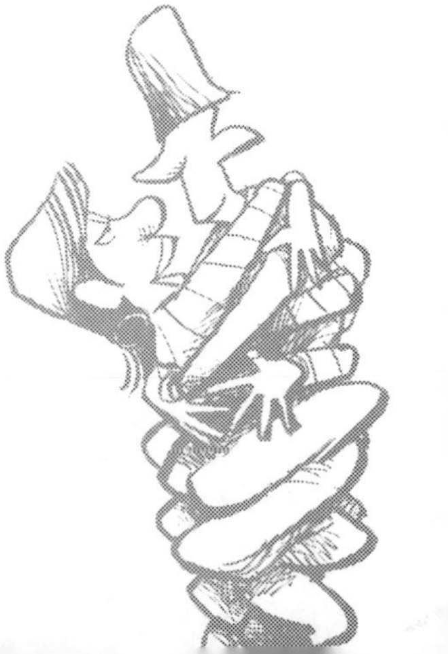

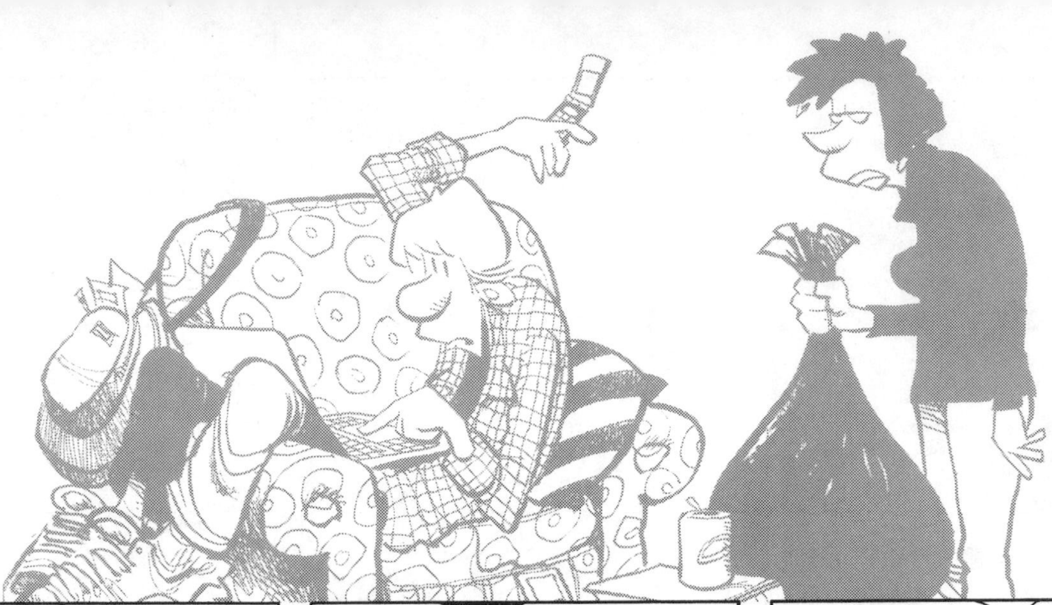

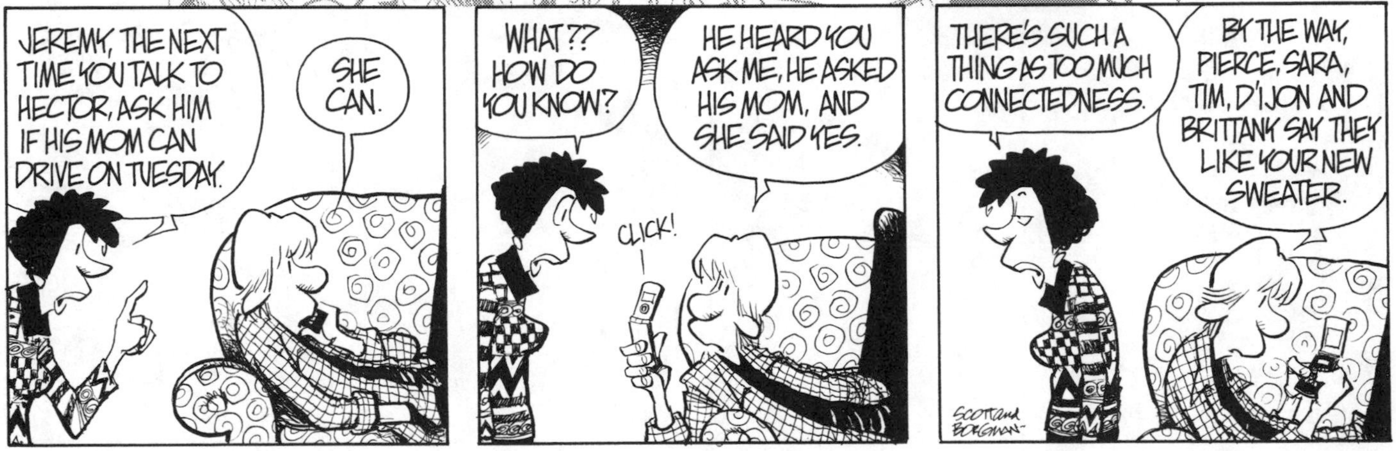
JEREMY, THE NEXT TIME YOU TALK TO HECTOR, ASK HIM IF HIS MOM CAN DRIVE ON TUESDAY.
SHE CAN.
WHAT?? HOW DO YOU KNOW?
HE HEARD YOU ASK ME, HE ASKED HIS MOM, AND SHE SAID YES.
CLICK!
THERE'S SUCH A THING AS TOO MUCH CONNECTEDNESS.
BY THE WAY, PIERCE, SARA, TIM, D'IJON AND BRITTANY SAY THEY LIKE YOUR NEW SWEATER.
SCOTT and BORGMAN

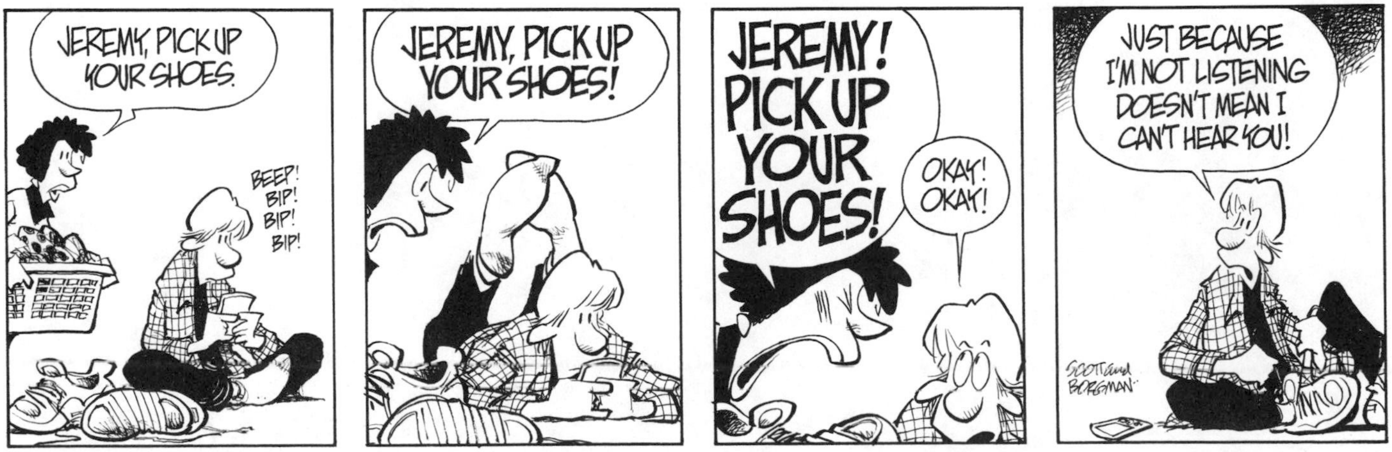
JEREMY, PICK UP YOUR SHOES.
BEEP! BIP! BIP! BIP!
JEREMY, PICK UP YOUR SHOES!
JEREMY! PICK UP YOUR SHOES!
OKAY! OKAY!
JUST BECAUSE I'M NOT LISTENING DOESN'T MEAN I CAN'T HEAR YOU!
SCOTT and BORGMAN

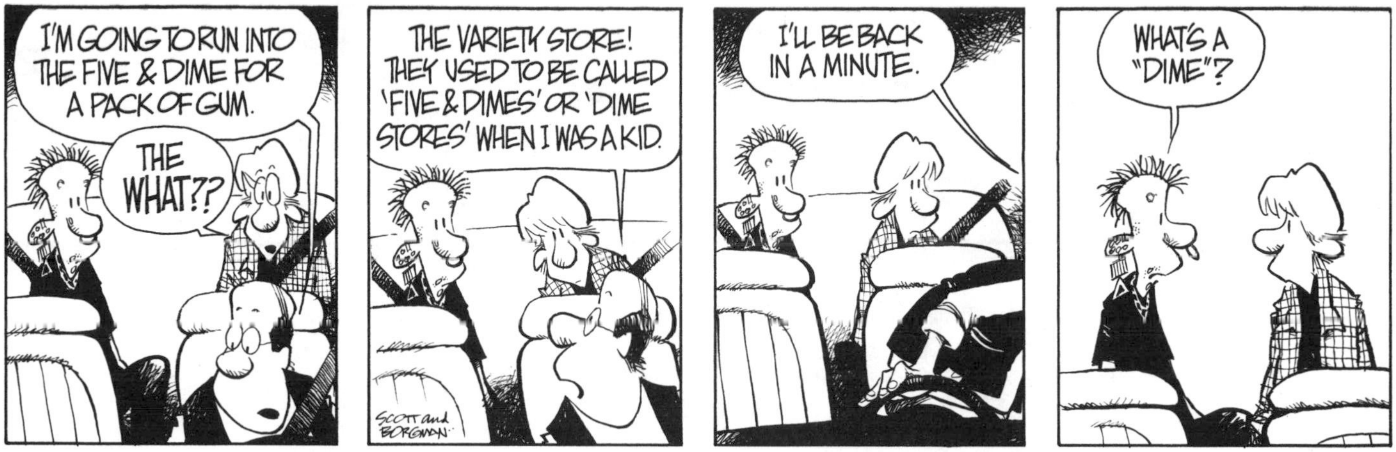
I'M GOING TO RUN INTO THE FIVE & DIME FOR A PACK OF GUM.
THE WHAT??
THE VARIETY STORE! THEY USED TO BE CALLED 'FIVE & DIMES' OR 'DIME STORES' WHEN I WAS A KID.
SCOTT and BORGMAN
I'LL BE BACK IN A MINUTE.
WHAT'S A "DIME"?

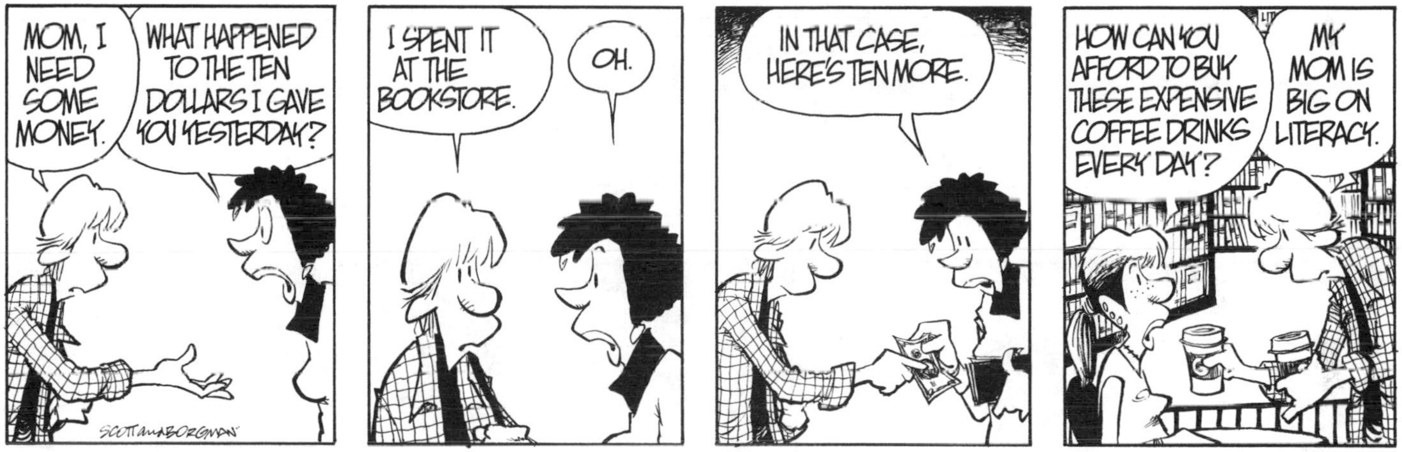
MOM, I NEED SOME MONEY.
WHAT HAPPENED TO THE TEN DOLLARS I GAVE YOU YESTERDAY?
SCOTT and BORGMAN
I SPENT IT AT THE BOOKSTORE.
OH.
IN THAT CASE, HERE'S TEN MORE.
HOW CAN YOU AFFORD TO BUY THESE EXPENSIVE COFFEE DRINKS EVERY DAY?
MY MOM IS BIG ON LITERACY.

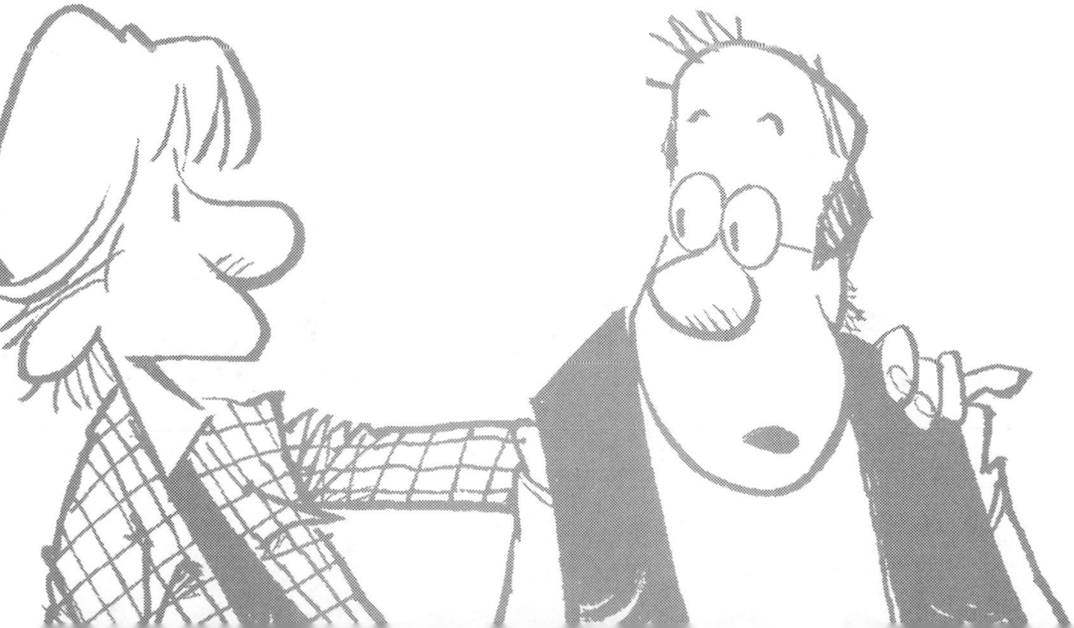

Zits
by JERRY SCOTT and JIM BORGMAN

ANOTHER ONE OF THOSE DAYS WITH MORE QUESTIONS THAN ANSWERS?
YUH-HUH. THANKS FOR ASKING.

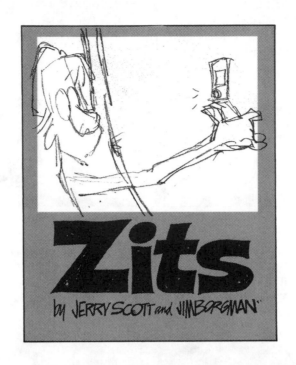

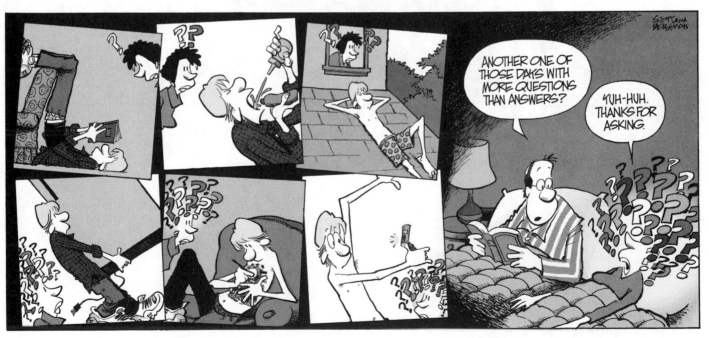

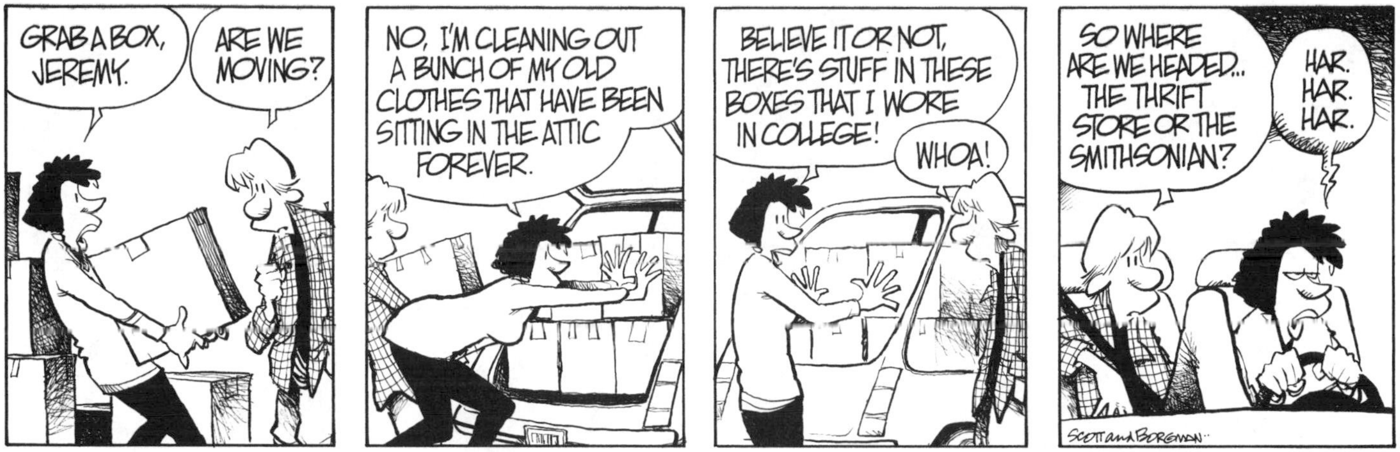
GRAB A BOX, JEREMY.
ARE WE MOVING?
NO, I'M CLEANING OUT A BUNCH OF MY OLD CLOTHES THAT HAVE BEEN SITTING IN THE ATTIC FOREVER.
BELIEVE IT OR NOT, THERE'S STUFF IN THESE BOXES THAT I WORE IN COLLEGE!
WHOA!
SO WHERE ARE WE HEADED... THE THRIFT STORE OR THE SMITHSONIAN?
HAR. HAR. HAR.
SCOTT and BORGMAN

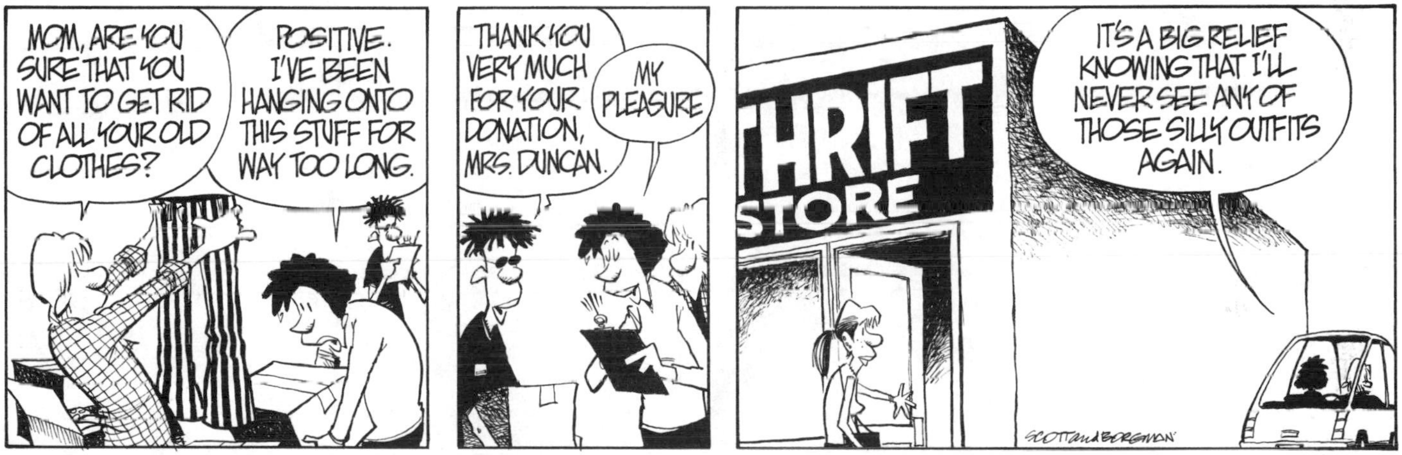
MOM, ARE YOU SURE THAT YOU WANT TO GET RID OF ALL YOUR OLD CLOTHES?
POSITIVE. I'VE BEEN HANGING ONTO THIS STUFF FOR WAY TOO LONG.
THANK YOU VERY MUCH FOR YOUR DONATION, MRS. DUNCAN.
MY PLEASURE
THRIFT STORE
IT'S A BIG RELIEF KNOWING THAT I'LL NEVER SEE ANY OF THOSE SILLY OUTFITS AGAIN.
SCOTT and BORGMAN

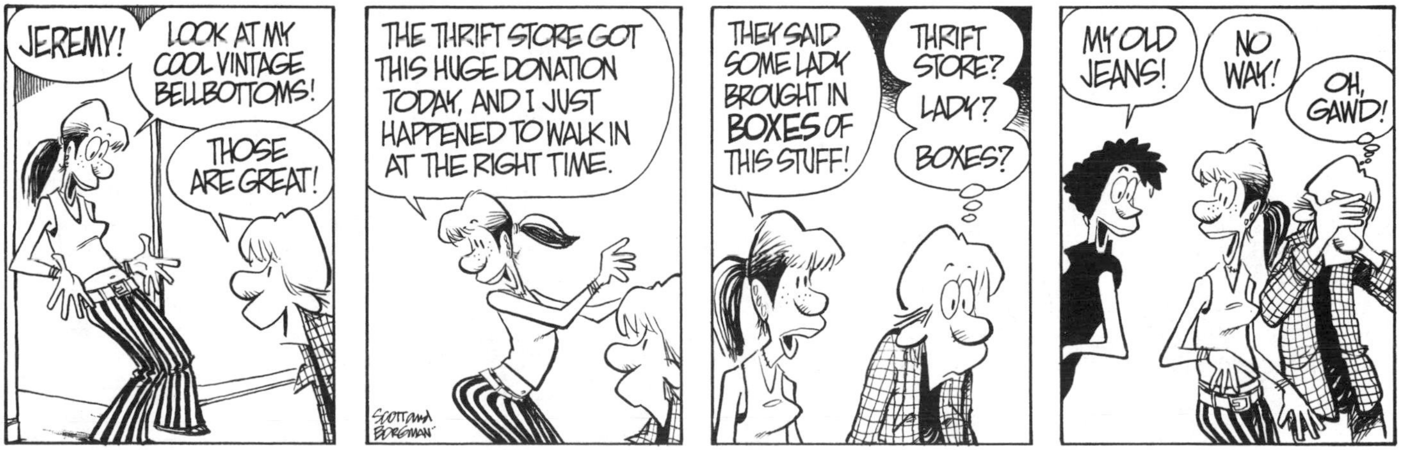
JEREMY!
LOOK AT MY COOL VINTAGE BELLBOTTOMS!
THOSE ARE GREAT!
THE THRIFT STORE GOT THIS HUGE DONATION TODAY, AND I JUST HAPPENED TO WALK IN AT THE RIGHT TIME.
SCOTT and BORGMAN
THEY SAID SOME LADY BROUGHT IN BOXES OF THIS STUFF!
THRIFT STORE?
LADY?
BOXES?
MY OLD JEANS!
NO WAY!
OH, GAWD!

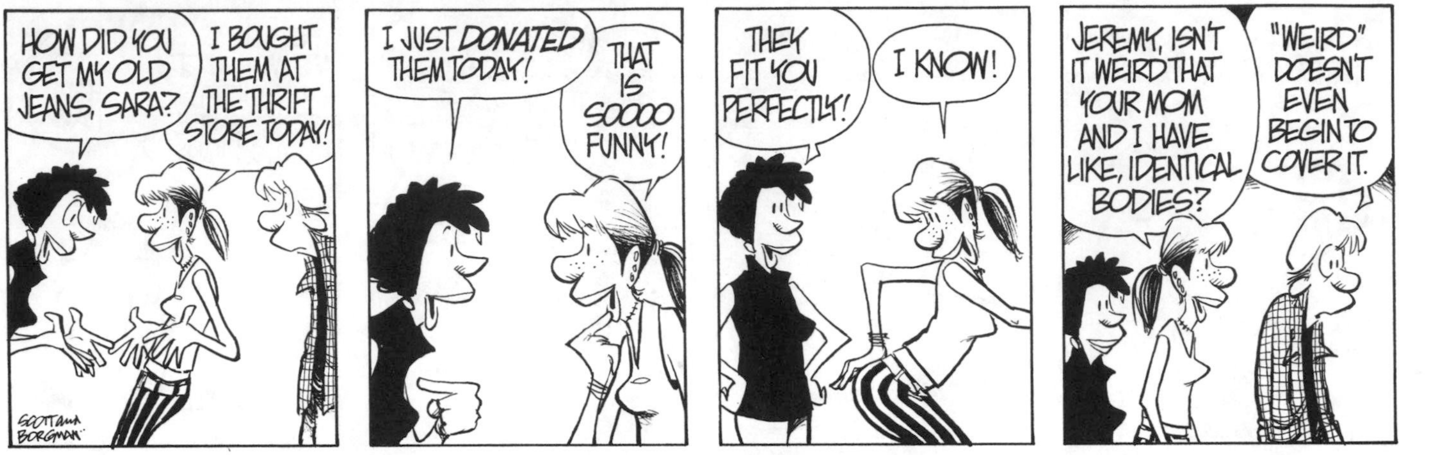
HOW DID YOU GET MY OLD JEANS, SARA?
I BOUGHT THEM AT THE THRIFT STORE TODAY!
SCOTT and BORGMAN
I JUST *DONATED* THEM TODAY!
THAT IS SOOOO FUNNY!
THEY FIT YOU PERFECTLY!
I KNOW!
JEREMY, ISN'T IT WEIRD THAT YOUR MOM AND I HAVE LIKE, IDENTICAL BODIES?
"WEIRD" DOESN'T EVEN BEGIN TO COVER IT.

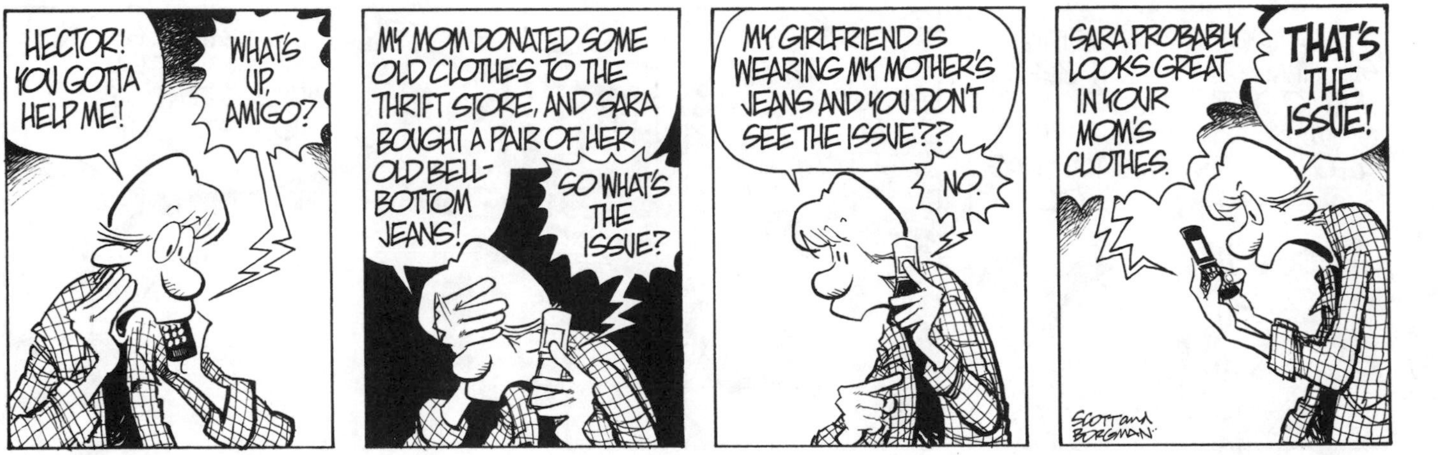
HECTOR! YOU GOTTA HELP ME!
WHAT'S UP, AMIGO?
MY MOM DONATED SOME OLD CLOTHES TO THE THRIFT STORE, AND SARA BOUGHT A PAIR OF HER OLD BELL-BOTTOM JEANS!
SO WHAT'S THE ISSUE?
MY GIRLFRIEND IS WEARING MY MOTHER'S JEANS AND YOU DON'T SEE THE ISSUE??
NO.
SARA PROBABLY LOOKS GREAT IN YOUR MOM'S CLOTHES.
THAT'S THE ISSUE!
SCOTT and BORGMAN

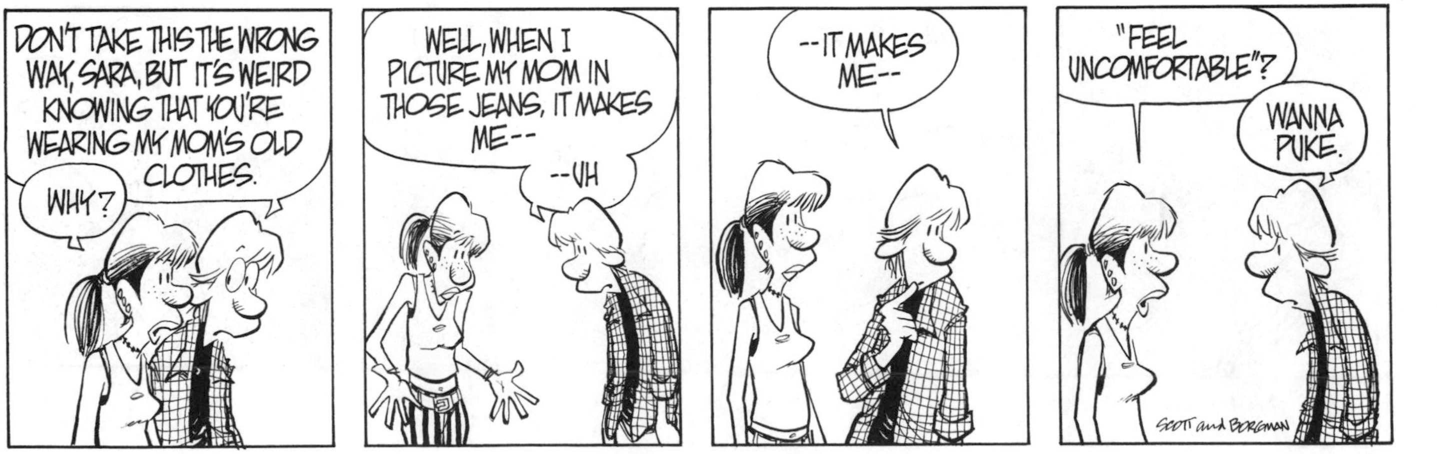
DON'T TAKE THIS THE WRONG WAY, SARA, BUT IT'S WEIRD KNOWING THAT YOU'RE WEARING MY MOM'S OLD CLOTHES.
WHY?
WELL, WHEN I PICTURE MY MOM IN THOSE JEANS, IT MAKES ME--
--UH
--IT MAKES ME--
"FEEL UNCOMFORTABLE"?
WANNA PUKE.
SCOTT and BORGMAN

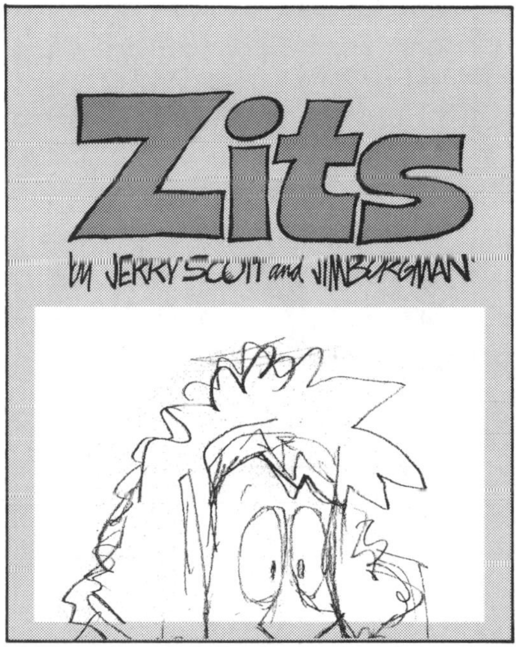
Zits
by JERRY SCOTT and JIM BORGMAN

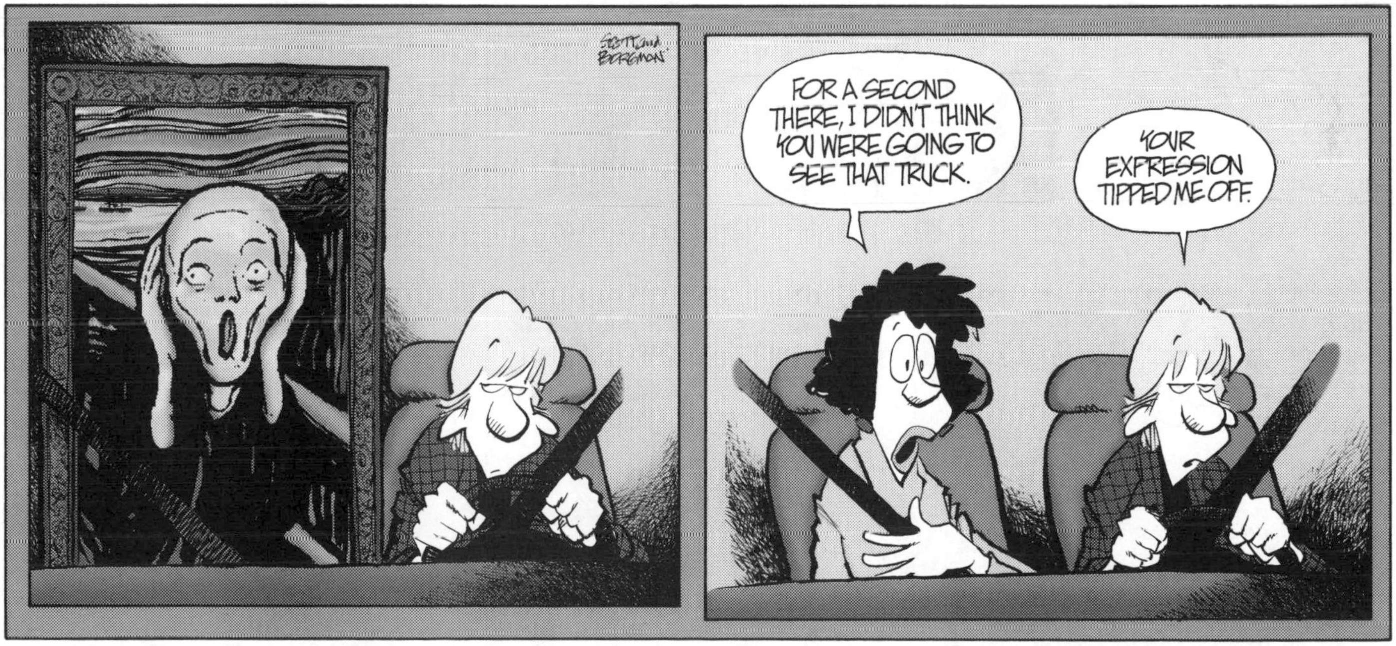
SCOTT and BORGMAN
FOR A SECOND THERE, I DIDN'T THINK YOU WERE GOING TO SEE THAT TRUCK.
YOUR EXPRESSION TIPPED ME OFF.

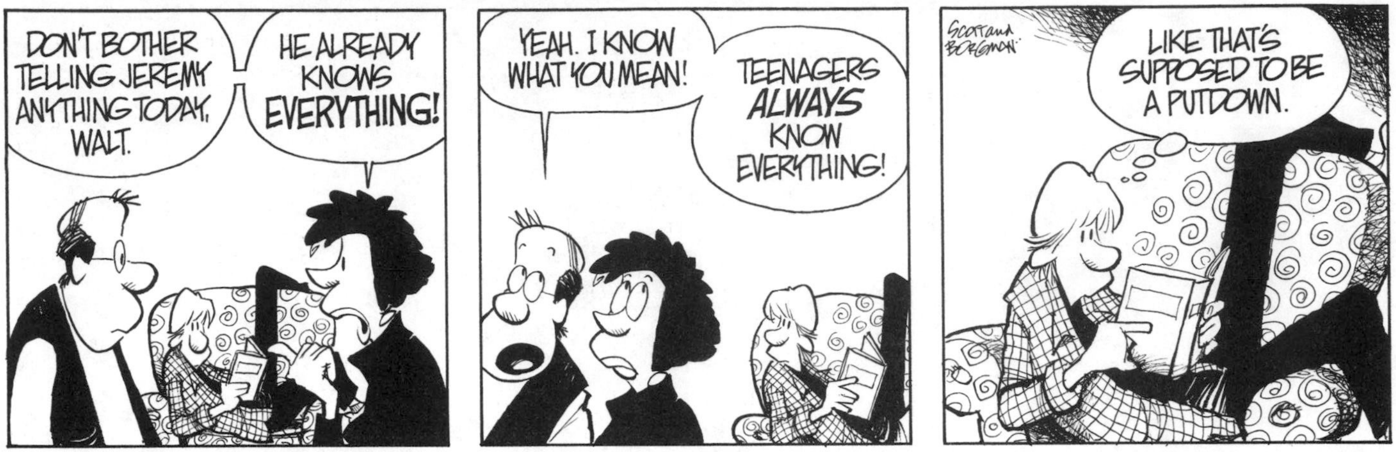
DON'T BOTHER TELLING JEREMY ANYTHING TODAY, WALT.
HE ALREADY KNOWS EVERYTHING!
YEAH. I KNOW WHAT YOU MEAN!
TEENAGERS ALWAYS KNOW EVERYTHING!
LIKE THAT'S SUPPOSED TO BE A PUTDOWN.

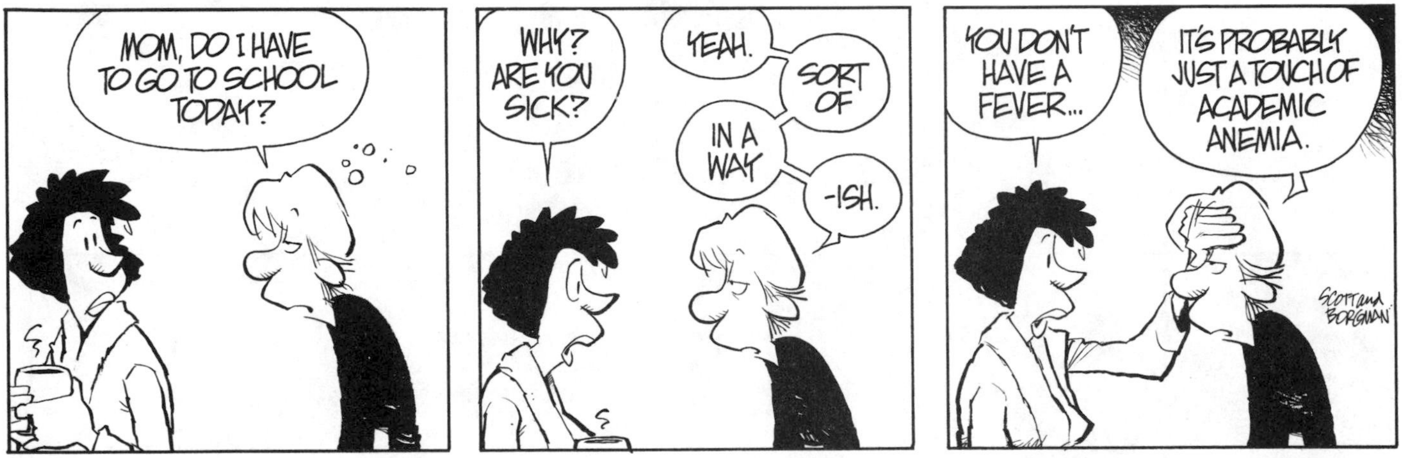
MOM, DO I HAVE TO GO TO SCHOOL TODAY?
WHY? ARE YOU SICK?
YEAH.
SORT OF
IN A WAY
-ISH.
YOU DON'T HAVE A FEVER...
IT'S PROBABLY JUST A TOUCH OF ACADEMIC ANEMIA.

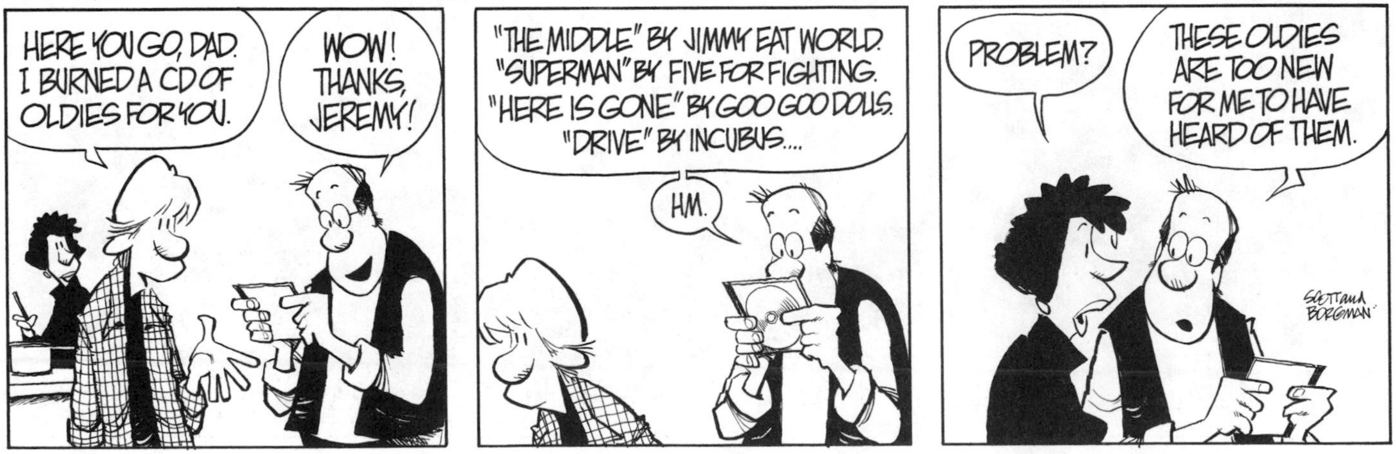
HERE YOU GO, DAD. I BURNED A CD OF OLDIES FOR YOU.
WOW! THANKS, JEREMY!
"THE MIDDLE" BY JIMMY EAT WORLD. "SUPERMAN" BY FIVE FOR FIGHTING. "HERE IS GONE" BY GOO GOO DOLLS. "DRIVE" BY INCUBUS....
HM.
PROBLEM?
THESE OLDIES ARE TOO NEW FOR ME TO HAVE HEARD OF THEM.

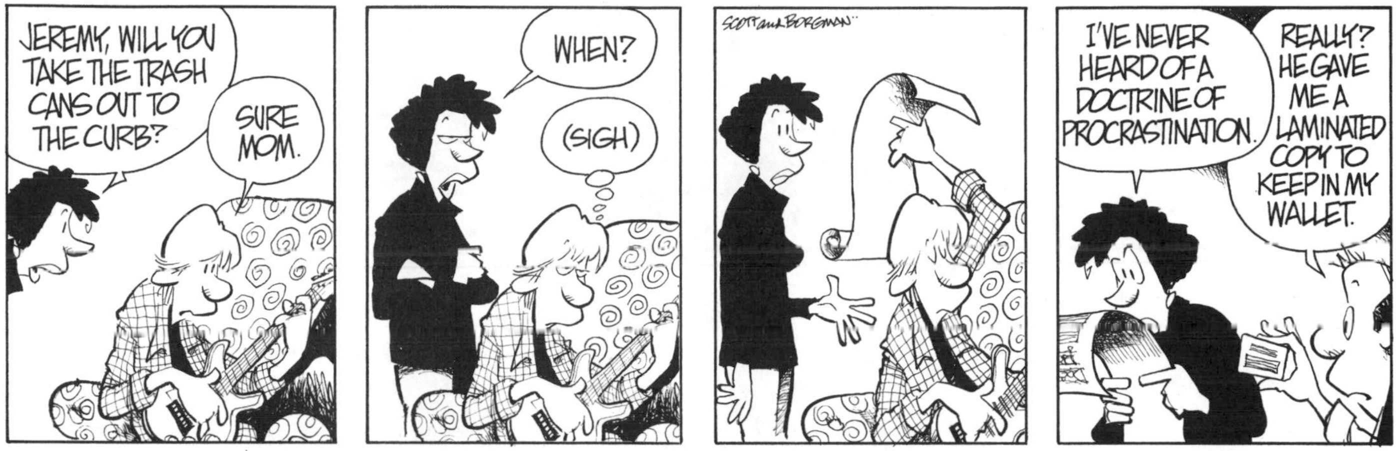
JEREMY, WILL YOU TAKE THE TRASH CANS OUT TO THE CURB?
SURE MOM.
WHEN?
(SIGH)
SCOTT and BORGMAN
I'VE NEVER HEARD OF A DOCTRINE OF PROCRASTINATION.
REALLY? HE GAVE ME A LAMINATED COPY TO KEEP IN MY WALLET.

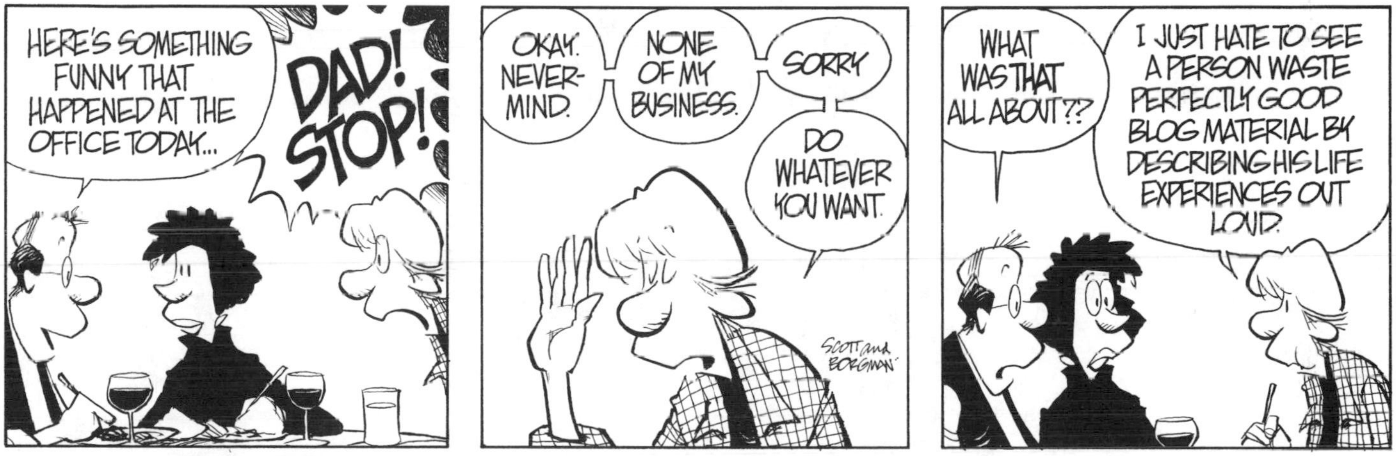
HERE'S SOMETHING FUNNY THAT HAPPENED AT THE OFFICE TODAY...
DAD! STOP!
OKAY. NEVER-MIND.
NONE OF MY BUSINESS.
SORRY
DO WHATEVER YOU WANT.
SCOTT and BORGMAN
WHAT WAS THAT ALL ABOUT??
I JUST HATE TO SEE A PERSON WASTE PERFECTLY GOOD BLOG MATERIAL BY DESCRIBING HIS LIFE EXPERIENCES OUT LOUD.

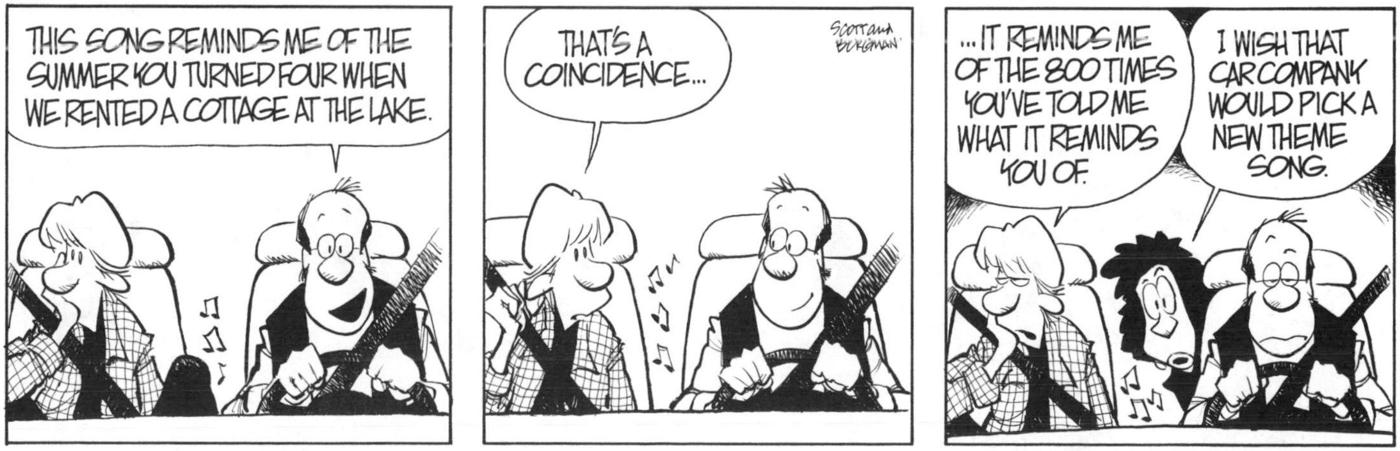
THIS SONG REMINDS ME OF THE SUMMER YOU TURNED FOUR WHEN WE RENTED A COTTAGE AT THE LAKE.
THAT'S A COINCIDENCE...
SCOTT and BORGMAN
...IT REMINDS ME OF THE 800 TIMES YOU'VE TOLD ME WHAT IT REMINDS YOU OF.
I WISH THAT CAR COMPANY WOULD PICK A NEW THEME SONG.

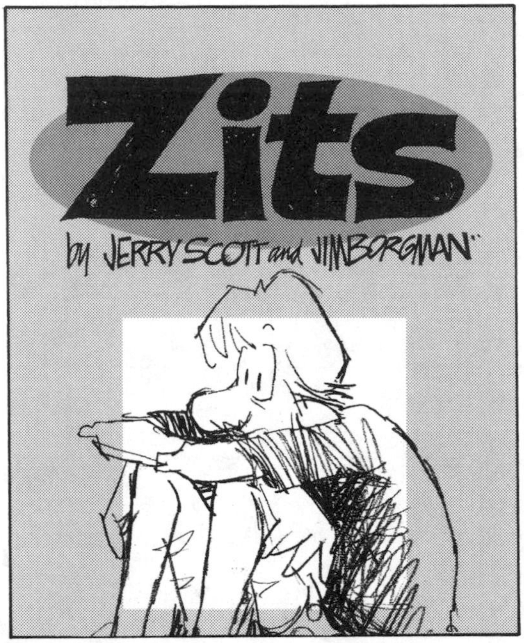
Zits
by JERRY SCOTT and JIMBORGMAN

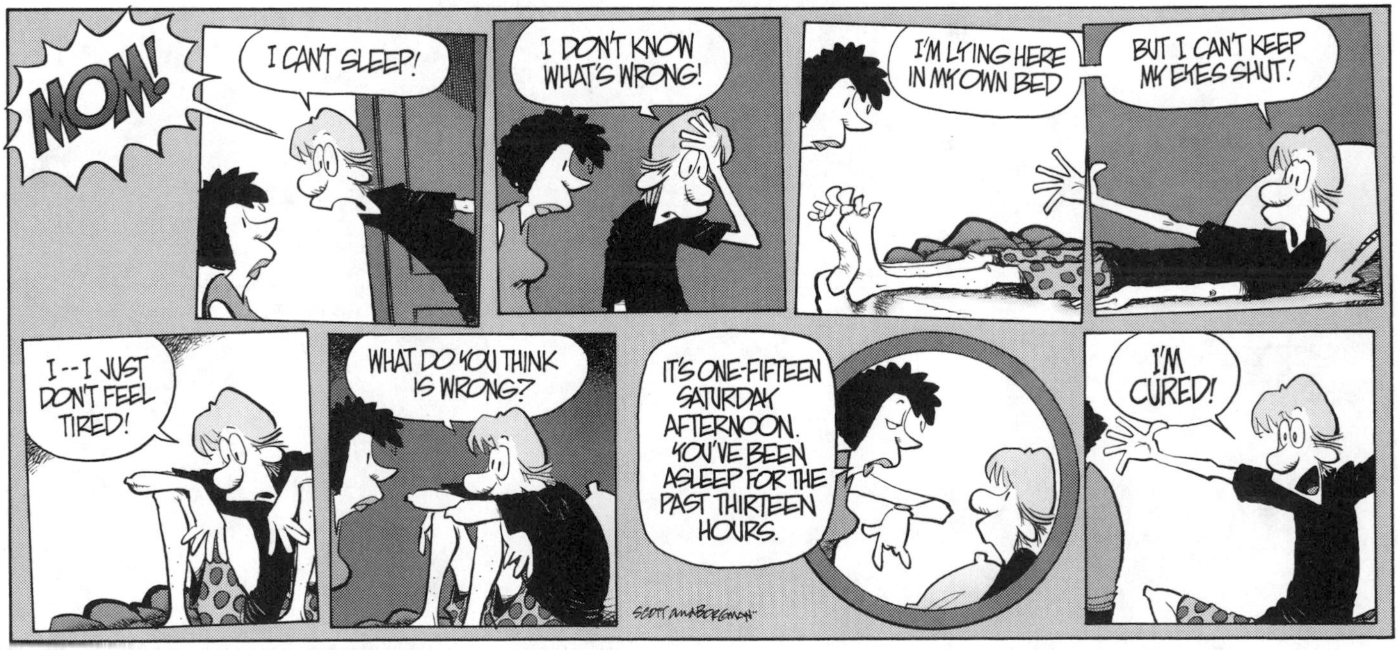
MOM!
I CAN'T SLEEP!
I DON'T KNOW WHAT'S WRONG!
I'M LYING HERE IN MY OWN BED
BUT I CAN'T KEEP MY EYES SHUT!
I--I JUST DON'T FEEL TIRED!
WHAT DO YOU THINK IS WRONG?
IT'S ONE-FIFTEEN SATURDAY AFTERNOON. YOU'VE BEEN ASLEEP FOR THE PAST THIRTEEN HOURS.
I'M CURED!

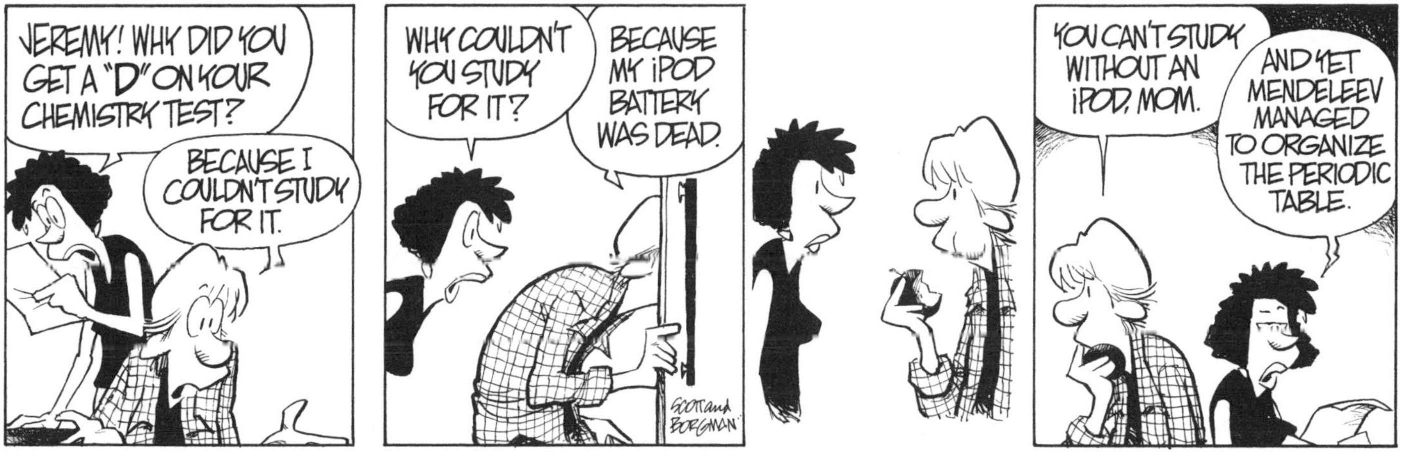
JEREMY! WHY DID YOU GET A "D" ON YOUR CHEMISTRY TEST?
BECAUSE I COULDN'T STUDY FOR IT.
WHY COULDN'T YOU STUDY FOR IT?
BECAUSE MY iPOD BATTERY WAS DEAD.
YOU CAN'T STUDY WITHOUT AN iPOD, MOM.
AND YET MENDELEEV MANAGED TO ORGANIZE THE PERIODIC TABLE.
SCOTT and BORGMAN

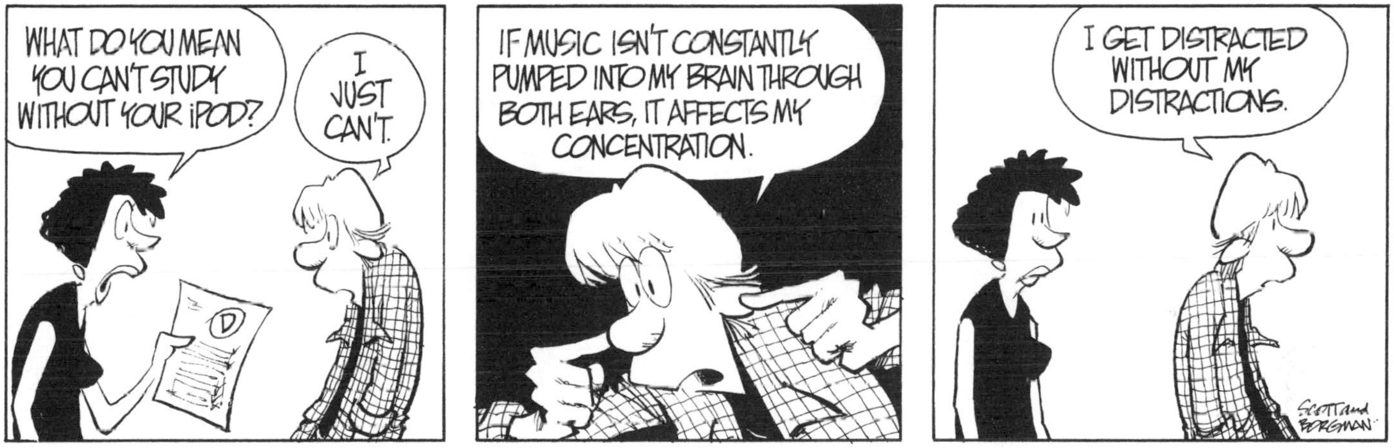
WHAT DO YOU MEAN YOU CAN'T STUDY WITHOUT YOUR iPOD?
I JUST CAN'T.
IF MUSIC ISN'T CONSTANTLY PUMPED INTO MY BRAIN THROUGH BOTH EARS, IT AFFECTS MY CONCENTRATION.
I GET DISTRACTED WITHOUT MY DISTRACTIONS.
SCOTT and BORGMAN

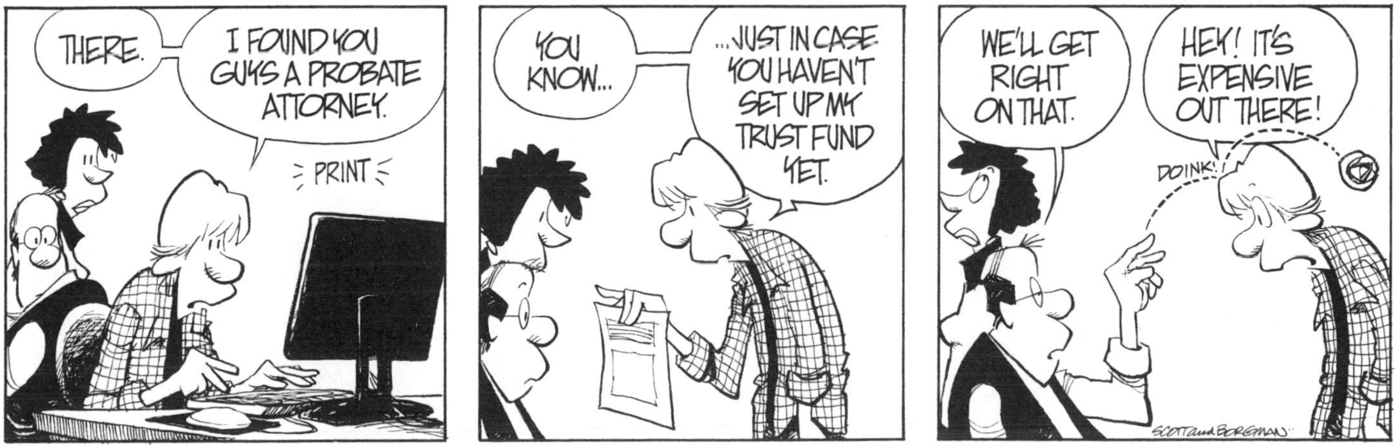
THERE.
I FOUND YOU GUYS A PROBATE ATTORNEY.
PRINT
YOU KNOW...
...JUST IN CASE YOU HAVEN'T SET UP MY TRUST FUND YET.
WE'LL GET RIGHT ON THAT.
HEY! IT'S EXPENSIVE OUT THERE!
DOINK!
SCOTT and BORGMAN

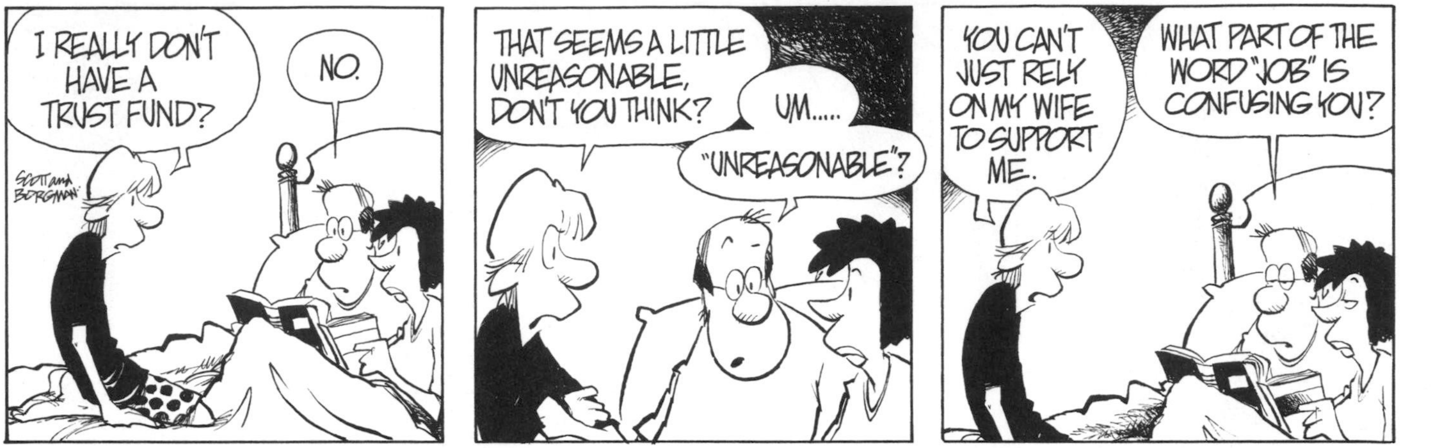
I REALLY DON'T HAVE A TRUST FUND?
NO.
THAT SEEMS A LITTLE UNREASONABLE, DON'T YOU THINK?
UM.....
"UNREASONABLE"?
YOU CAN'T JUST RELY ON MY WIFE TO SUPPORT ME.
WHAT PART OF THE WORD "JOB" IS CONFUSING YOU?

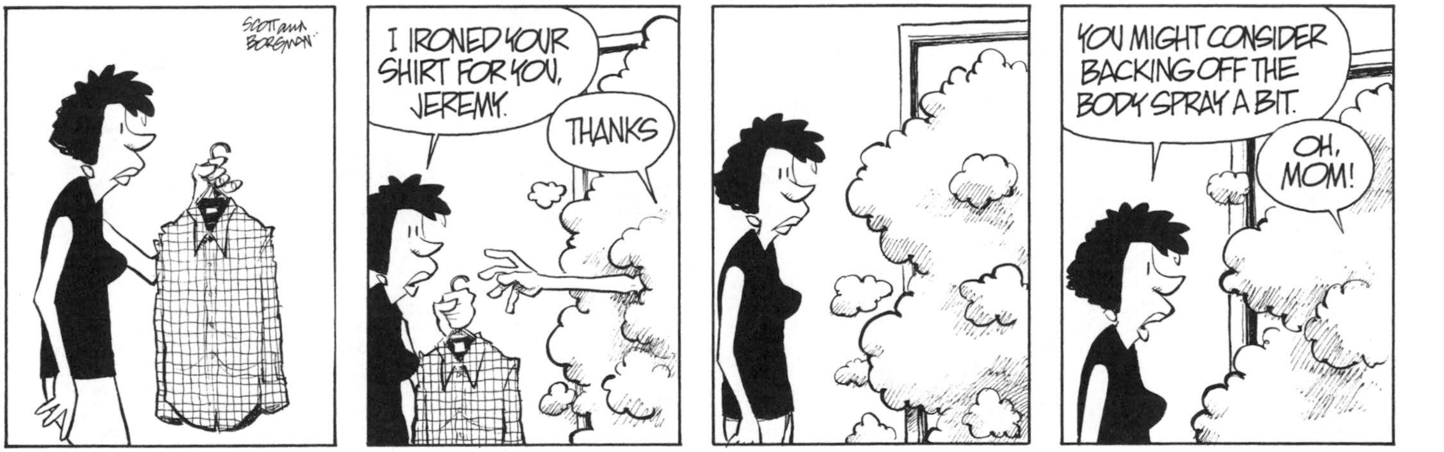
I IRONED YOUR SHIRT FOR YOU, JEREMY.
THANKS
YOU MIGHT CONSIDER BACKING OFF THE BODY SPRAY A BIT.
OH, MOM!

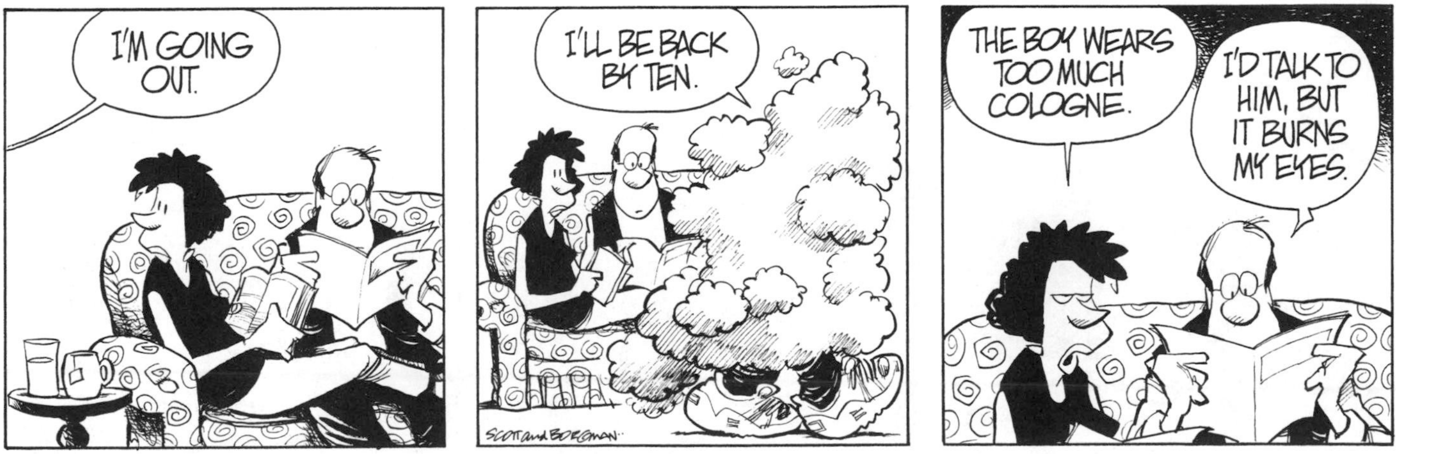
I'M GOING OUT.
I'LL BE BACK BY TEN.
THE BOY WEARS TOO MUCH COLOGNE.
I'D TALK TO HIM, BUT IT BURNS MY EYES.

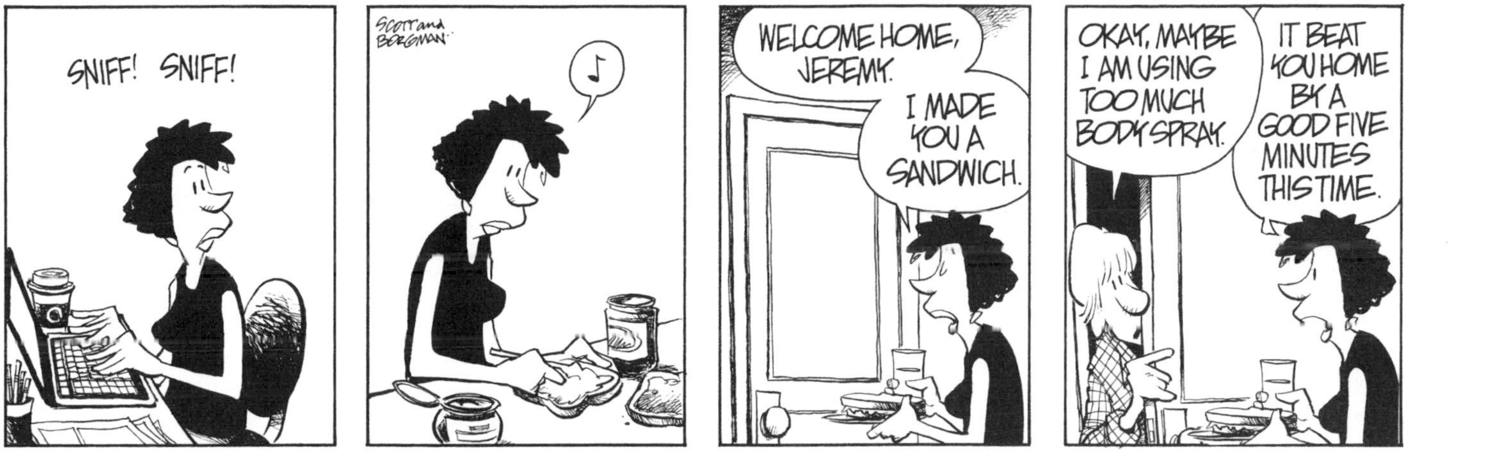
SNIFF! SNIFF!
SCOTT and BORGMAN
♪
WELCOME HOME, JEREMY.
I MADE YOU A SANDWICH.
OKAY, MAYBE I AM USING TOO MUCH BODY SPRAY.
IT BEAT YOU HOME BY A GOOD FIVE MINUTES THIS TIME.

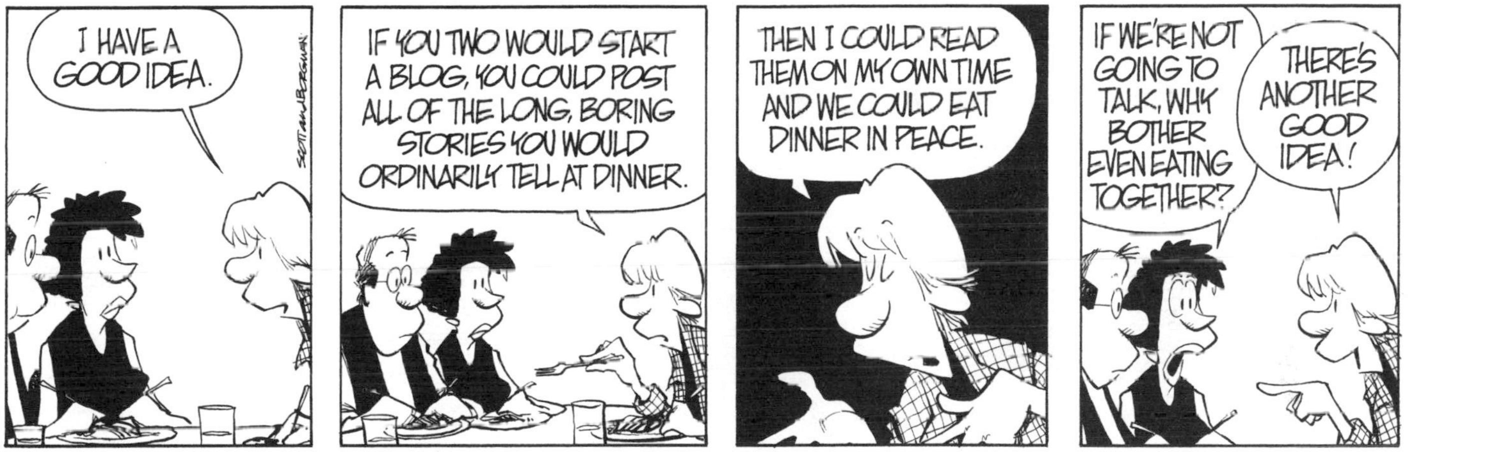
I HAVE A GOOD IDEA.
IF YOU TWO WOULD START A BLOG, YOU COULD POST ALL OF THE LONG, BORING STORIES YOU WOULD ORDINARILY TELL AT DINNER.
THEN I COULD READ THEM ON MY OWN TIME AND WE COULD EAT DINNER IN PEACE.
IF WE'RE NOT GOING TO TALK, WHY BOTHER EVEN EATING TOGETHER?
THERE'S ANOTHER GOOD IDEA!

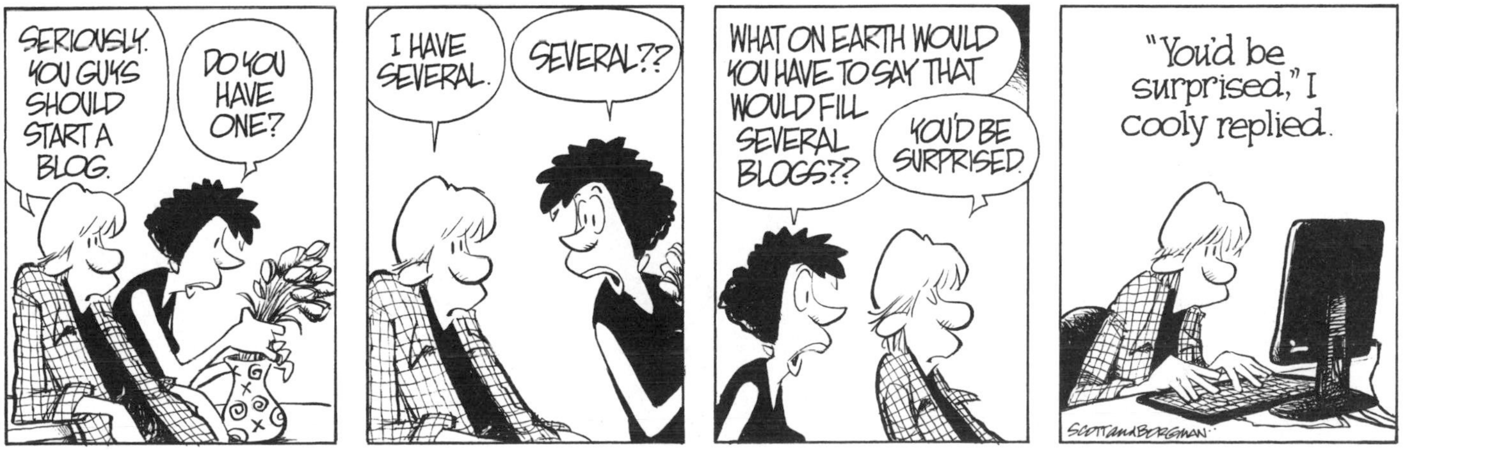
SERIOUSLY. YOU GUYS SHOULD START A BLOG.
DO YOU HAVE ONE?
I HAVE SEVERAL.
SEVERAL??
WHAT ON EARTH WOULD YOU HAVE TO SAY THAT WOULD FILL SEVERAL BLOGS??
YOU'D BE SURPRISED.
"You'd be surprised," I cooly replied.
SCOTT and BORGMAN

Zits
by
JERRY SCOTT and
JIM BORGMAN

BRILLIANT!
PHENOMENAL!
CUTE.
A NEW RECORD!
ANOTHER PERFECT QUIZ SCORE!
HOW WAS YOUR DAY, JEREMY?
SARA LIKED MY SHIRT.
SCOTT and BORGMAN

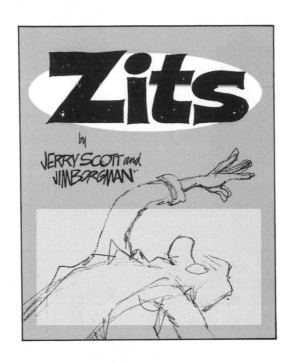

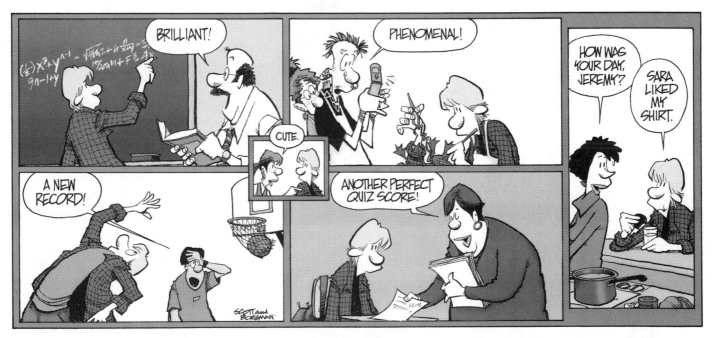

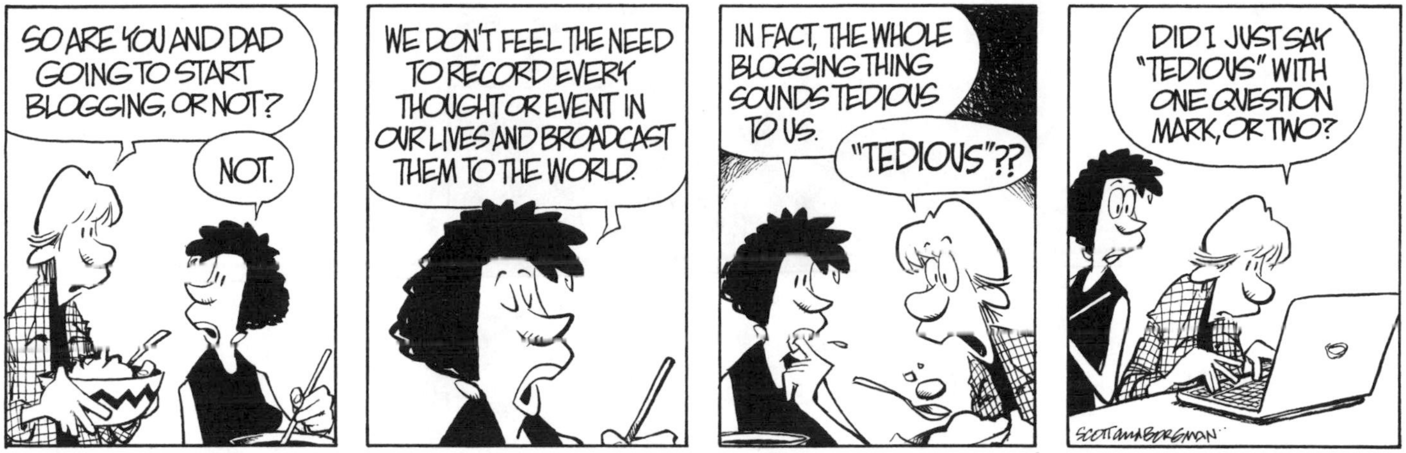
SO ARE YOU AND DAD GOING TO START BLOGGING, OR NOT?
NOT.
WE DON'T FEEL THE NEED TO RECORD EVERY THOUGHT OR EVENT IN OUR LIVES AND BROADCAST THEM TO THE WORLD.
IN FACT, THE WHOLE BLOGGING THING SOUNDS TEDIOUS TO US.
"TEDIOUS"??
DID I JUST SAY "TEDIOUS" WITH ONE QUESTION MARK, OR TWO?
SCOTT and BORGMAN

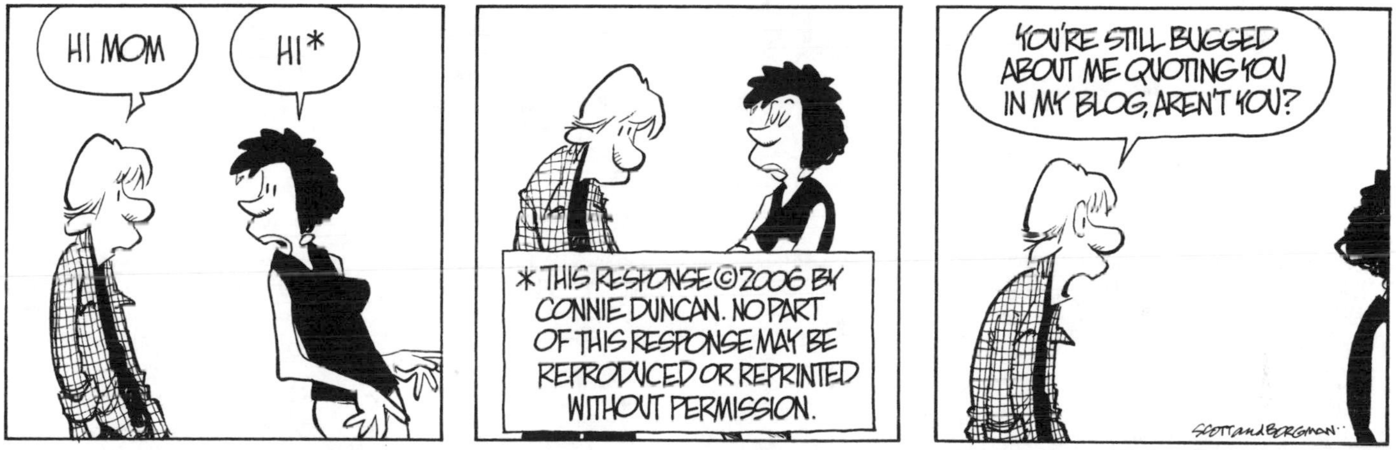
HI MOM
HI*
* THIS RESPONSE © 2006 BY CONNIE DUNCAN. NO PART OF THIS RESPONSE MAY BE REPRODUCED OR REPRINTED WITHOUT PERMISSION.
YOU'RE STILL BUGGED ABOUT ME QUOTING YOU IN MY BLOG, AREN'T YOU?
SCOTT and BORGMAN

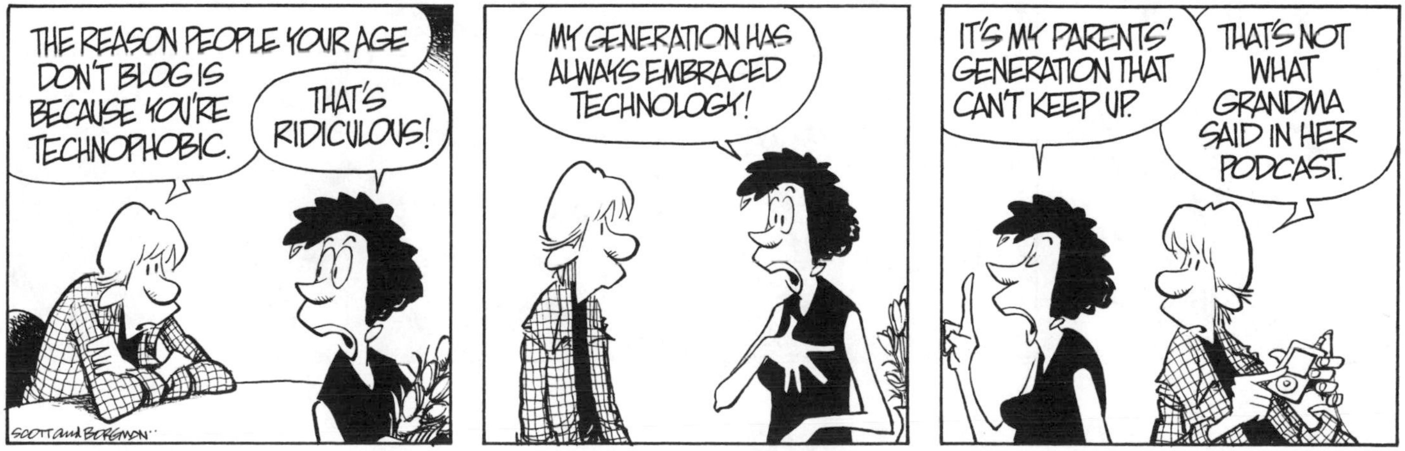
THE REASON PEOPLE YOUR AGE DON'T BLOG IS BECAUSE YOU'RE TECHNOPHOBIC.
THAT'S RIDICULOUS!
MY GENERATION HAS ALWAYS EMBRACED TECHNOLOGY!
IT'S MY PARENTS' GENERATION THAT CAN'T KEEP UP.
THAT'S NOT WHAT GRANDMA SAID IN HER PODCAST.
SCOTT and BORGMAN

Zits

by JERRY SCOTT and JIM BORGMAN

JEREMY, DO I GET ANY CHANGE BACK FROM THE TWENTY BUCKS I GAVE YOU LAST NIGHT?

OH, YEAH. ABOUT THAT...

THE MOVIE WAS EIGHT BUCKS, AND SARA WAS STARVING SO I GOT THE JUMBO POPCORN.

THAT WAS LIKE, SIX DOLLARS

AND HECTOR BORROWED A FIVE.

AFTER THE MOVIE WE WALKED BY THE FOOD COURT WHERE THE MOST INCREDIBLE PIZZA WAS JUST COMING OUT OF THE OVEN!

THEN WE ALL WENT OVER TO THE BOOK-STORE FOR COFFEE, SO....

SO I OWE YOU?

GIVE ME ANOTHER TWENTY AND WE'LL CALL IT EVEN.

SCOTT and BORGMAN

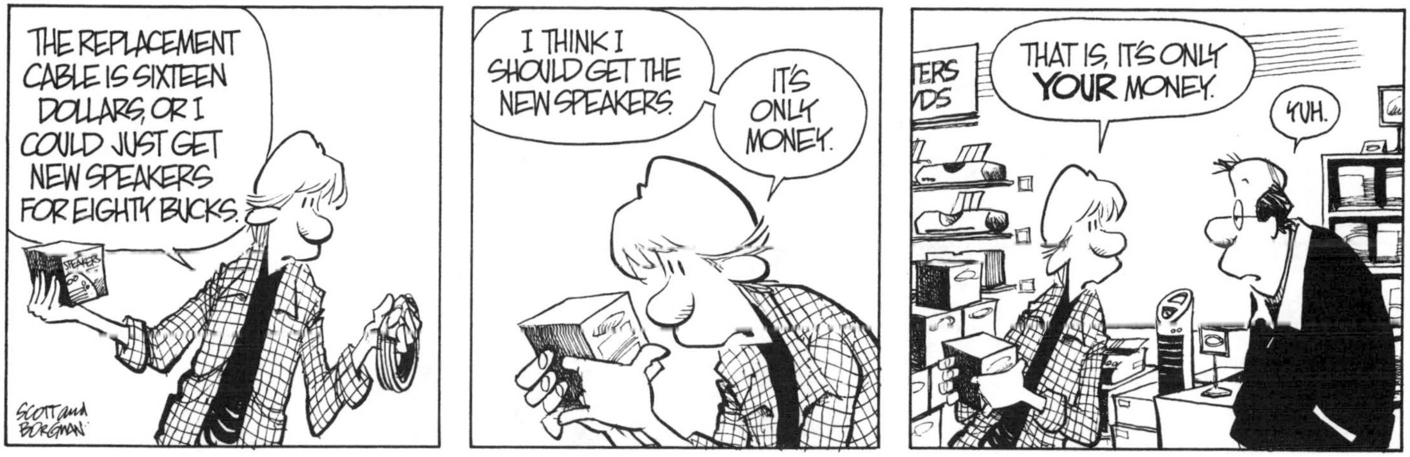
THE REPLACEMENT CABLE IS SIXTEEN DOLLARS, OR I COULD JUST GET NEW SPEAKERS FOR EIGHTY BUCKS.
I THINK I SHOULD GET THE NEW SPEAKERS.
IT'S ONLY MONEY.
THAT IS, IT'S ONLY YOUR MONEY.
YUH.

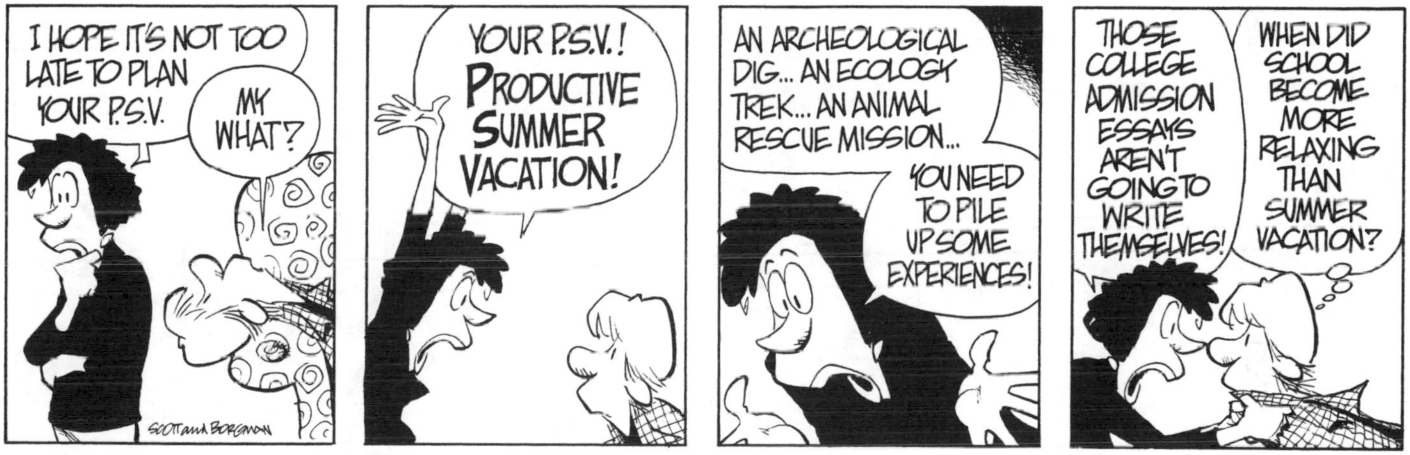
I HOPE IT'S NOT TOO LATE TO PLAN YOUR P.S.V.
MY WHAT?
YOUR P.S.V.! PRODUCTIVE SUMMER VACATION!
AN ARCHEOLOGICAL DIG... AN ECOLOGY TREK... AN ANIMAL RESCUE MISSION...
YOU NEED TO PILE UP SOME EXPERIENCES!
THOSE COLLEGE ADMISSION ESSAYS AREN'T GOING TO WRITE THEMSELVES!
WHEN DID SCHOOL BECOME MORE RELAXING THAN SUMMER VACATION?

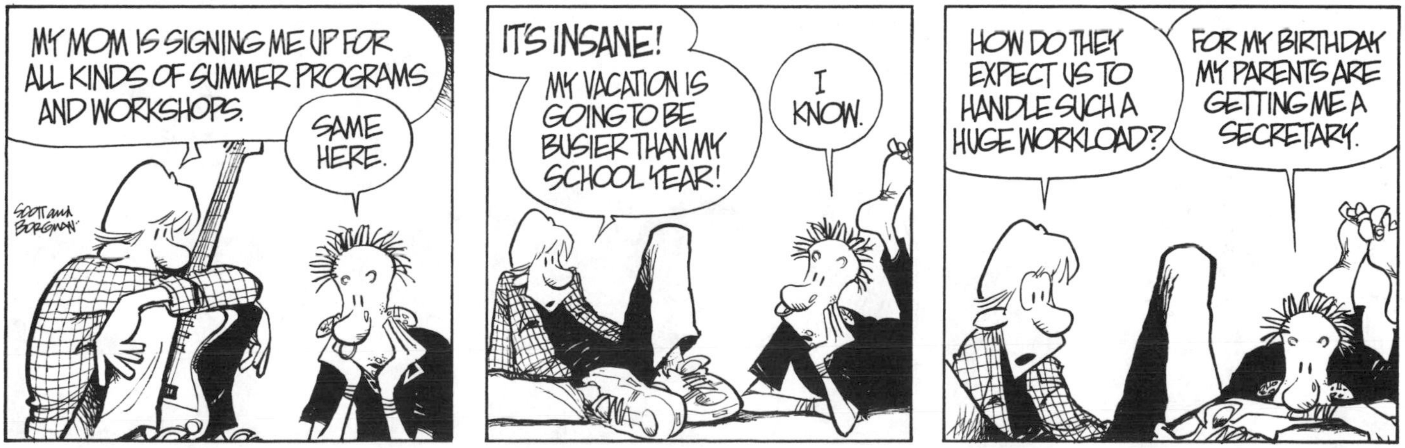
MY MOM IS SIGNING ME UP FOR ALL KINDS OF SUMMER PROGRAMS AND WORKSHOPS.
SAME HERE.
IT'S INSANE!
MY VACATION IS GOING TO BE BUSIER THAN MY SCHOOL YEAR!
I KNOW.
HOW DO THEY EXPECT US TO HANDLE SUCH A HUGE WORKLOAD?
FOR MY BIRTHDAY MY PARENTS ARE GETTING ME A SECRETARY.

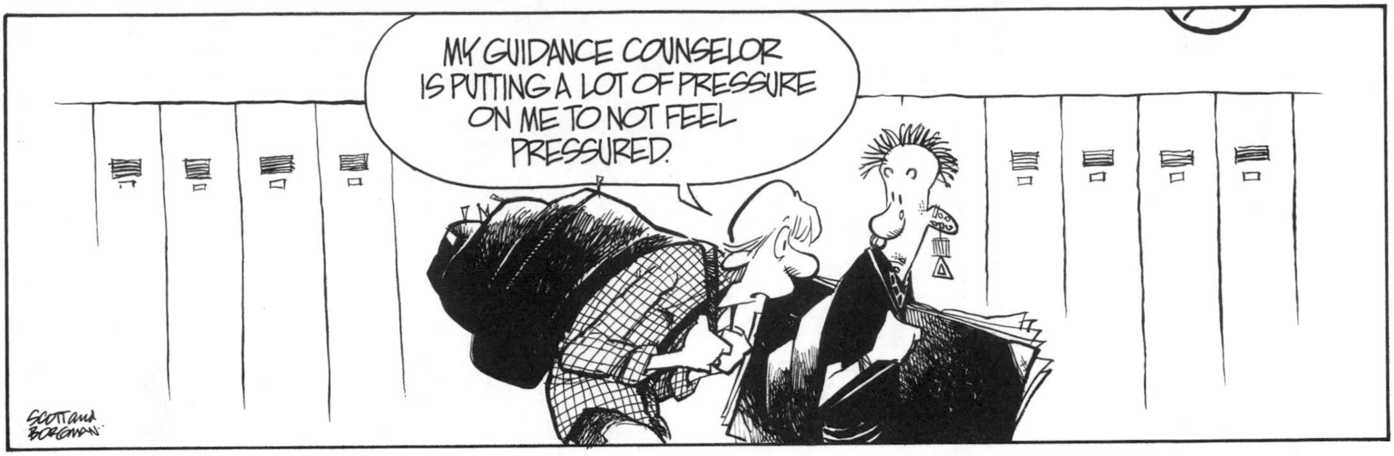
MY GUIDANCE COUNSELOR IS PUTTING A LOT OF PRESSURE ON ME TO NOT FEEL PRESSURED.
SCOTT and BORGMAN

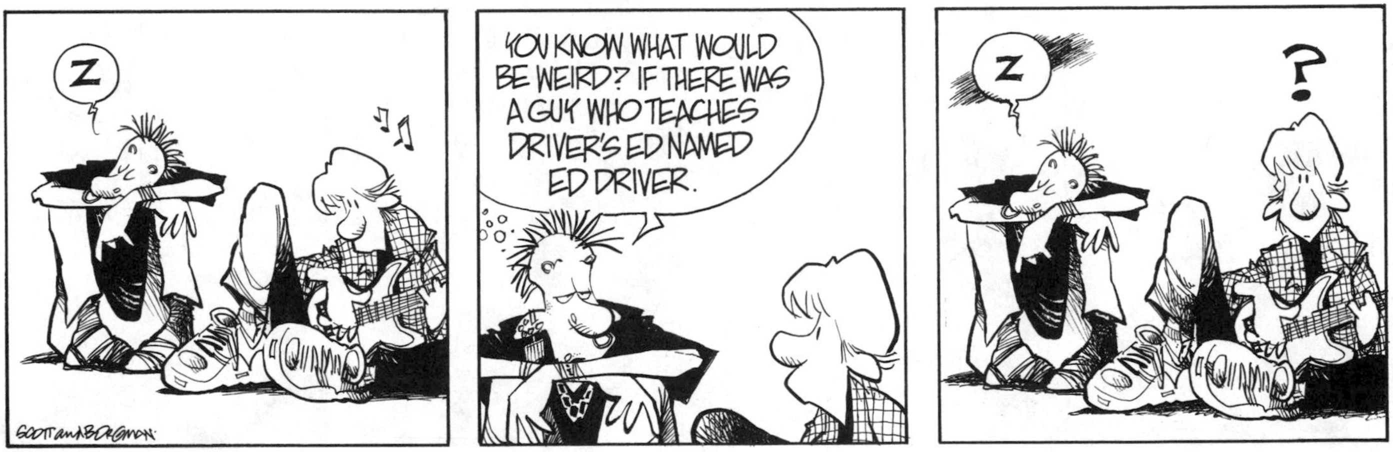
Z
YOU KNOW WHAT WOULD BE WEIRD? IF THERE WAS A GUY WHO TEACHES DRIVER'S ED NAMED ED DRIVER.
Z
?
SCOTT and BORGMAN

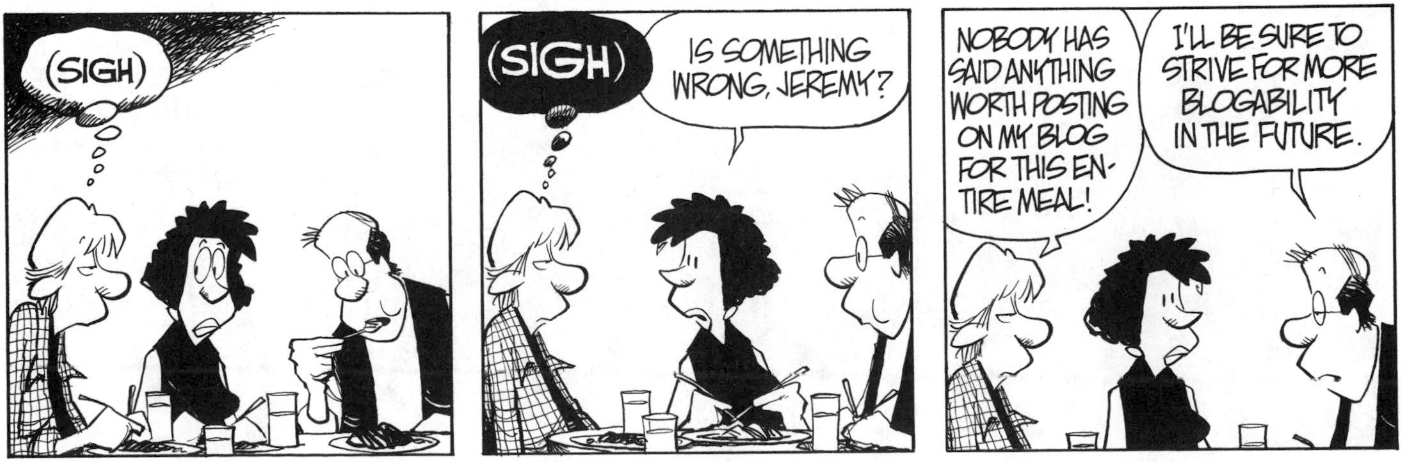
(SIGH)
(SIGH)
IS SOMETHING WRONG, JEREMY?
NOBODY HAS SAID ANYTHING WORTH POSTING ON MY BLOG FOR THIS ENTIRE MEAL!
I'LL BE SURE TO STRIVE FOR MORE BLOGABILITY IN THE FUTURE.

SO THAT'S THE SITUATION.

DO YOU HAVE ANY ADVICE?

YES

I THINK YOU SHOULD ADMIT YOUR MISTAKE AND QUIT WORRYING ABOUT WHAT OTHER PEOPLE THINK.

SCOTT and BORGMAN

I MEANT ADVICE THAT I MIGHT ACTUALLY USE.

I TOLD HIM TO GET SOMETHING TATTOOED, BUT HE WON'T LISTEN TO ME, EITHER.

SEE?? I TOLD YOU WE WERE GOING TO JEREMY'S HOUSE!

MY MOM HAS ME G.P.S.'D

OKAY. I'LL BE SURE TO GIVE HIM THE MESSAGE AS SOON AS HE GETS HOME.

CLICK! SCAN! PRINT!

DAD-
CALL
HOME.
-J

PIERCE!

OHMYGAWD! D'IJON DECIDED TO BREAK UP WITH YOU THIS MORNING BUT WE HAD A LONG TALK AND I CONVINCED HER THAT YOU STILL HAD POTENTIAL SO SHE TOTALLY CHANGED HER MIND AND NOW SHE'S OUT BUYING THIS NEW SHIRT FOR YOU BECAUSE IT MATCHES YOUR EYES, SO BE SURPRISED WHEN

WAIT-- WHAT?? RELATIONSHIPS ARE LIKE SAUSAGE.... IT'S REALLY BETTER NOT KNOWING HOW THEY'RE MADE.

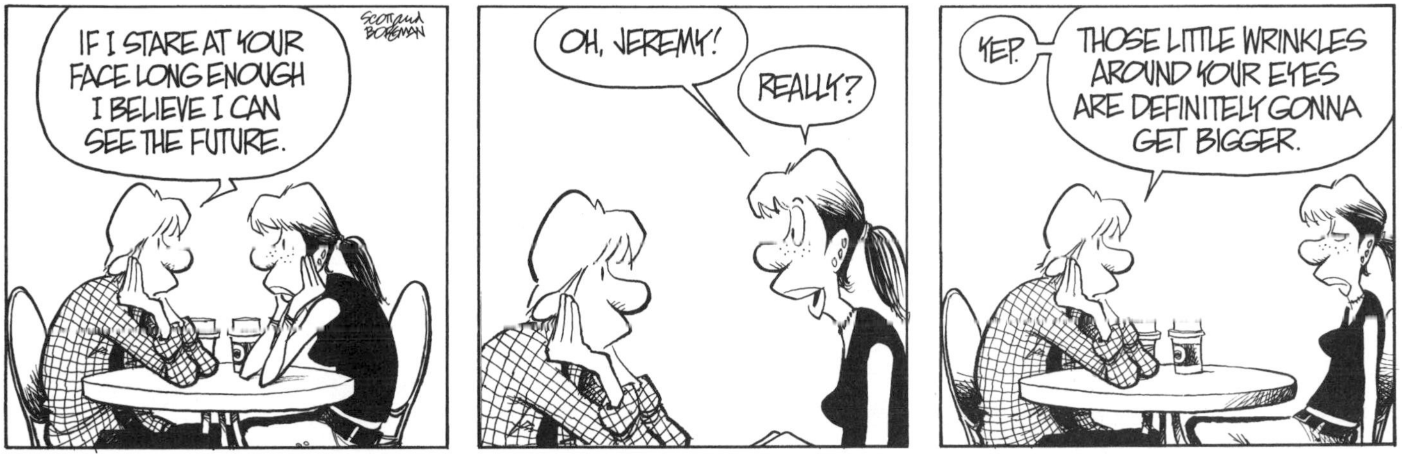
IF I STARE AT YOUR FACE LONG ENOUGH I BELIEVE I CAN SEE THE FUTURE.
SCOTT and BORGMAN
OH, JEREMY!
REALLY?
YEP.
THOSE LITTLE WRINKLES AROUND YOUR EYES ARE DEFINITELY GONNA GET BIGGER.

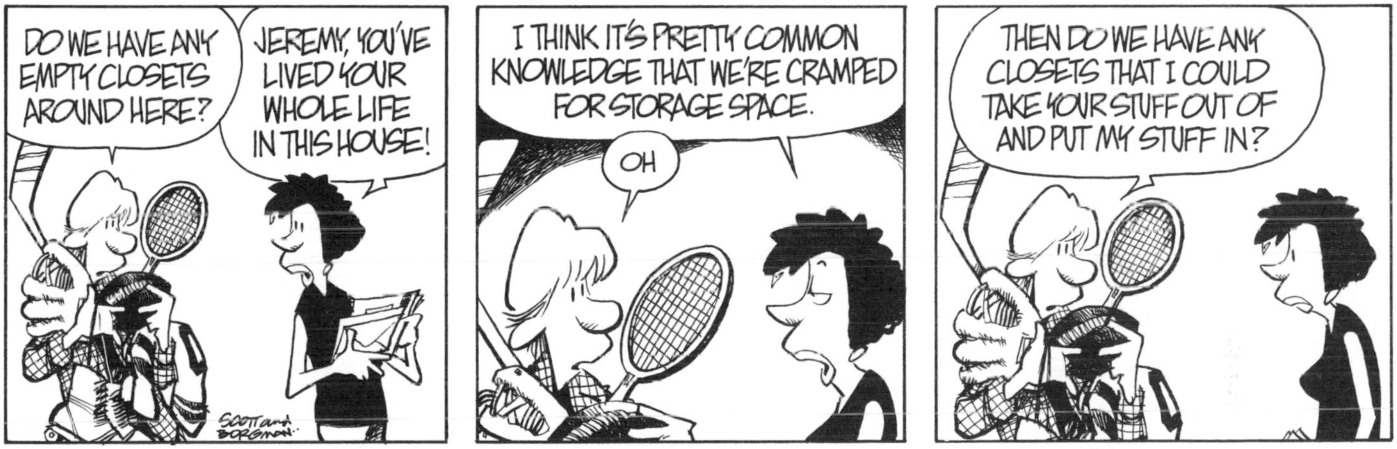
DO WE HAVE ANY EMPTY CLOSETS AROUND HERE?
JEREMY, YOU'VE LIVED YOUR WHOLE LIFE IN THIS HOUSE!
SCOTT and BORGMAN
I THINK IT'S PRETTY COMMON KNOWLEDGE THAT WE'RE CRAMPED FOR STORAGE SPACE.
OH
THEN DO WE HAVE ANY CLOSETS THAT I COULD TAKE YOUR STUFF OUT OF AND PUT MY STUFF IN?

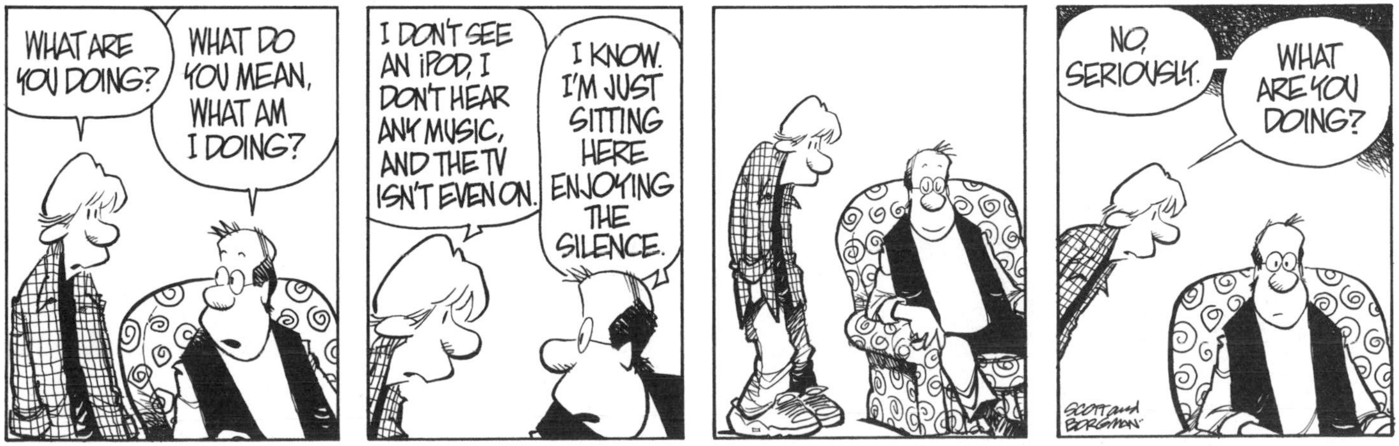
WHAT ARE YOU DOING?
WHAT DO YOU MEAN, WHAT AM I DOING?
I DON'T SEE AN iPOD, I DON'T HEAR ANY MUSIC, AND THE TV ISN'T EVEN ON.
I KNOW. I'M JUST SITTING HERE ENJOYING THE SILENCE.
NO, SERIOUSLY.
WHAT ARE YOU DOING?
SCOTT and BORGMAN

Zits

by JERRY SCOTT and JIM BORGMAN

DUDE—HELP ME OUT HERE.

CAN YOU READ QUESTION 8?

WHAT IS THIS?

THE HISTORY TEST WE'RE TAKING IN TEN MINUTES.

MOE TOOK A PICTURE OF IT LAST PERIOD WITH HER CELL PHONE CAMERA AND POSTED IT ON HER MYSPACE PAGE, WHICH I'VE BEEN TRYING TO MAKE OUT ON MY TEENIE BLACKBERRY SCREEN FOR THE PAST FORTY-FIVE MINUTES.

GOOD USE OF YOUR STUDY HOUR.

WHY DO PEOPLE KEEP SAYING THAT TO ME?

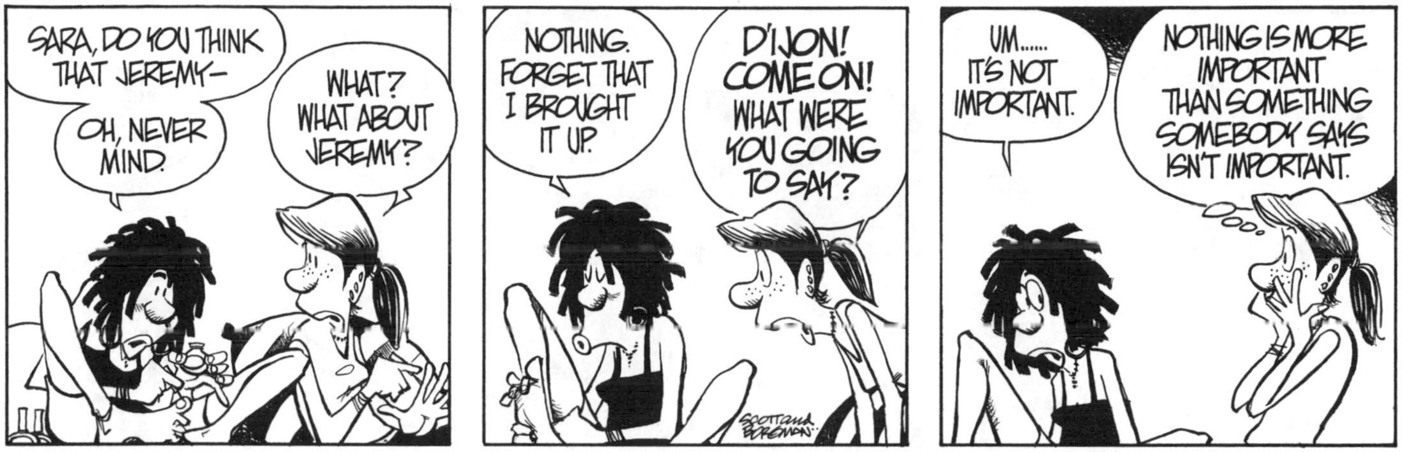
SARA, DO YOU THINK THAT JEREMY–
OH, NEVER MIND.
WHAT? WHAT ABOUT JEREMY?
NOTHING. FORGET THAT I BROUGHT IT UP.
D'JON! COME ON! WHAT WERE YOU GOING TO SAY?
UM...... IT'S NOT IMPORTANT.
NOTHING IS MORE IMPORTANT THAN SOMETHING SOMEBODY SAYS ISN'T IMPORTANT.

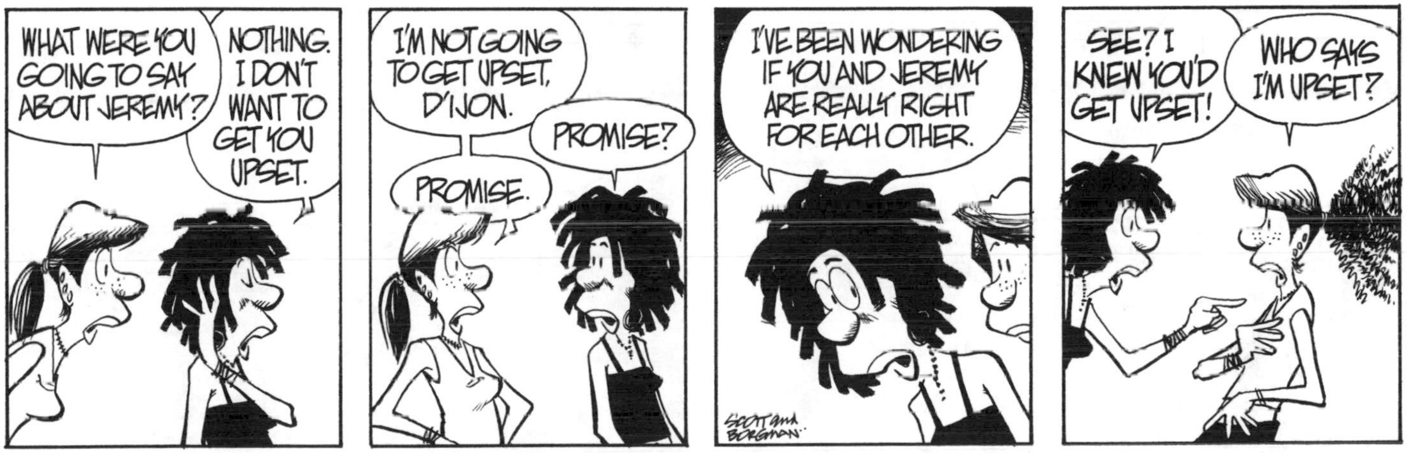
WHAT WERE YOU GOING TO SAY ABOUT JEREMY?
NOTHING. I DON'T WANT TO GET YOU UPSET.
I'M NOT GOING TO GET UPSET, D'JON.
PROMISE?
PROMISE.
I'VE BEEN WONDERING IF YOU AND JEREMY ARE REALLY RIGHT FOR EACH OTHER.
SEE? I KNEW YOU'D GET UPSET!
WHO SAYS I'M UPSET?

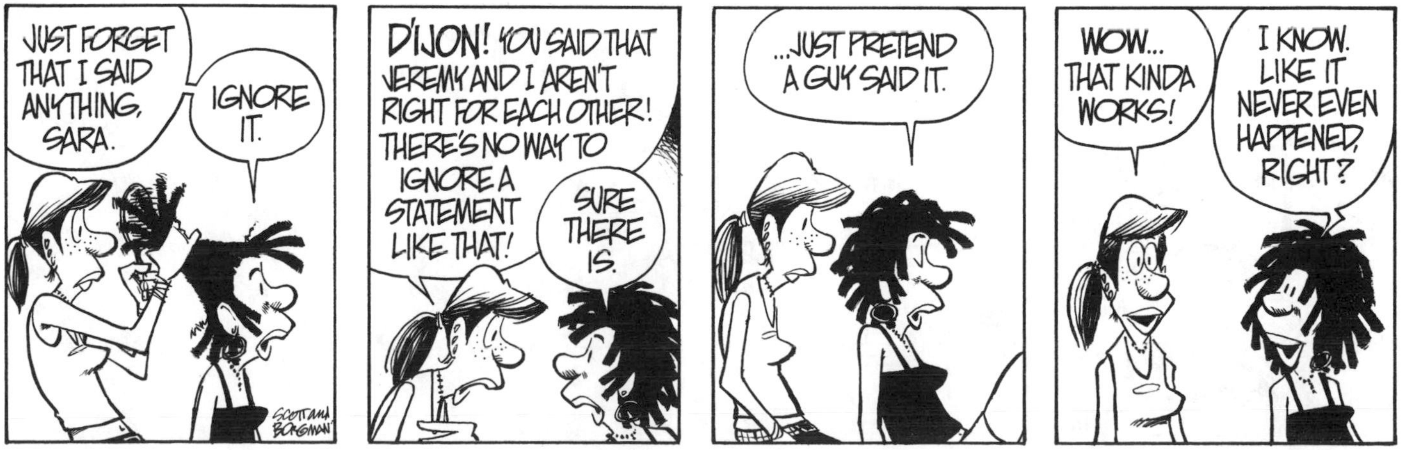
JUST FORGET THAT I SAID ANYTHING, SARA.
IGNORE IT.
D'JON! YOU SAID THAT JEREMY AND I AREN'T RIGHT FOR EACH OTHER! THERE'S NO WAY TO IGNORE A STATEMENT LIKE THAT!
SURE THERE IS.
...JUST PRETEND A GUY SAID IT.
WOW... THAT KINDA WORKS!
I KNOW. LIKE IT NEVER EVEN HAPPENED, RIGHT?

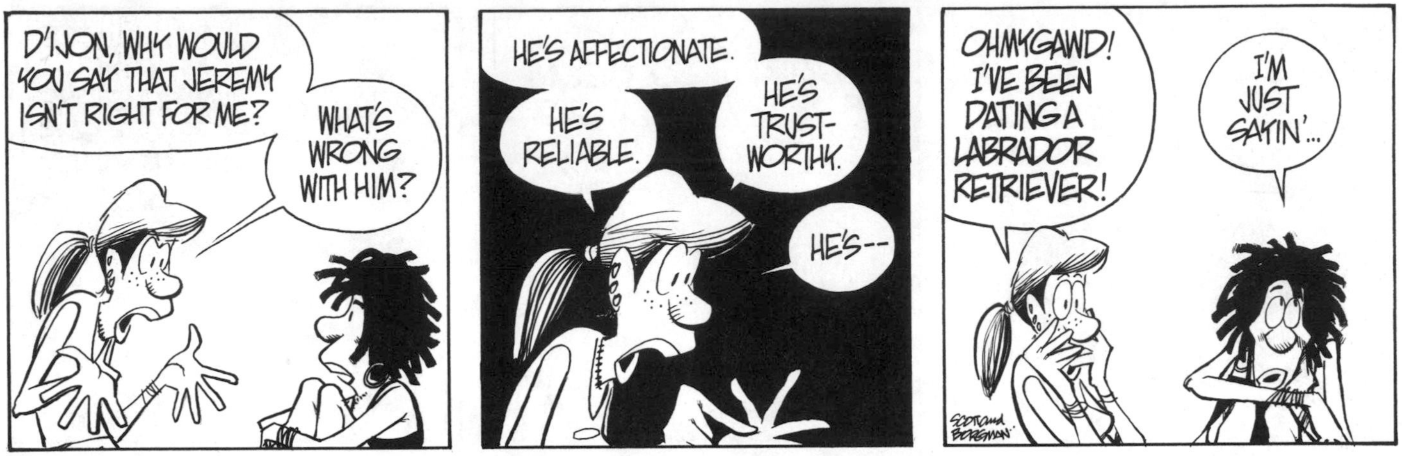
D'IJON, WHY WOULD YOU SAY THAT JEREMY ISN'T RIGHT FOR ME?
WHAT'S WRONG WITH HIM?
HE'S AFFECTIONATE.
HE'S RELIABLE.
HE'S TRUST-WORTHY.
HE'S--
OHMYGAWD! I'VE BEEN DATING A LABRADOR RETRIEVER!
I'M JUST SAYIN'...

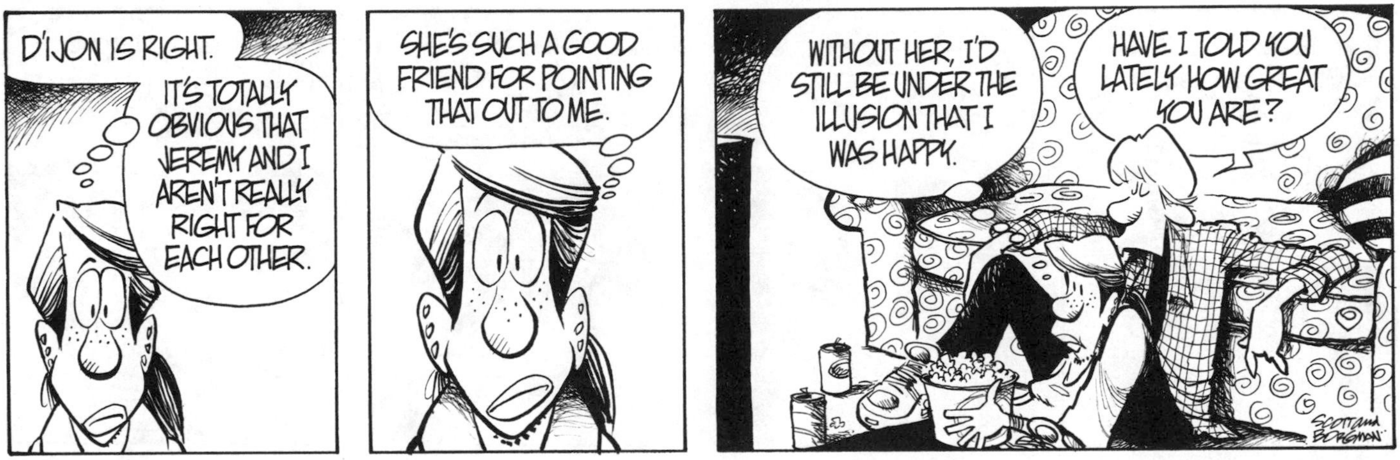
D'IJON IS RIGHT.
IT'S TOTALLY OBVIOUS THAT JEREMY AND I AREN'T REALLY RIGHT FOR EACH OTHER.
SHE'S SUCH A GOOD FRIEND FOR POINTING THAT OUT TO ME.
WITHOUT HER, I'D STILL BE UNDER THE ILLUSION THAT I WAS HAPPY.
HAVE I TOLD YOU LATELY HOW GREAT YOU ARE?

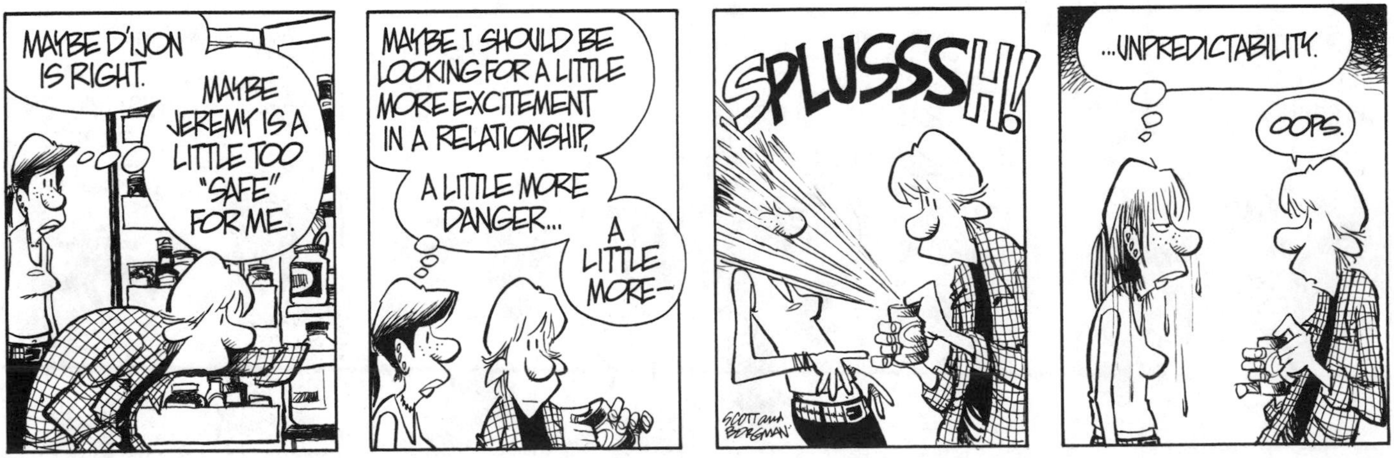
MAYBE D'IJON IS RIGHT.
MAYBE JEREMY IS A LITTLE TOO "SAFE" FOR ME.
MAYBE I SHOULD BE LOOKING FOR A LITTLE MORE EXCITEMENT IN A RELATIONSHIP,
A LITTLE MORE DANGER...
A LITTLE MORE-
SPLUSSSH!
...UNPREDICTABILITY.
OOPS.

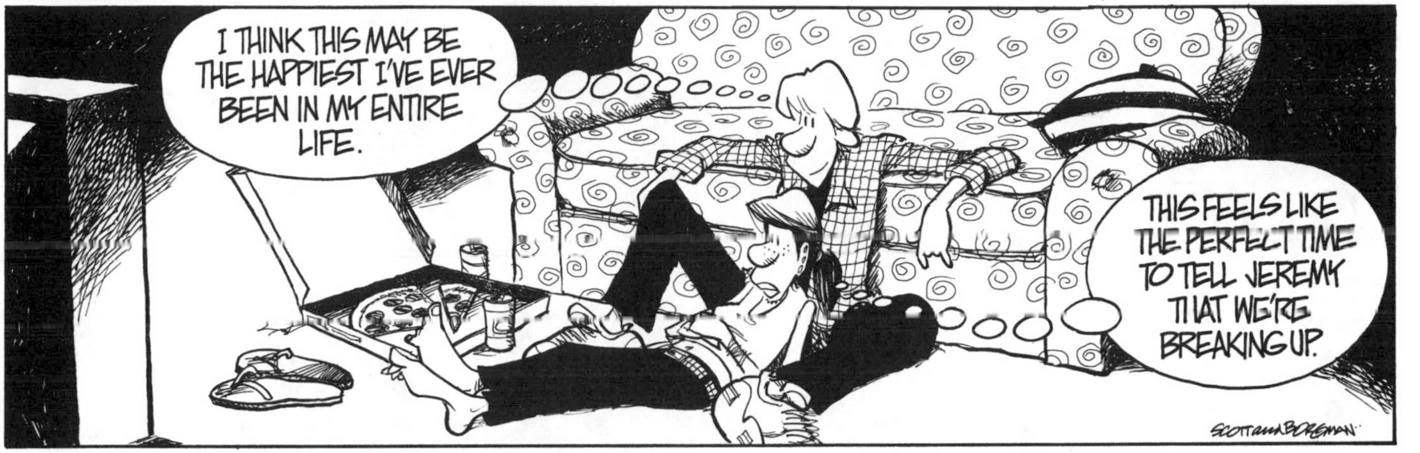
I THINK THIS MAY BE THE HAPPIEST I'VE EVER BEEN IN MY ENTIRE LIFE.
THIS FEELS LIKE THE PERFECT TIME TO TELL JEREMY THAT WE'RE BREAKING UP.
SCOTT and BORGMAN

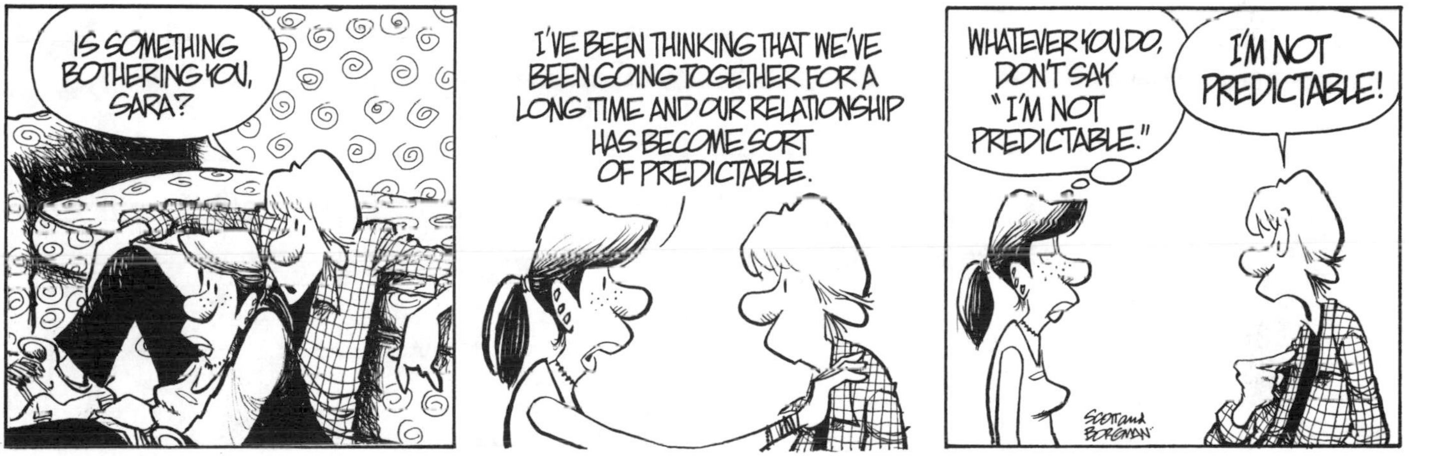
IS SOMETHING BOTHERING YOU, SARA?
I'VE BEEN THINKING THAT WE'VE BEEN GOING TOGETHER FOR A LONG TIME AND OUR RELATIONSHIP HAS BECOME SORT OF PREDICTABLE.
WHATEVER YOU DO, DON'T SAY "I'M NOT PREDICTABLE."
I'M NOT PREDICTABLE!
SCOTT and BORGMAN

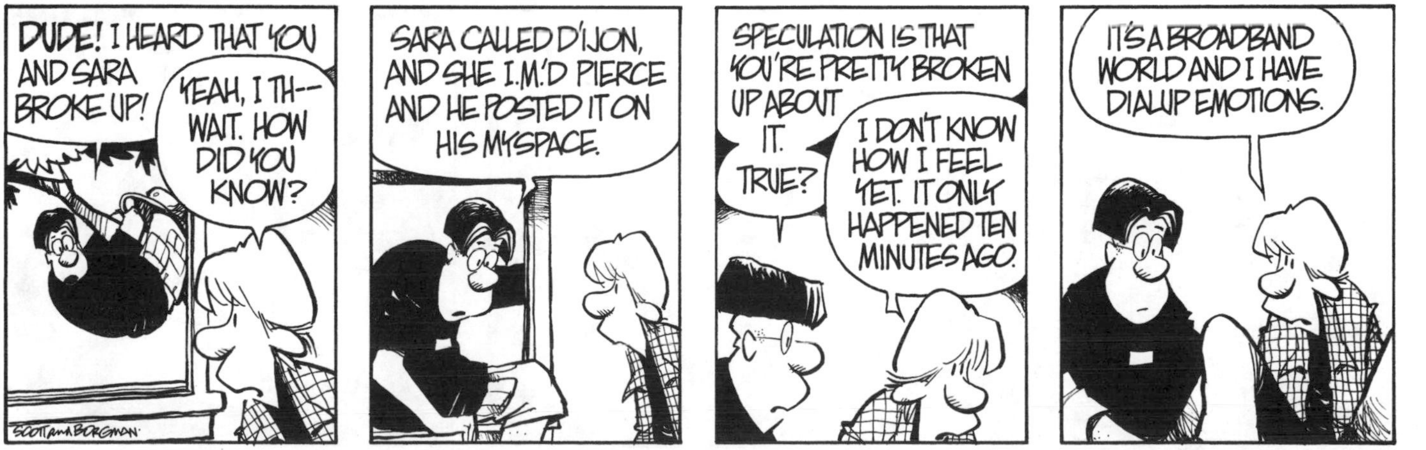
DUDE! I HEARD THAT YOU AND SARA BROKE UP!
YEAH, I TH-- WAIT. HOW DID YOU KNOW?
SARA CALLED D'IJON, AND SHE I.M.'D PIERCE AND HE POSTED IT ON HIS MYSPACE.
SPECULATION IS THAT YOU'RE PRETTY BROKEN UP ABOUT IT.
TRUE?
I DON'T KNOW HOW I FEEL YET. IT ONLY HAPPENED TEN MINUTES AGO.
IT'S A BROADBAND WORLD AND I HAVE DIALUP EMOTIONS.
SCOTT and BORGMAN

YOUR GENERATION HAS TOTALLY MESSED UP THIS PLANET THROUGH ITS GREED, INCOMPETENCE AND APATHY!

SCOTT and BORGMAN

YOU'RE PROBABLY THE MOST ARROGANT GROUP OF PEOPLE IN HISTORY!

WELL, I'M SURE YOUR GENERATION WILL DO A BETTER JOB...

...SHOULD ANY OF YOU EVER MANAGE TO GET OUT OF BED BEFORE NOON.

AND WHY DO YOU ALWAYS HAVE TO BE SO CRITICAL?

MOM, CAN YOU PICK ME UP?

SCOTT and BORGMAN

OH, WAIT, NEVER MIND. PIERCE SAID THAT HIS DAD CAN GIVE ME A R-- WHAT? HE CAN'T GIVE ME A RIDE? WHY NOT? WHOA! DID YOU SEE THAT?

THAT GUY JUST ABOUT-- DUDE! MOVE! YOU'RE STANDING RIGHT IN FRONT OF THE TV, YOU--OW! OH, YOU ARE SO GONNA GET IT! THUMP! BAM! HA! HA! HA!

FLUSH!

SO, CAN YOU PICK ME UP?

I'M THE KIND OF PERSON WHO REALLY LOVES PEOPLE.

SCOTT and BORGMAN

ALL KINDS OF PEOPLE, REALLY.

IT DOESN'T MATTER TO ME...

TAP TAP

...I MEAN, AS LONG AS THEY'RE HOT YOUNG GIRLS.

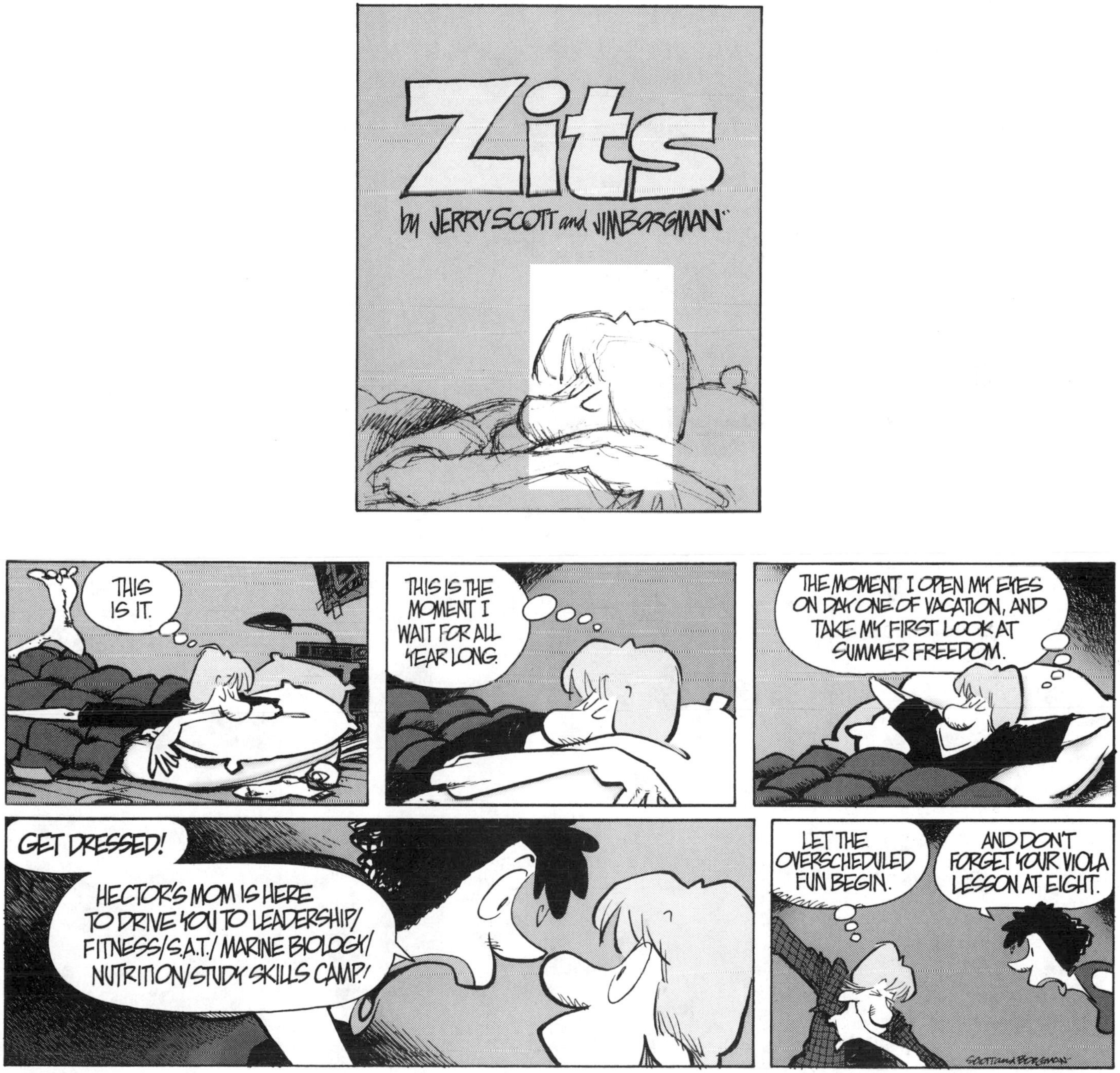
Zits
by JERRY SCOTT and JIM BORGMAN
THIS IS IT.
THIS IS THE MOMENT I WAIT FOR ALL YEAR LONG.
THE MOMENT I OPEN MY EYES ON DAY ONE OF VACATION, AND TAKE MY FIRST LOOK AT SUMMER FREEDOM.
GET DRESSED!
HECTOR'S MOM IS HERE TO DRIVE YOU TO LEADERSHIP/ FITNESS/S.A.T./ MARINE BIOLOGY/ NUTRITION/STUDY SKILLS CAMP!
LET THE OVERSCHEDULED FUN BEGIN.
AND DON'T FORGET YOUR VIOLA LESSON AT EIGHT.
SCOTT and BORGMAN

Zits
by
JERRY SCOTT and JIM BORGMAN

HEY.
THERE GOES SARA.
SARA!
HEY SARA!
SA-RA!
YO!
SCOTT and BORGMAN
SARA!
SARA!
SARA TOOMEY!
FWEEEEET!
OH, HI JEREMY.
SOMETIMES I FEEL SMOTHERED IN THIS RELATIONSHIP.

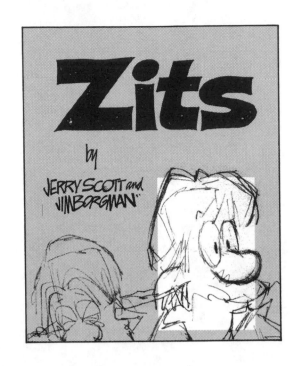

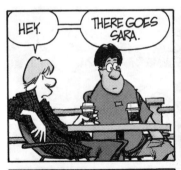

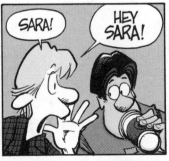

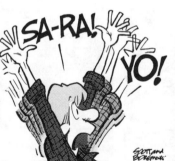

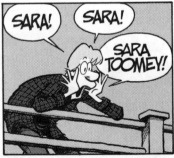

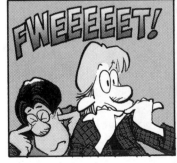

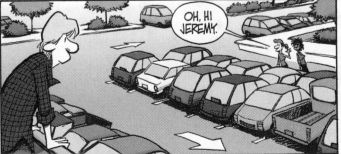

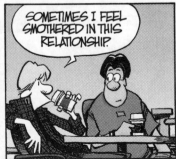

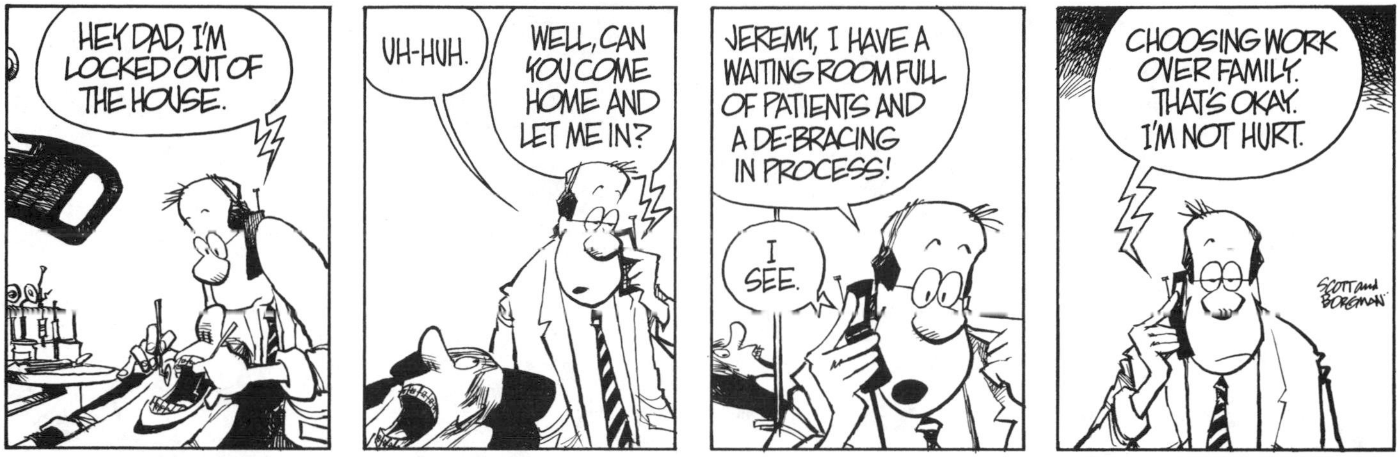
HEY DAD, I'M LOCKED OUT OF THE HOUSE.
UH-HUH.
WELL, CAN YOU COME HOME AND LET ME IN?
JEREMY, I HAVE A WAITING ROOM FULL OF PATIENTS AND A DE-BRACING IN PROCESS!
I SEE.
CHOOSING WORK OVER FAMILY. THAT'S OKAY. I'M NOT HURT.
SCOTT and BORGMAN

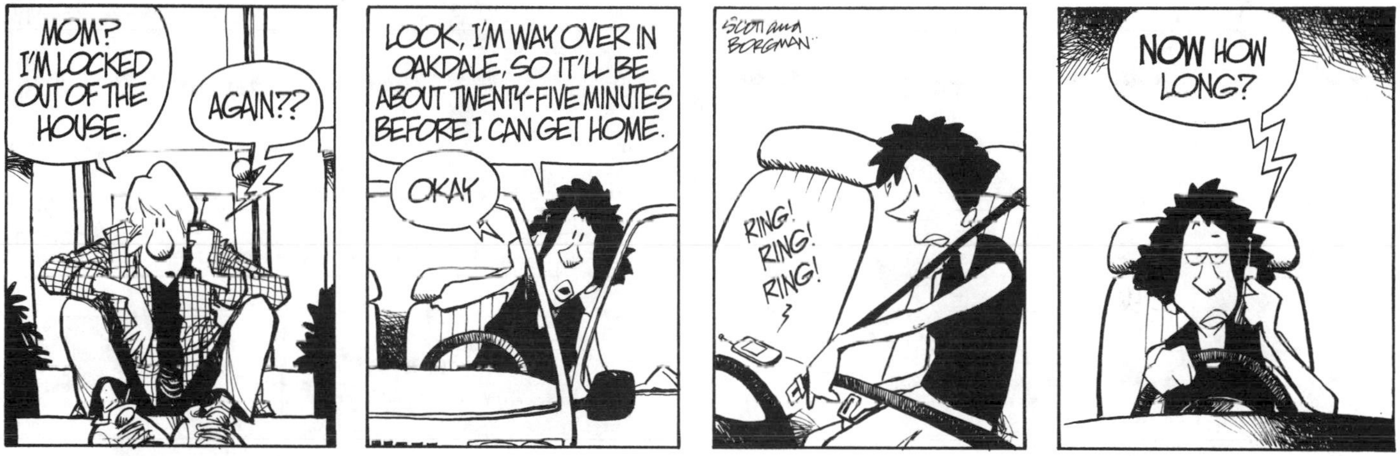
MOM? I'M LOCKED OUT OF THE HOUSE.
AGAIN??
LOOK, I'M WAY OVER IN OAKDALE, SO IT'LL BE ABOUT TWENTY-FIVE MINUTES BEFORE I CAN GET HOME.
OKAY
SCOTT and BORGMAN
RING! RING! RING!
NOW HOW LONG?

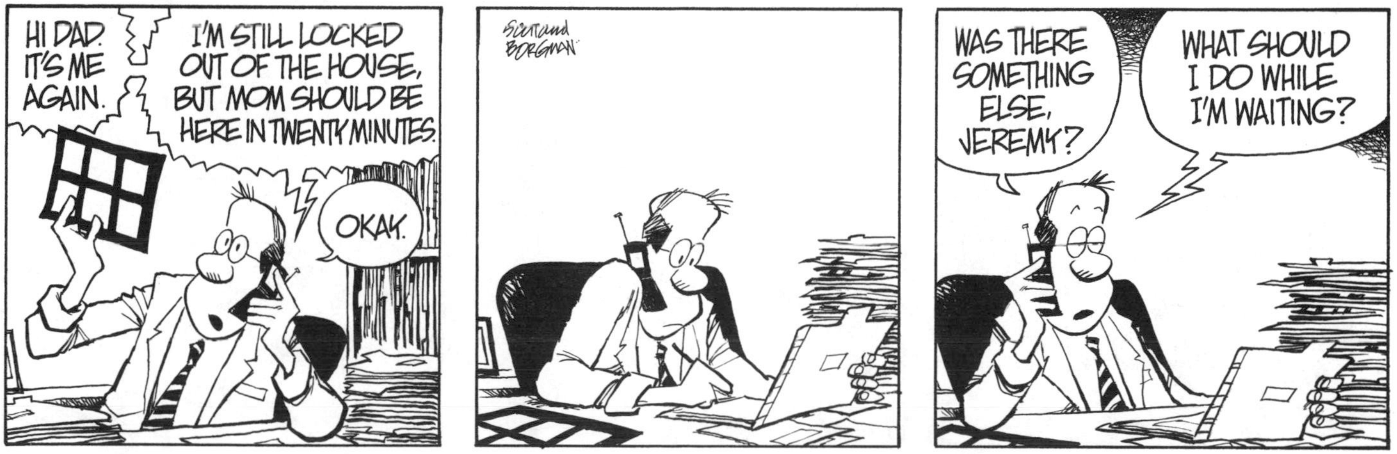
HI DAD. IT'S ME AGAIN.
I'M STILL LOCKED OUT OF THE HOUSE, BUT MOM SHOULD BE HERE IN TWENTY MINUTES.
OKAY.
SCOTT and BORGMAN
WAS THERE SOMETHING ELSE, JEREMY?
WHAT SHOULD I DO WHILE I'M WAITING?

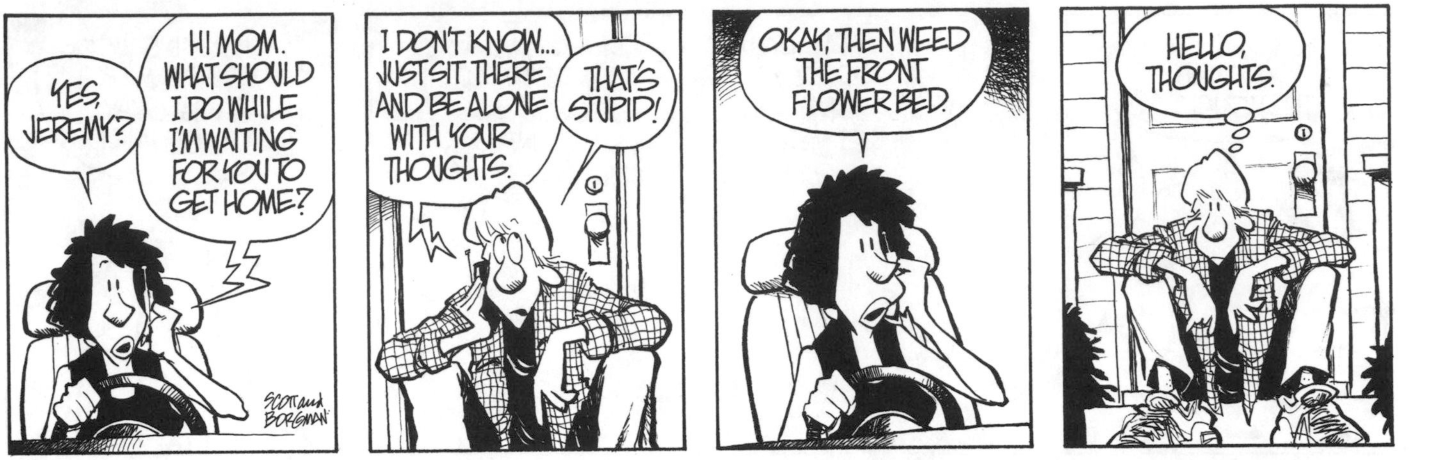
YES, JEREMY?
HI MOM. WHAT SHOULD I DO WHILE I'M WAITING FOR YOU TO GET HOME?
I DON'T KNOW... JUST SIT THERE AND BE ALONE WITH YOUR THOUGHTS.
THAT'S STUPID!
OKAY, THEN WEED THE FRONT FLOWER BED.
HELLO, THOUGHTS.

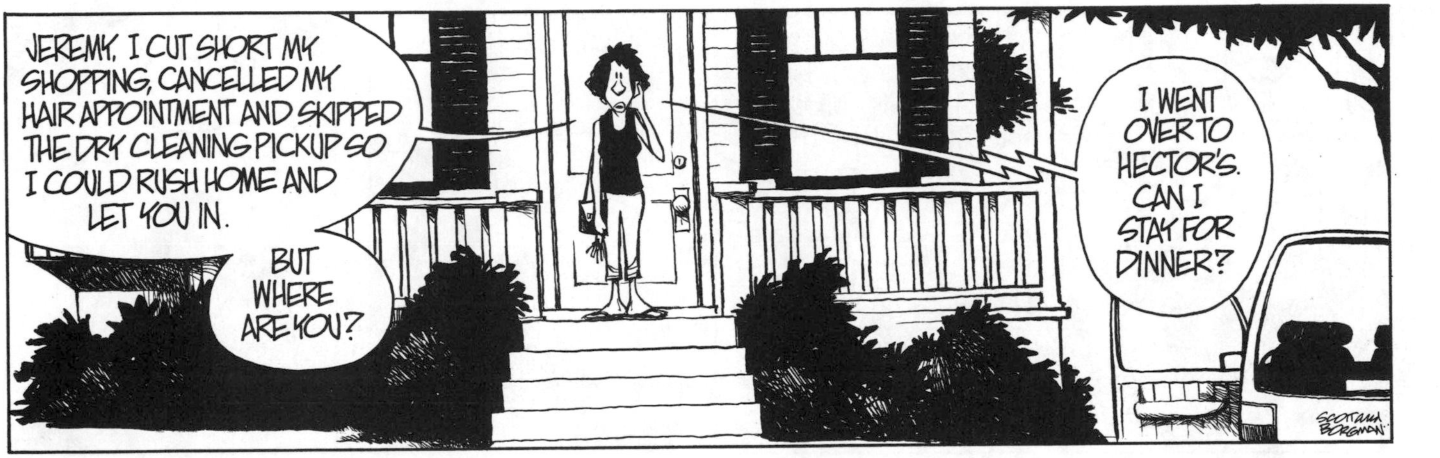
JEREMY, I CUT SHORT MY SHOPPING, CANCELLED MY HAIR APPOINTMENT AND SKIPPED THE DRY CLEANING PICKUP SO I COULD RUSH HOME AND LET YOU IN.
BUT WHERE ARE YOU?
I WENT OVER TO HECTOR'S. CAN I STAY FOR DINNER?

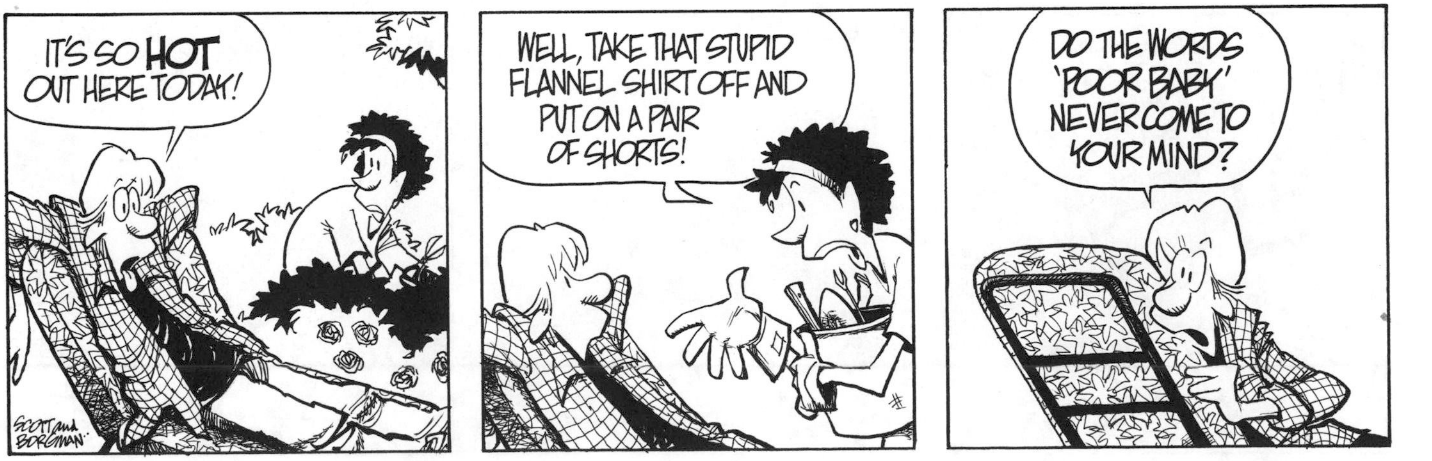
IT'S SO **HOT** OUT HERE TODAY!
WELL, TAKE THAT STUPID FLANNEL SHIRT OFF AND PUT ON A PAIR OF SHORTS!
DO THE WORDS 'POOR BABY' NEVER COME TO YOUR MIND?

Zits
by JERRY SCOTT and JIM BORGMAN

...PLUS I ALSO HAVE TO HAUL THE TRASH CANS TO THE CURB AND EMPTY THE DISHWASHER ONCE A WEEK!
DUDE, THIS PLACE WOULD FALL APART WITHOUT YOU!

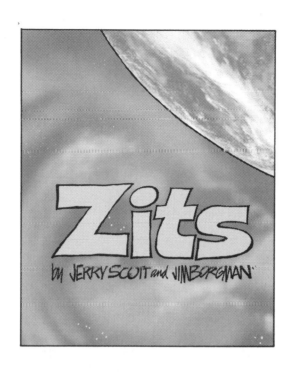

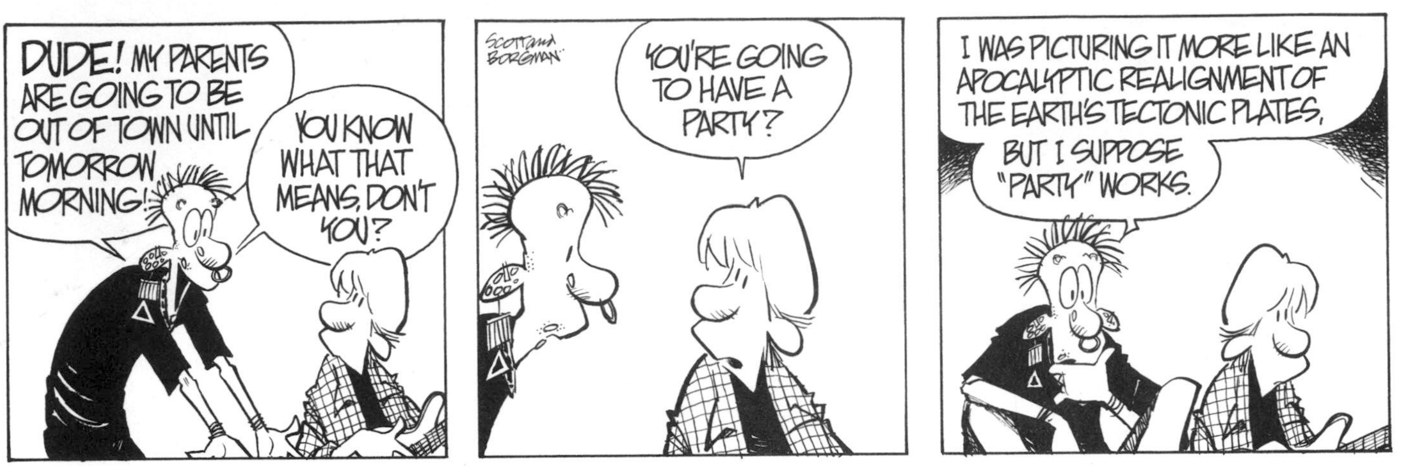
DUDE! MY PARENTS ARE GOING TO BE OUT OF TOWN UNTIL TOMORROW MORNING!
YOU KNOW WHAT THAT MEANS, DON'T YOU?
YOU'RE GOING TO HAVE A PARTY?
I WAS PICTURING IT MORE LIKE AN APOCALYPTIC REALIGNMENT OF THE EARTH'S TECTONIC PLATES,
BUT I SUPPOSE "PARTY" WORKS.

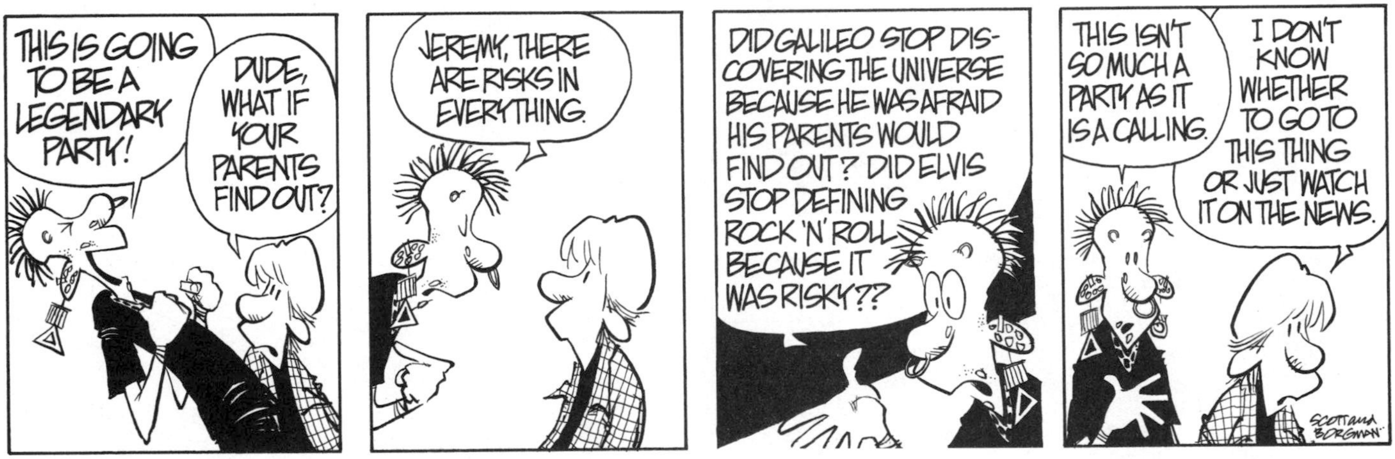
THIS IS GOING TO BE A LEGENDARY PARTY!
DUDE, WHAT IF YOUR PARENTS FIND OUT?
JEREMY, THERE ARE RISKS IN EVERYTHING.
DID GALILEO STOP DISCOVERING THE UNIVERSE BECAUSE HE WAS AFRAID HIS PARENTS WOULD FIND OUT? DID ELVIS STOP DEFINING ROCK 'N' ROLL BECAUSE IT WAS RISKY??
THIS ISN'T SO MUCH A PARTY AS IT IS A CALLING.
I DON'T KNOW WHETHER TO GO TO THIS THING OR JUST WATCH IT ON THE NEWS.

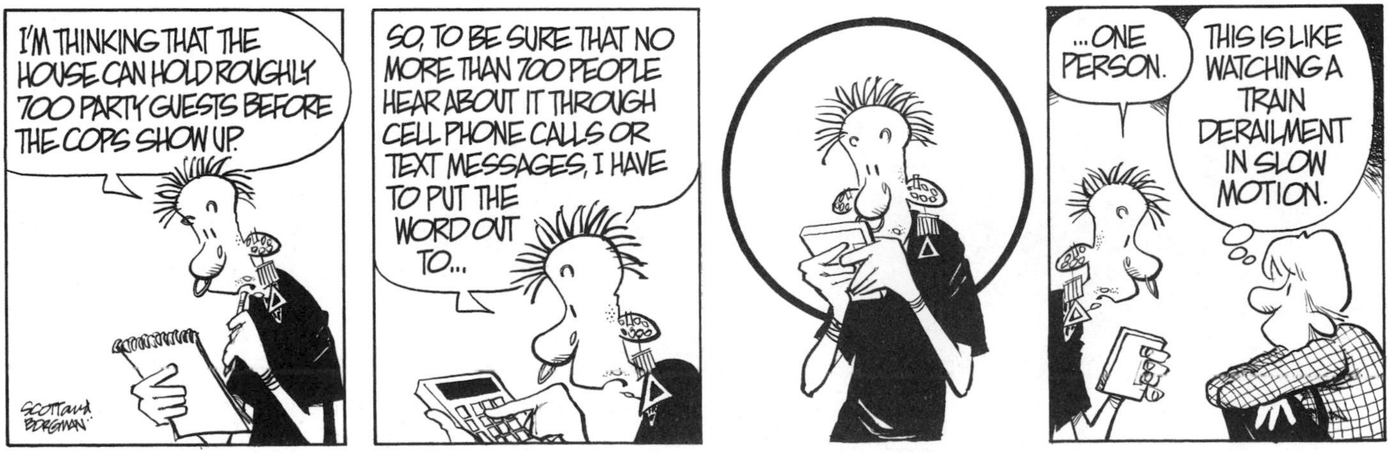
I'M THINKING THAT THE HOUSE CAN HOLD ROUGHLY 700 PARTY GUESTS BEFORE THE COPS SHOW UP.
SO, TO BE SURE THAT NO MORE THAN 700 PEOPLE HEAR ABOUT IT THROUGH CELL PHONE CALLS OR TEXT MESSAGES, I HAVE TO PUT THE WORD OUT TO...
...ONE PERSON.
THIS IS LIKE WATCHING A TRAIN DERAILMENT IN SLOW MOTION.

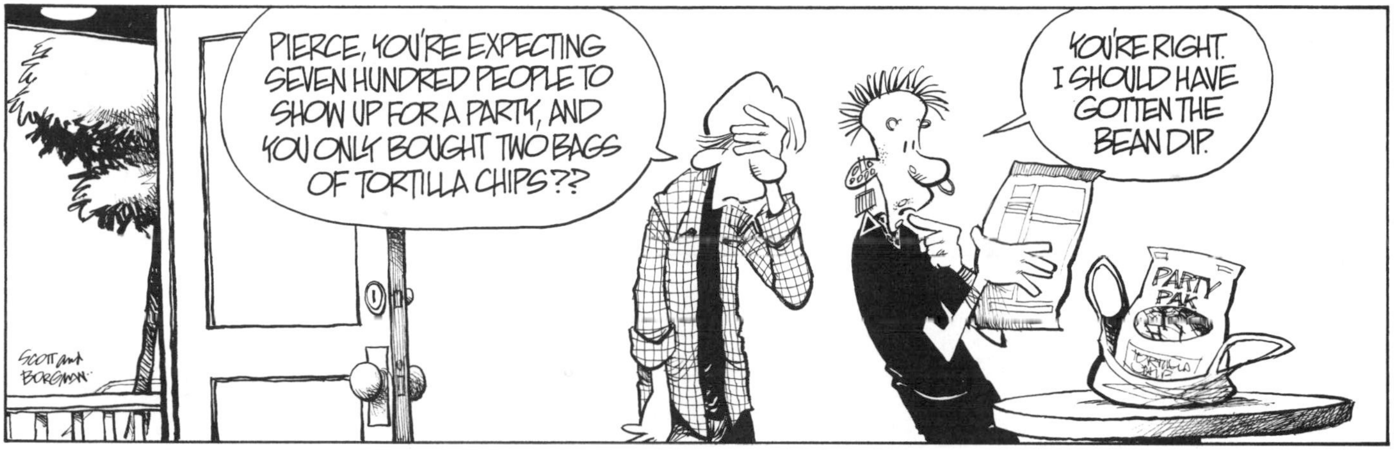
PIERCE, YOU'RE EXPECTING SEVEN HUNDRED PEOPLE TO SHOW UP FOR A PARTY, AND YOU ONLY BOUGHT TWO BAGS OF TORTILLA CHIPS??
YOU'RE RIGHT. I SHOULD HAVE GOTTEN THE BEAN DIP.
PARTY PAK
SCOTT and BORGMAN

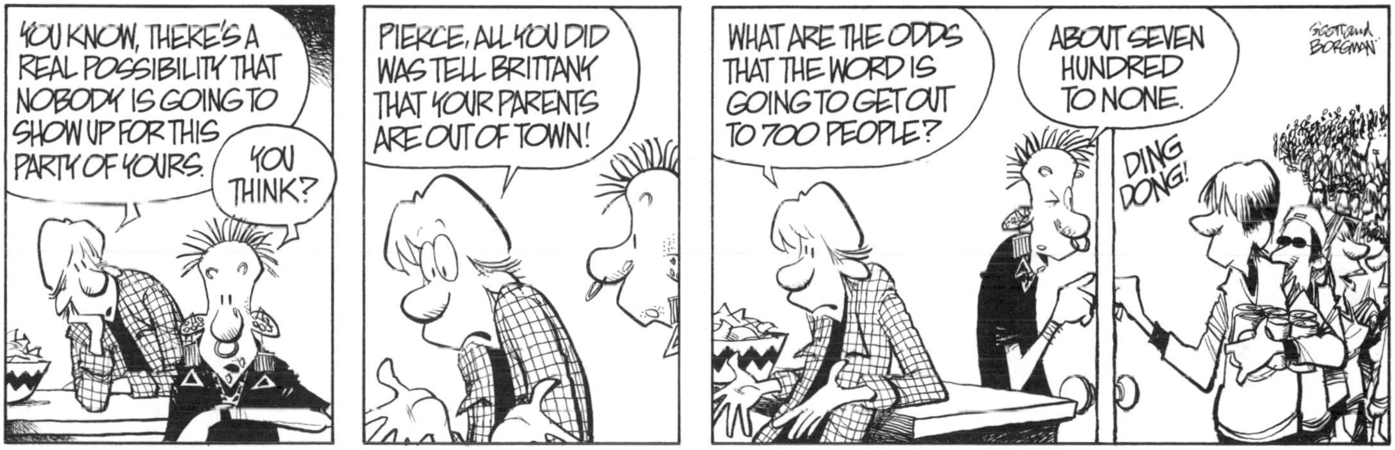
YOU KNOW, THERE'S A REAL POSSIBILITY THAT NOBODY IS GOING TO SHOW UP FOR THIS PARTY OF YOURS.
YOU THINK?
PIERCE, ALL YOU DID WAS TELL BRITTANY THAT YOUR PARENTS ARE OUT OF TOWN!
WHAT ARE THE ODDS THAT THE WORD IS GOING TO GET OUT TO 700 PEOPLE?
ABOUT SEVEN HUNDRED TO NONE.
DING DONG!
SCOTT and BORGMAN

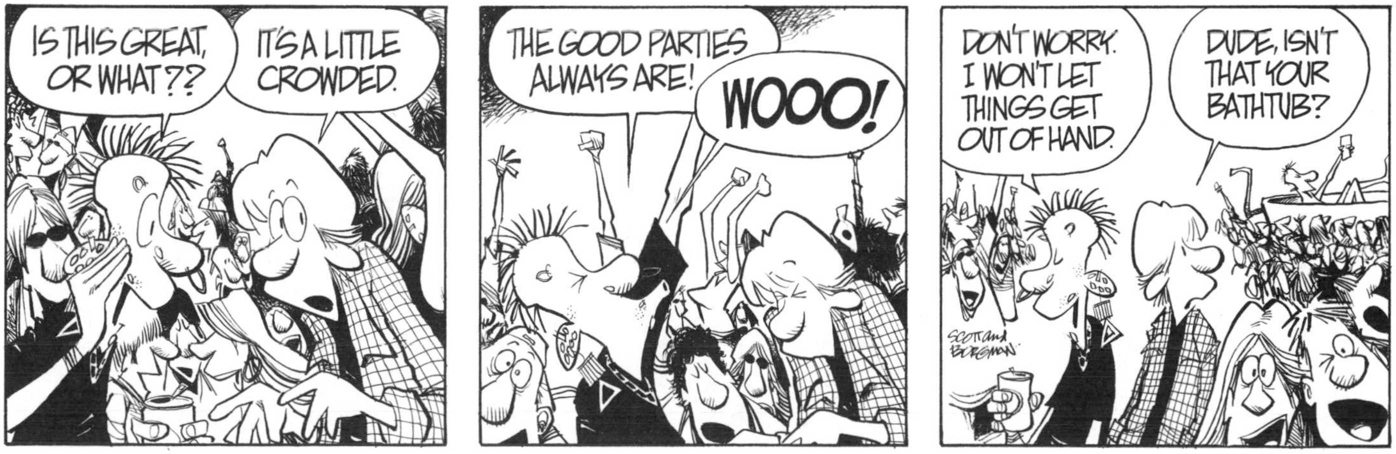
IS THIS GREAT, OR WHAT??
IT'S A LITTLE CROWDED.
THE GOOD PARTIES ALWAYS ARE!
WOOO!
DON'T WORRY. I WON'T LET THINGS GET OUT OF HAND.
DUDE, ISN'T THAT YOUR BATHTUB?
SCOTT and BORGMAN

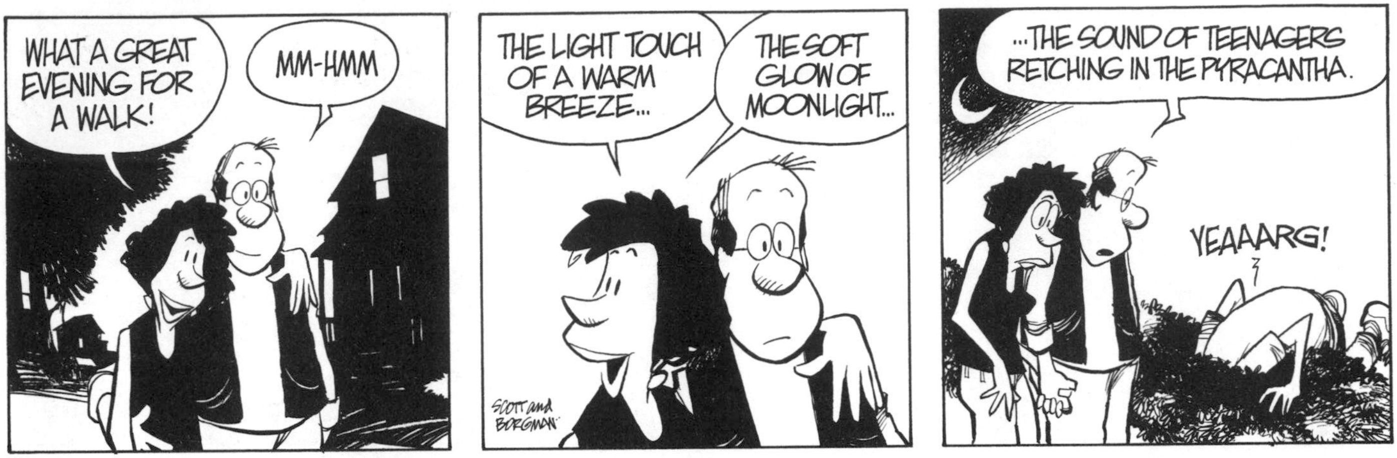
WHAT A GREAT EVENING FOR A WALK!
MM-HMM
THE LIGHT TOUCH OF A WARM BREEZE...
THE SOFT GLOW OF MOONLIGHT...
SCOTT and BORGMAN
...THE SOUND OF TEENAGERS RETCHING IN THE PYRACANTHA.
YEAAARG!

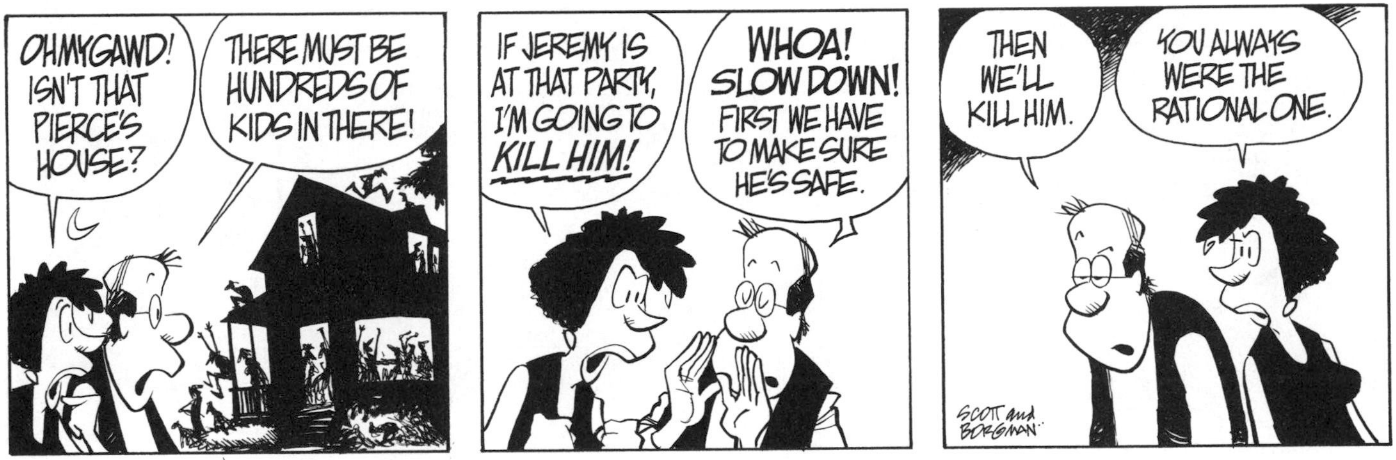
OHMYGAWD! ISN'T THAT PIERCE'S HOUSE?
THERE MUST BE HUNDREDS OF KIDS IN THERE!
IF JEREMY IS AT THAT PARTY, I'M GOING TO KILL HIM!
WHOA! SLOW DOWN! FIRST WE HAVE TO MAKE SURE HE'S SAFE.
THEN WE'LL KILL HIM.
YOU ALWAYS WERE THE RATIONAL ONE.
SCOTT and BORGMAN

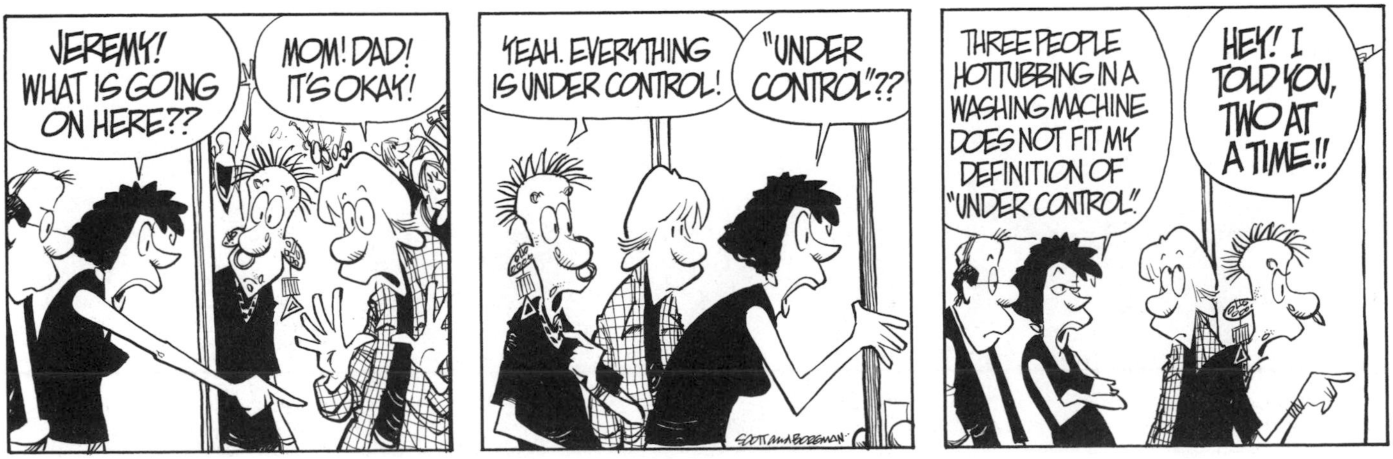
JEREMY! WHAT IS GOING ON HERE??
MOM! DAD! IT'S OKAY!
YEAH. EVERYTHING IS UNDER CONTROL!
"UNDER CONTROL"??
SCOTT and BORGMAN
THREE PEOPLE HOTTUBBING IN A WASHING MACHINE DOES NOT FIT MY DEFINITION OF "UNDER CONTROL."
HEY! I TOLD YOU, TWO AT A TIME!!

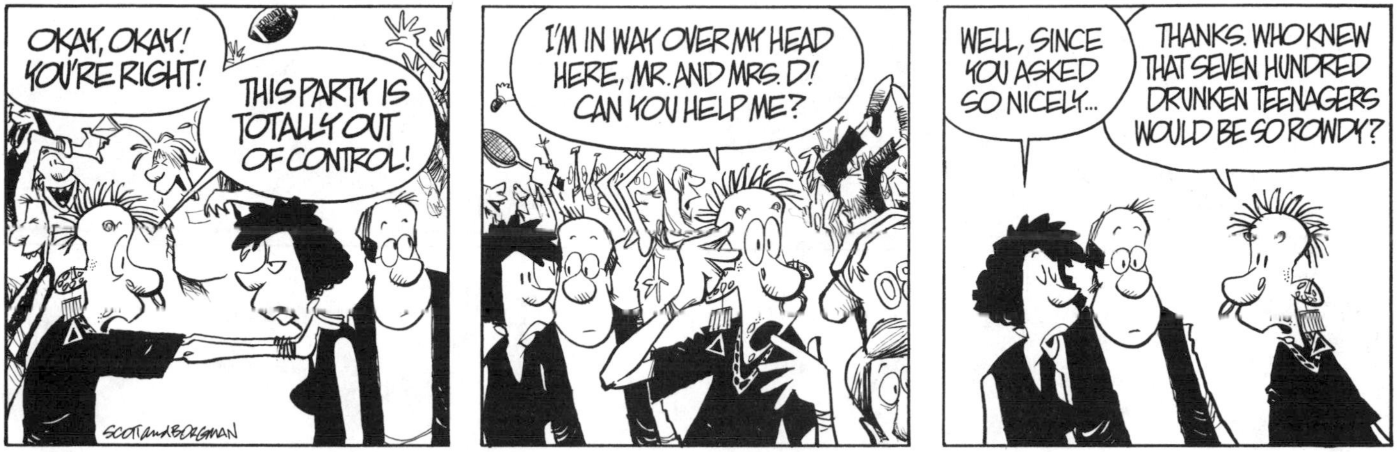
OKAY, OKAY! YOU'RE RIGHT!
THIS PARTY IS TOTALLY OUT OF CONTROL!
I'M IN WAY OVER MY HEAD HERE, MR. AND MRS. D! CAN YOU HELP ME?
WELL, SINCE YOU ASKED SO NICELY...
THANKS. WHO KNEW THAT SEVEN HUNDRED DRUNKEN TEENAGERS WOULD BE SO ROWDY?

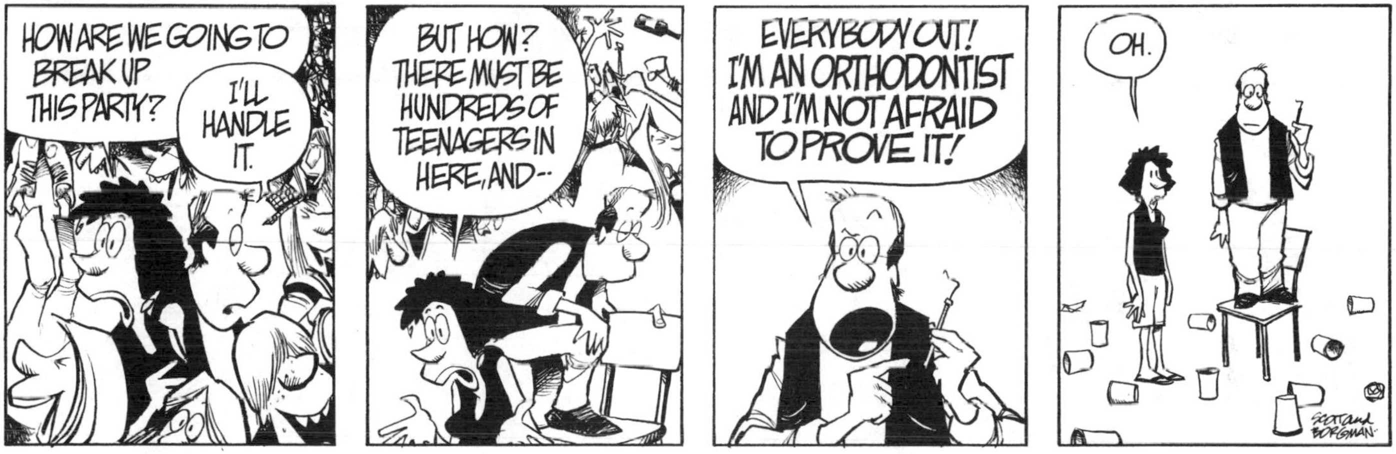
HOW ARE WE GOING TO BREAK UP THIS PARTY?
I'LL HANDLE IT.
BUT HOW? THERE MUST BE HUNDREDS OF TEENAGERS IN HERE, AND--
EVERYBODY OUT! I'M AN ORTHODONTIST AND I'M NOT AFRAID TO PROVE IT!
OH.

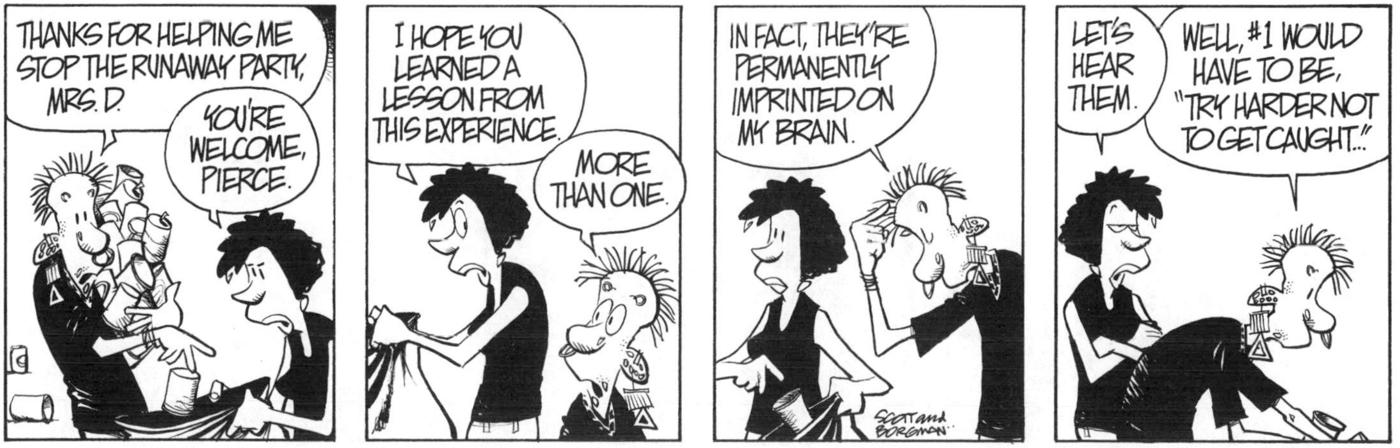
THANKS FOR HELPING ME STOP THE RUNAWAY PARTY, MRS. D.
YOU'RE WELCOME, PIERCE.
I HOPE YOU LEARNED A LESSON FROM THIS EXPERIENCE.
MORE THAN ONE.
IN FACT, THEY'RE PERMANENTLY IMPRINTED ON MY BRAIN.
LET'S HEAR THEM.
WELL, #1 WOULD HAVE TO BE, "TRY HARDER NOT TO GET CAUGHT."

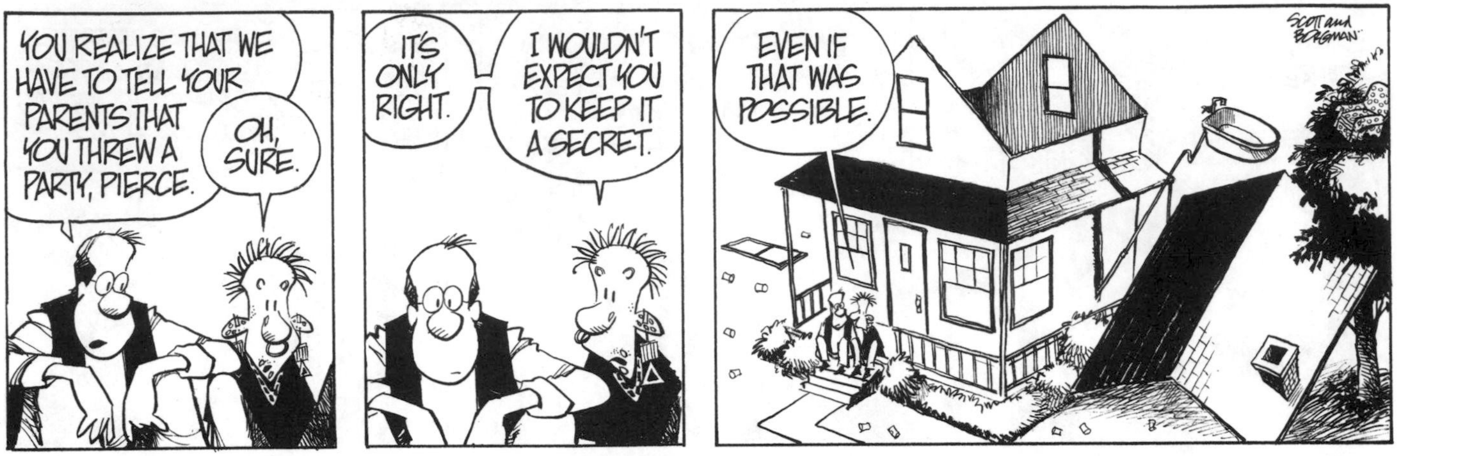
YOU REALIZE THAT WE HAVE TO TELL YOUR PARENTS THAT YOU THREW A PARTY, PIERCE.
OH, SURE.
IT'S ONLY RIGHT.
I WOULDN'T EXPECT YOU TO KEEP IT A SECRET.
EVEN IF THAT WAS POSSIBLE.

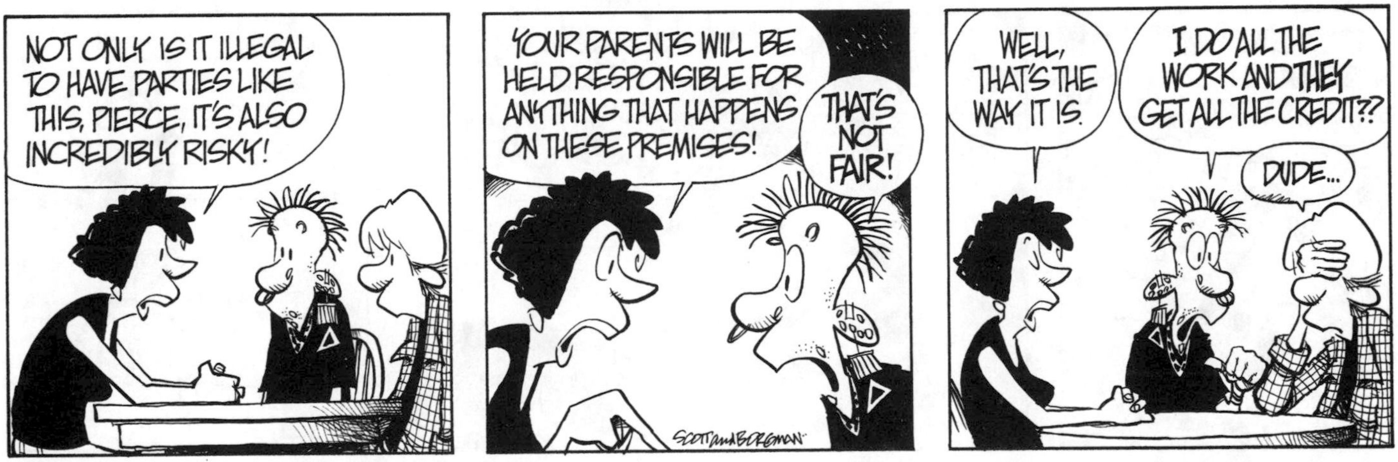
NOT ONLY IS IT ILLEGAL TO HAVE PARTIES LIKE THIS, PIERCE, IT'S ALSO INCREDIBLY RISKY!
YOUR PARENTS WILL BE HELD RESPONSIBLE FOR ANYTHING THAT HAPPENS ON THESE PREMISES!
THAT'S NOT FAIR!
WELL, THAT'S THE WAY IT IS.
I DO ALL THE WORK AND THEY GET ALL THE CREDIT??
DUDE...

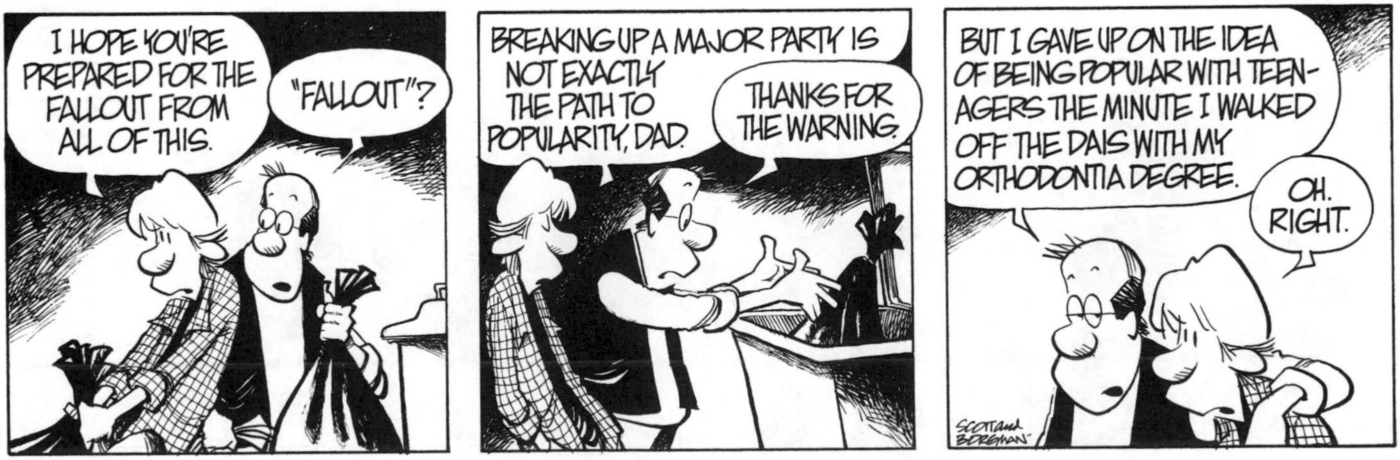
I HOPE YOU'RE PREPARED FOR THE FALLOUT FROM ALL OF THIS.
"FALLOUT"?
BREAKING UP A MAJOR PARTY IS NOT EXACTLY THE PATH TO POPULARITY, DAD.
THANKS FOR THE WARNING.
BUT I GAVE UP ON THE IDEA OF BEING POPULAR WITH TEEN-AGERS THE MINUTE I WALKED OFF THE DAIS WITH MY ORTHODONTIA DEGREE.
OH. RIGHT.

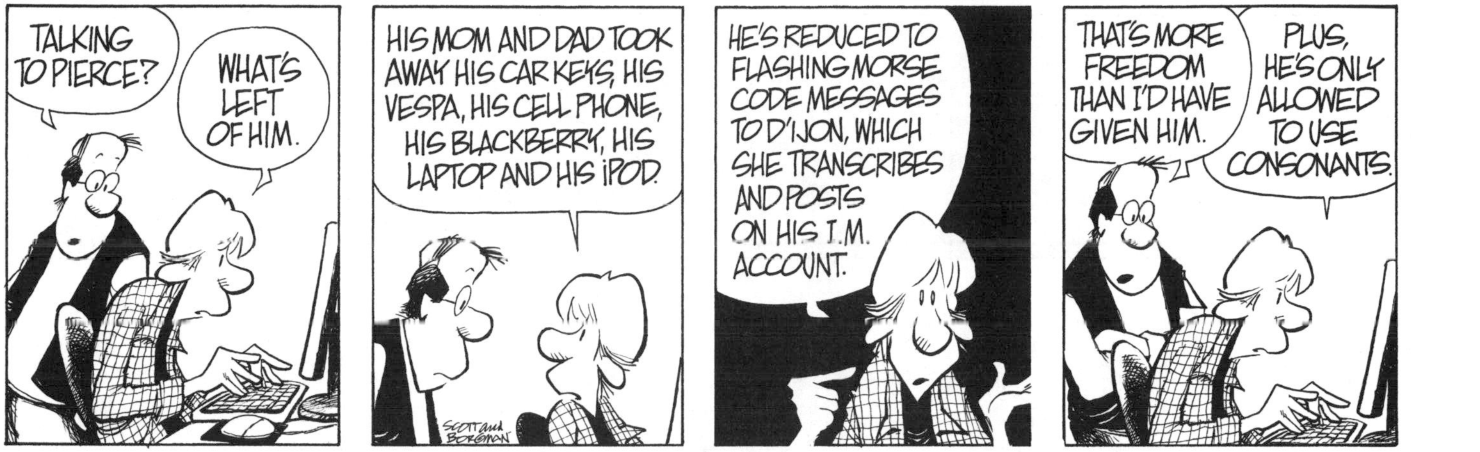
TALKING TO PIERCE?
WHAT'S LEFT OF HIM.
HIS MOM AND DAD TOOK AWAY HIS CAR KEYS, HIS VESPA, HIS CELL PHONE, HIS BLACKBERRY, HIS LAPTOP AND HIS iPOD.
SCOTT and BORGMAN
HE'S REDUCED TO FLASHING MORSE CODE MESSAGES TO D'JON, WHICH SHE TRANSCRIBES AND POSTS ON HIS I.M. ACCOUNT.
THAT'S MORE FREEDOM THAN I'D HAVE GIVEN HIM.
PLUS, HE'S ONLY ALLOWED TO USE CONSONANTS.

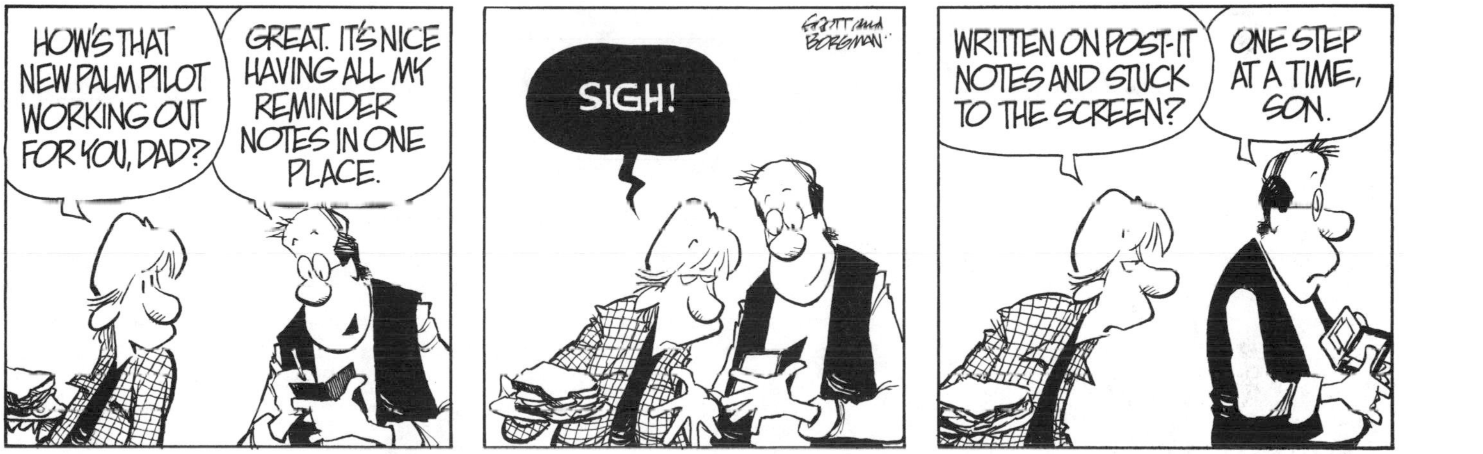
HOW'S THAT NEW PALM PILOT WORKING OUT FOR YOU, DAD?
GREAT. IT'S NICE HAVING ALL MY REMINDER NOTES IN ONE PLACE.
SCOTT and BORGMAN
SIGH!
WRITTEN ON POST-IT NOTES AND STUCK TO THE SCREEN?
ONE STEP AT A TIME, SON.

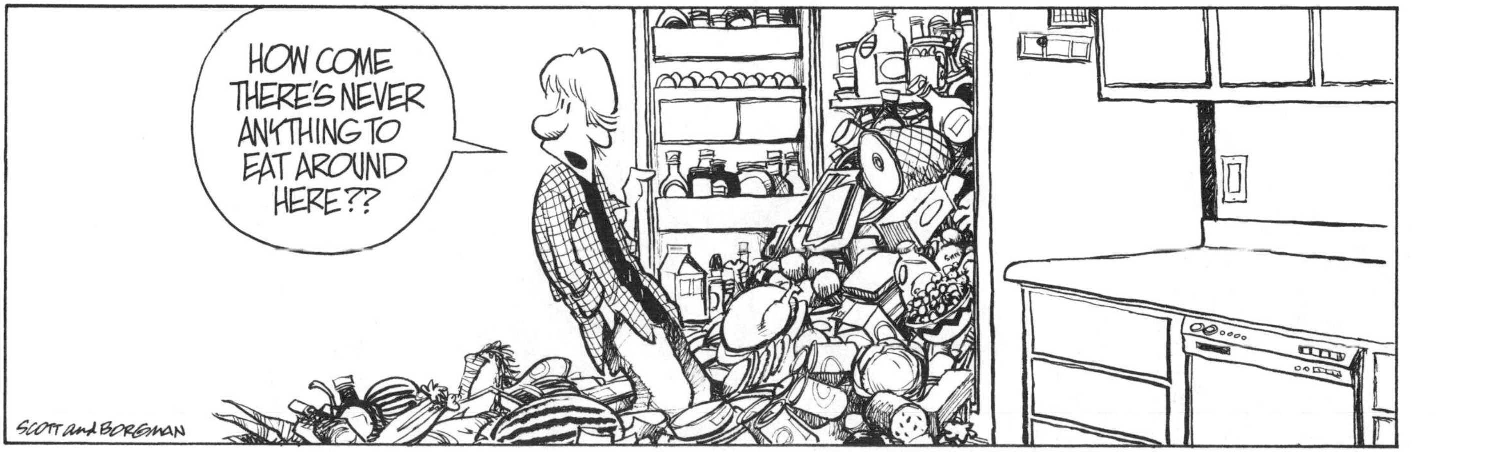
HOW COME THERE'S NEVER ANYTHING TO EAT AROUND HERE??
SCOTT and BORGMAN

Zits
JERRY SCOTT and JIM BORGMAN

SCOTT and BORGMAN
JEREMY? ARE YOU IN THERE?
YEAH!
HANG ON!
I'LL BE RIGHT THERE!
QUICK!
PUT IT AWAY!
HURRY!
HI MRS. D!
HI PIERCE.
WHAT'S GOING ON, GUYS?
NOTHING.
OKAY... JUST CHECKING.
DO YOU THINK SHE SAW ANYTHING?
I CAN'T TELL.... I DON'T THINK SO.
DUDE, IF YOU'RE WORRIED ABOUT YOUR IMAGE, MAYBE SCRAP-BOOKING SHOULDN'T BE YOUR HOBBY.
MAYBE. PASS THE PINKING SHEARS.

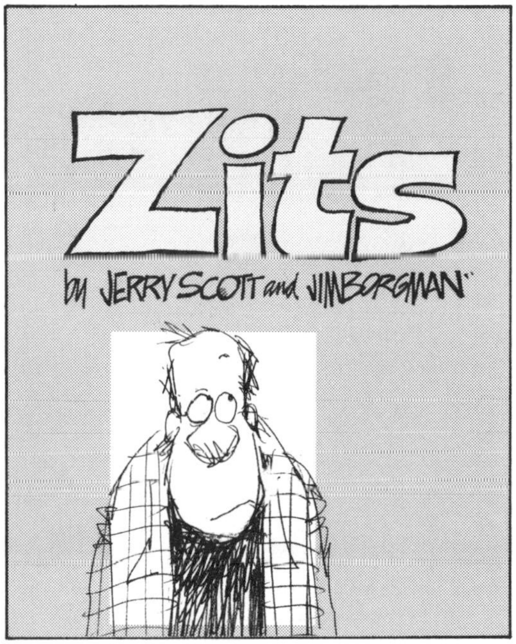
Zits
by JERRY SCOTT and JIM BORGMAN

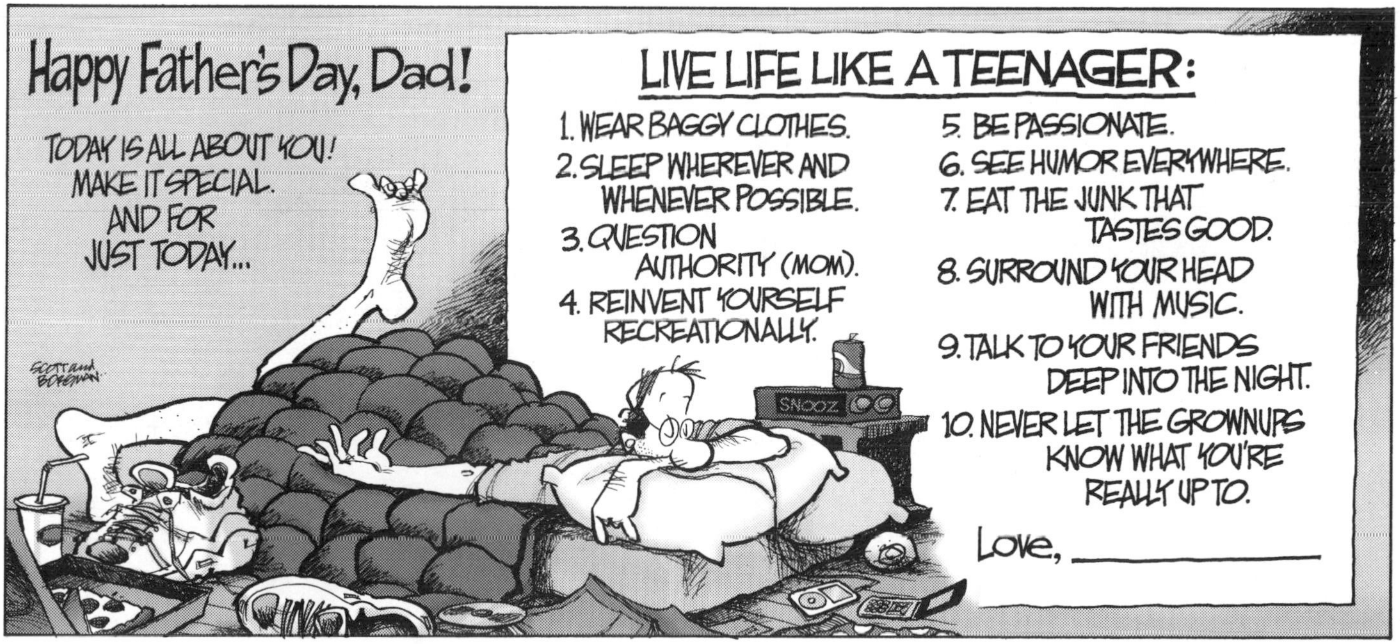
Happy Father's Day, Dad!
TODAY IS ALL ABOUT YOU! MAKE IT SPECIAL. AND FOR JUST TODAY...
LIVE LIFE LIKE A TEENAGER:
1. WEAR BAGGY CLOTHES.
2. SLEEP WHEREVER AND WHENEVER POSSIBLE.
3. QUESTION AUTHORITY (MOM).
4. REINVENT YOURSELF RECREATIONALLY.
5. BE PASSIONATE.
6. SEE HUMOR EVERYWHERE.
7. EAT THE JUNK THAT TASTES GOOD.
8. SURROUND YOUR HEAD WITH MUSIC.
9. TALK TO YOUR FRIENDS DEEP INTO THE NIGHT.
10. NEVER LET THE GROWNUPS KNOW WHAT YOU'RE REALLY UP TO.
Love, ___________
SNOOZ
SCOTT and BORGMAN

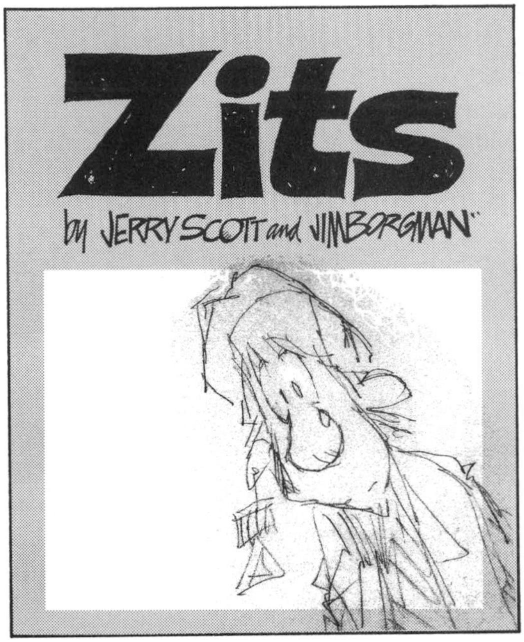
Zits
by JERRY SCOTT and JIM BORGMAN

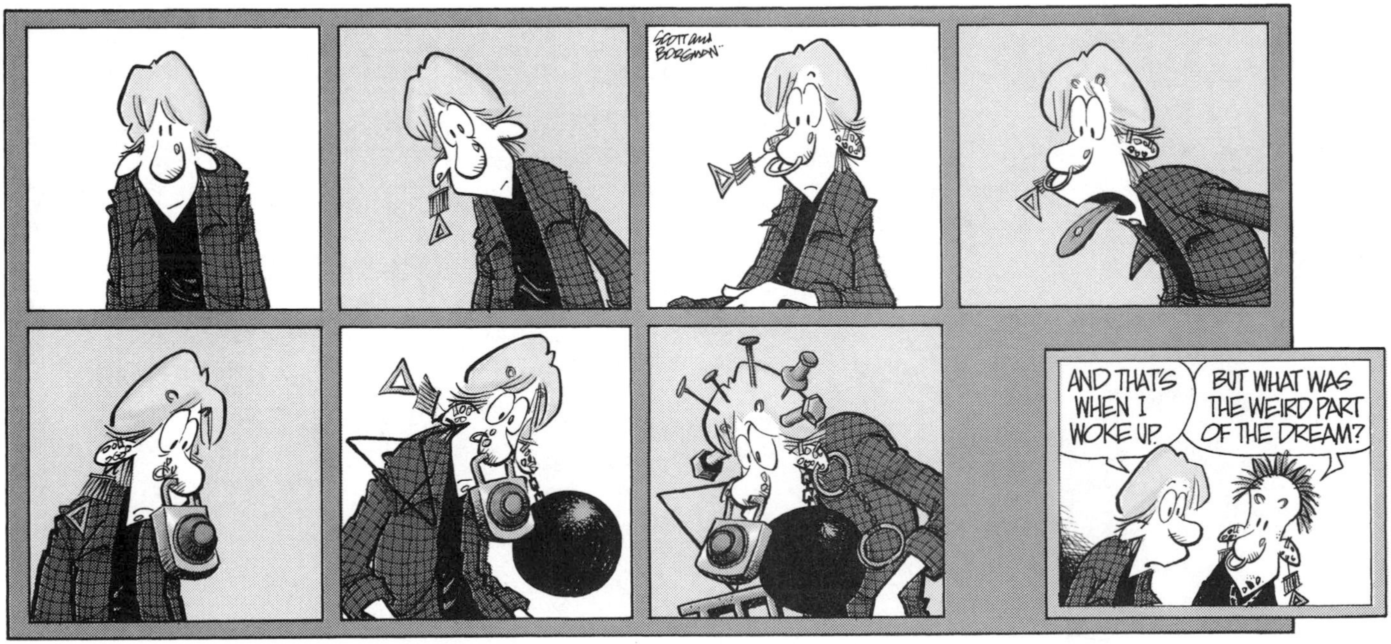
SCOTT and BORGMAN
AND THAT'S WHEN I WOKE UP.
BUT WHAT WAS THE WEIRD PART OF THE DREAM?

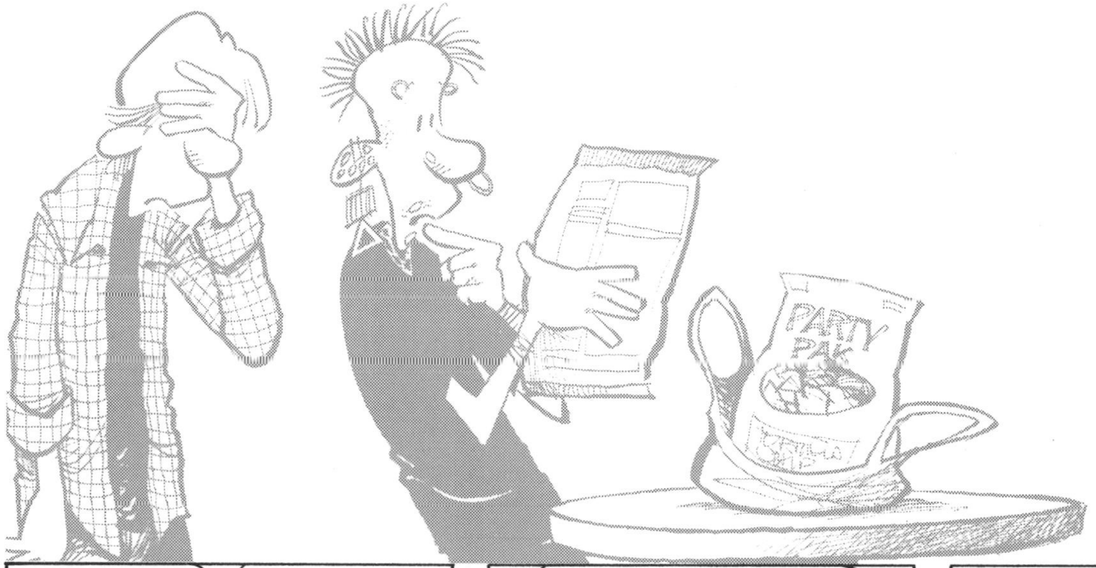
PARTY PAK

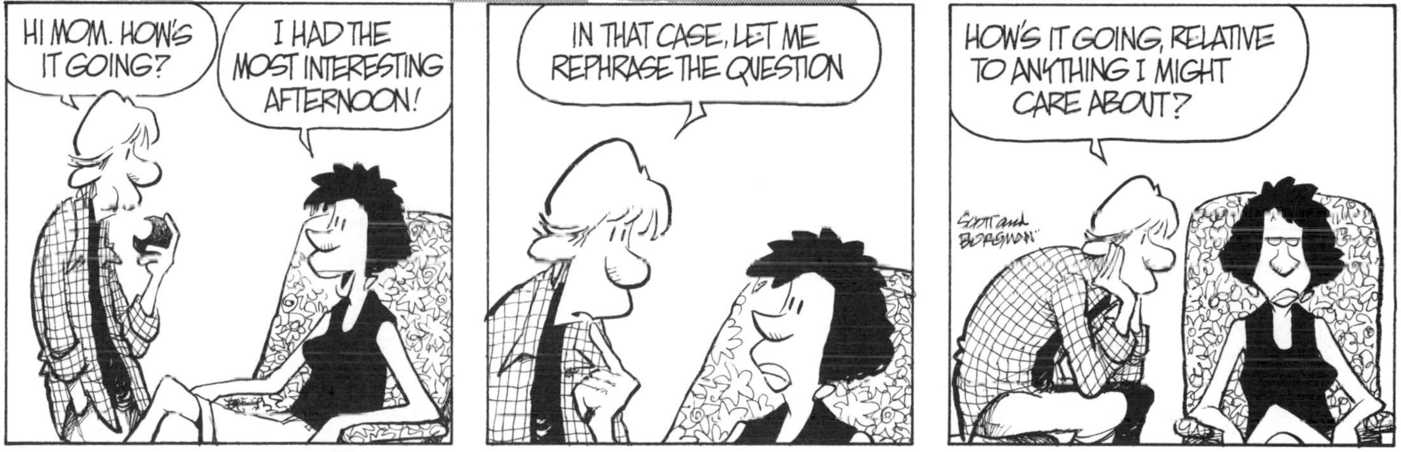
HI MOM. HOW'S IT GOING?
I HAD THE MOST INTERESTING AFTERNOON!
IN THAT CASE, LET ME REPHRASE THE QUESTION
HOW'S IT GOING, RELATIVE TO ANYTHING I MIGHT CARE ABOUT?

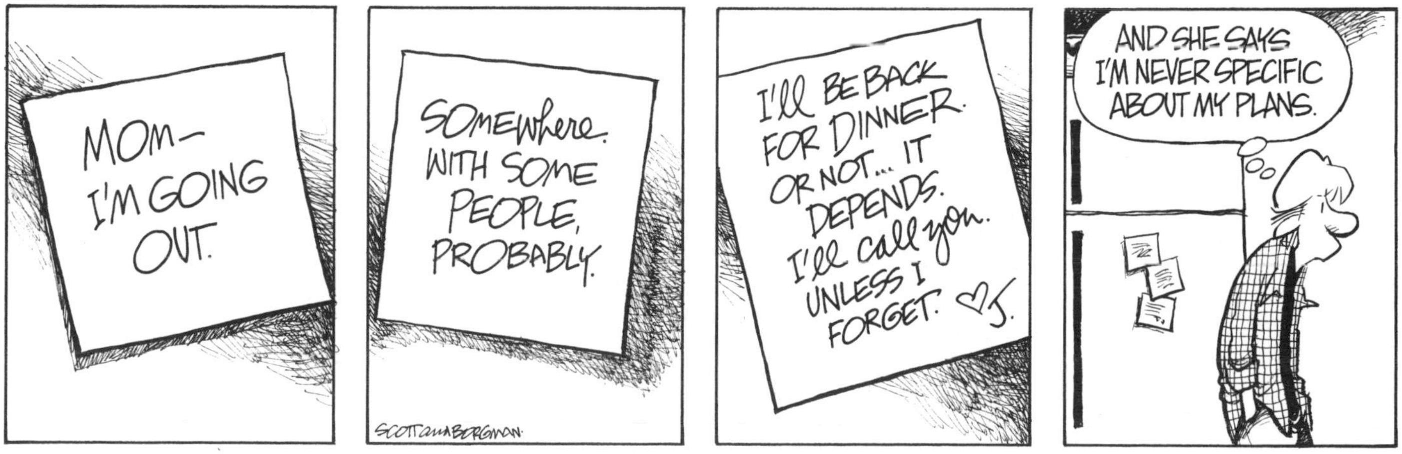
MOM— I'M GOING OUT.
SOMEWHERE. WITH SOME PEOPLE, PROBABLY.
I'LL BE BACK FOR DINNER. OR NOT... IT DEPENDS. I'LL CALL YOU. UNLESS I FORGET. ♡ J.
AND SHE SAYS I'M NEVER SPECIFIC ABOUT MY PLANS.

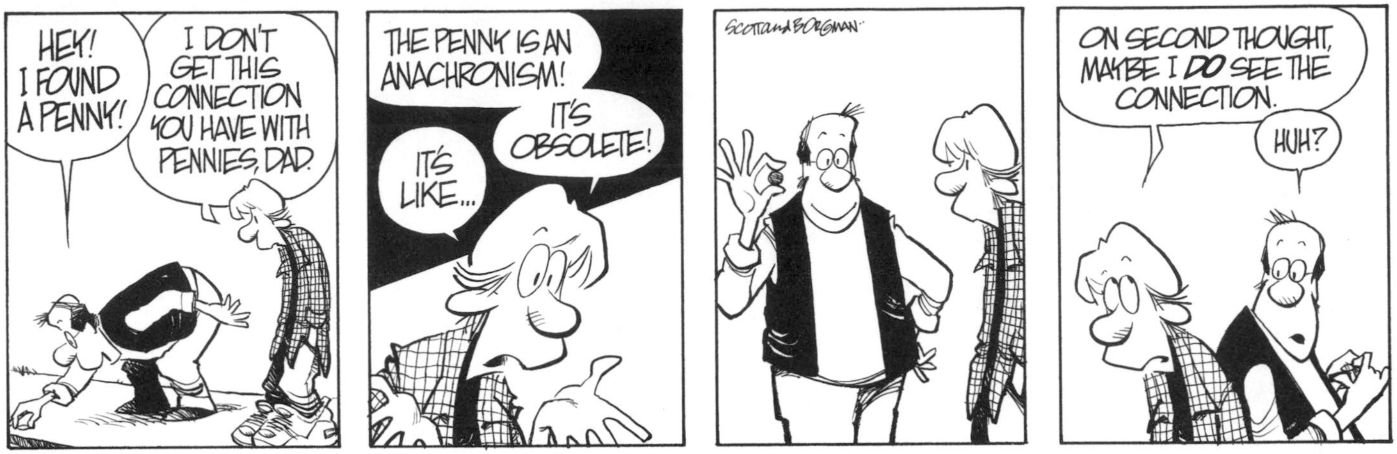
HEY! I FOUND A PENNY!
I DON'T GET THIS CONNECTION YOU HAVE WITH PENNIES, DAD.
THE PENNY IS AN ANACHRONISM!
IT'S LIKE...
IT'S OBSOLETE!
SCOTT and BORGMAN
ON SECOND THOUGHT, MAYBE I DO SEE THE CONNECTION.
HUH?

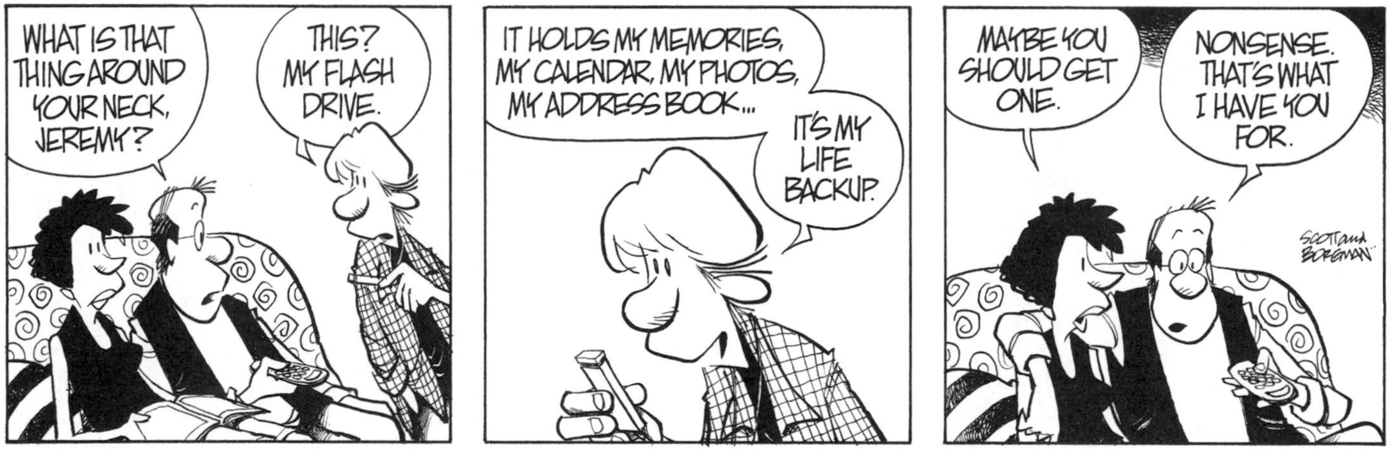
WHAT IS THAT THING AROUND YOUR NECK, JEREMY?
THIS? MY FLASH DRIVE.
IT HOLDS MY MEMORIES, MY CALENDAR, MY PHOTOS, MY ADDRESS BOOK...
IT'S MY LIFE BACKUP.
MAYBE YOU SHOULD GET ONE.
NONSENSE. THAT'S WHAT I HAVE YOU FOR.
SCOTT and BORGMAN

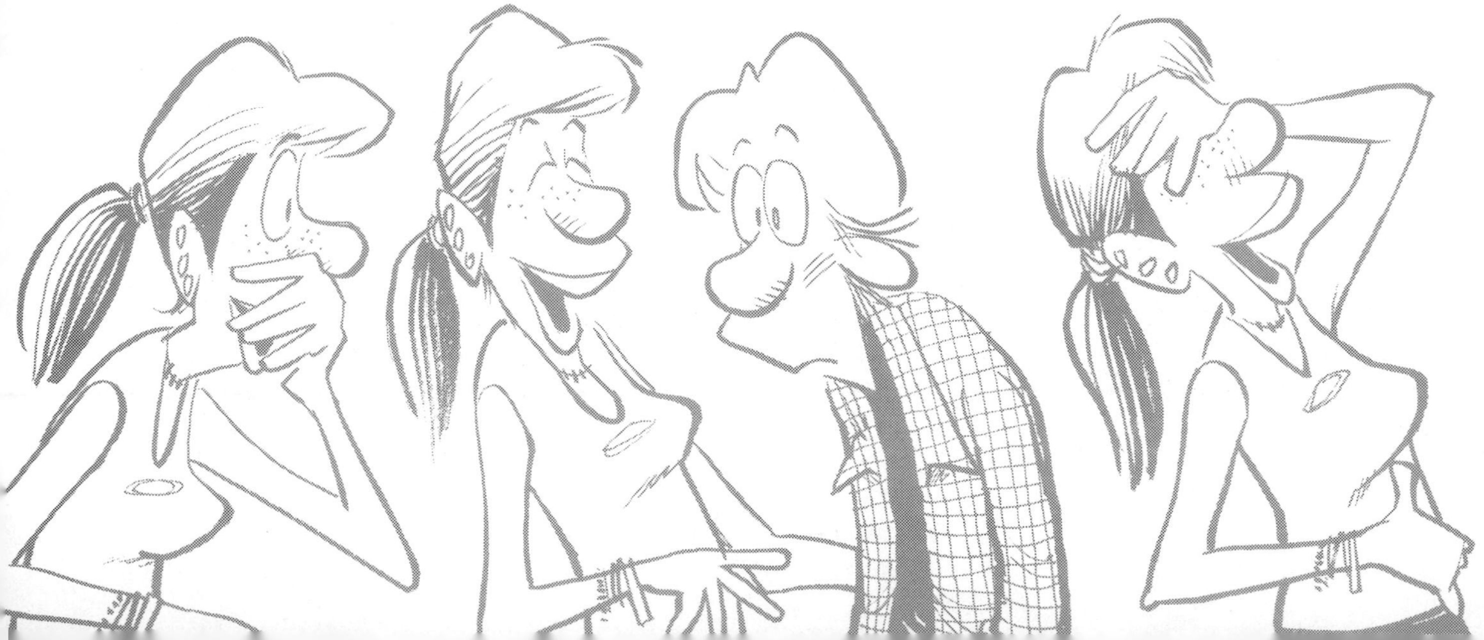

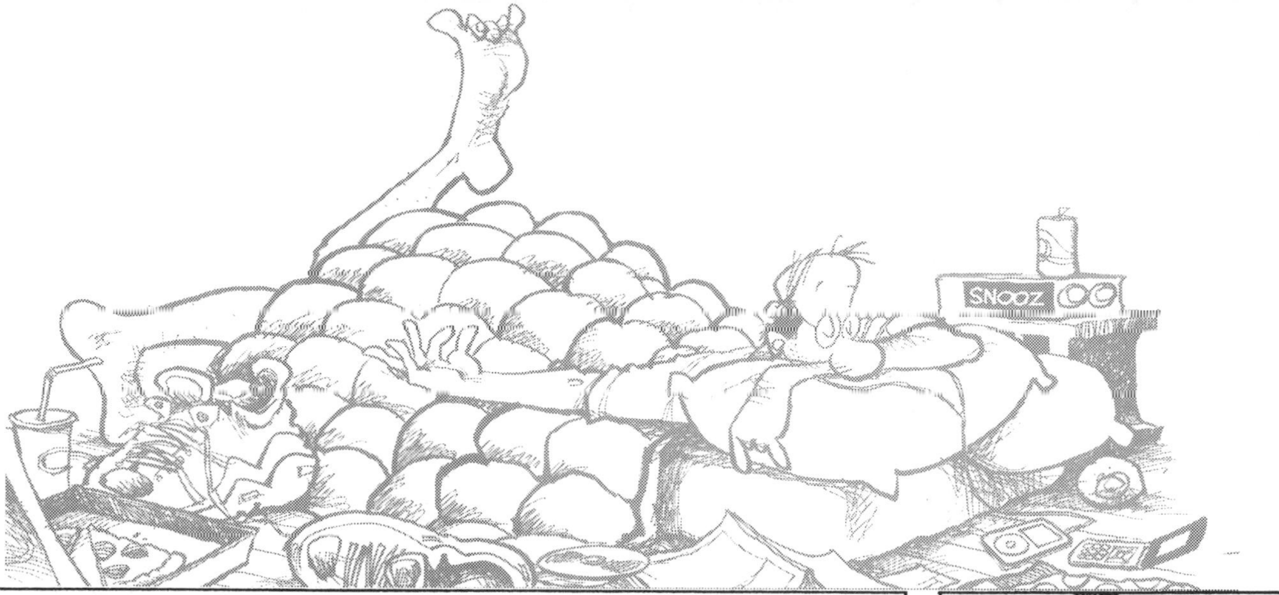
SNOOZ

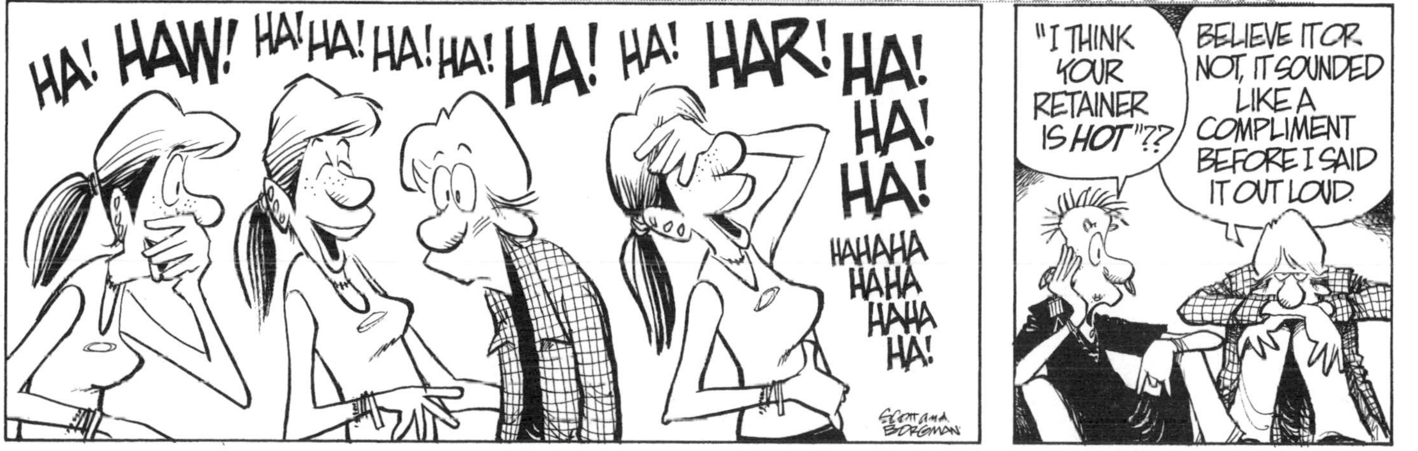
HA! HAW! HA! HA! HA! HA! HA! HA! HAR! HA! HA! HA!
HAHAHA HAHA HAHA HA!
SCOTT AND BORGMAN
"I THINK YOUR RETAINER IS *HOT*"??
BELIEVE IT OR NOT, IT SOUNDED LIKE A COMPLIMENT BEFORE I SAID IT OUT LOUD.

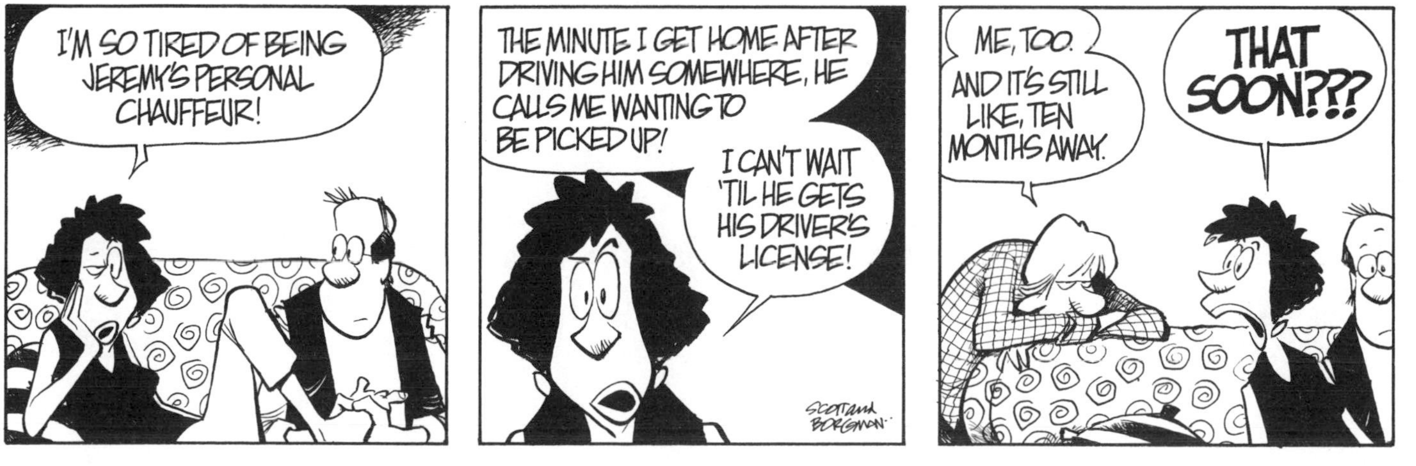
I'M SO TIRED OF BEING JEREMY'S PERSONAL CHAUFFEUR!
THE MINUTE I GET HOME AFTER DRIVING HIM SOMEWHERE, HE CALLS ME WANTING TO BE PICKED UP!
I CAN'T WAIT 'TIL HE GETS HIS DRIVER'S LICENSE!
SCOTT AND BORGMAN
ME, TOO.
AND IT'S STILL LIKE, TEN MONTHS AWAY.
THAT SOON???

Zits
by
JERRY SCOTT and
JIM BORGMAN

SCOTT and BORGMAN
I SUPPOSE YOU HAVEN'T EVEN NOTICED THAT I CLEANED OUT MY CLOSET.

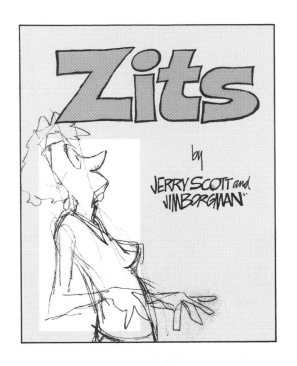

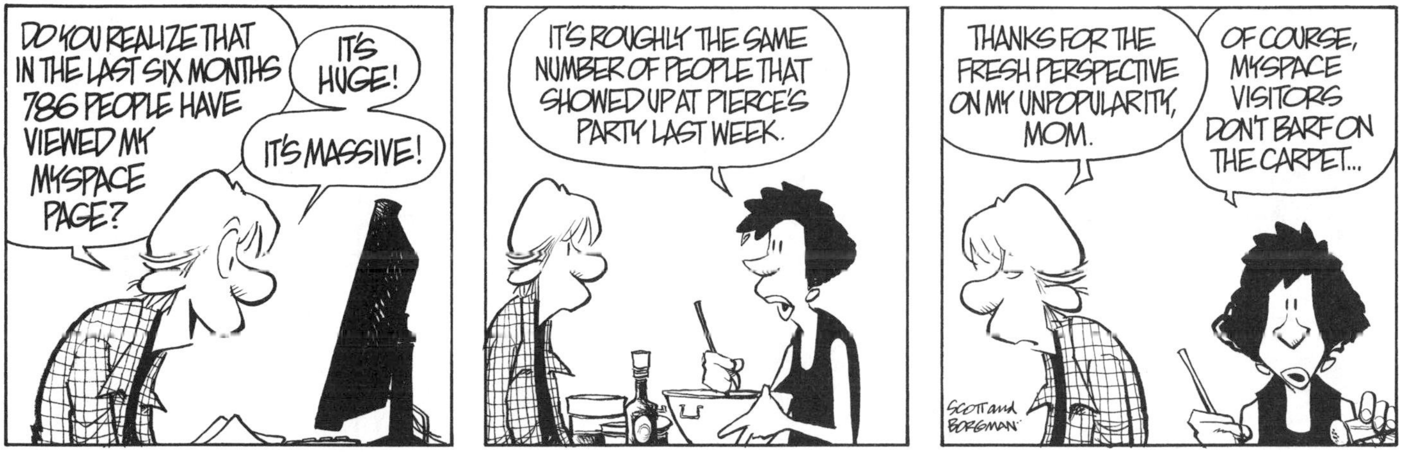
DO YOU REALIZE THAT IN THE LAST SIX MONTHS 786 PEOPLE HAVE VIEWED MY MYSPACE PAGE?
IT'S HUGE!
IT'S MASSIVE!
IT'S ROUGHLY THE SAME NUMBER OF PEOPLE THAT SHOWED UP AT PIERCE'S PARTY LAST WEEK.
THANKS FOR THE FRESH PERSPECTIVE ON MY UNPOPULARITY, MOM.
OF COURSE, MYSPACE VISITORS DON'T BARF ON THE CARPET...
SCOTT and BORGMAN

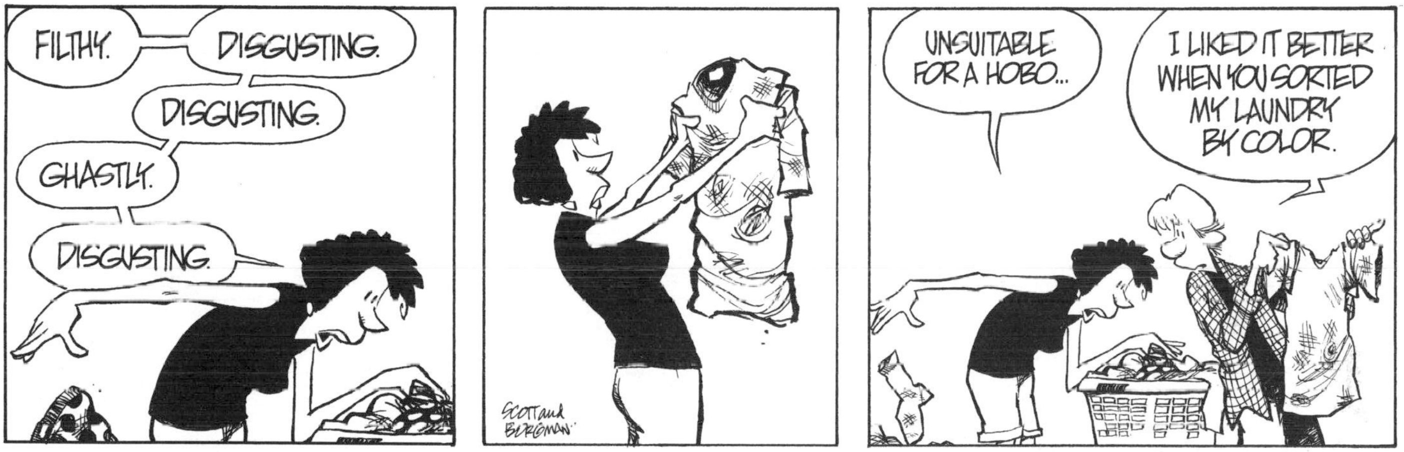
FILTHY.
DISGUSTING.
DISGUSTING.
GHASTLY.
DISGUSTING.
SCOTT and BORGMAN
UNSUITABLE FOR A HOBO...
I LIKED IT BETTER WHEN YOU SORTED MY LAUNDRY BY COLOR.

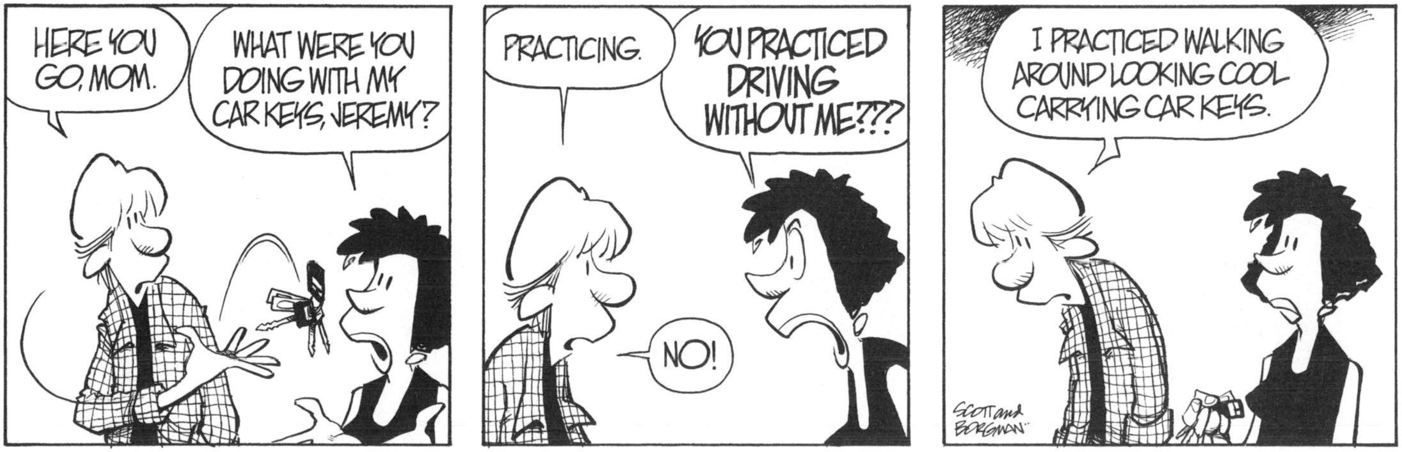
HERE YOU GO, MOM.
WHAT WERE YOU DOING WITH MY CAR KEYS, JEREMY?
PRACTICING.
YOU PRACTICED DRIVING WITHOUT ME???
NO!
I PRACTICED WALKING AROUND LOOKING COOL CARRYING CAR KEYS.
SCOTT and BORGMAN

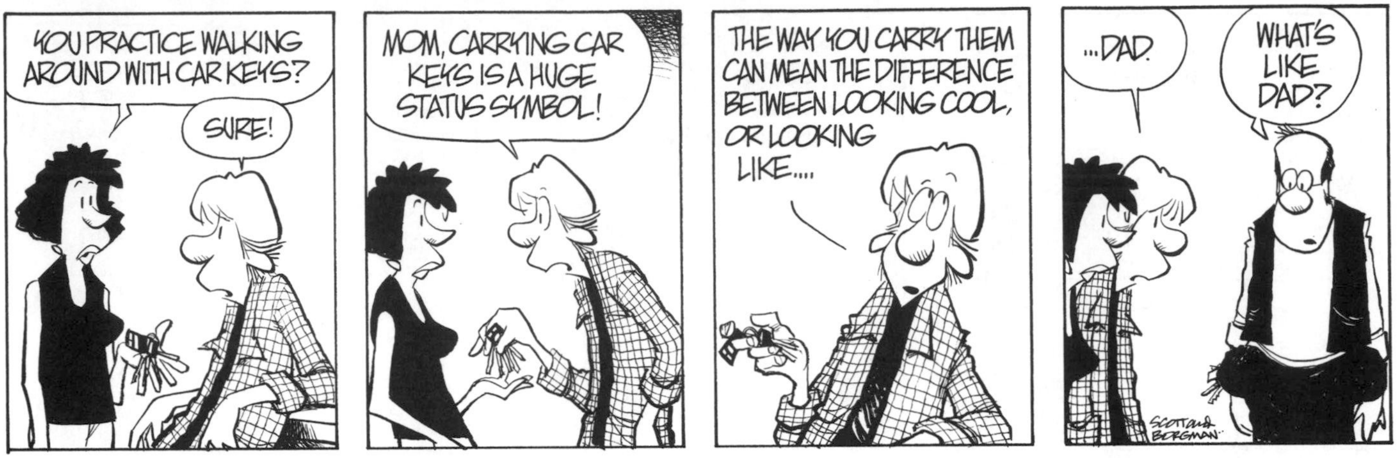
YOU PRACTICE WALKING AROUND WITH CAR KEYS?
SURE!
MOM, CARRYING CAR KEYS IS A HUGE STATUS SYMBOL!
THE WAY YOU CARRY THEM CAN MEAN THE DIFFERENCE BETWEEN LOOKING COOL, OR LOOKING LIKE....
...DAD.
WHAT'S LIKE DAD?

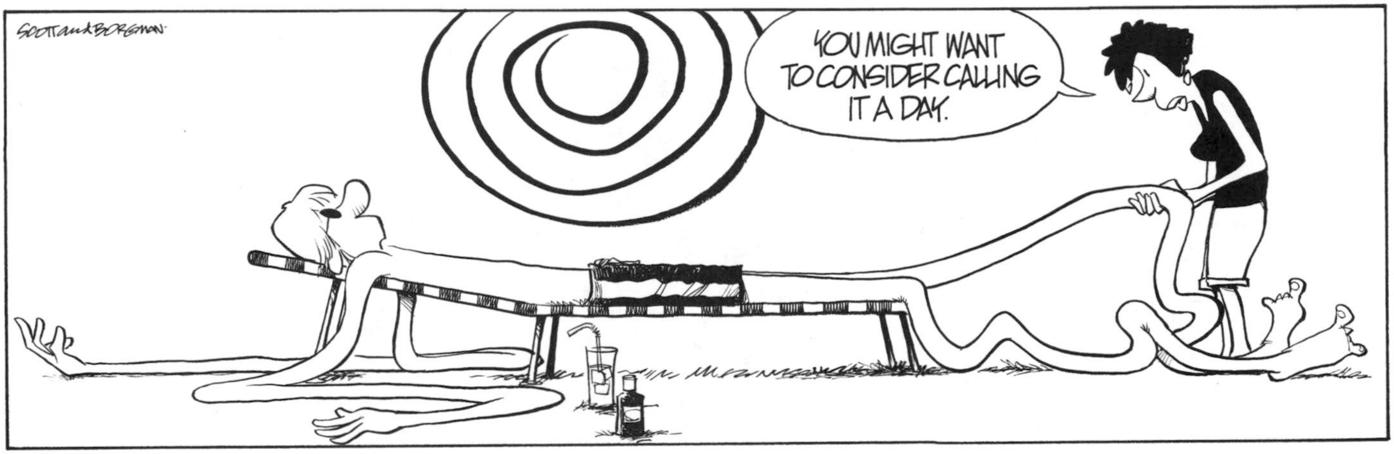
YOU MIGHT WANT TO CONSIDER CALLING IT A DAY.

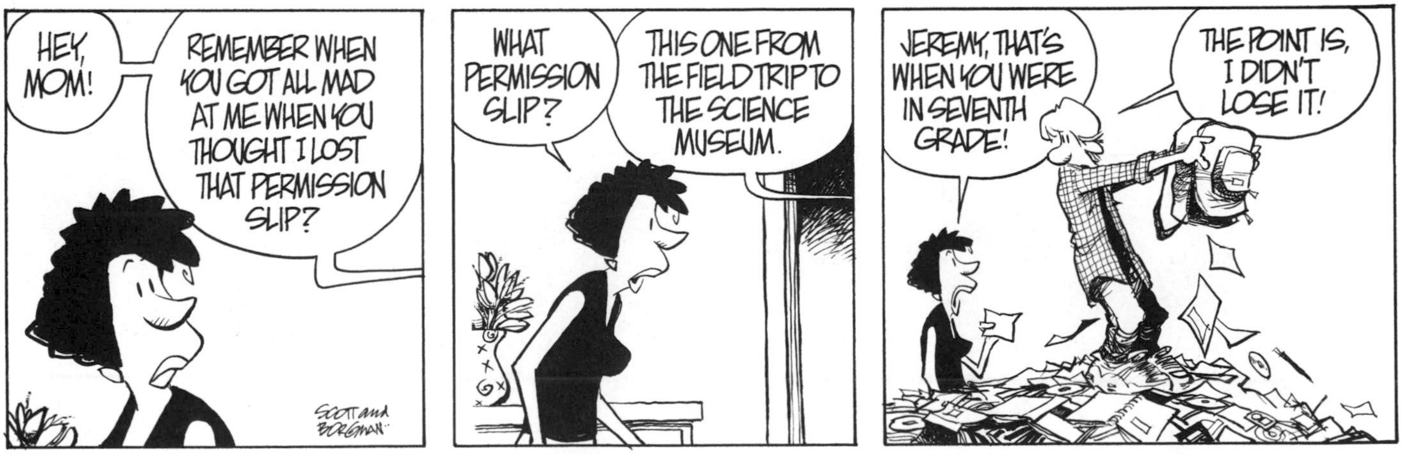
HEY, MOM!
REMEMBER WHEN YOU GOT ALL MAD AT ME WHEN YOU THOUGHT I LOST THAT PERMISSION SLIP?
WHAT PERMISSION SLIP?
THIS ONE FROM THE FIELD TRIP TO THE SCIENCE MUSEUM.
JEREMY, THAT'S WHEN YOU WERE IN SEVENTH GRADE!
THE POINT IS, I DIDN'T LOSE IT!

Zits

by JERRY SCOTT and JIM BORGMAN

SORRY I'M LATE, GUYS.

IT'S ABOUT TIME!

TODAY IS MY MOM'S BIRTHDAY, AND I HAD TO GIVE HER MY GIFT.

WHAT DID YOU GET HER?

IT'S MORE LIKE A RITUAL THAN A GIFT REALLY.

EVERY YEAR I ASK HER WHAT SHE WANTS, AND EVERY YEAR SHE SAYS THE SAME THING, SO THAT'S WHAT I DO.

BUY HER FLOWERS?

HAVE A TATTOO REMOVED.

SCOTT and BORGMAN

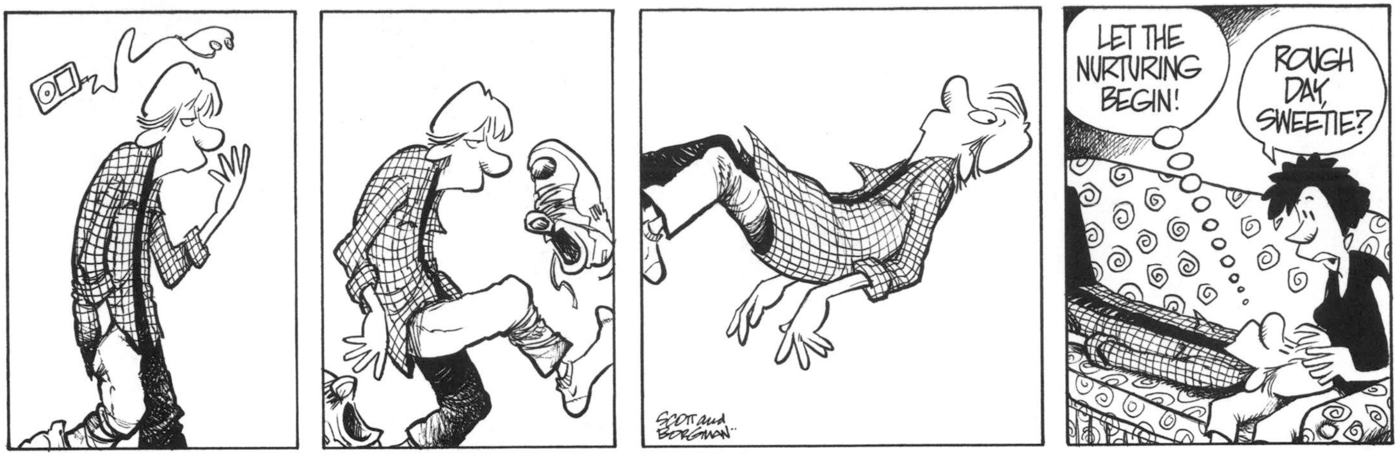
SCOTT and BORGMAN
LET THE NURTURING BEGIN!
ROUGH DAY, SWEETIE?

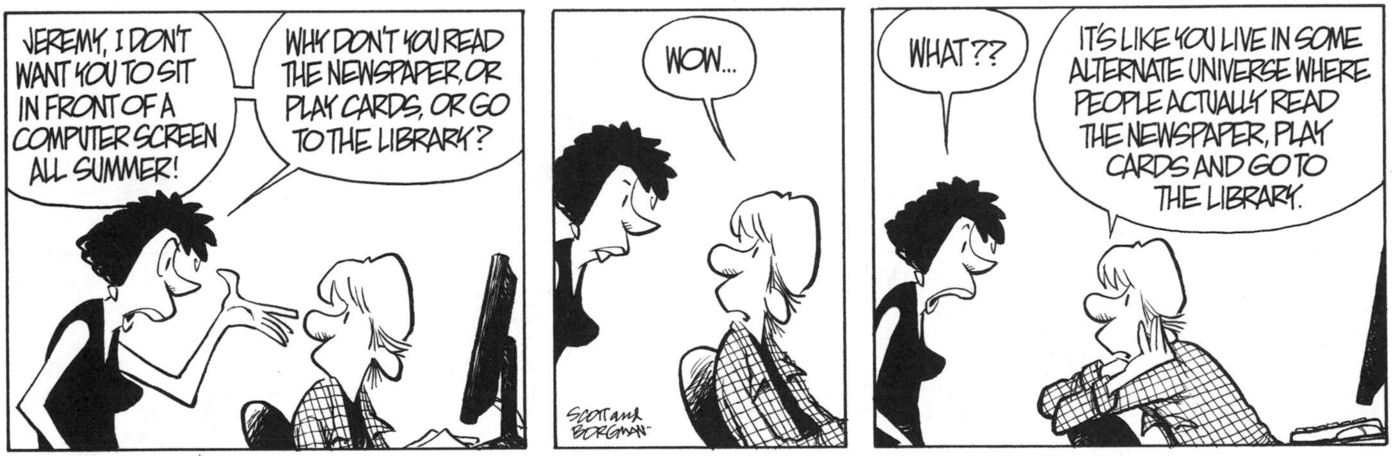
JEREMY, I DON'T WANT YOU TO SIT IN FRONT OF A COMPUTER SCREEN ALL SUMMER!
WHY DON'T YOU READ THE NEWSPAPER, OR PLAY CARDS, OR GO TO THE LIBRARY?
WOW...
SCOTT and BORGMAN
WHAT??
IT'S LIKE YOU LIVE IN SOME ALTERNATE UNIVERSE WHERE PEOPLE ACTUALLY READ THE NEWSPAPER, PLAY CARDS AND GO TO THE LIBRARY.

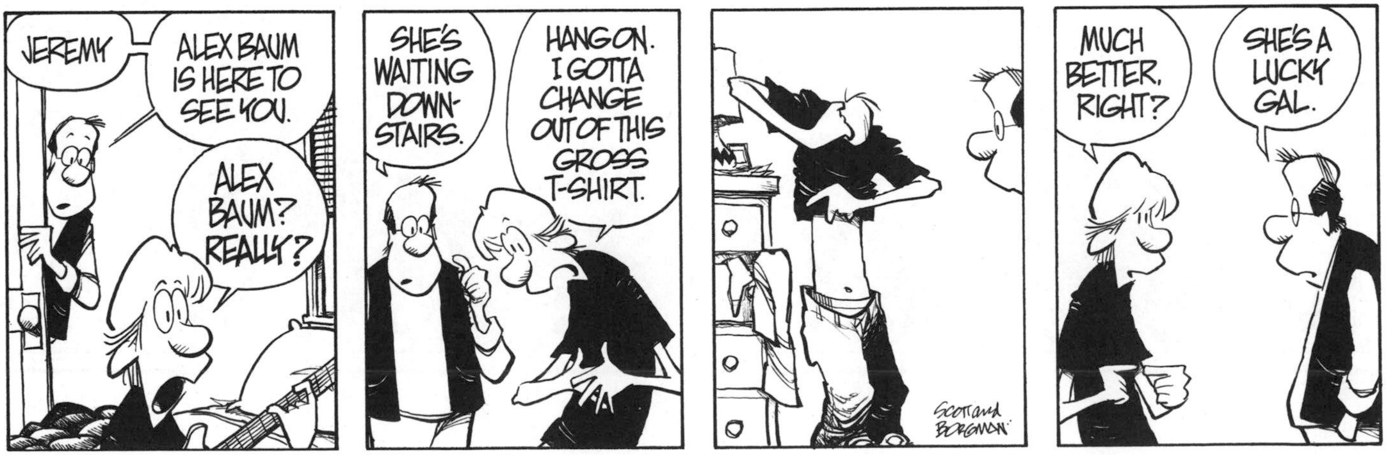
JEREMY
ALEX BAUM IS HERE TO SEE YOU.
ALEX BAUM? REALLY?
SHE'S WAITING DOWN-STAIRS.
HANG ON. I GOTTA CHANGE OUT OF THIS GROSS T-SHIRT.
SCOTT and BORGMAN
MUCH BETTER, RIGHT?
SHE'S A LUCKY GAL.

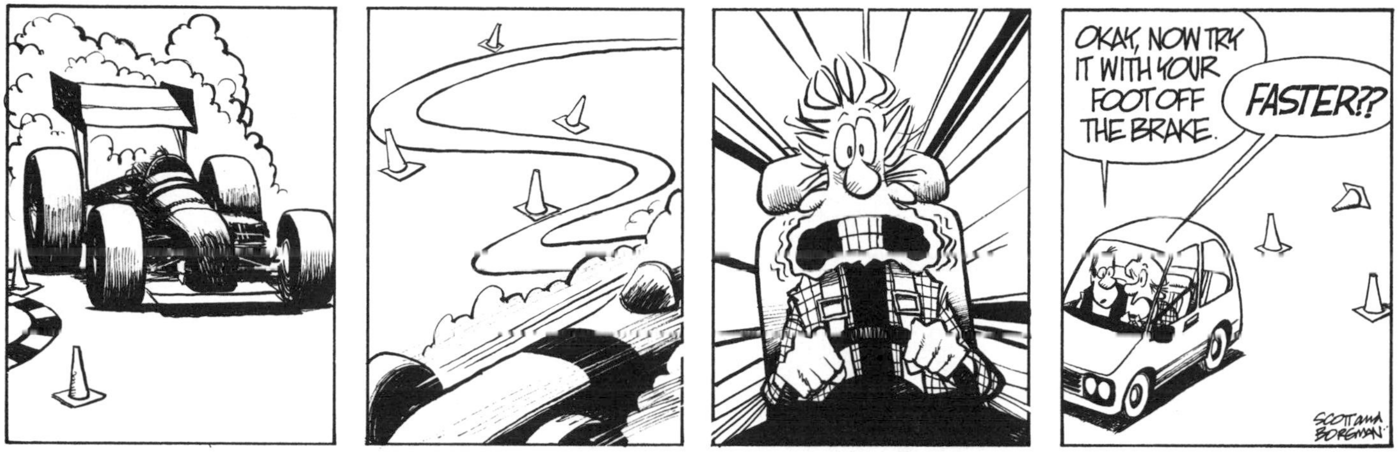
OKAY, NOW TRY IT WITH YOUR FOOT OFF THE BRAKE.
FASTER??
SCOTT and BORGMAN

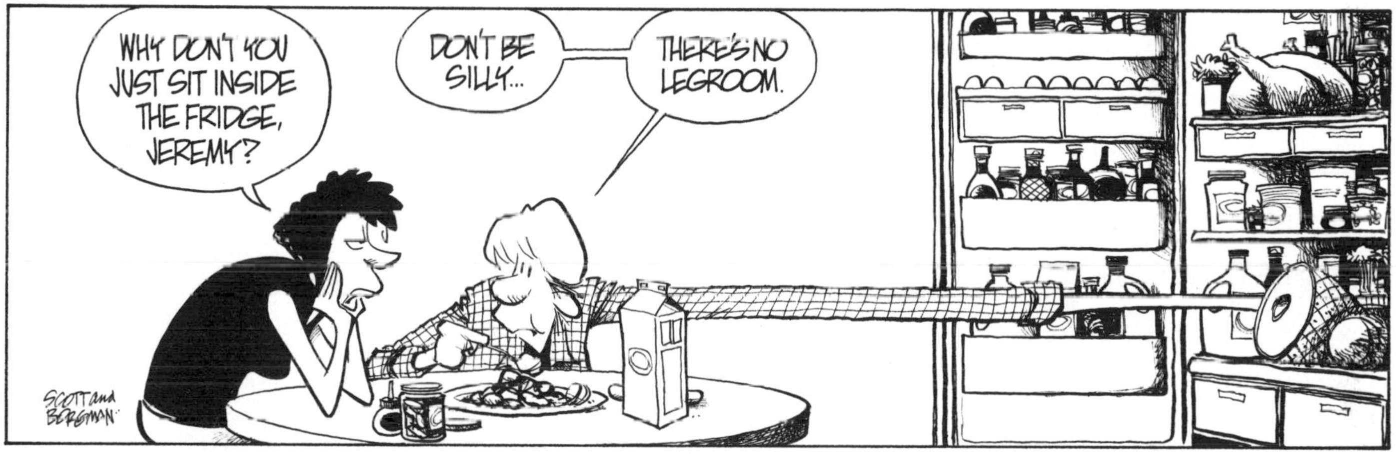
WHY DON'T YOU JUST SIT INSIDE THE FRIDGE, JEREMY?
DON'T BE SILLY...
THERE'S NO LEGROOM.
SCOTT and BORGMAN

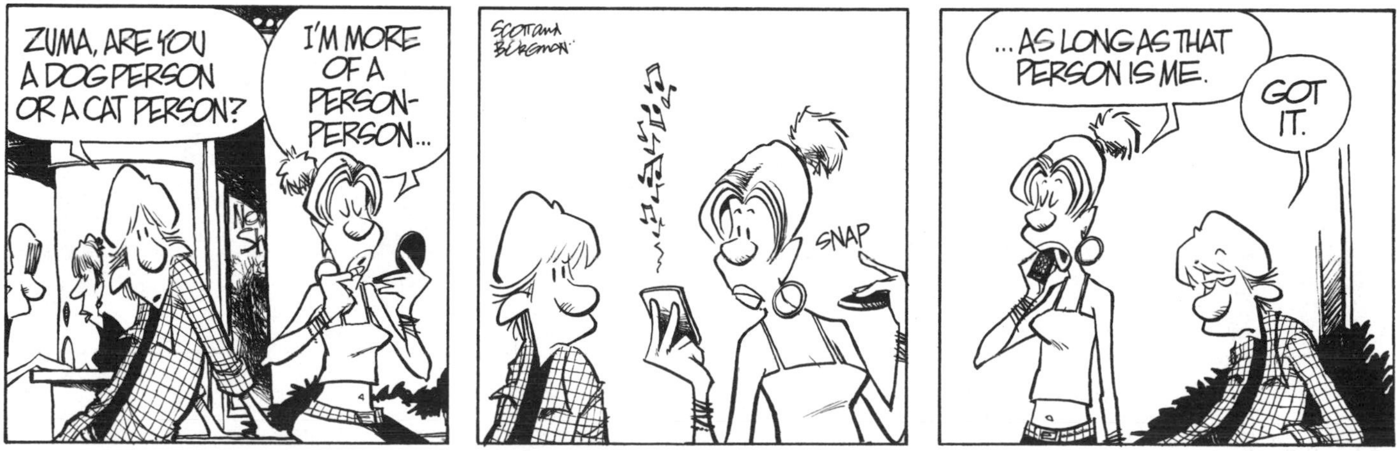
ZUMA, ARE YOU A DOG PERSON OR A CAT PERSON?
I'M MORE OF A PERSON-PERSON...
SCOTT and BORGMAN
SNAP
...AS LONG AS THAT PERSON IS ME.
GOT IT.

Zits

by
JERRY SCOTT and
JIM BORGMAN"

JEREMY, I--

HANG ON, MOM.

LET ME ADJUST THIS VOLUME.

I JUST WANTED TO SAY THAT THE NEXT TIME WE HAVE A MAJOR DISAGREEMENT, I SUGGEST THAT INSTEAD OF IMMEDIATELY JUST ASSUMING THAT THERE IS SOME SORT OF AGENDA BEHIND IT, THAT WE TALK AND SEE IF WE CAN FIND SOME COMMON GROUND BECAUSE WE'RE ACTUALLY A LOT ALIKE AND IT SURPRISES...

THANKS FOR LETTING ME GET THAT OFF MY CHEST!

SCOTT and BORGMAN"

THAT WAS RESPECTFUL OF YOU TO TURN YOUR iPOD DOWN WHEN YOUR MOTHER SPOKE TO YOU.

"DOWN"?

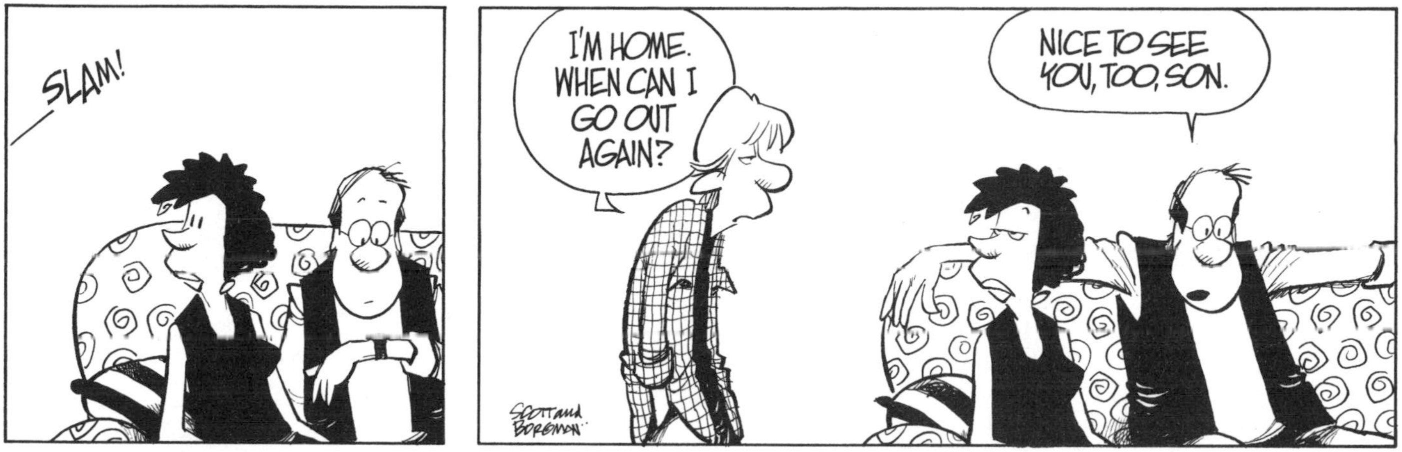
SLAM!
I'M HOME. WHEN CAN I GO OUT AGAIN?
NICE TO SEE YOU, TOO, SON.

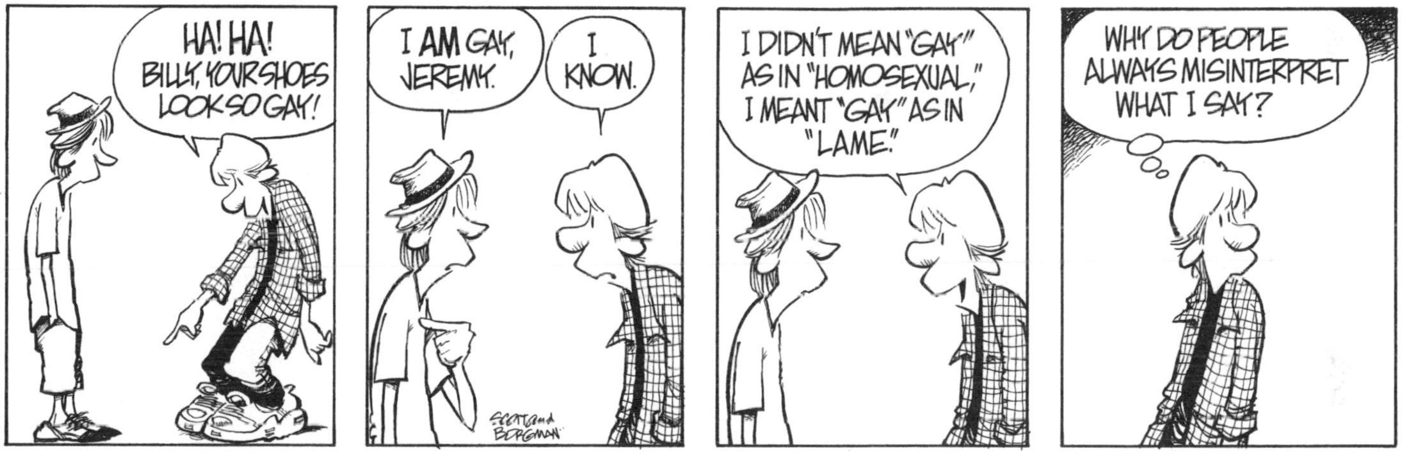
HA! HA! BILLY, YOUR SHOES LOOK SO GAY!
I AM GAY, JEREMY.
I KNOW.
I DIDN'T MEAN "GAY" AS IN "HOMOSEXUAL," I MEANT "GAY" AS IN "LAME."
WHY DO PEOPLE ALWAYS MISINTERPRET WHAT I SAY?

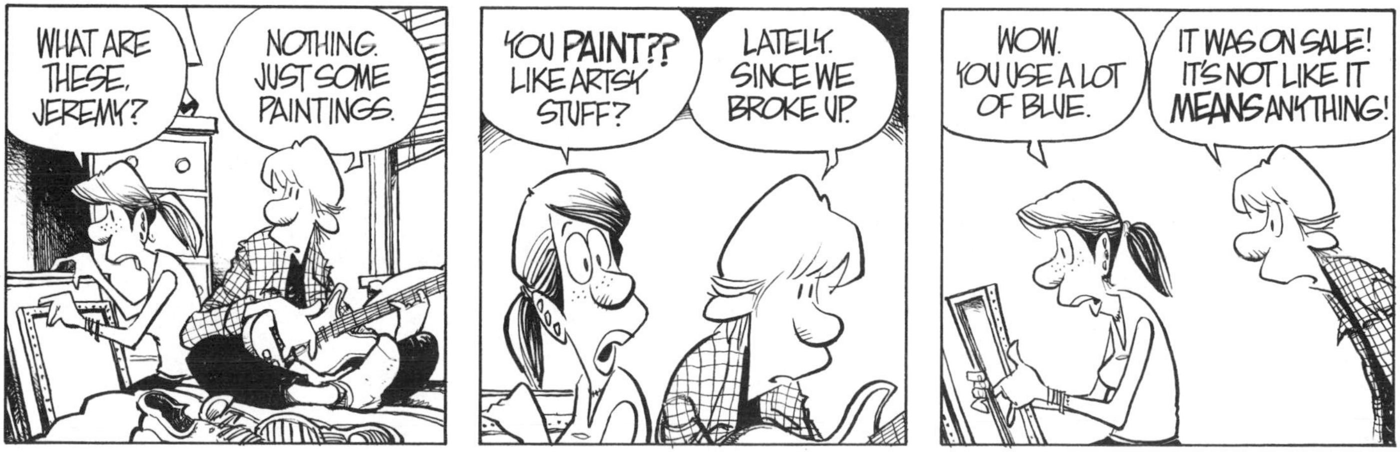
WHAT ARE THESE, JEREMY?
NOTHING. JUST SOME PAINTINGS.
YOU PAINT?? LIKE ARTSY STUFF?
LATELY. SINCE WE BROKE UP.
WOW. YOU USE A LOT OF BLUE.
IT WAS ON SALE! IT'S NOT LIKE IT MEANS ANYTHING!

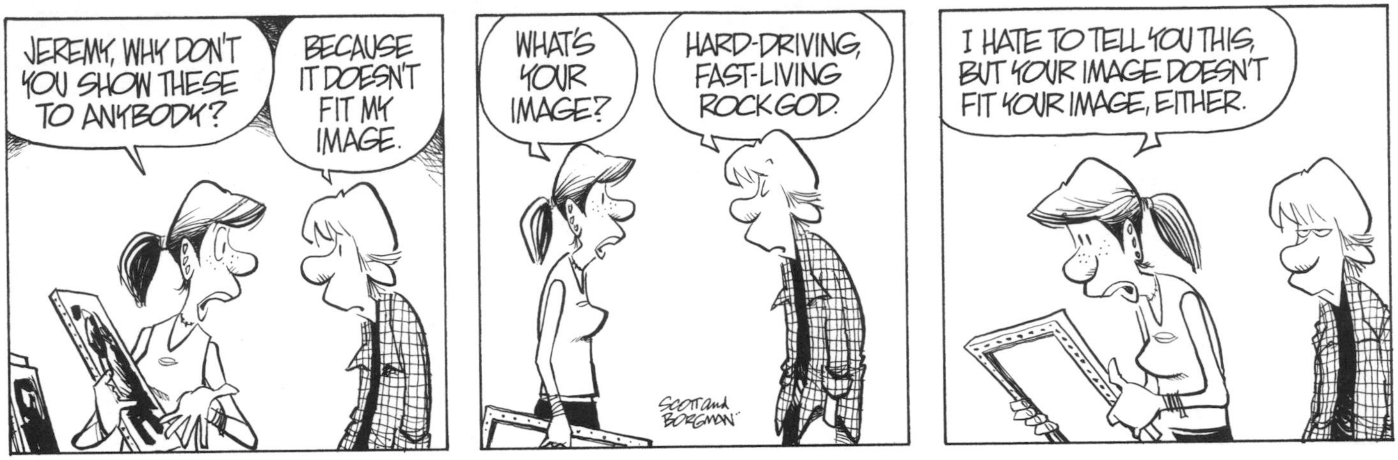
JEREMY, WHY DON'T YOU SHOW THESE TO ANYBODY?
BECAUSE IT DOESN'T FIT MY IMAGE.
WHAT'S YOUR IMAGE?
HARD-DRIVING, FAST-LIVING ROCK GOD.
I HATE TO TELL YOU THIS, BUT YOUR IMAGE DOESN'T FIT YOUR IMAGE, EITHER.

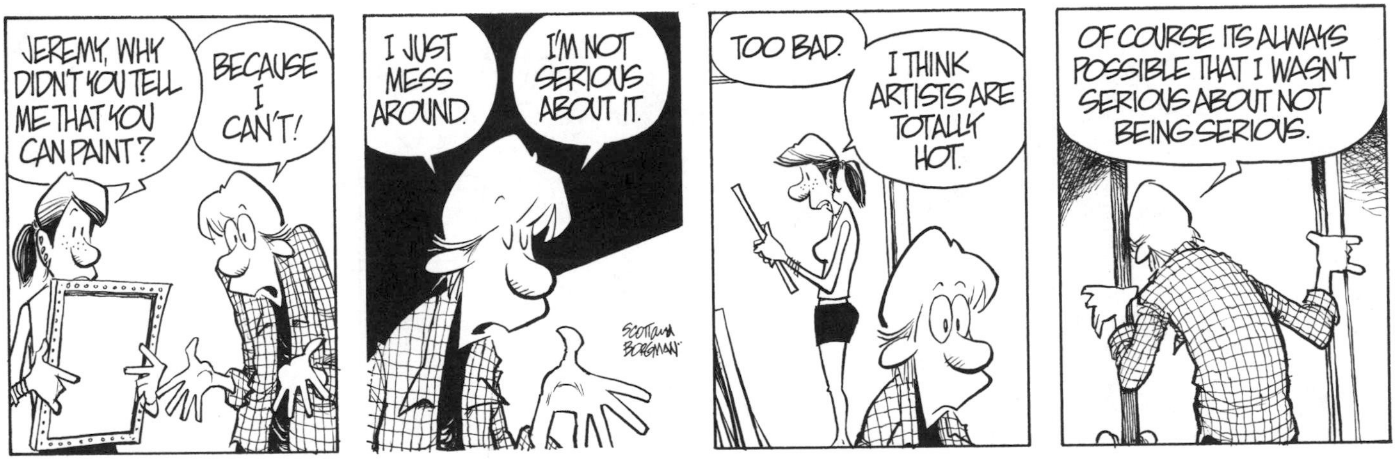
JEREMY, WHY DIDN'T YOU TELL ME THAT YOU CAN PAINT?
BECAUSE I CAN'T!
I JUST MESS AROUND.
I'M NOT SERIOUS ABOUT IT.
TOO BAD.
I THINK ARTISTS ARE TOTALLY HOT.
OF COURSE ITS ALWAYS POSSIBLE THAT I WASN'T SERIOUS ABOUT NOT BEING SERIOUS.

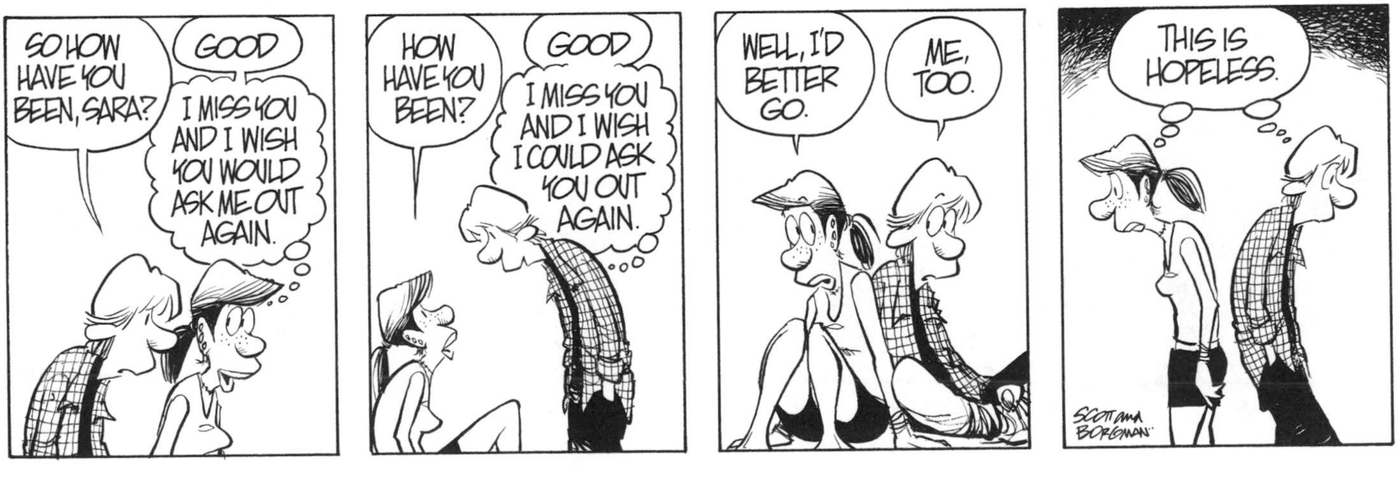
SO HOW HAVE YOU BEEN, SARA?
GOOD
I MISS YOU AND I WISH YOU WOULD ASK ME OUT AGAIN.
HOW HAVE YOU BEEN?
GOOD
I MISS YOU AND I WISH I COULD ASK YOU OUT AGAIN.
WELL, I'D BETTER GO.
ME, TOO.
THIS IS HOPELESS.

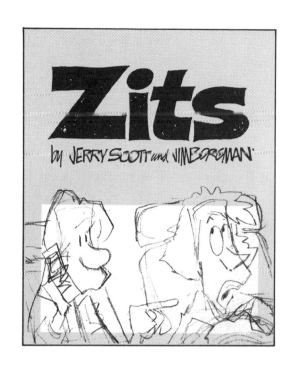

Zits by Jerry Scott and Jim Borgman

MOM, PIERCE AND HECTOR WANT ME TO GO TO A MOVIE. CAN YOU DROP ME OFF AT THE MALL?

SURE.

WAIT— WE'RE NOT GOING TO A MOVIE NOW. JUST DROP ME OFF AT HECTOR'S.

OKAY.

HOLD IT— NOT HECTOR'S. THE MUSIC STORE.

FINE.

NO, THE MALL. DEFINITELY THE MALL.

(SIGH)

BUT FIRST GO BY THE MUSIC STORE — I MEAN, TIM'S HOUSE!

IT'S TIM'S HOUSE, MUSIC STORE, MALL.

WAIT— WHAT? OKAY. COOL.

NEVER MIND. EVERYBODY IS COMING TO OUR HOUSE.

FLINK!

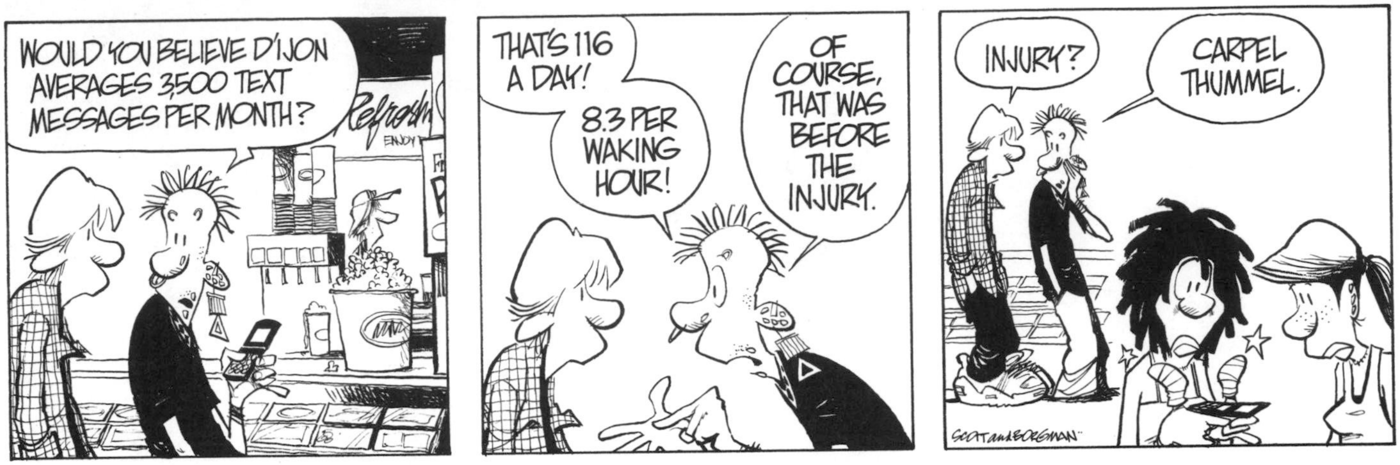
WOULD YOU BELIEVE D'IJON AVERAGES 3,500 TEXT MESSAGES PER MONTH?
THAT'S 116 A DAY!
8.3 PER WAKING HOUR!
OF COURSE, THAT WAS BEFORE THE INJURY.
INJURY?
CARPEL THUMMEL.
SCOTT and BORGMAN

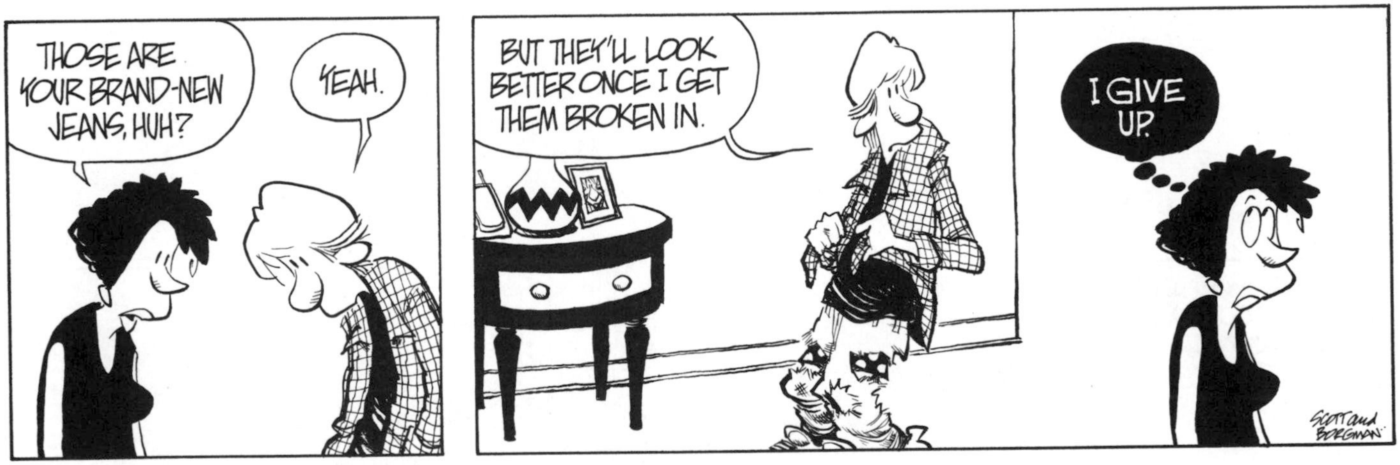
THOSE ARE YOUR BRAND-NEW JEANS, HUH?
YEAH.
BUT THEY'LL LOOK BETTER ONCE I GET THEM BROKEN IN.
I GIVE UP.
SCOTT and BORGMAN

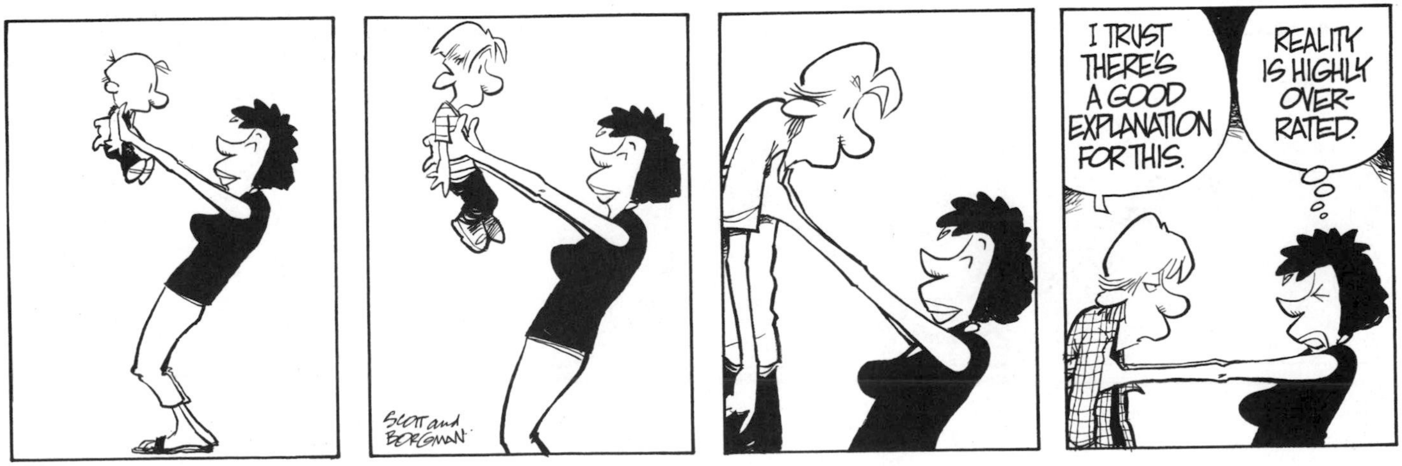
SCOTT and BORGMAN
I TRUST THERE'S A GOOD EXPLANATION FOR THIS.
REALITY IS HIGHLY OVER-RATED.

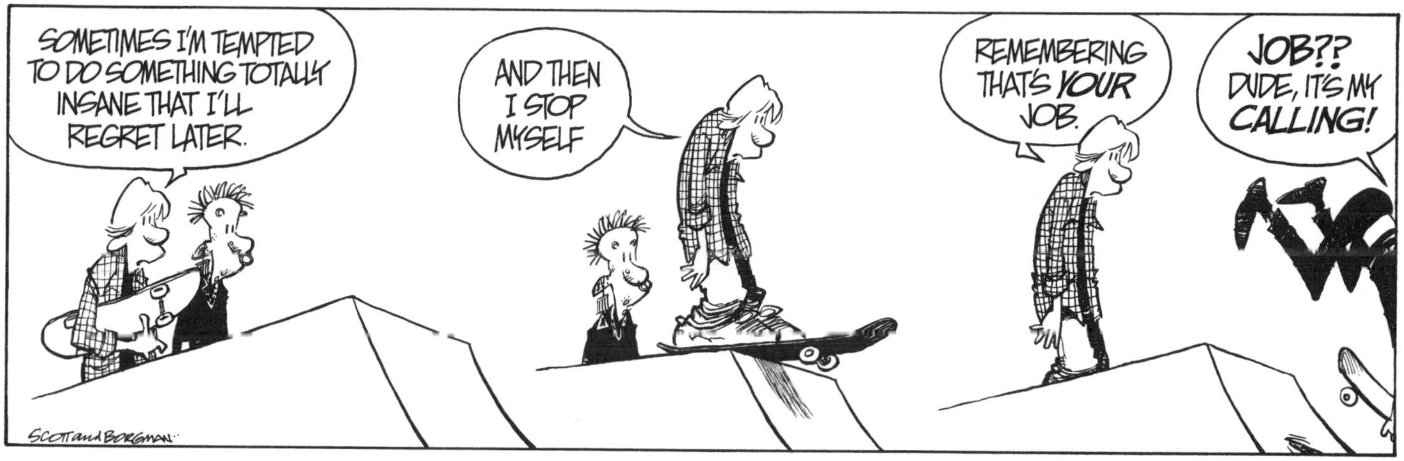
SOMETIMES I'M TEMPTED TO DO SOMETHING TOTALLY INSANE THAT I'LL REGRET LATER.
AND THEN I STOP MYSELF
REMEMBERING THAT'S YOUR JOB.
JOB?? DUDE, IT'S MY CALLING!
SCOTT and BORGMAN

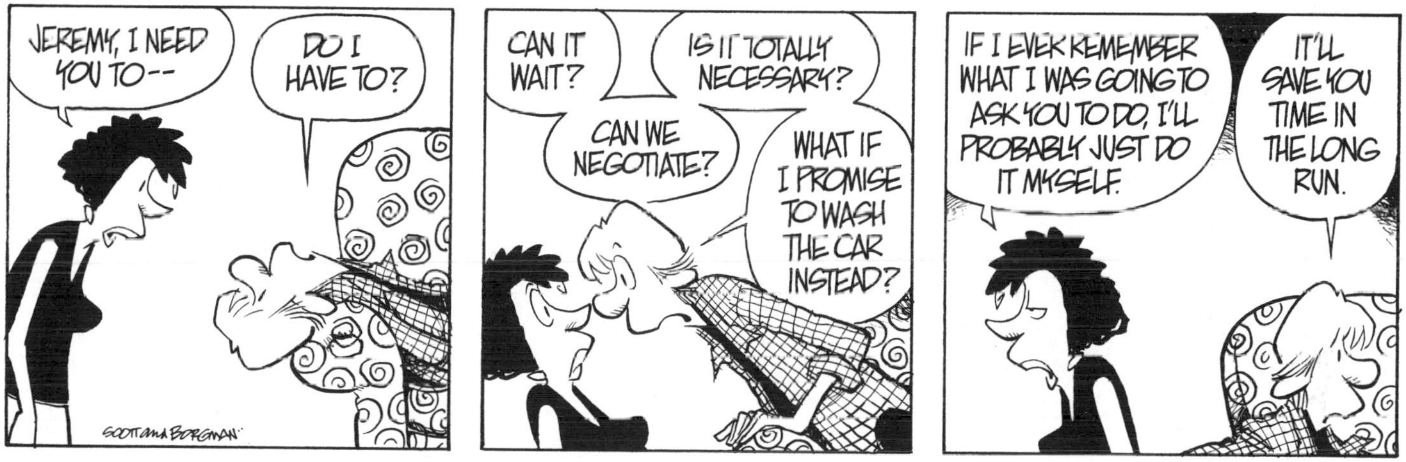
JEREMY, I NEED YOU TO--
DO I HAVE TO?
CAN IT WAIT?
IS IT TOTALLY NECESSARY?
CAN WE NEGOTIATE?
WHAT IF I PROMISE TO WASH THE CAR INSTEAD?
IF I EVER REMEMBER WHAT I WAS GOING TO ASK YOU TO DO, I'LL PROBABLY JUST DO IT MYSELF.
IT'LL SAVE YOU TIME IN THE LONG RUN.
SCOTT and BORGMAN

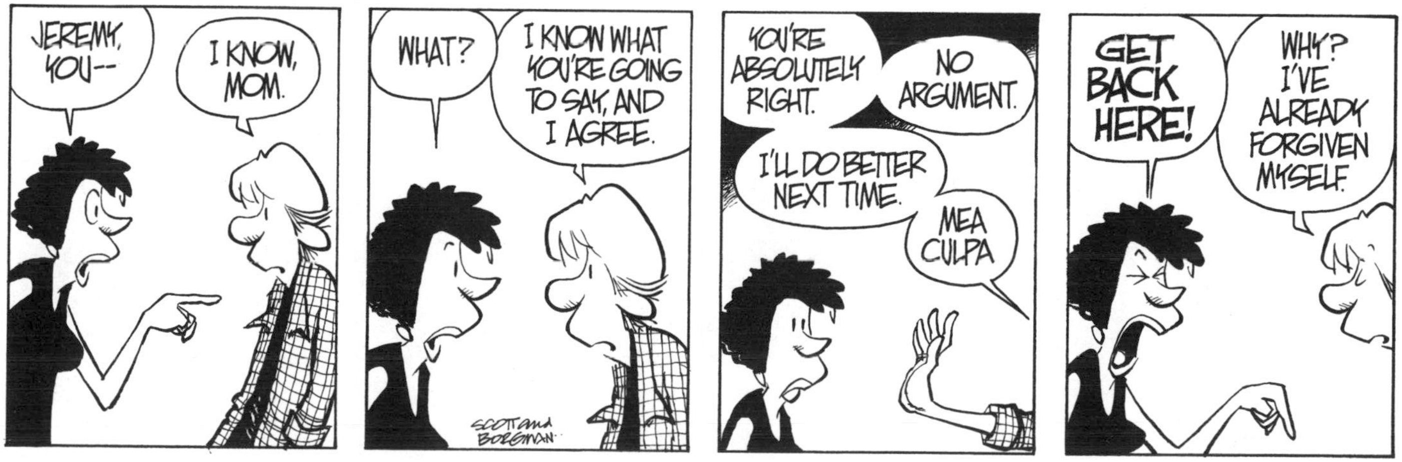
JEREMY, YOU--
I KNOW, MOM.
WHAT?
I KNOW WHAT YOU'RE GOING TO SAY, AND I AGREE.
YOU'RE ABSOLUTELY RIGHT.
NO ARGUMENT.
I'LL DO BETTER NEXT TIME.
MEA CULPA
GET BACK HERE!
WHY? I'VE ALREADY FORGIVEN MYSELF.
SCOTT and BORGMAN

Zits
by
JERRY SCOTT and
JIM BORGMAN

NO WAY! YOU'RE CRAZY!
I'M RIGHT!
POOK!
WATCH! I'LL PROVE IT!
SCOTT and BORGMAN
SEE? I TOLD YOU ROB ZOMBIE IS HEAVY METAL!
WEIRD, I TOTALLY HAD HIM ON MY "EASY LISTENING" PLAYLIST.

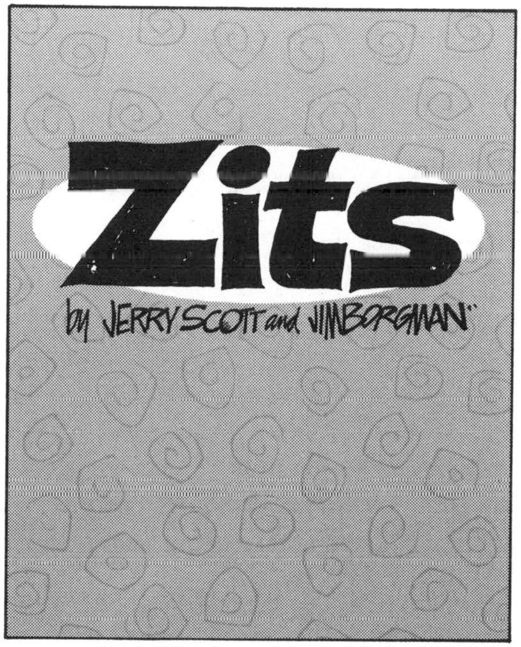
Zits
by JERRY SCOTT and JIM BORGMAN

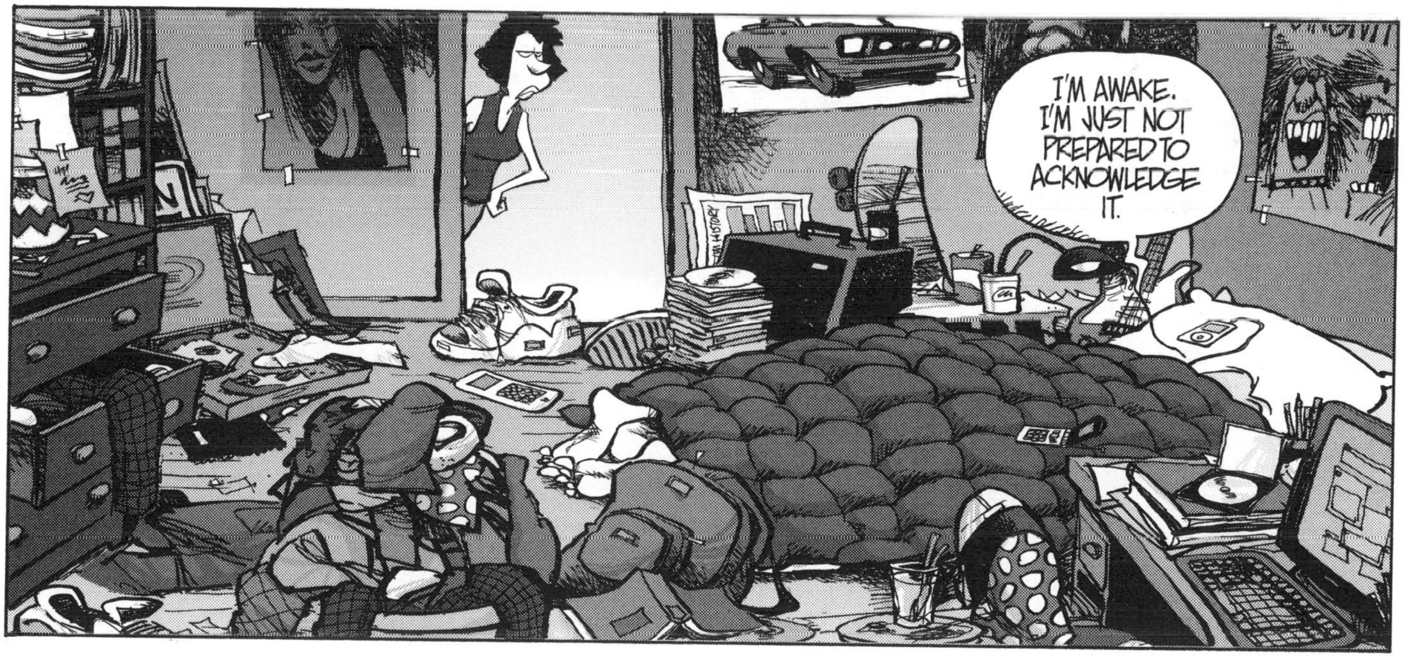
I'M AWAKE. I'M JUST NOT PREPARED TO ACKNOWLEDGE IT.

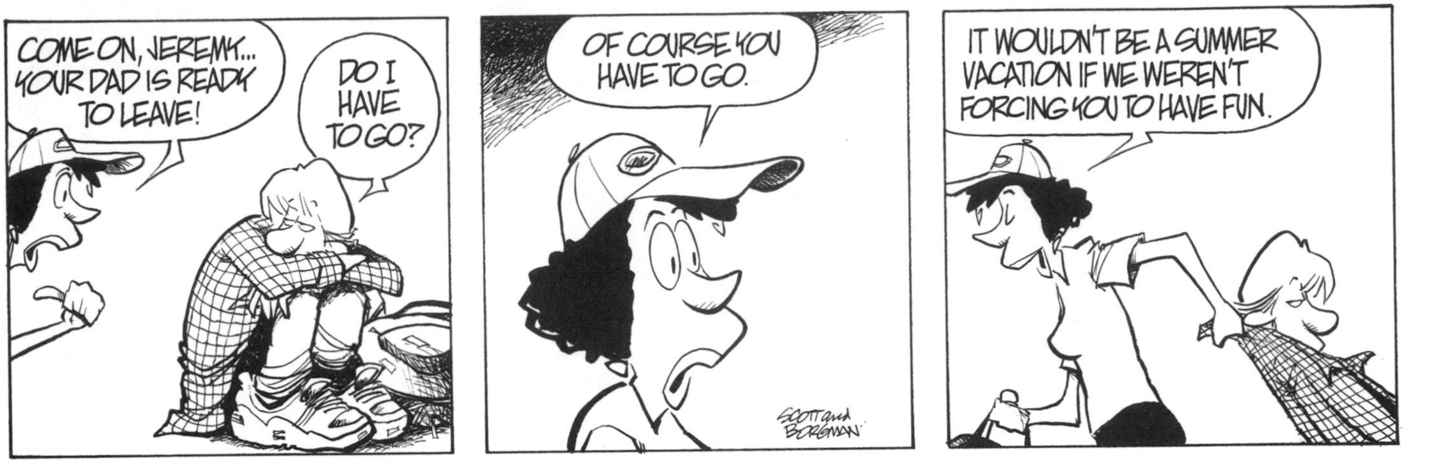
COME ON, JEREMY... YOUR DAD IS READY TO LEAVE!
DO I HAVE TO GO?
OF COURSE YOU HAVE TO GO.
IT WOULDN'T BE A SUMMER VACATION IF WE WEREN'T FORCING YOU TO HAVE FUN.

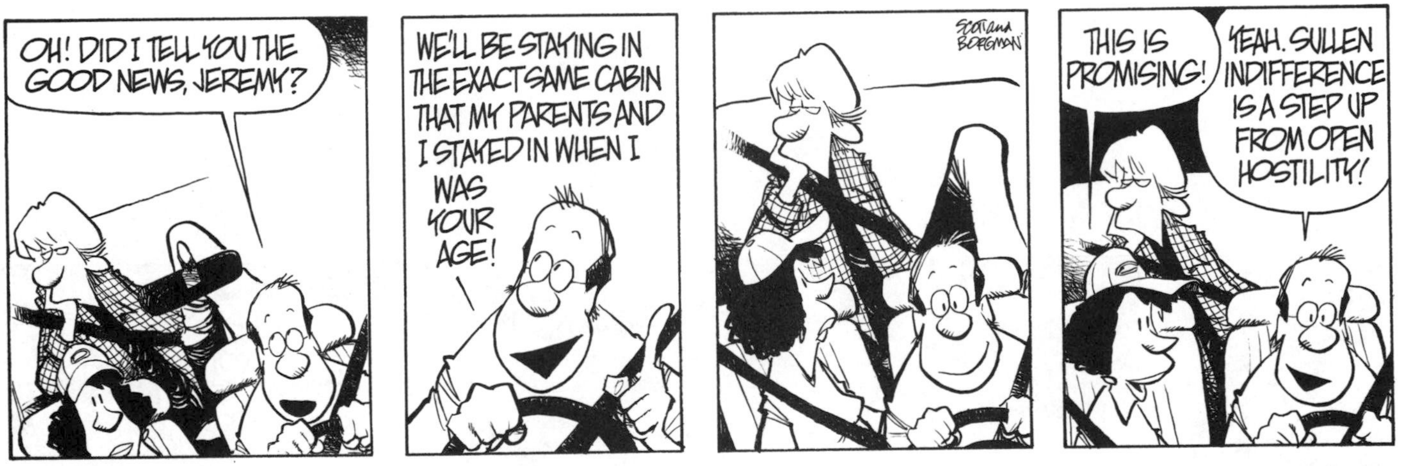
OH! DID I TELL YOU THE GOOD NEWS, JEREMY?
WE'LL BE STAYING IN THE EXACT SAME CABIN THAT MY PARENTS AND I STAYED IN WHEN I WAS YOUR AGE!
THIS IS PROMISING!
YEAH. SULLEN INDIFFERENCE IS A STEP UP FROM OPEN HOSTILITY!

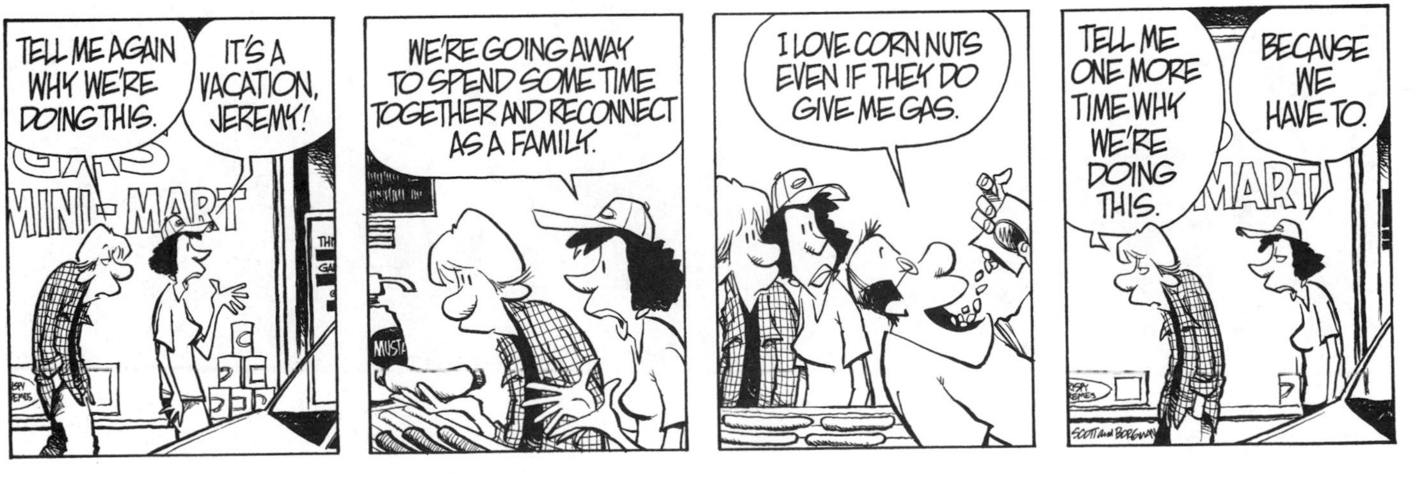
TELL ME AGAIN WHY WE'RE DOING THIS.
IT'S A VACATION, JEREMY!
WE'RE GOING AWAY TO SPEND SOME TIME TOGETHER AND RECONNECT AS A FAMILY.
I LOVE CORN NUTS EVEN IF THEY DO GIVE ME GAS.
TELL ME ONE MORE TIME WHY WE'RE DOING THIS.
BECAUSE WE HAVE TO.

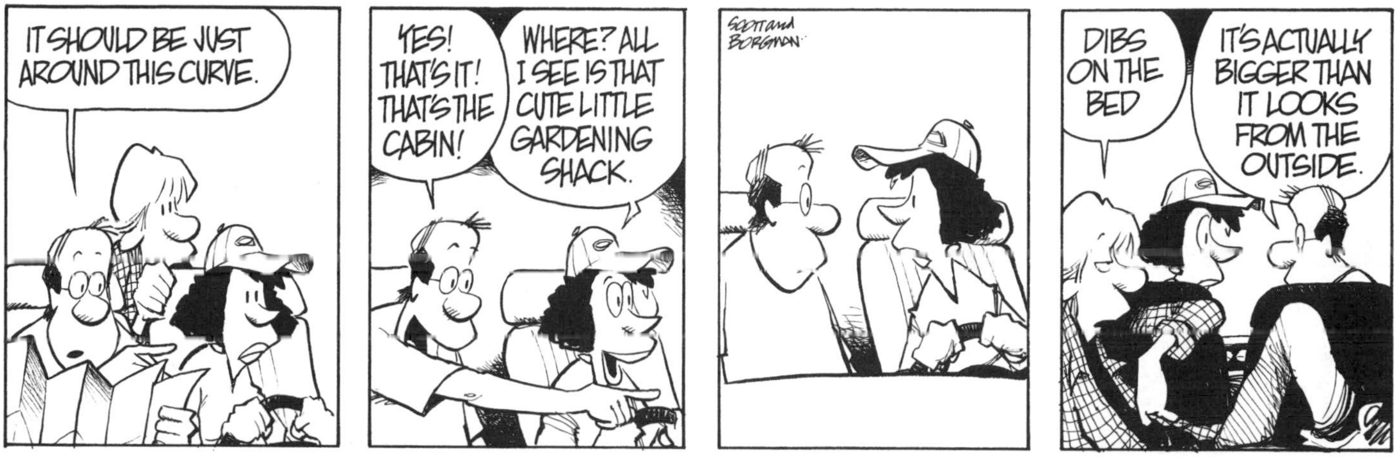
IT SHOULD BE JUST AROUND THIS CURVE.
YES! THAT'S IT! THAT'S THE CABIN!
WHERE? ALL I SEE IS THAT CUTE LITTLE GARDENING SHACK.
SCOTT and BORGMAN
DIBS ON THE BED
IT'S ACTUALLY BIGGER THAN IT LOOKS FROM THE OUTSIDE.

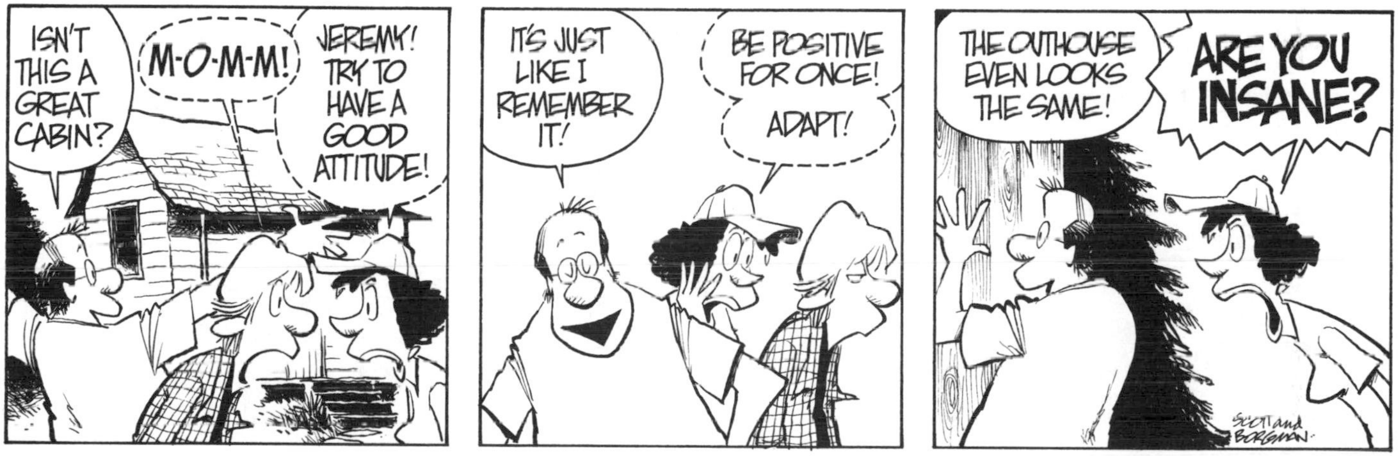
ISN'T THIS A GREAT CABIN?
M-O-M-M!
JEREMY! TRY TO HAVE A GOOD ATTITUDE!
IT'S JUST LIKE I REMEMBER IT!
BE POSITIVE FOR ONCE!
ADAPT!
THE OUTHOUSE EVEN LOOKS THE SAME!
ARE YOU INSANE?
SCOTT and BORGMAN

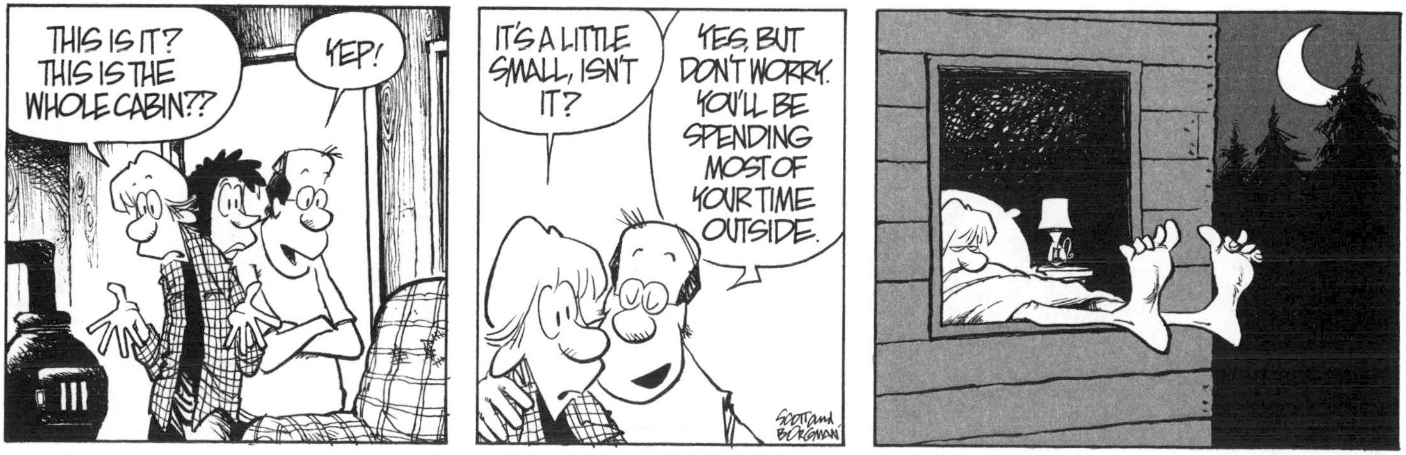
THIS IS IT? THIS IS THE WHOLE CABIN??
YEP!
IT'S A LITTLE SMALL, ISN'T IT?
YES, BUT DON'T WORRY. YOU'LL BE SPENDING MOST OF YOUR TIME OUTSIDE.
SCOTT and BORGMAN

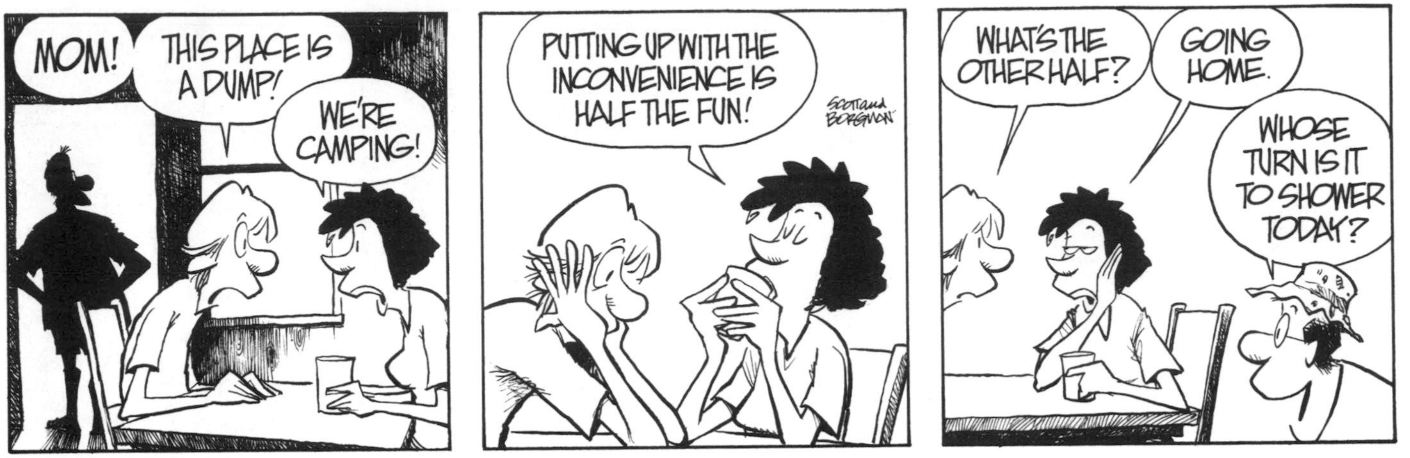
MOM!
THIS PLACE IS A DUMP!
WE'RE CAMPING!
PUTTING UP WITH THE INCONVENIENCE IS HALF THE FUN!
WHAT'S THE OTHER HALF?
GOING HOME.
WHOSE TURN IS IT TO SHOWER TODAY?

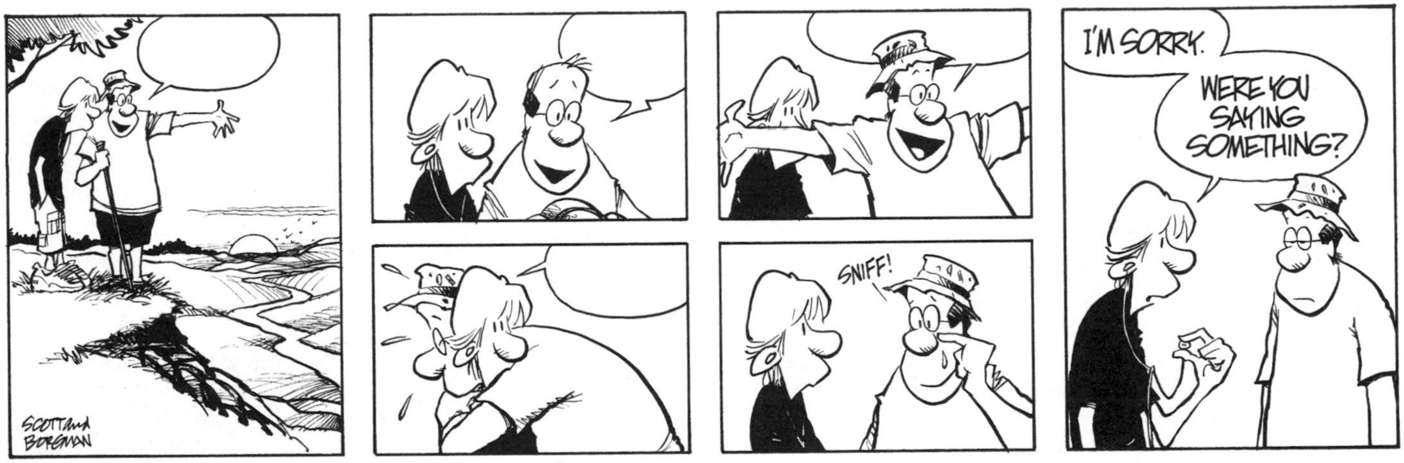
SNIFF!
I'M SORRY.
WERE YOU SAYING SOMETHING?

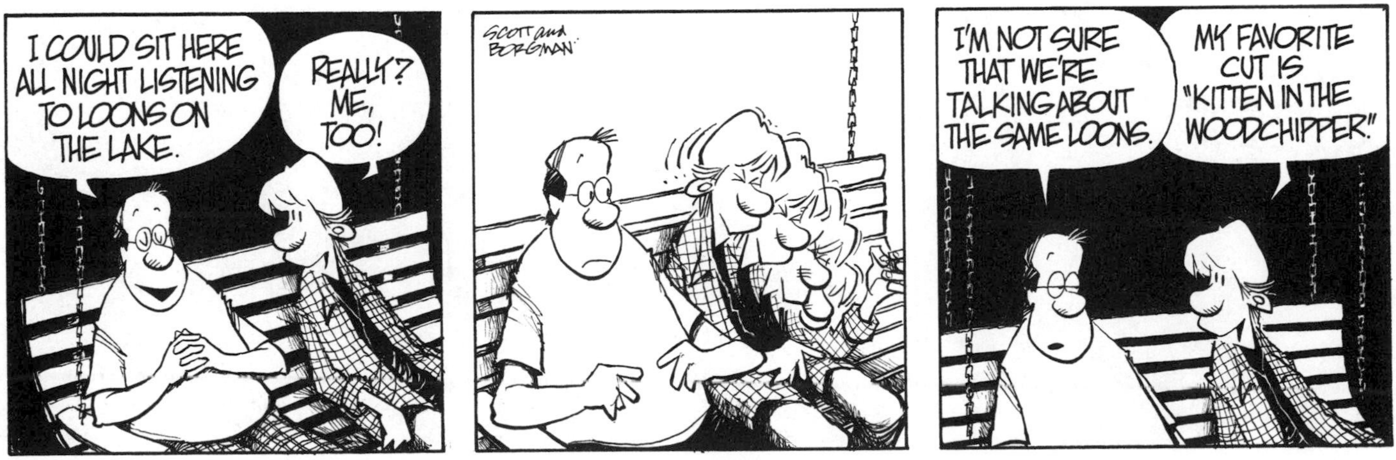
I COULD SIT HERE ALL NIGHT LISTENING TO LOONS ON THE LAKE.
REALLY? ME, TOO!
I'M NOT SURE THAT WE'RE TALKING ABOUT THE SAME LOONS.
MY FAVORITE CUT IS "KITTEN IN THE WOODCHIPPER."

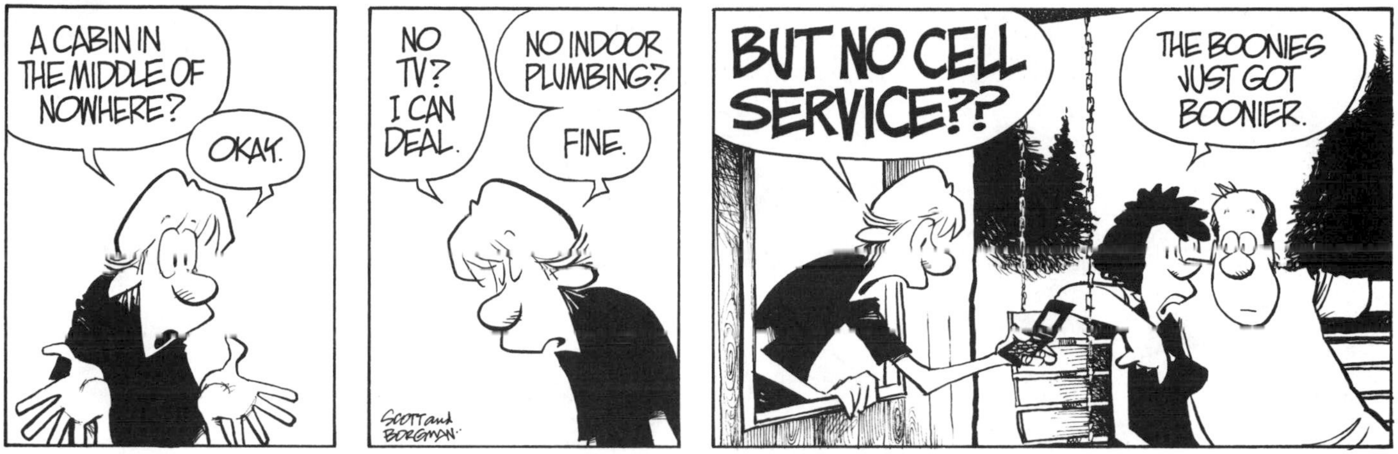
A CABIN IN THE MIDDLE OF NOWHERE?
OKAY.
NO TV? I CAN DEAL.
NO INDOOR PLUMBING?
FINE.
SCOTT and BORGMAN
BUT NO CELL SERVICE??
THE BOONIES JUST GOT BOONIER.

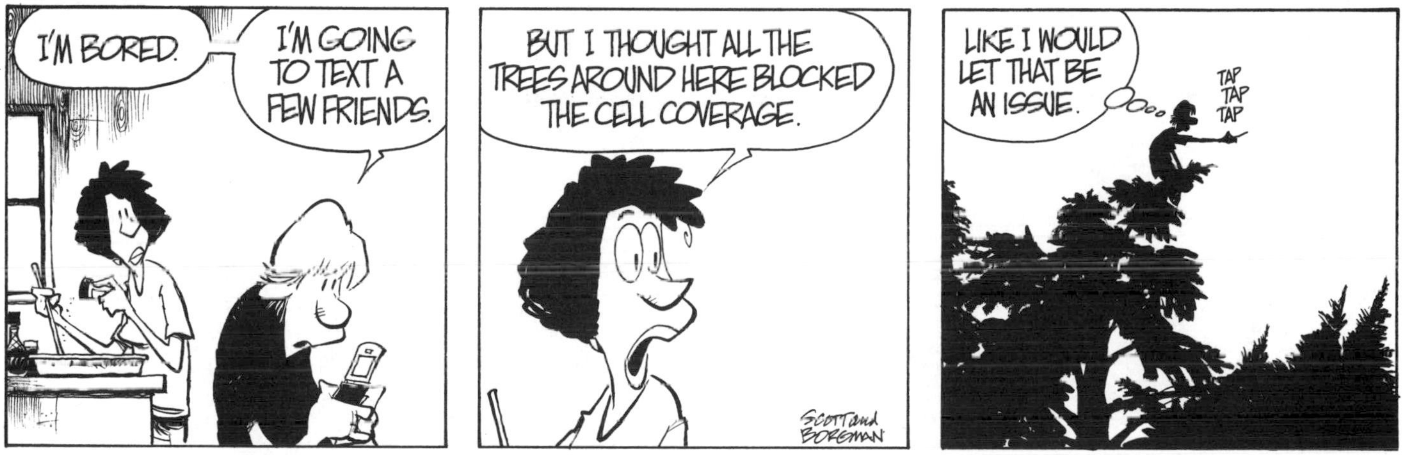
I'M BORED.
I'M GOING TO TEXT A FEW FRIENDS.
BUT I THOUGHT ALL THE TREES AROUND HERE BLOCKED THE CELL COVERAGE.
SCOTT and BORGMAN
LIKE I WOULD LET THAT BE AN ISSUE.
TAP TAP TAP

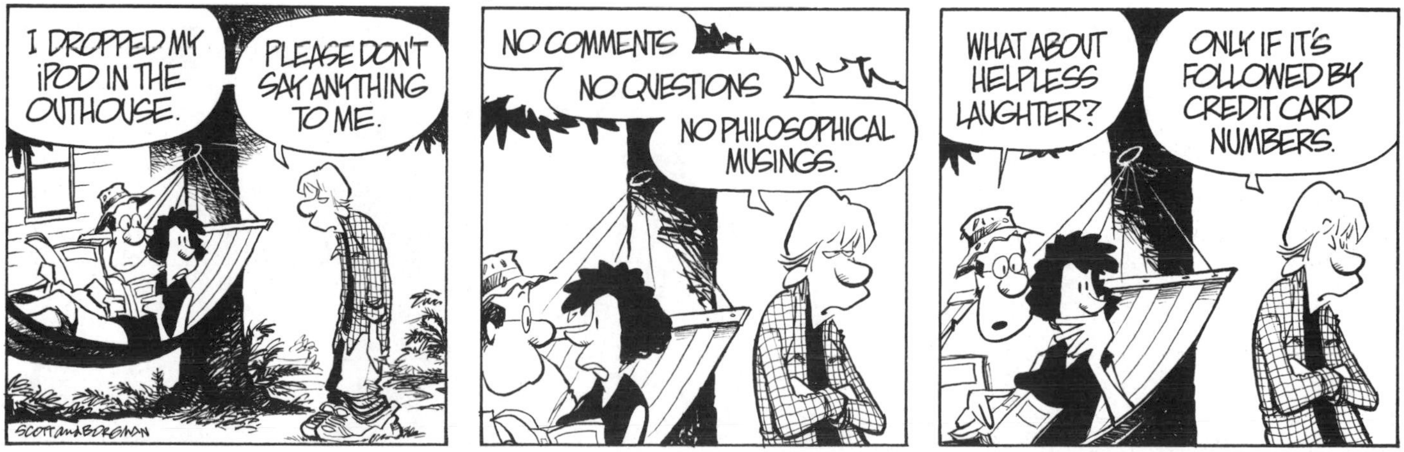
I DROPPED MY iPOD IN THE OUTHOUSE.
PLEASE DON'T SAY ANYTHING TO ME.
SCOTT and BORGMAN
NO COMMENTS.
NO QUESTIONS.
NO PHILOSOPHICAL MUSINGS.
WHAT ABOUT HELPLESS LAUGHTER?
ONLY IF IT'S FOLLOWED BY CREDIT CARD NUMBERS.

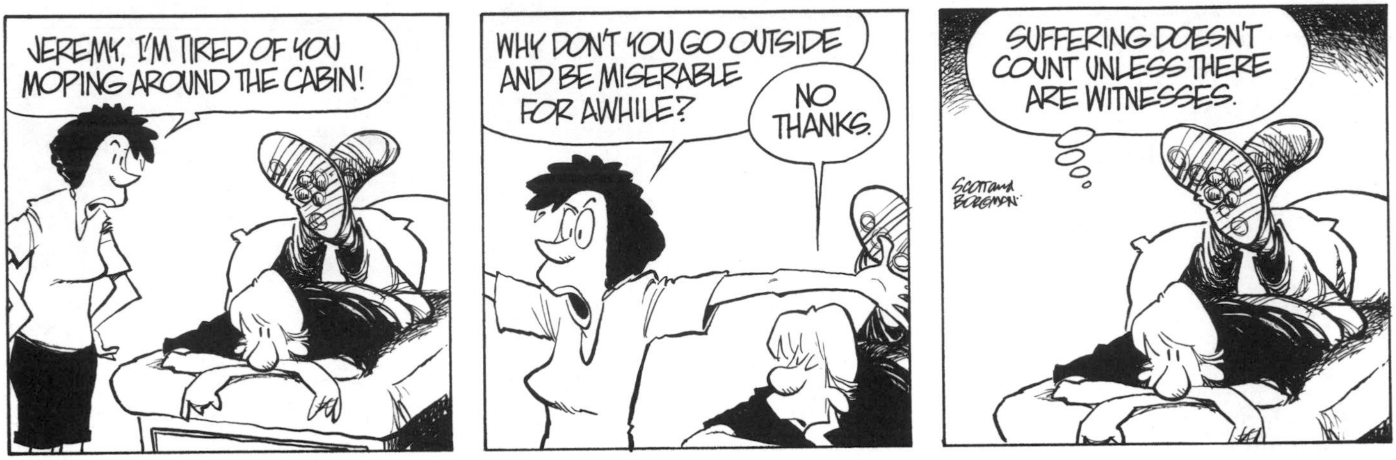
JEREMY, I'M TIRED OF YOU MOPING AROUND THE CABIN!
WHY DON'T YOU GO OUTSIDE AND BE MISERABLE FOR AWHILE?
NO THANKS.
SUFFERING DOESN'T COUNT UNLESS THERE ARE WITNESSES.
SCOTT and BORGMAN

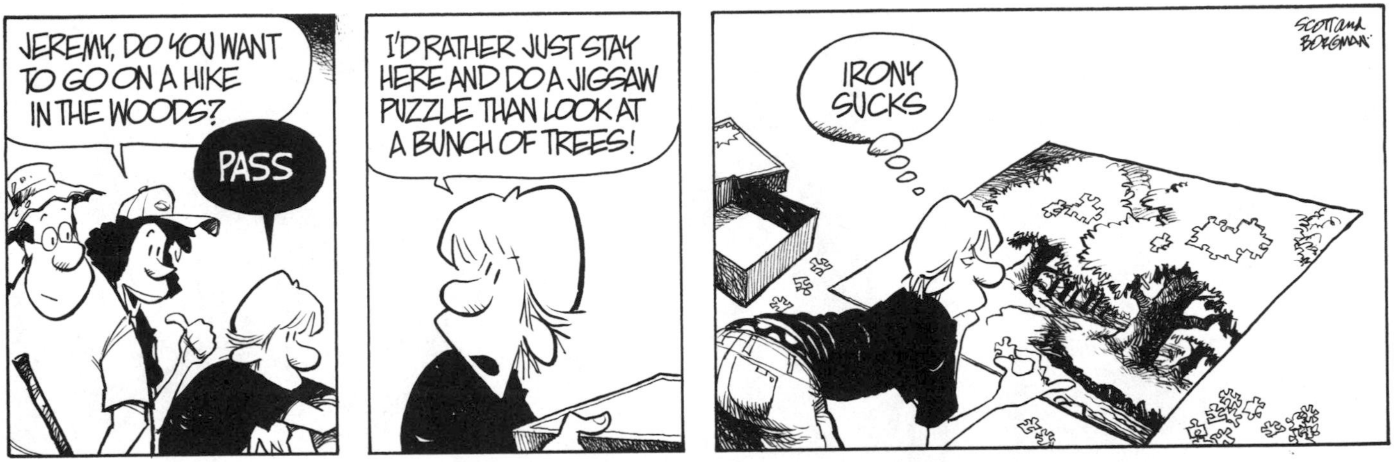
JEREMY, DO YOU WANT TO GO ON A HIKE IN THE WOODS?
PASS
I'D RATHER JUST STAY HERE AND DO A JIGSAW PUZZLE THAN LOOK AT A BUNCH OF TREES!
SCOTT and BORGMAN
IRONY SUCKS

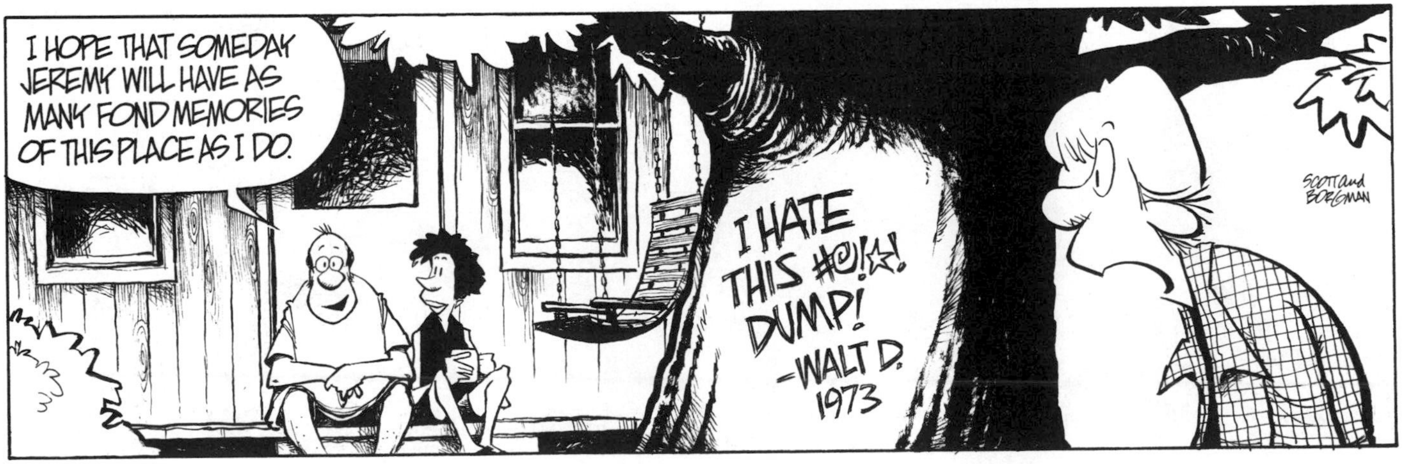
I HOPE THAT SOMEDAY JEREMY WILL HAVE AS MANY FOND MEMORIES OF THIS PLACE AS I DO.
I HATE THIS #@!☆! DUMP! -WALT D. 1973
SCOTT and BORGMAN

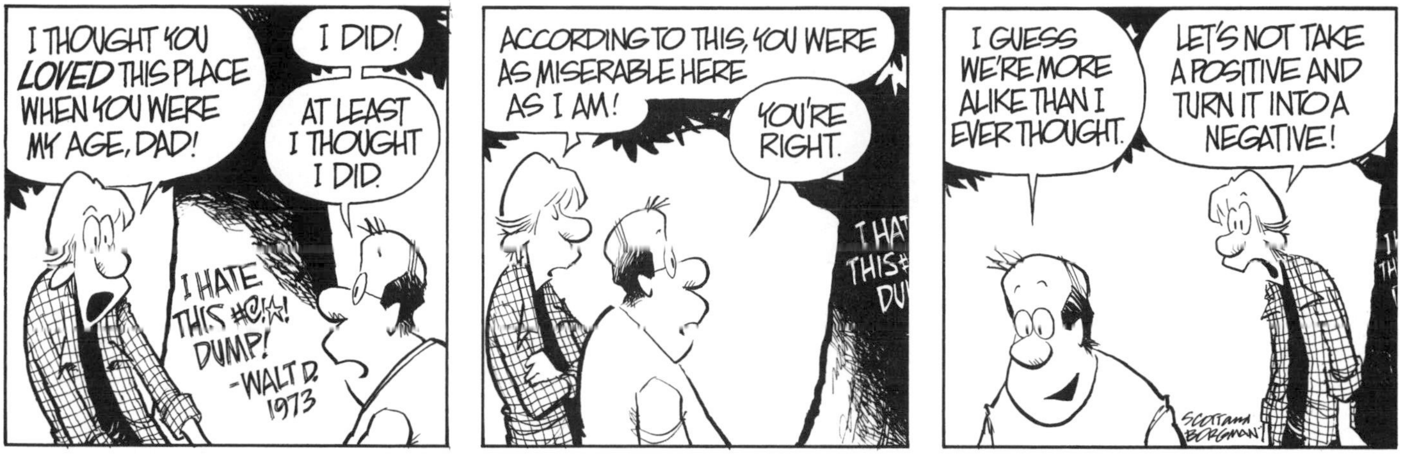
I THOUGHT YOU LOVED THIS PLACE WHEN YOU WERE MY AGE, DAD!
I DID!
AT LEAST I THOUGHT I DID.
I HATE THIS #C☆☆! DUMP! -WALT D. 1973
ACCORDING TO THIS, YOU WERE AS MISERABLE HERE AS I AM!
YOU'RE RIGHT.
I GUESS WE'RE MORE ALIKE THAN I EVER THOUGHT.
LET'S NOT TAKE A POSITIVE AND TURN IT INTO A NEGATIVE!
SCOTT and BORGMAN

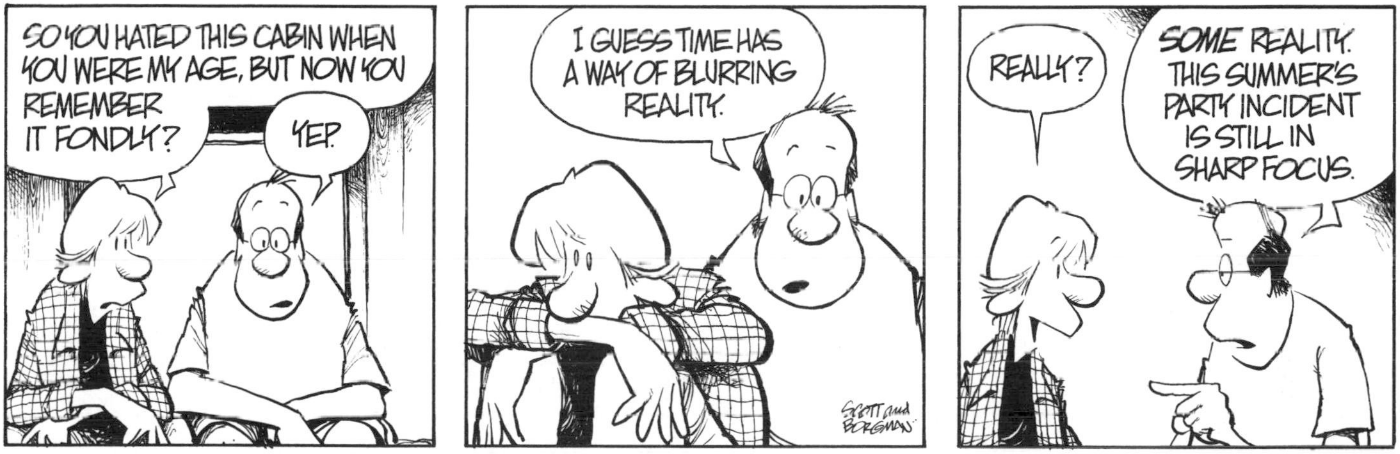
SO YOU HATED THIS CABIN WHEN YOU WERE MY AGE, BUT NOW YOU REMEMBER IT FONDLY?
YEP.
I GUESS TIME HAS A WAY OF BLURRING REALITY.
SCOTT and BORGMAN
REALLY?
SOME REALITY. THIS SUMMER'S PARTY INCIDENT IS STILL IN SHARP FOCUS.

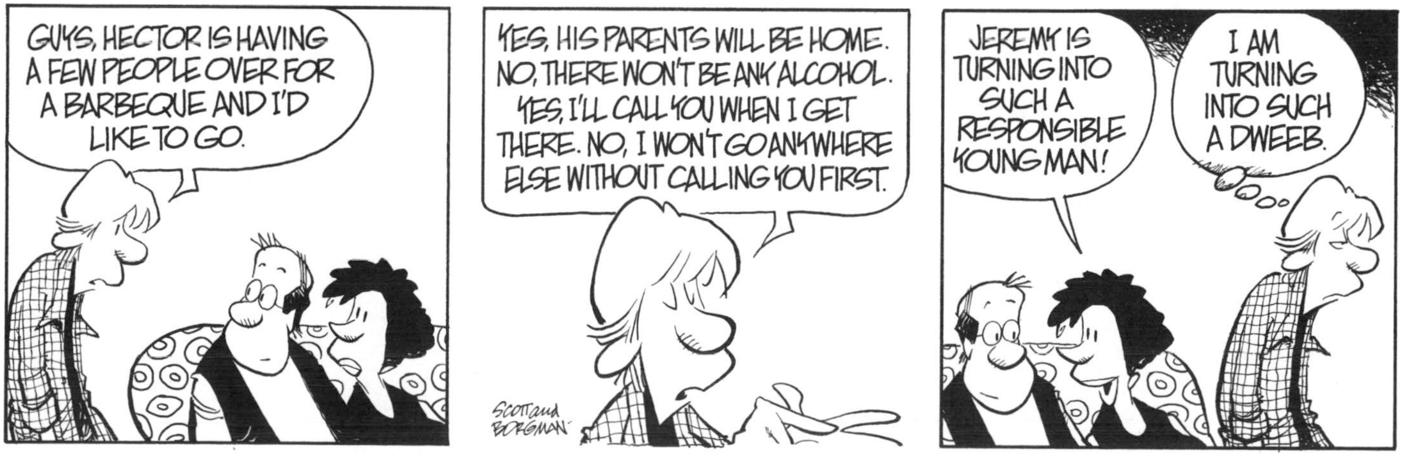
GUYS, HECTOR IS HAVING A FEW PEOPLE OVER FOR A BARBEQUE AND I'D LIKE TO GO.
YES, HIS PARENTS WILL BE HOME. NO, THERE WON'T BE ANY ALCOHOL. YES, I'LL CALL YOU WHEN I GET THERE. NO, I WON'T GO ANYWHERE ELSE WITHOUT CALLING YOU FIRST.
SCOTT and BORGMAN
JEREMY IS TURNING INTO SUCH A RESPONSIBLE YOUNG MAN!
I AM TURNING INTO SUCH A DWEEB.

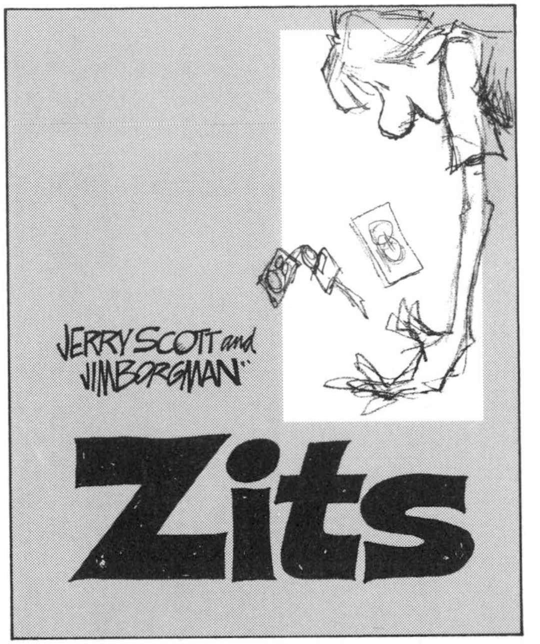
JERRY SCOTT and JIM BORGMAN
Zits

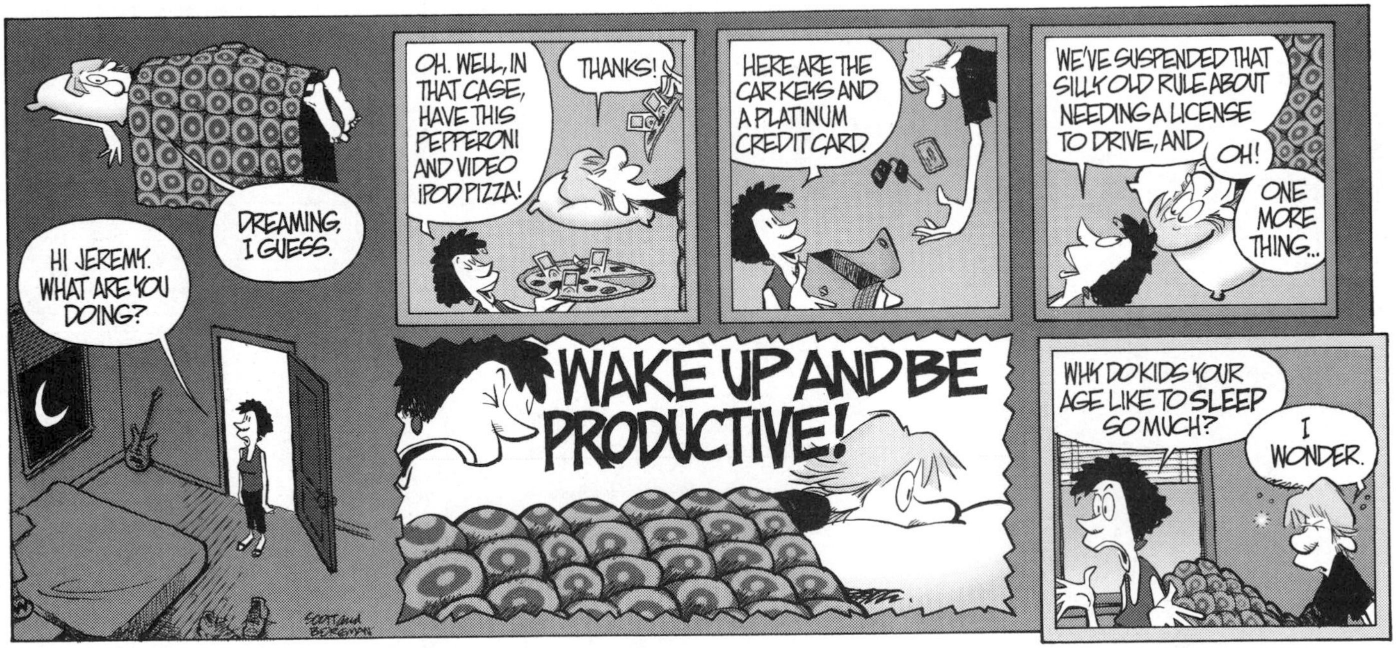
HI JEREMY. WHAT ARE YOU DOING?
DREAMING, I GUESS.
OH. WELL, IN THAT CASE, HAVE THIS PEPPERONI AND VIDEO iPOD PIZZA!
THANKS!
HERE ARE THE CAR KEYS AND A PLATINUM CREDIT CARD.
WE'VE SUSPENDED THAT SILLY OLD RULE ABOUT NEEDING A LICENSE TO DRIVE, AND
OH!
ONE MORE THING...
WAKE UP AND BE PRODUCTIVE!
WHY DO KIDS YOUR AGE LIKE TO SLEEP SO MUCH?
I WONDER.
SCOTT and BORGMAN

Zits
by
JERRY SCOTT and
JIM BORGMAN

DO YOU THINK WE'LL EVER GET THIS VAN RUNNING?
WE HAVE TO.
WE DON'T HAVE A CHOICE!
ANYBODY WANT SOME LEMONADE?
THIS ISN'T SOME HOBBY, HECTOR...
...IT'S A PROMISE THAT WE MADE TO OURSELVES!
SANDWICH?
OUR CROSS-COUNTRY ODYSSEY OF ADVENTURE AND AWAKENING IS LESS THAN A YEAR AWAY!
YES, WE'LL GET IT RUNNING!
OF THIS YOU CAN BE SURE.
IF YOU'D LIKE TO STAY FOR DINNER, I'M MAKING FAJITAS.
MY FRIEND, THE VAN IS OUR TICKET OUT OF THIS HELLHOLE!

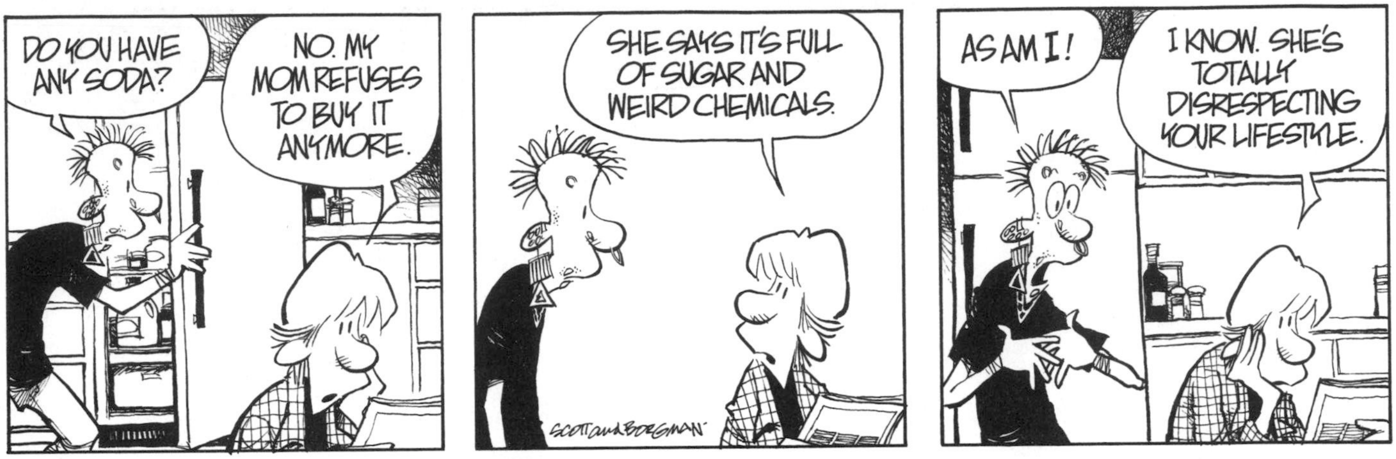
DO YOU HAVE ANY SODA?
NO. MY MOM REFUSES TO BUY IT ANYMORE.
SHE SAYS IT'S FULL OF SUGAR AND WEIRD CHEMICALS.
AS AM I!
I KNOW. SHE'S TOTALLY DISRESPECTING YOUR LIFESTYLE.
SCOTT and BORGMAN

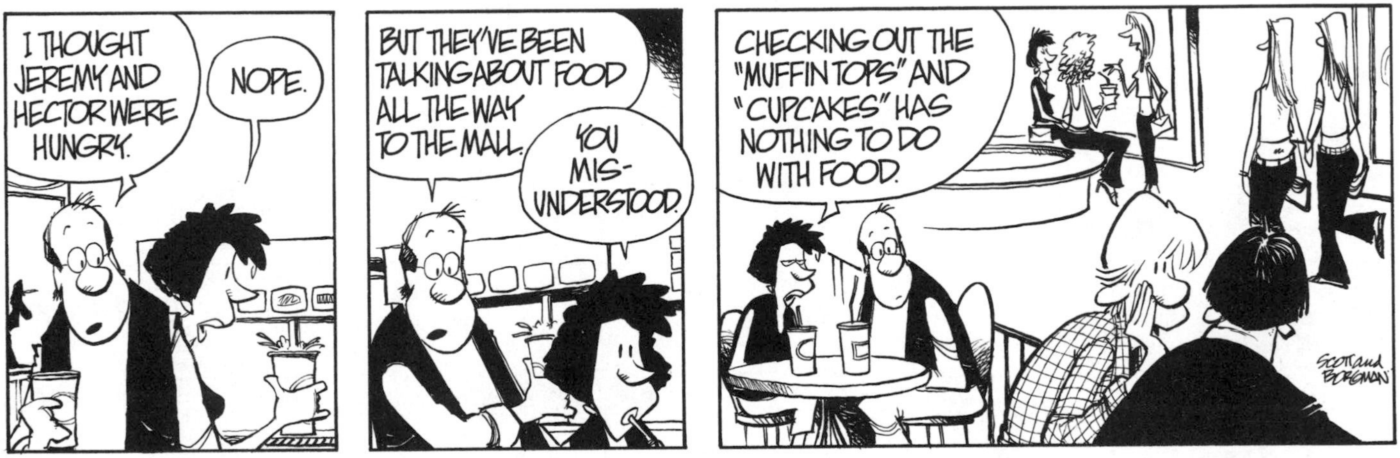
I THOUGHT JEREMY AND HECTOR WERE HUNGRY.
NOPE.
BUT THEY'VE BEEN TALKING ABOUT FOOD ALL THE WAY TO THE MALL.
YOU MIS-UNDERSTOOD.
CHECKING OUT THE "MUFFIN TOPS" AND "CUPCAKES" HAS NOTHING TO DO WITH FOOD.
SCOTT and BORGMAN

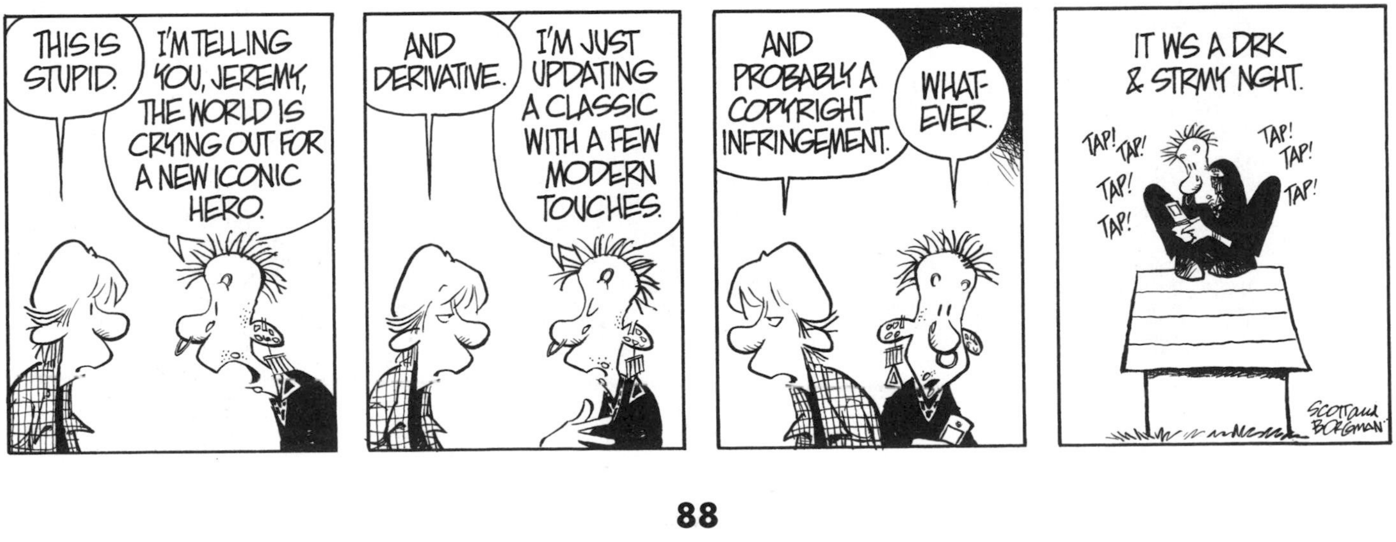
THIS IS STUPID.
I'M TELLING YOU, JEREMY, THE WORLD IS CRYING OUT FOR A NEW ICONIC HERO.
AND DERIVATIVE.
I'M JUST UPDATING A CLASSIC WITH A FEW MODERN TOUCHES.
AND PROBABLY A COPYRIGHT INFRINGEMENT.
WHAT-EVER.
IT WS A DRK & STRMY NGHT.
TAP! TAP! TAP! TAP!
TAP! TAP! TAP!
SCOTT and BORGMAN

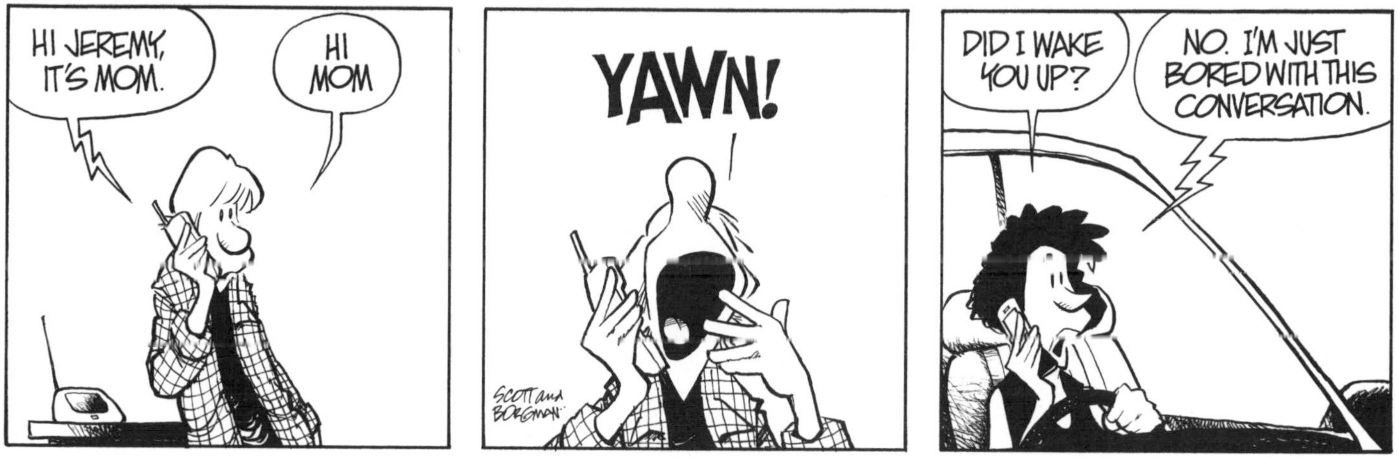
HI JEREMY, IT'S MOM.
HI MOM
YAWN!
DID I WAKE YOU UP?
NO. I'M JUST BORED WITH THIS CONVERSATION.

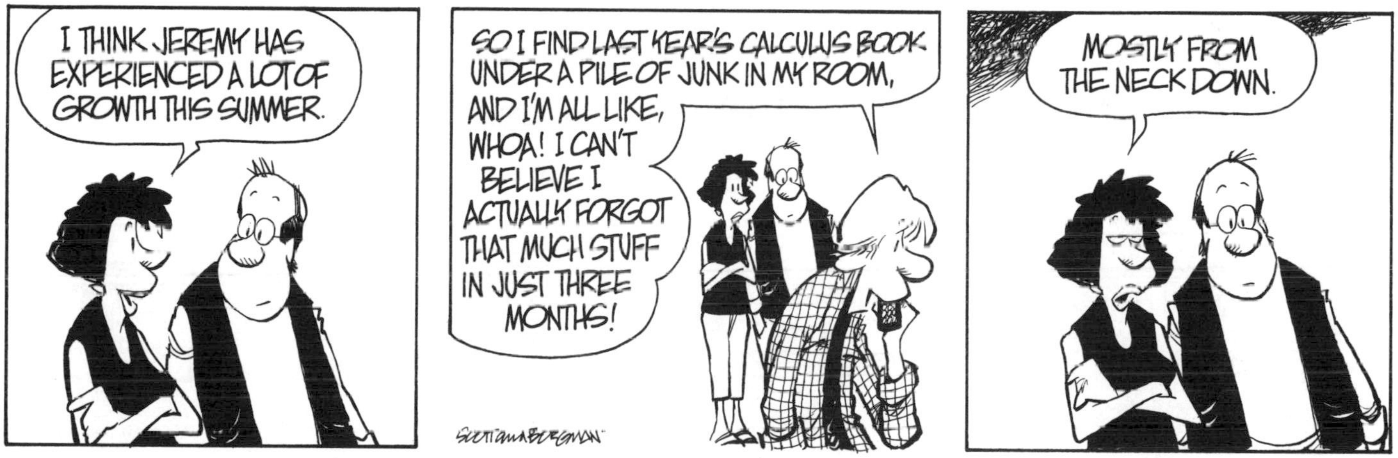
I THINK JEREMY HAS EXPERIENCED A LOT OF GROWTH THIS SUMMER.
SO I FIND LAST YEAR'S CALCULUS BOOK UNDER A PILE OF JUNK IN MY ROOM, AND I'M ALL LIKE, WHOA! I CAN'T BELIEVE I ACTUALLY FORGOT THAT MUCH STUFF IN JUST THREE MONTHS!
MOSTLY FROM THE NECK DOWN.

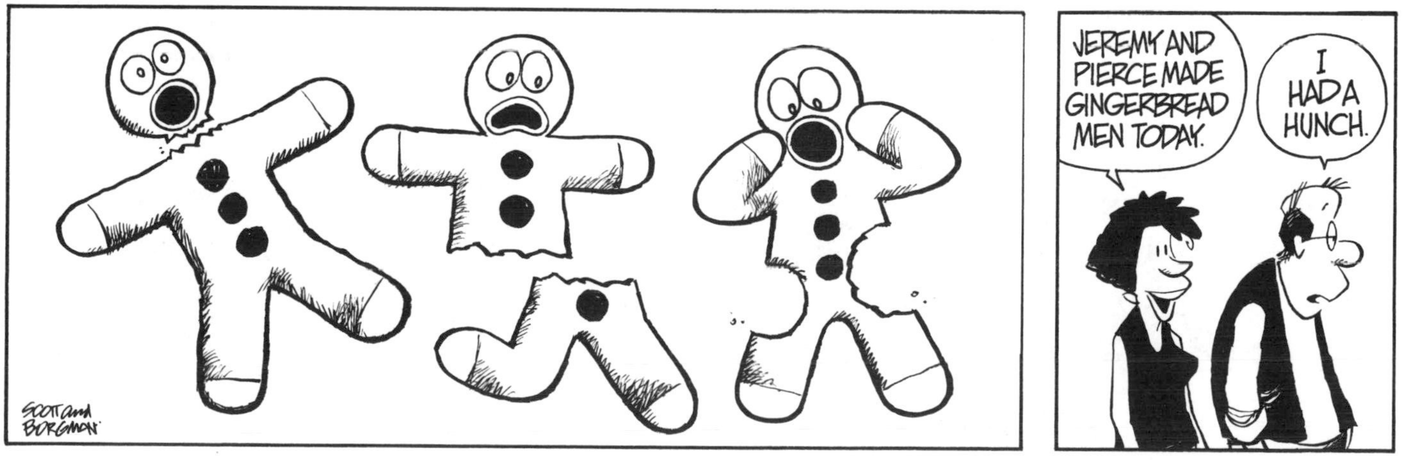
JEREMY AND PIERCE MADE GINGERBREAD MEN TODAY.
I HAD A HUNCH.

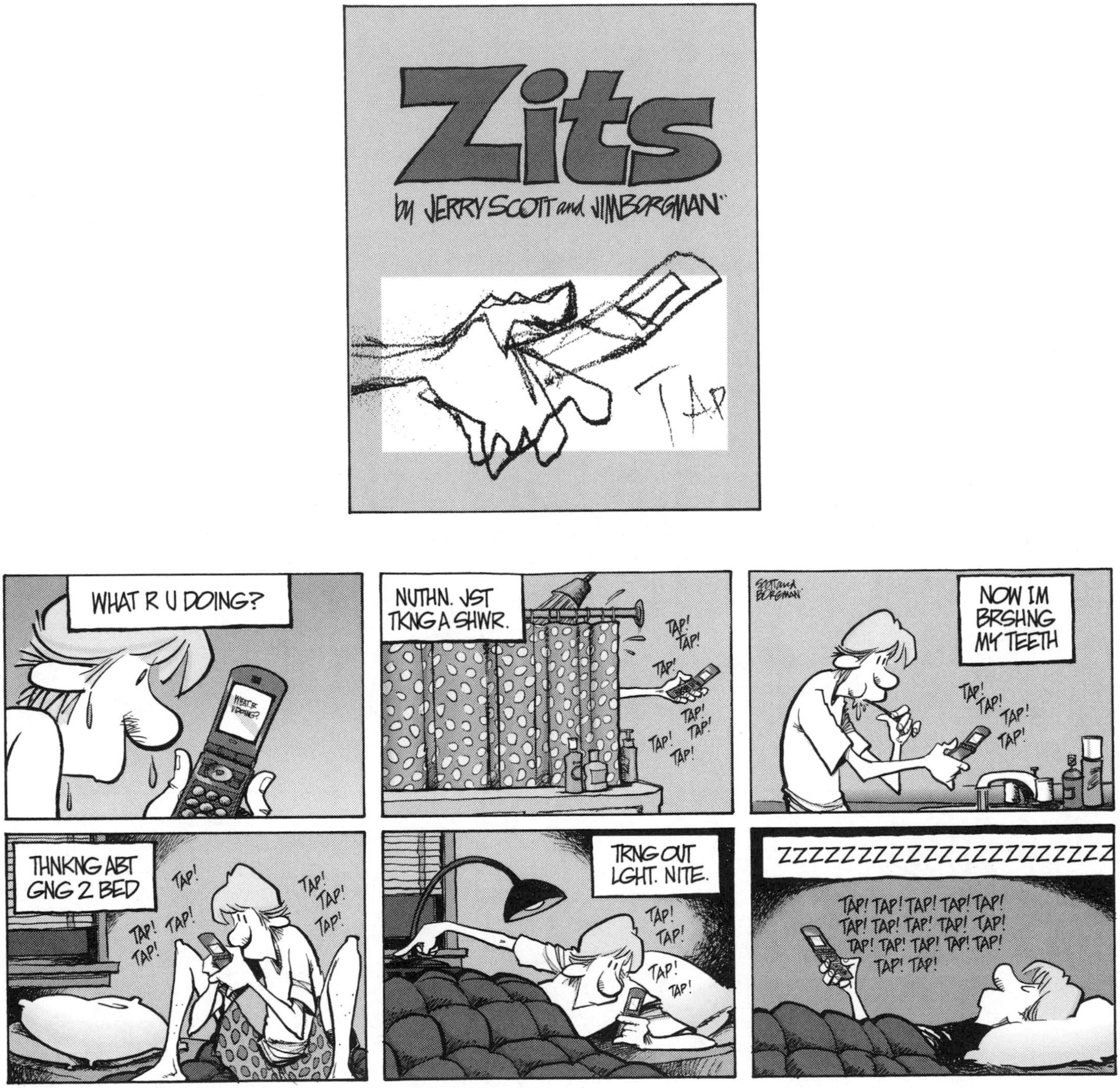

Zits
by JERRY SCOTT and JIM BORGMAN
TAP
WHAT R U DOING?
NUTHN. JST TKNG A SHWR.
TAP! TAP! TAP! TAP! TAP! TAP! TAP!
SCOTT and BORGMAN
NOW IM BRSHNG MY TEETH
TAP! TAP! TAP! TAP!
THNKNG ABT GNG 2 BED
TAP! TAP! TAP! TAP! TAP! TAP! TAP!
TRNG OUT LGHT. NITE.
TAP! TAP! TAP! TAP!
ZZZZZZZZZZZZZZZZZZZZZ
TAP! TAP! TAP! TAP! TAP! TAP! TAP! TAP! TAP! TAP! TAP! TAP! TAP! TAP! TAP! TAP! TAP!

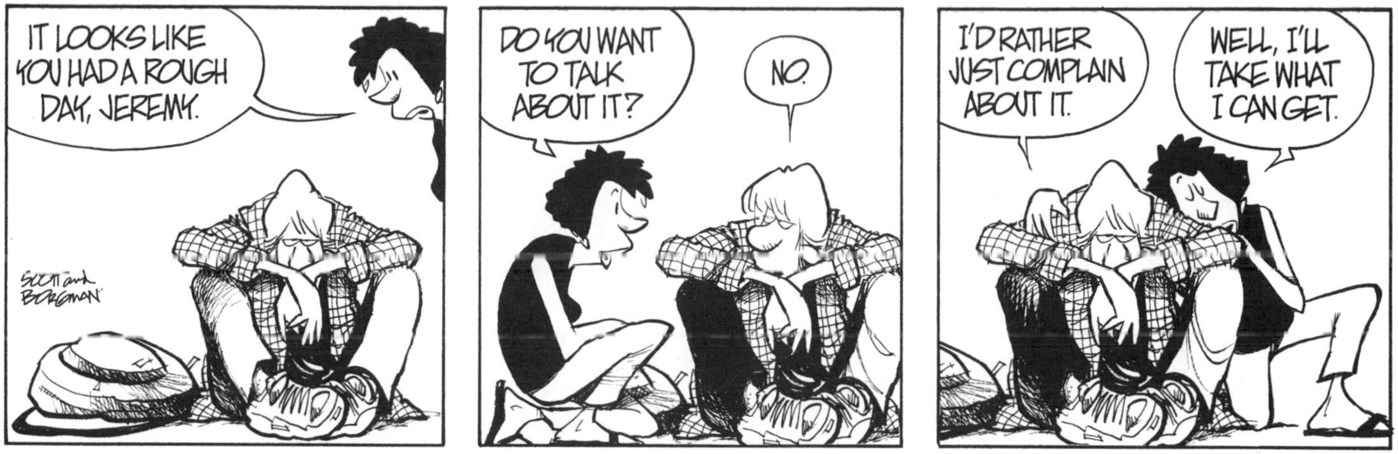
IT LOOKS LIKE YOU HAD A ROUGH DAY, JEREMY.
DO YOU WANT TO TALK ABOUT IT?
NO.
I'D RATHER JUST COMPLAIN ABOUT IT.
WELL, I'LL TAKE WHAT I CAN GET.

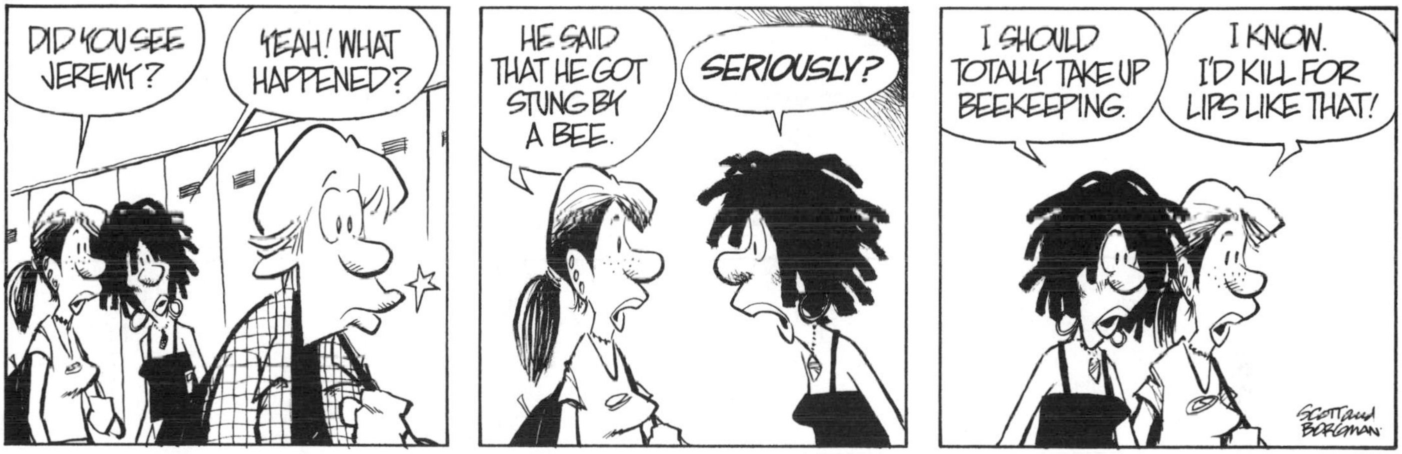
DID YOU SEE JEREMY?
YEAH! WHAT HAPPENED?
HE SAID THAT HE GOT STUNG BY A BEE.
SERIOUSLY?
I SHOULD TOTALLY TAKE UP BEEKEEPING.
I KNOW. I'D KILL FOR LIPS LIKE THAT!

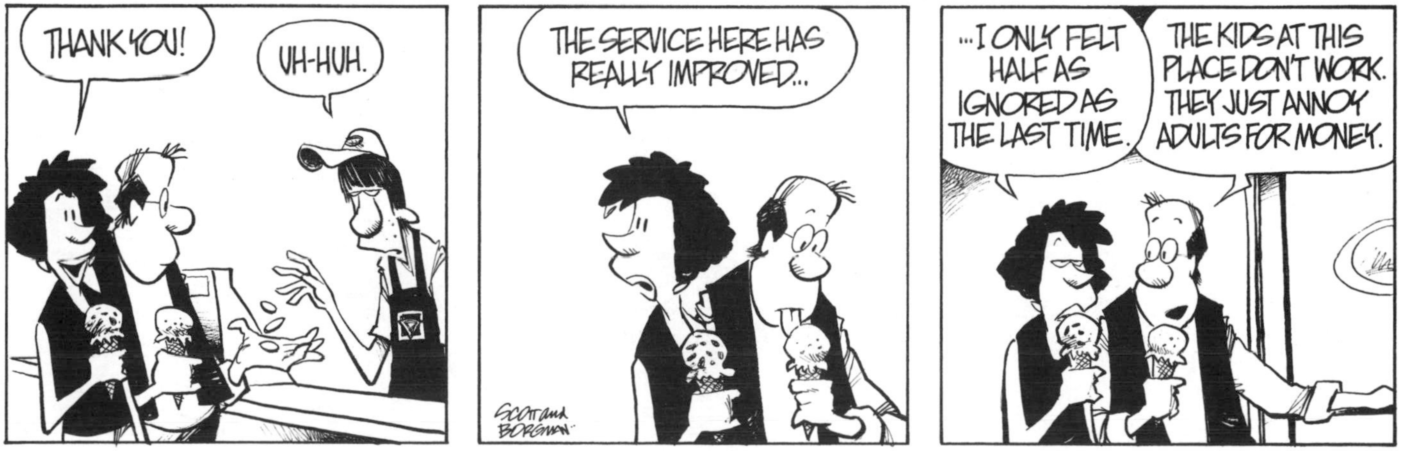
THANK YOU!
UH-HUH.
THE SERVICE HERE HAS REALLY IMPROVED...
...I ONLY FELT HALF AS IGNORED AS THE LAST TIME.
THE KIDS AT THIS PLACE DON'T WORK. THEY JUST ANNOY ADULTS FOR MONEY.

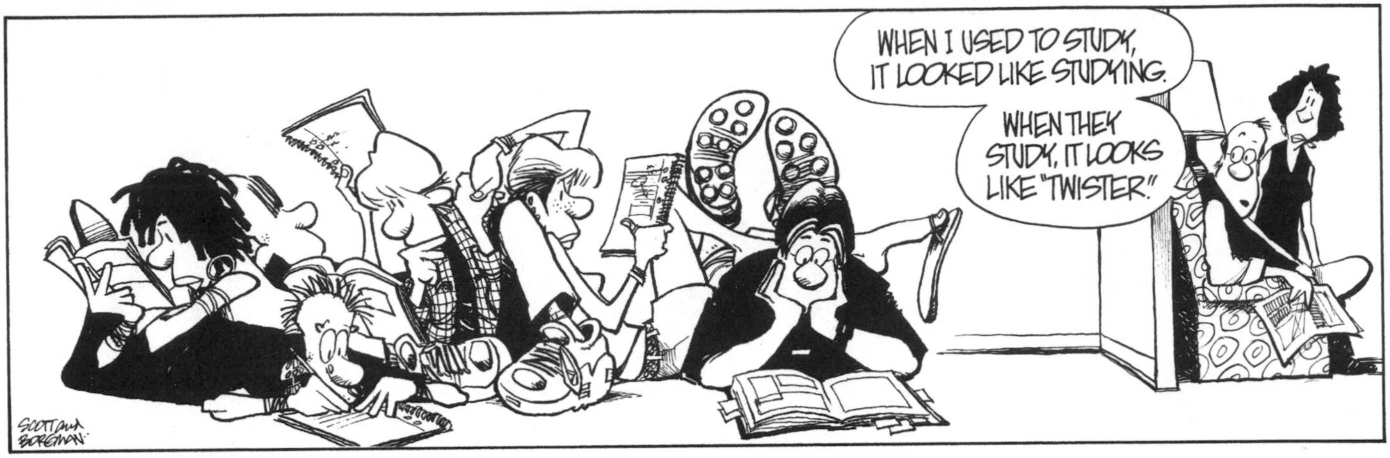
WHEN I USED TO STUDY, IT LOOKED LIKE STUDYING.
WHEN THEY STUDY, IT LOOKS LIKE "TWISTER."

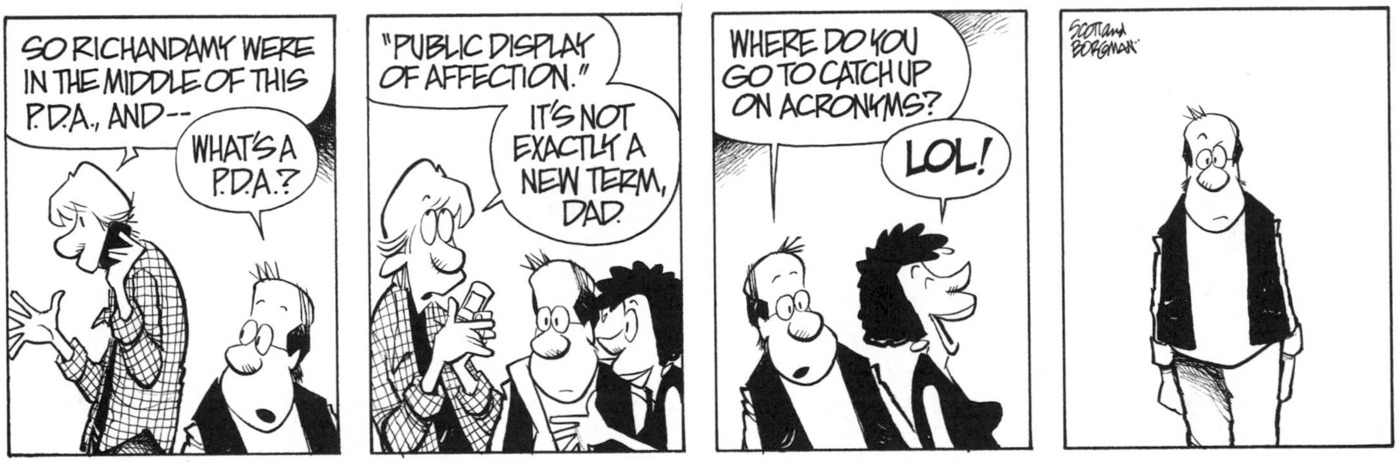
SO RICHANDAMY WERE IN THE MIDDLE OF THIS P.D.A., AND--
WHAT'S A P.D.A.?
"PUBLIC DISPLAY OF AFFECTION."
IT'S NOT EXACTLY A NEW TERM, DAD.
WHERE DO YOU GO TO CATCH UP ON ACRONYMS?
LOL!

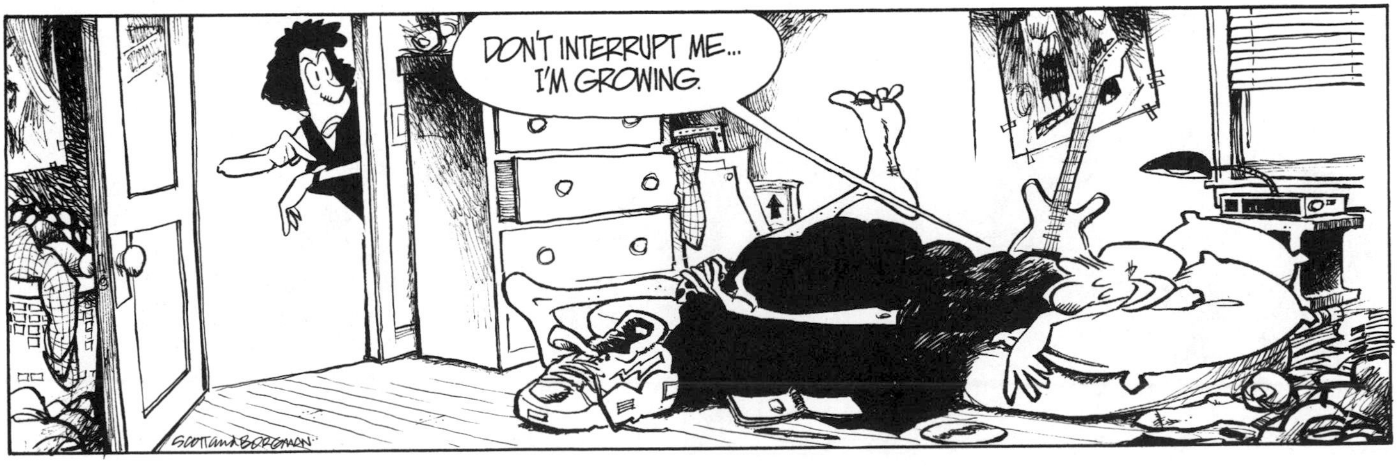
DON'T INTERRUPT ME... I'M GROWING.

Zits
by JERRY SCOTT and JIM BORGMAN

HI
WE'D LIKE A ROOM.
TWO ROOMS
RECEPTI
UH...
DAD, IT'S BEEN A LONG DAY CRAMMED IN THE CAR TOGETHER. DON'T YOU THINK WE NEED A LITTLE SPACE?
TWO ROOMS.
YES, SIR.
WALT, ARE YOU CRAZY?? YOU'RE GOING TO PAY FOR AN EXTRA HOTEL ROOM JUST BECAUSE *SOMEBODY* "NEEDS A LITTLE SPACE"?
SCOTT and BORGMAN
THREE ROOMS.

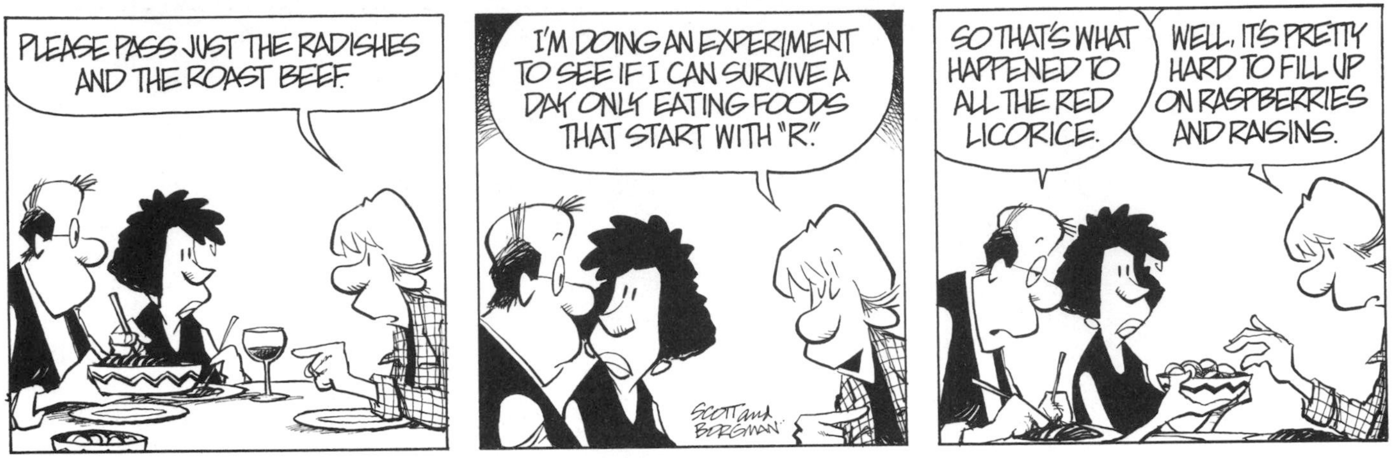
PLEASE PASS JUST THE RADISHES AND THE ROAST BEEF.
I'M DOING AN EXPERIMENT TO SEE IF I CAN SURVIVE A DAY ONLY EATING FOODS THAT START WITH "R."
SCOTT and BORGMAN
SO THAT'S WHAT HAPPENED TO ALL THE RED LICORICE.
WELL, IT'S PRETTY HARD TO FILL UP ON RASPBERRIES AND RAISINS.

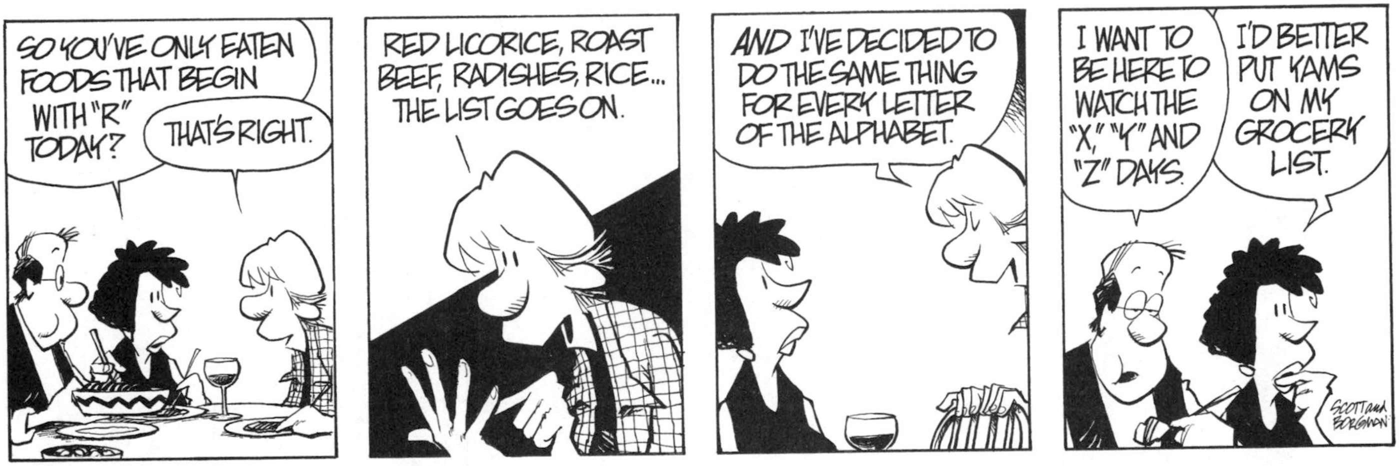
SO YOU'VE ONLY EATEN FOODS THAT BEGIN WITH "R" TODAY?
THAT'S RIGHT.
RED LICORICE, ROAST BEEF, RADISHES, RICE... THE LIST GOES ON.
AND I'VE DECIDED TO DO THE SAME THING FOR EVERY LETTER OF THE ALPHABET.
I WANT TO BE HERE TO WATCH THE "X," "Y" AND "Z" DAYS.
I'D BETTER PUT YAMS ON MY GROCERY LIST.
SCOTT and BORGMAN

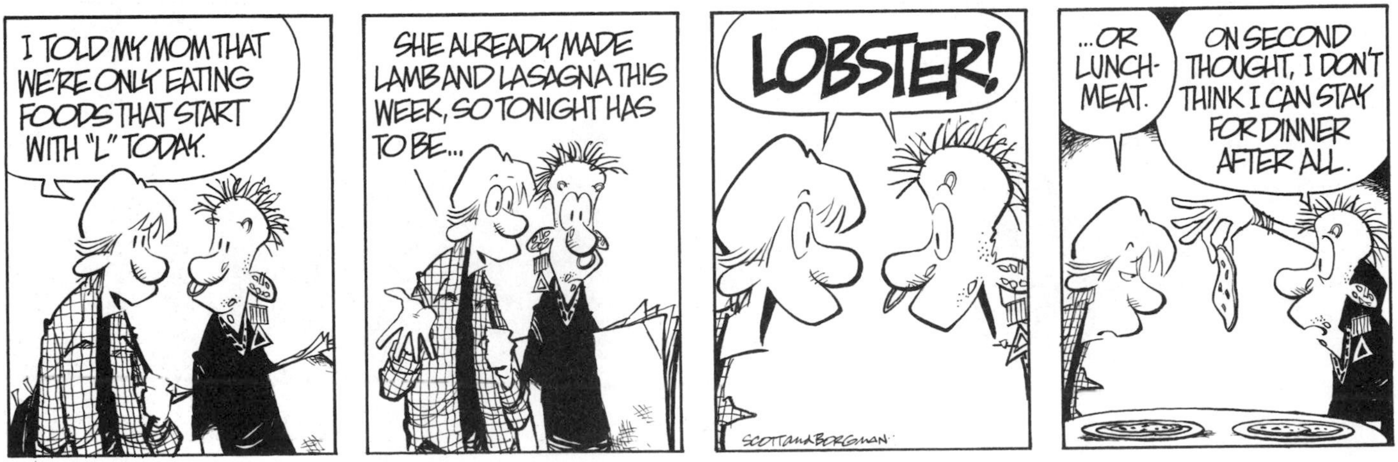
I TOLD MY MOM THAT WE'RE ONLY EATING FOODS THAT START WITH "L" TODAY.
SHE ALREADY MADE LAMB AND LASAGNA THIS WEEK, SO TONIGHT HAS TO BE...
LOBSTER!
SCOTT and BORGMAN
...OR LUNCH-MEAT.
ON SECOND THOUGHT, I DON'T THINK I CAN STAY FOR DINNER AFTER ALL.

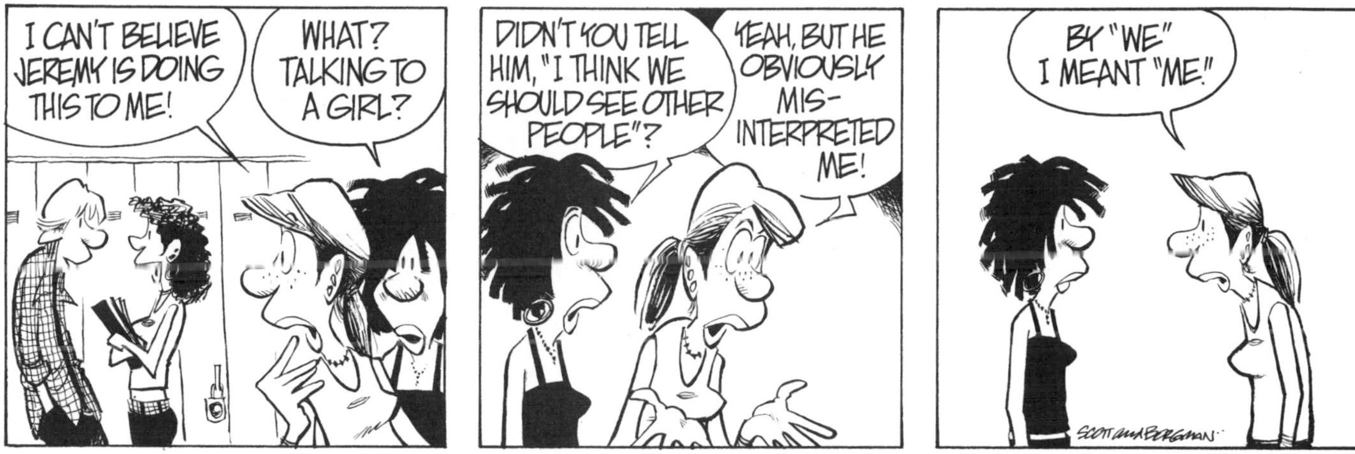
I CAN'T BELIEVE JEREMY IS DOING THIS TO ME!
WHAT? TALKING TO A GIRL?
DIDN'T YOU TELL HIM, "I THINK WE SHOULD SEE OTHER PEOPLE"?
YEAH, BUT HE OBVIOUSLY MIS-INTERPRETED ME!
BY "WE" I MEANT "ME."

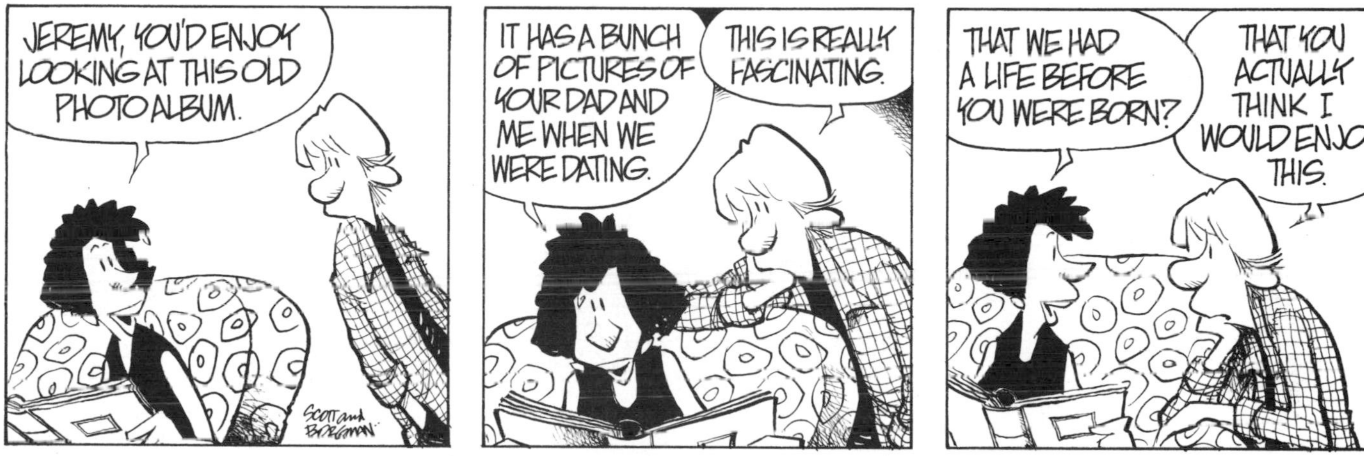
JEREMY, YOU'D ENJOY LOOKING AT THIS OLD PHOTO ALBUM.
IT HAS A BUNCH OF PICTURES OF YOUR DAD AND ME WHEN WE WERE DATING.
THIS IS REALLY FASCINATING.
THAT WE HAD A LIFE BEFORE YOU WERE BORN?
THAT YOU ACTUALLY THINK I WOULD ENJOY THIS.

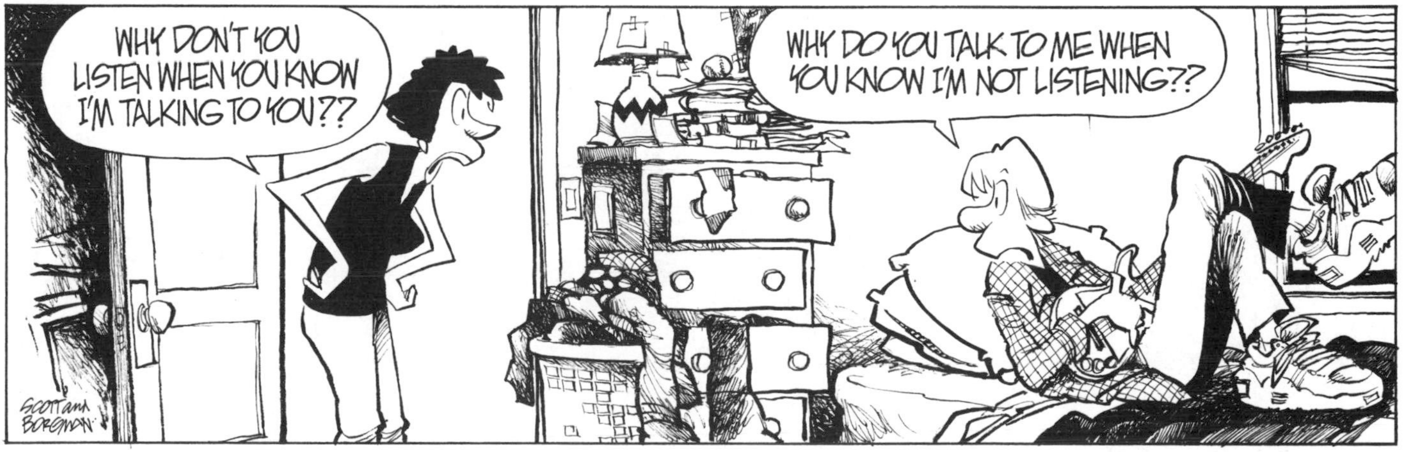
WHY DON'T YOU LISTEN WHEN YOU KNOW I'M TALKING TO YOU??
WHY DO YOU TALK TO ME WHEN YOU KNOW I'M NOT LISTENING??

Zits
by
JERRY SCOTT and
JIM BORGMAN

YOU SHOULD TOTALLY GET A BICEP TATTOO
WHAT KIND OF TATTOO?
I DON'T KNOW... SOMETHING THAT SAYS WHO YOU ARE AND WHAT YOU BELIEVE IN.
I GOT IT. HAND ME THAT PEN.
SOMETHING
LIKE
THIS?
SCOTT and BORGMAN
IT LOOKS LIKE A BARBED WIRE QUESTION MARK.
SIGNIFYING THAT I'M NOT SURE WHO I AM OR WHAT I BELIEVE IN
BUT WITH ATTITUDE!

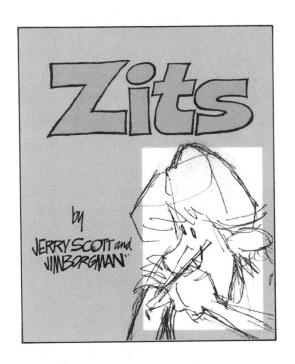

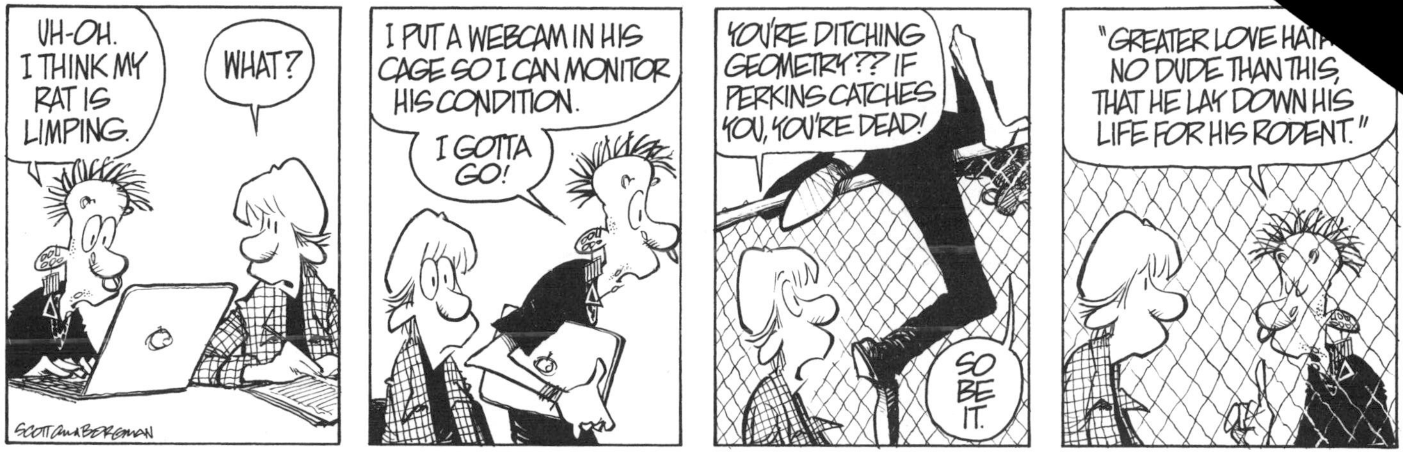
UH-OH. I THINK MY RAT IS LIMPING.
WHAT?
I PUT A WEBCAM IN HIS CAGE SO I CAN MONITOR HIS CONDITION.
I GOTTA GO!
YOU'RE DITCHING GEOMETRY?? IF PERKINS CATCHES YOU, YOU'RE DEAD!
SO BE IT.
"GREATER LOVE HAT
NO DUDE THAN THIS, THAT HE LAY DOWN HIS LIFE FOR HIS RODENT."
SCOTT and BORGMAN

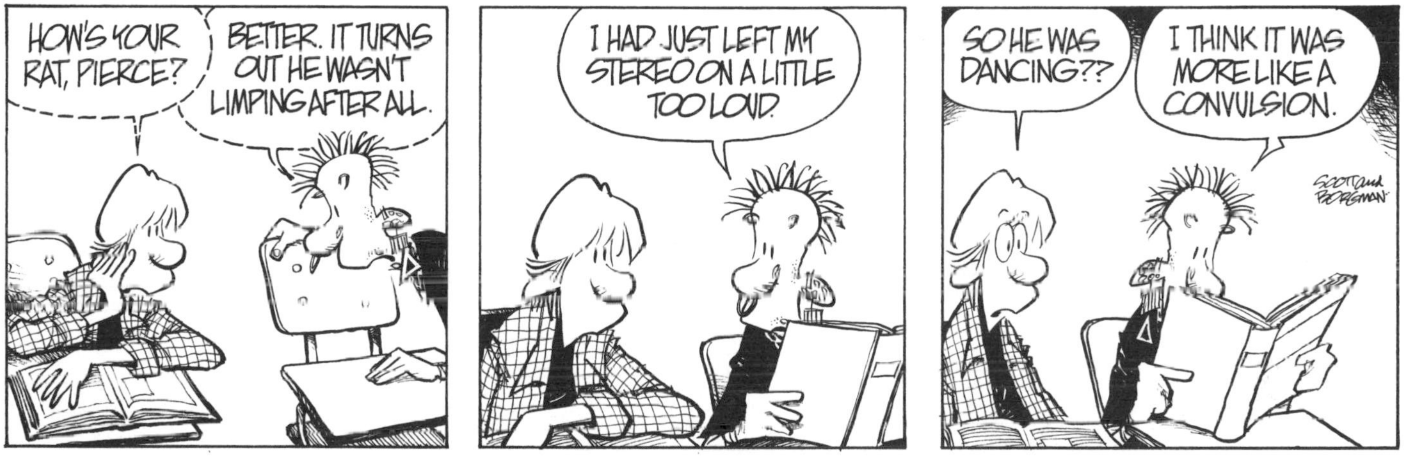
HOW'S YOUR RAT, PIERCE?
BETTER. IT TURNS OUT HE WASN'T LIMPING AFTER ALL.
I HAD JUST LEFT MY STEREO ON A LITTLE TOO LOUD.
SO HE WAS DANCING??
I THINK IT WAS MORE LIKE A CONVULSION.
SCOTT and BORGMAN

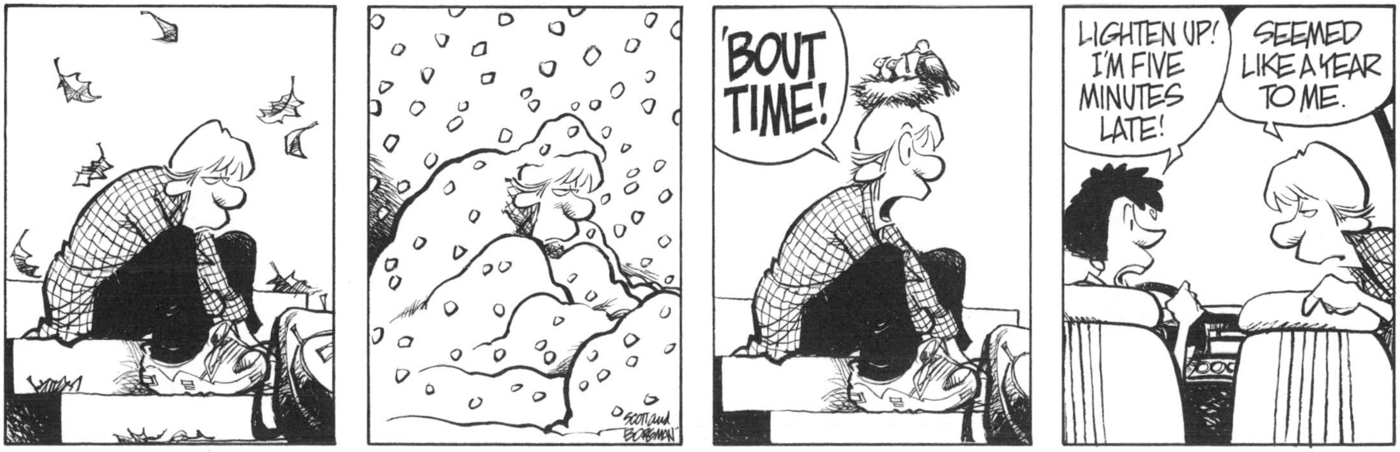
'BOUT TIME!
LIGHTEN UP! I'M FIVE MINUTES LATE!
SEEMED LIKE A YEAR TO ME.
SCOTT and BORGMAN

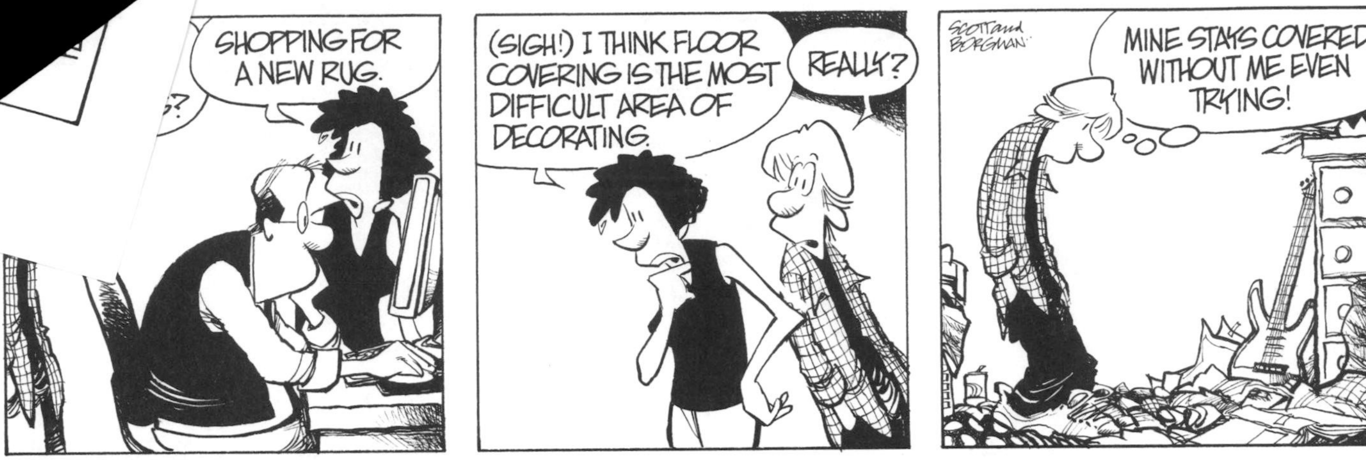
SHOPPING FOR A NEW RUG.
(SIGH!) I THINK FLOOR COVERING IS THE MOST DIFFICULT AREA OF DECORATING.
REALLY?
SCOTT and BORGMAN
MINE STAYS COVERED WITHOUT ME EVEN TRYING!

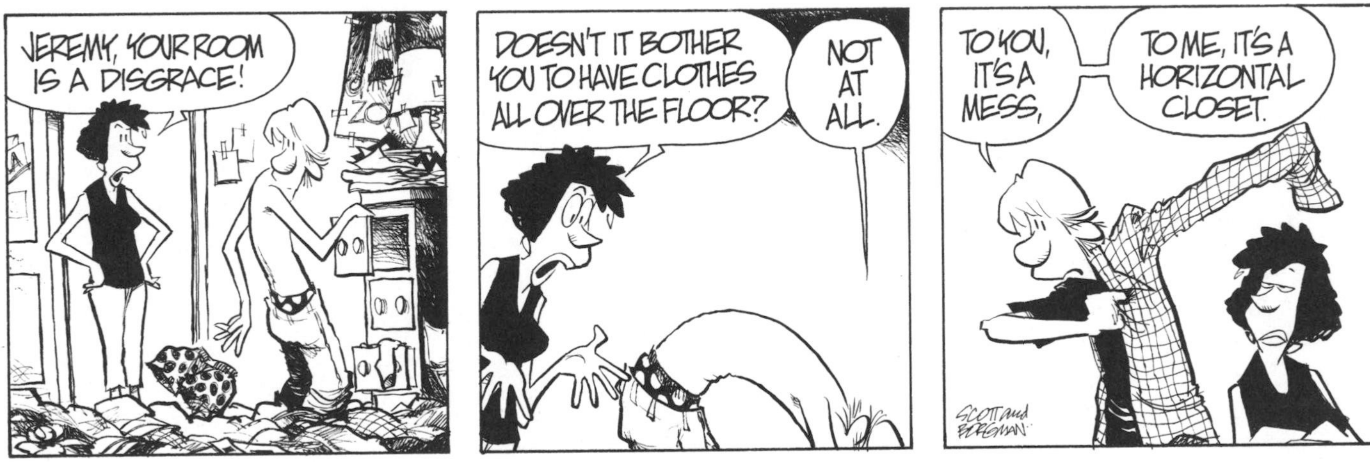
JEREMY, YOUR ROOM IS A DISGRACE!
DOESN'T IT BOTHER YOU TO HAVE CLOTHES ALL OVER THE FLOOR?
NOT AT ALL.
TO YOU, IT'S A MESS,
TO ME, IT'S A HORIZONTAL CLOSET.
SCOTT and BORGMAN

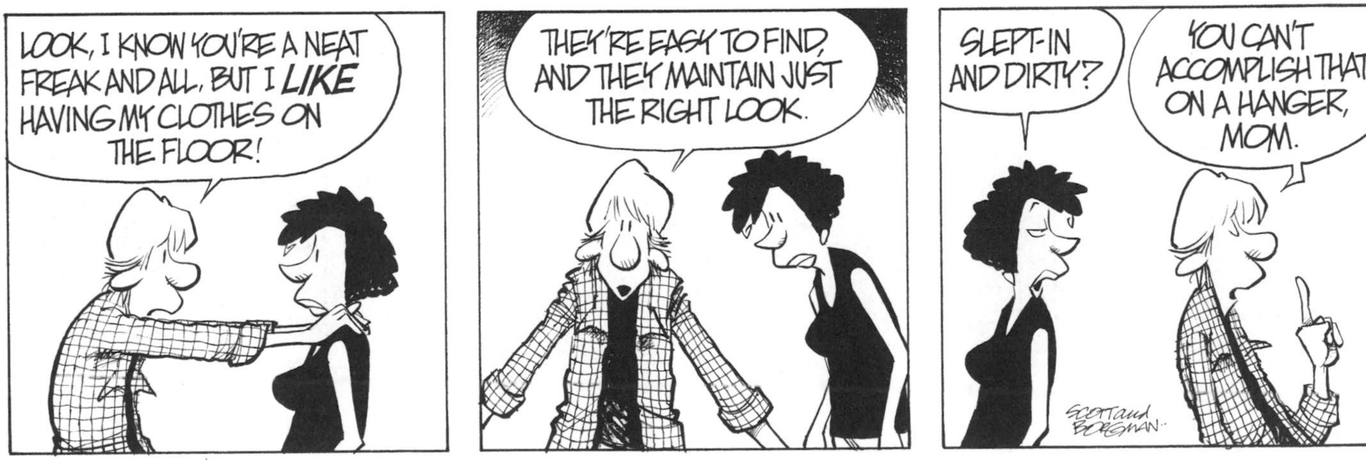
LOOK, I KNOW YOU'RE A NEAT FREAK AND ALL, BUT I LIKE HAVING MY CLOTHES ON THE FLOOR!
THEY'RE EASY TO FIND, AND THEY MAINTAIN JUST THE RIGHT LOOK.
SLEPT-IN AND DIRTY?
YOU CAN'T ACCOMPLISH THAT ON A HANGER, MOM.
SCOTT and BORGMAN

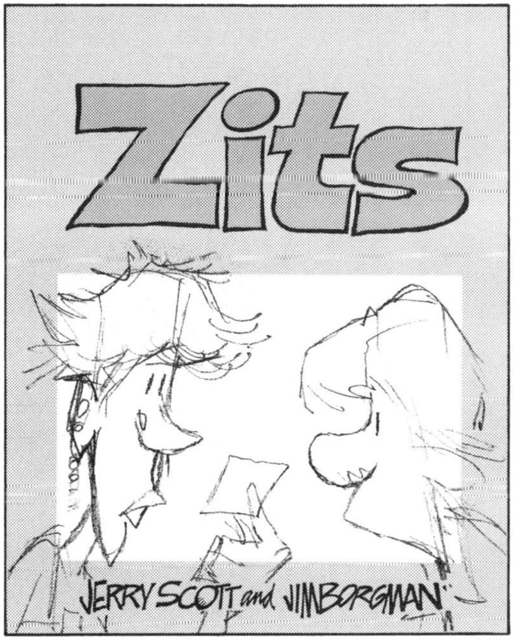
Zits
JERRY SCOTT and JIM BORGMAN

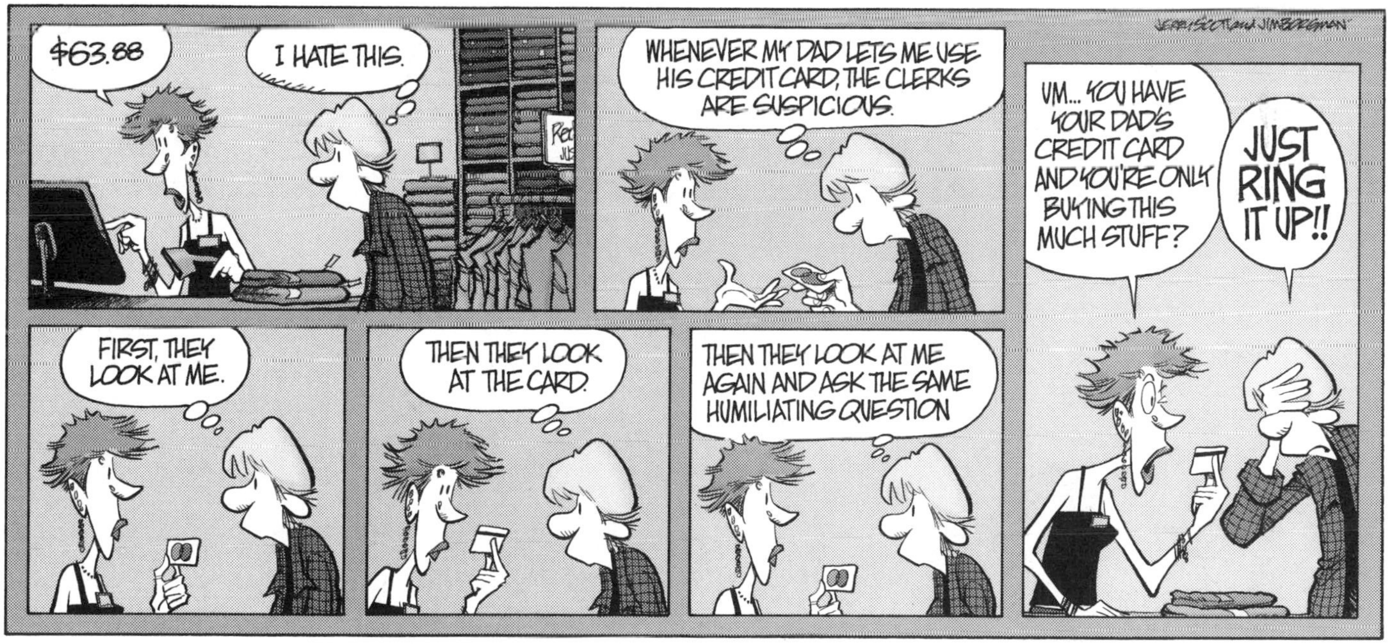
JERRY SCOTT and JIM BORGMAN
$63.88
I HATE THIS.
WHENEVER MY DAD LETS ME USE HIS CREDIT CARD, THE CLERKS ARE SUSPICIOUS.
FIRST, THEY LOOK AT ME.
THEN THEY LOOK AT THE CARD.
THEN THEY LOOK AT ME AGAIN AND ASK THE SAME HUMILIATING QUESTION
UM... YOU HAVE YOUR DAD'S CREDIT CARD AND YOU'RE ONLY BUYING THIS MUCH STUFF?
JUST RING IT UP!!

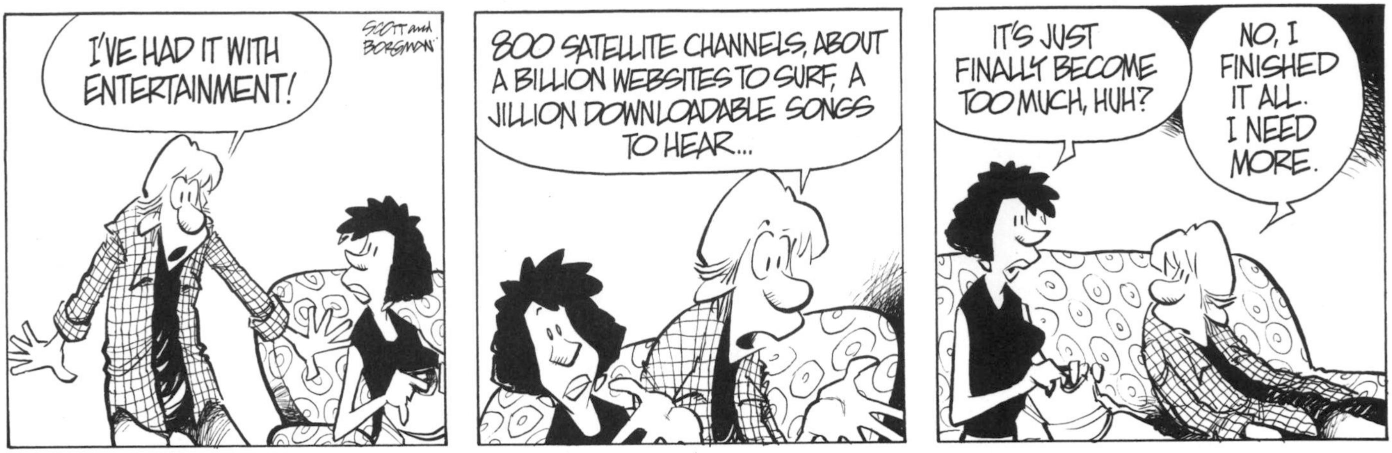
SCOTT and BORGMAN
I'VE HAD IT WITH ENTERTAINMENT!
800 SATELLITE CHANNELS, ABOUT A BILLION WEBSITES TO SURF, A JILLION DOWNLOADABLE SONGS TO HEAR...
IT'S JUST FINALLY BECOME TOO MUCH, HUH?
NO, I FINISHED IT ALL. I NEED MORE.

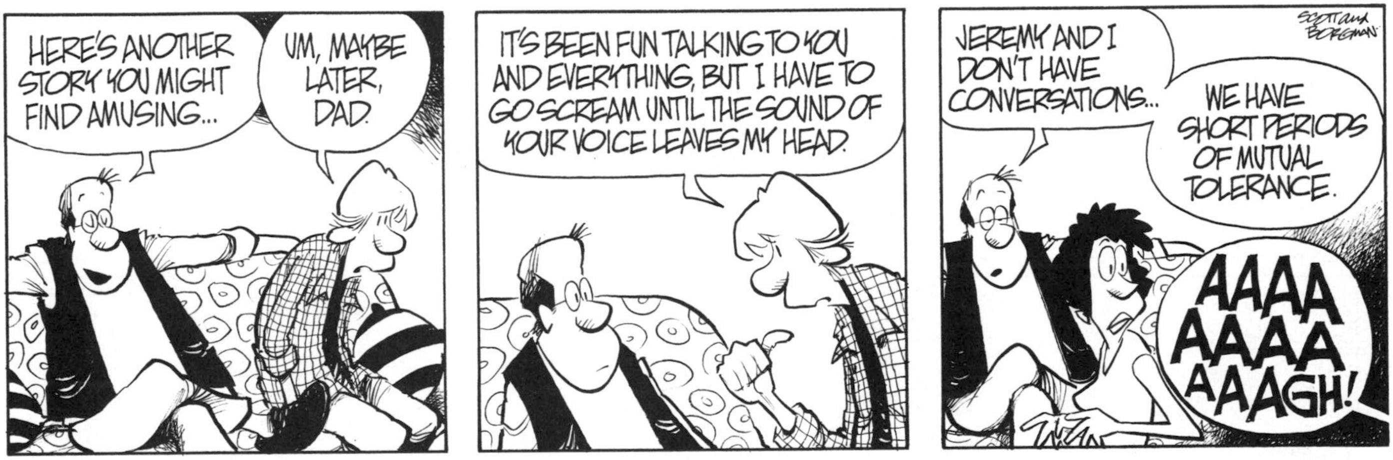
HERE'S ANOTHER STORY YOU MIGHT FIND AMUSING...
UM, MAYBE LATER, DAD.
IT'S BEEN FUN TALKING TO YOU AND EVERYTHING, BUT I HAVE TO GO SCREAM UNTIL THE SOUND OF YOUR VOICE LEAVES MY HEAD.
SCOTT and BORGMAN
JEREMY AND I DON'T HAVE CONVERSATIONS...
WE HAVE SHORT PERIODS OF MUTUAL TOLERANCE.
AAAA AAAA AAAGH!

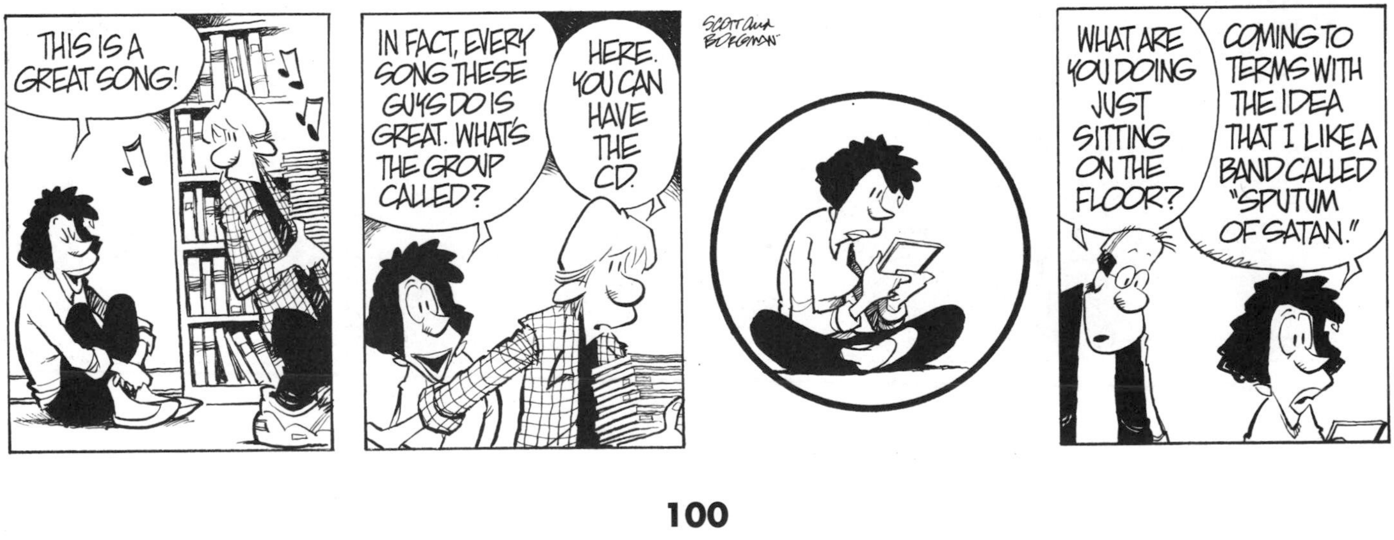
THIS IS A GREAT SONG!
IN FACT, EVERY SONG THESE GUYS DO IS GREAT. WHAT'S THE GROUP CALLED?
HERE. YOU CAN HAVE THE CD.
SCOTT and BORGMAN
WHAT ARE YOU DOING JUST SITTING ON THE FLOOR?
COMING TO TERMS WITH THE IDEA THAT I LIKE A BAND CALLED "SPUTUM OF SATAN."

Zits
by
JERRY SCOTT and
JIM BORGMAN

GUYS!
WHY AREN'T YOU DOING SOMETHING CONSTRUCTIVE?
TIME IS PASSING YOU BY!
YOU ONLY GET ONE SHOT AT LIFE... GRAB IT!
TALK!
LAUGH!
CREATE!
UM... OKAY.
VINYL
WOW
YEAH
WHAT ARE THE ODDS OF ALL FOUR OF US HAVING MOMS WHO ARE SLOB-OPHOBIC?
TOLD YA.

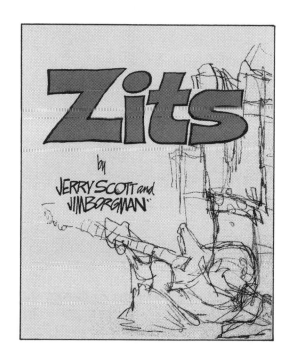

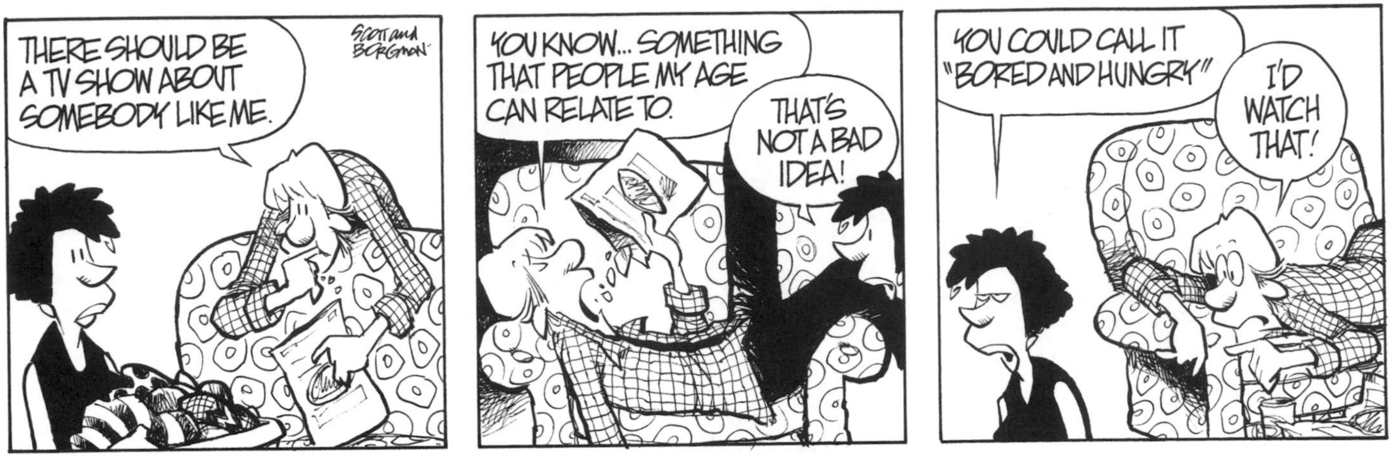
THERE SHOULD BE A TV SHOW ABOUT SOMEBODY LIKE ME.
SCOTT and BORGMAN
YOU KNOW... SOMETHING THAT PEOPLE MY AGE CAN RELATE TO.
THAT'S NOT A BAD IDEA!
YOU COULD CALL IT "BORED AND HUNGRY"
I'D WATCH THAT!

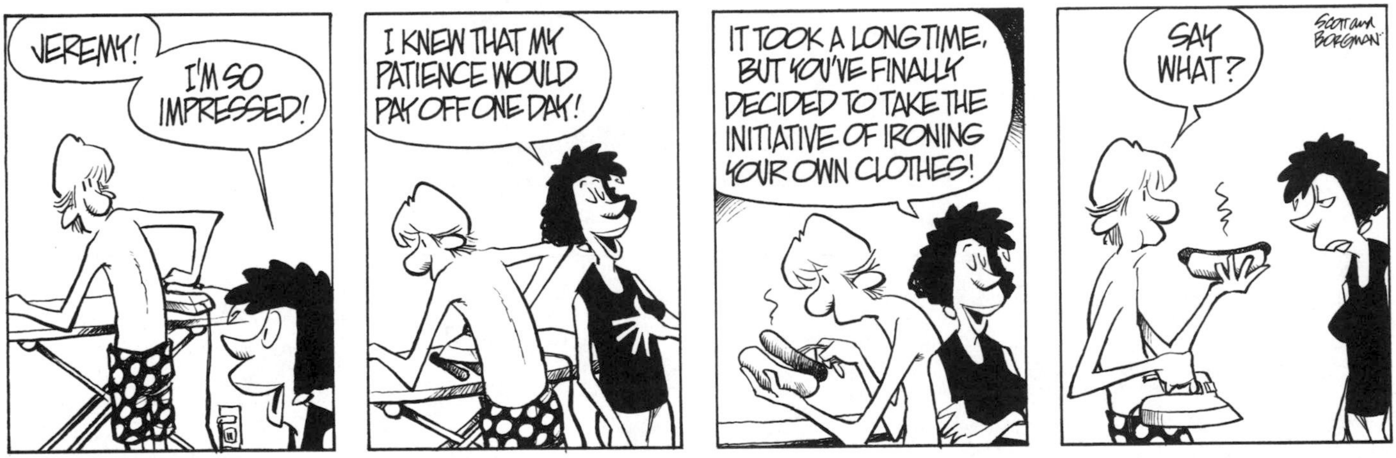
JEREMY!
I'M SO IMPRESSED!
I KNEW THAT MY PATIENCE WOULD PAY OFF ONE DAY!
IT TOOK A LONG TIME, BUT YOU'VE FINALLY DECIDED TO TAKE THE INITIATIVE OF IRONING YOUR OWN CLOTHES!
SAY WHAT?
SCOTT and BORGMAN

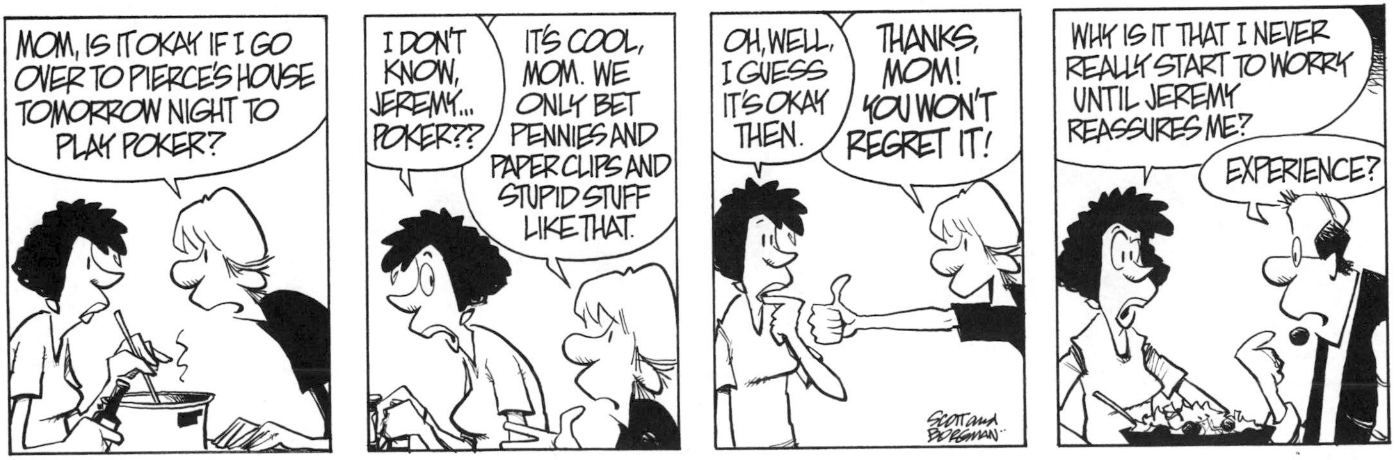
MOM, IS IT OKAY IF I GO OVER TO PIERCE'S HOUSE TOMORROW NIGHT TO PLAY POKER?
I DON'T KNOW, JEREMY... POKER??
IT'S COOL, MOM. WE ONLY BET PENNIES AND PAPER CLIPS AND STUPID STUFF LIKE THAT.
OH, WELL, I GUESS IT'S OKAY THEN.
THANKS, MOM! YOU WON'T REGRET IT!
SCOTT and BORGMAN
WHY IS IT THAT I NEVER REALLY START TO WORRY UNTIL JEREMY REASSURES ME?
EXPERIENCE?

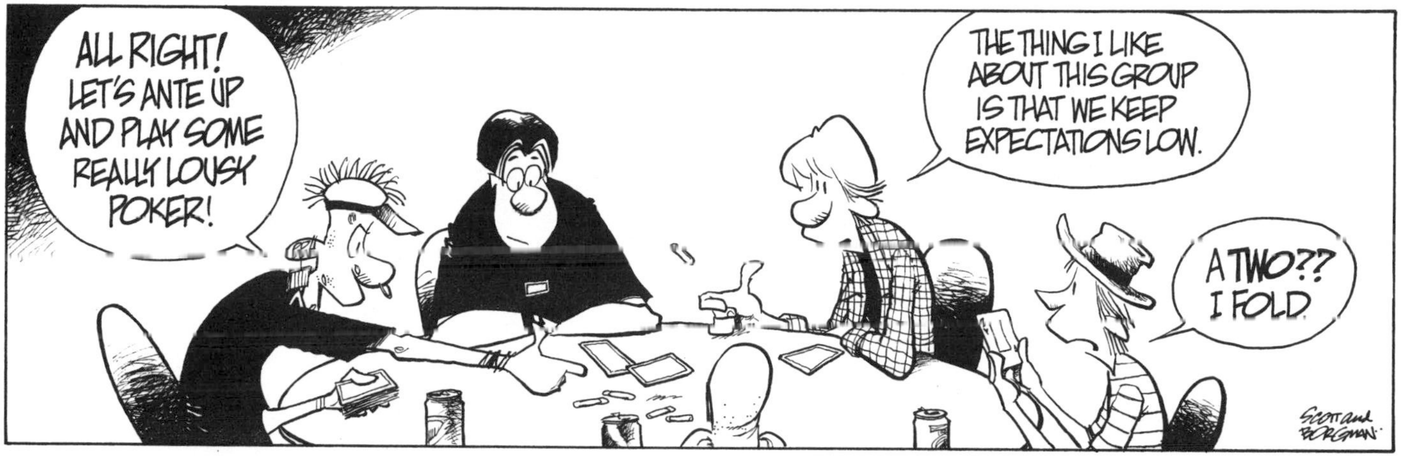
ALL RIGHT! LET'S ANTE UP AND PLAY SOME REALLY LOUSY POKER!
THE THING I LIKE ABOUT THIS GROUP IS THAT WE KEEP EXPECTATIONS LOW.
A TWO?? I FOLD.
SCOTT and BORGMAN

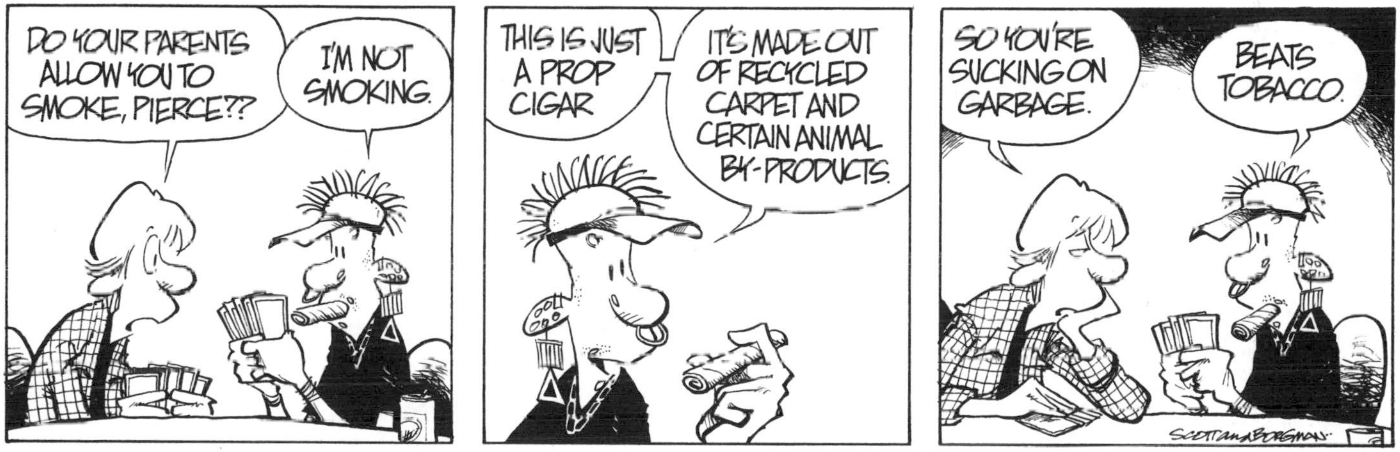
DO YOUR PARENTS ALLOW YOU TO SMOKE, PIERCE??
I'M NOT SMOKING.
THIS IS JUST A PROP CIGAR
IT'S MADE OUT OF RECYCLED CARPET AND CERTAIN ANIMAL BY-PRODUCTS.
SO YOU'RE SUCKING ON GARBAGE.
BEATS TOBACCO.
SCOTT and BORGMAN

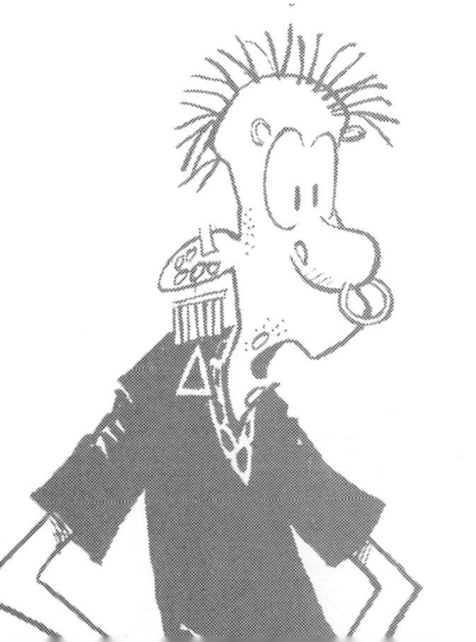

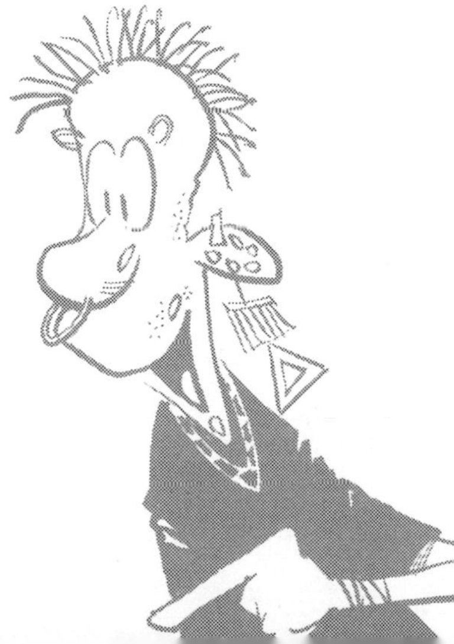

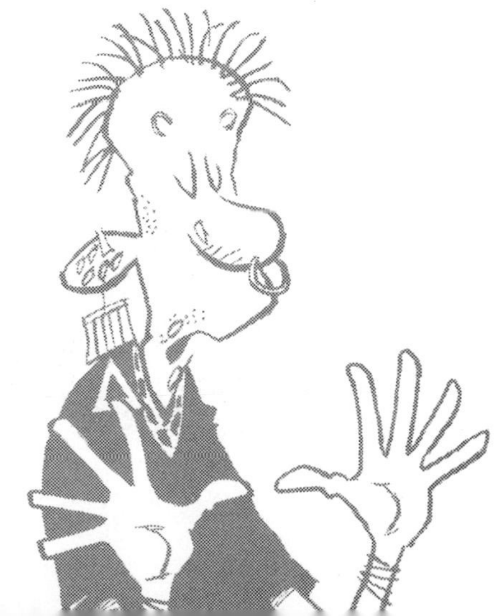

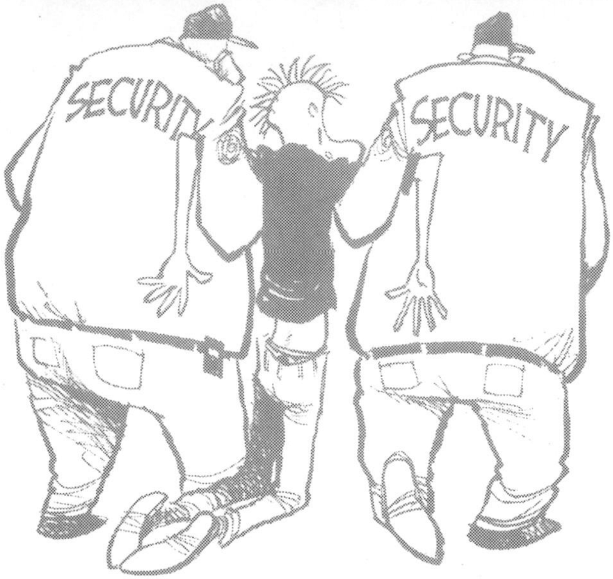

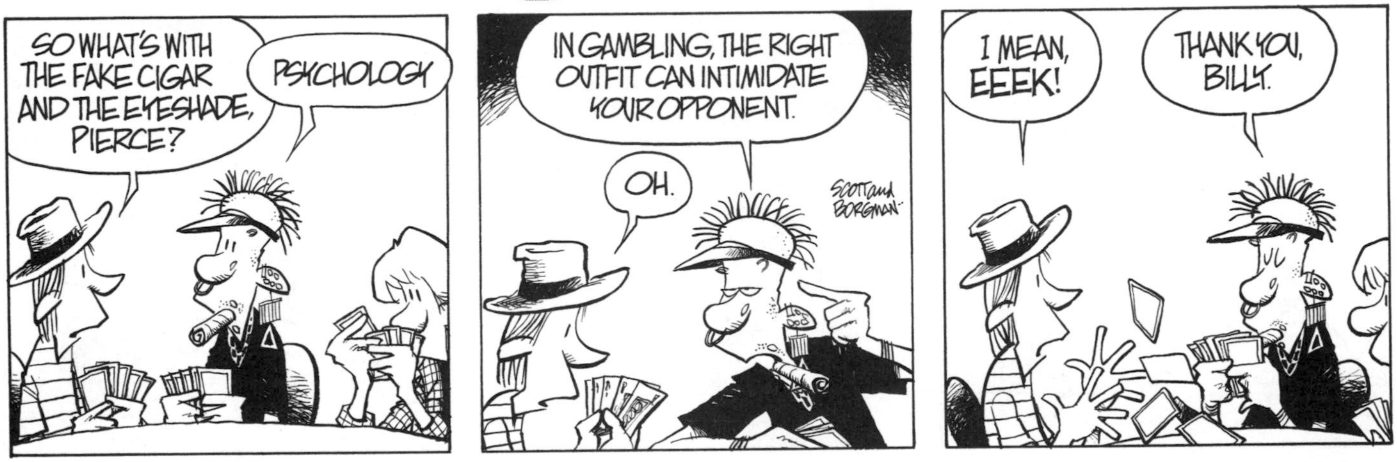
SO WHAT'S WITH THE FAKE CIGAR AND THE EYESHADE, PIERCE?
PSYCHOLOGY
IN GAMBLING, THE RIGHT OUTFIT CAN INTIMIDATE YOUR OPPONENT.
OH.
SCOTT and BORGMAN
I MEAN, EEEK!
THANK YOU, BILLY.

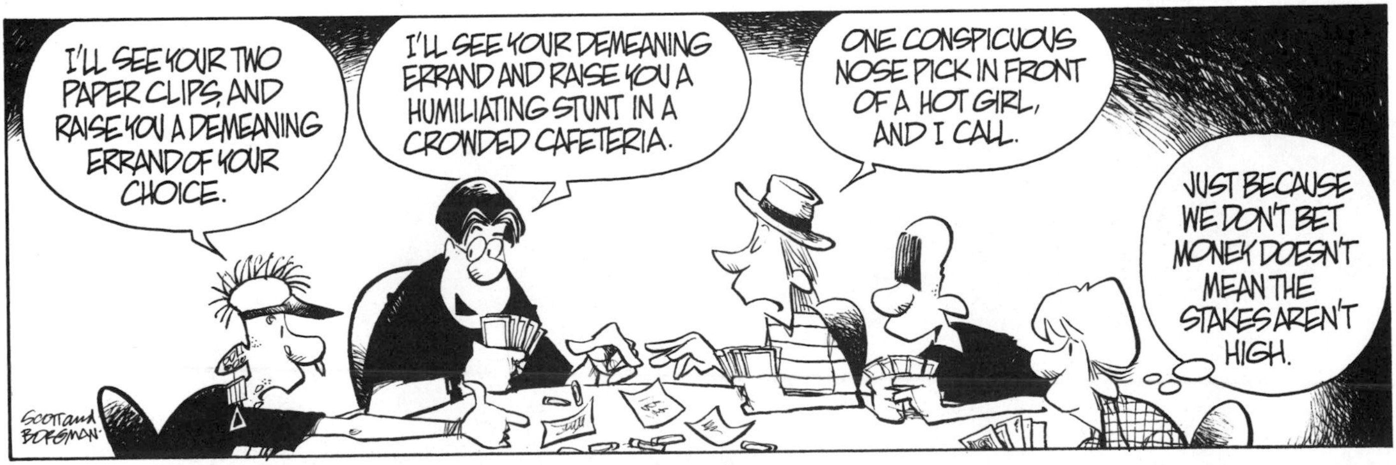
I'LL SEE YOUR TWO PAPER CLIPS, AND RAISE YOU A DEMEANING ERRAND OF YOUR CHOICE.
I'LL SEE YOUR DEMEANING ERRAND AND RAISE YOU A HUMILIATING STUNT IN A CROWDED CAFETERIA.
ONE CONSPICUOUS NOSE PICK IN FRONT OF A HOT GIRL, AND I CALL.
JUST BECAUSE WE DON'T BET MONEY DOESN'T MEAN THE STAKES AREN'T HIGH.
SCOTT and BORGMAN

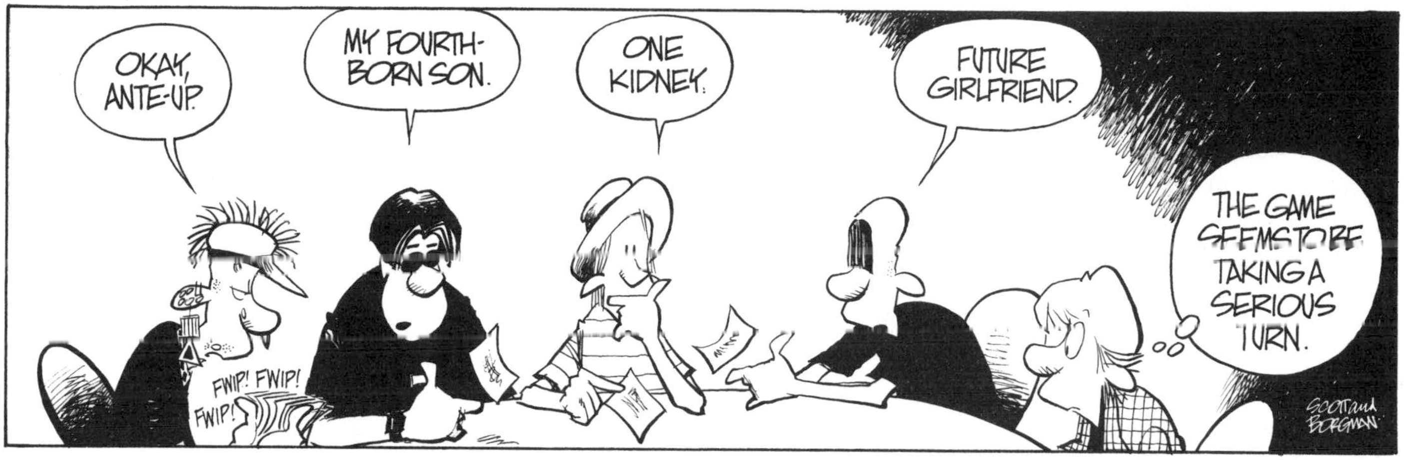
OKAY, ANTE-UP.
MY FOURTH-BORN SON.
ONE KIDNEY.
FUTURE GIRLFRIEND.
THE GAME SEEMS TO BE TAKING A SERIOUS TURN.
FWIP! FWIP! FWIP!
SCOTT and BORGMAN

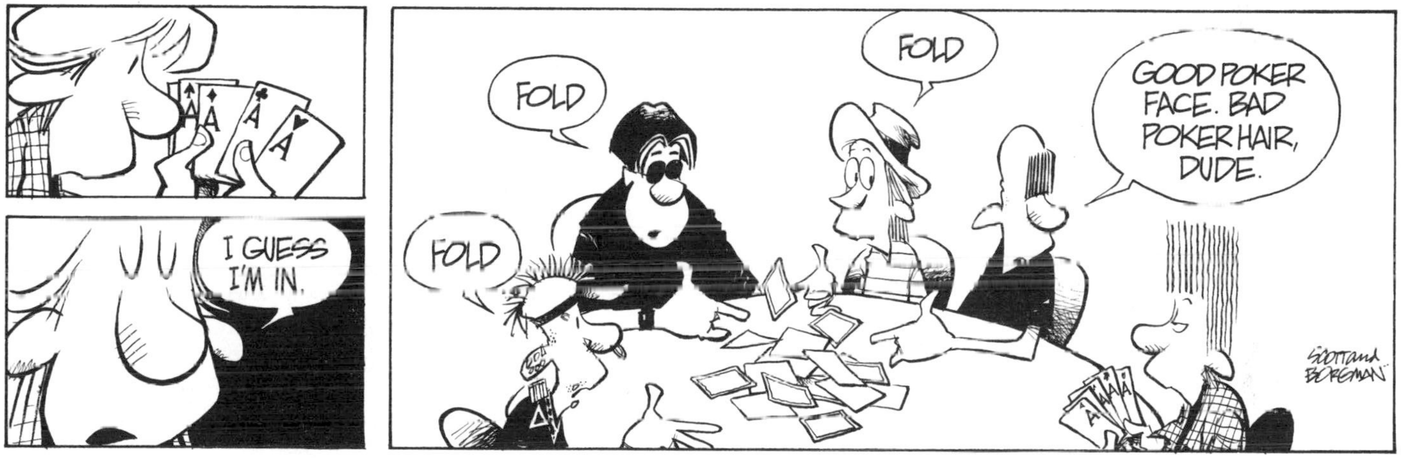
I GUESS I'M IN.
FOLD
FOLD
FOLD
GOOD POKER FACE. BAD POKER HAIR, DUDE.
SCOTT and BORGMAN

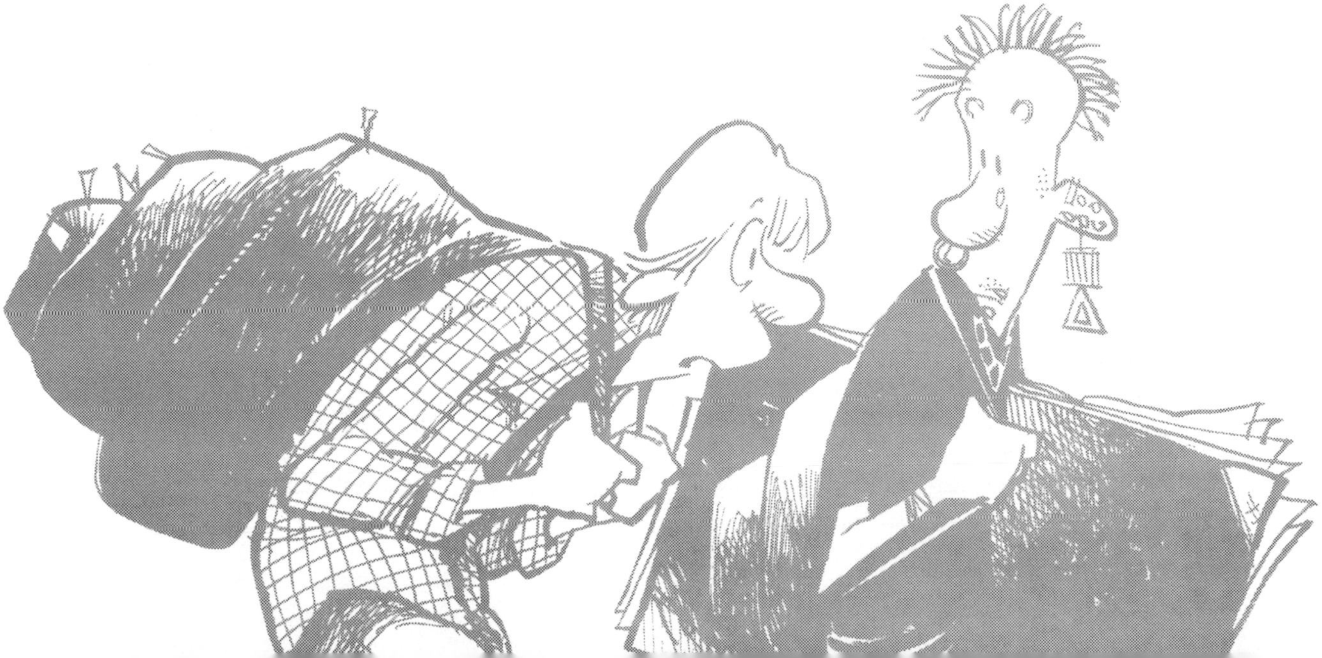

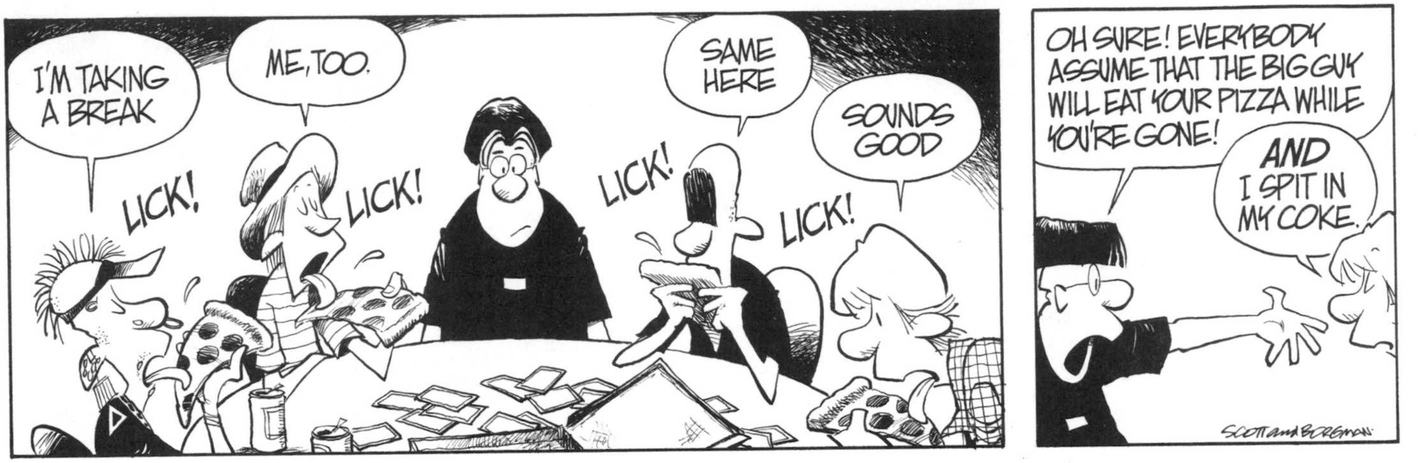
I'M TAKING A BREAK
ME, TOO.
SAME HERE
SOUNDS GOOD
LICK!
LICK!
LICK!
LICK!
OH SURE! EVERYBODY ASSUME THAT THE BIG GUY WILL EAT YOUR PIZZA WHILE YOU'RE GONE!
AND I SPIT IN MY COKE.
SCOTT and BORGMAN

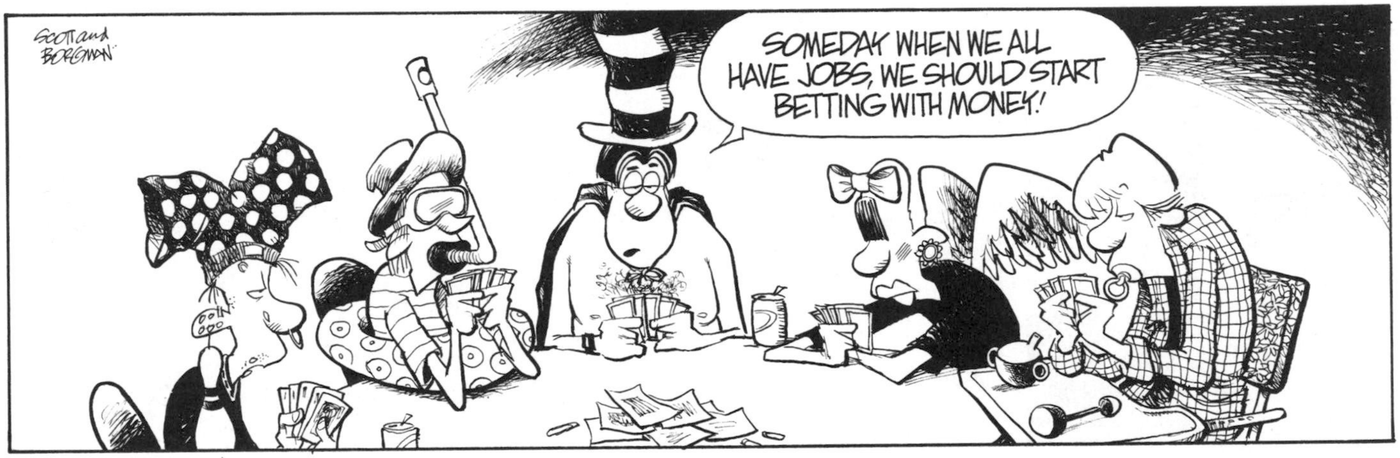
SCOTT and BORGMAN
SOMEDAY WHEN WE ALL HAVE JOBS, WE SHOULD START BETTING WITH MONEY!

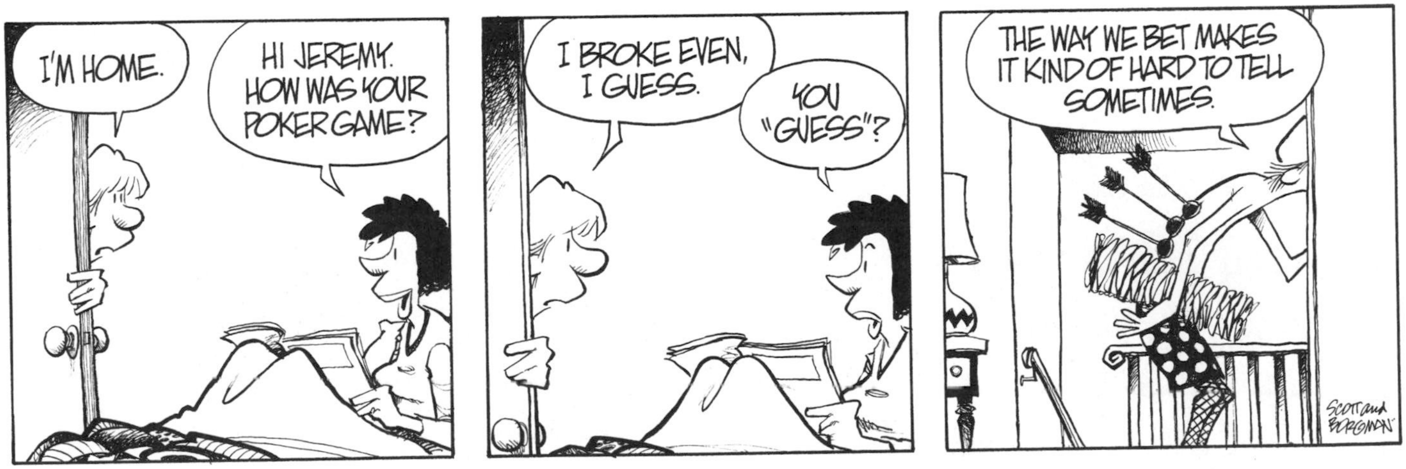
I'M HOME.
HI JEREMY. HOW WAS YOUR POKER GAME?
I BROKE EVEN, I GUESS.
YOU "GUESS"?
THE WAY WE BET MAKES IT KIND OF HARD TO TELL SOMETIMES.
SCOTT and BORGMAN

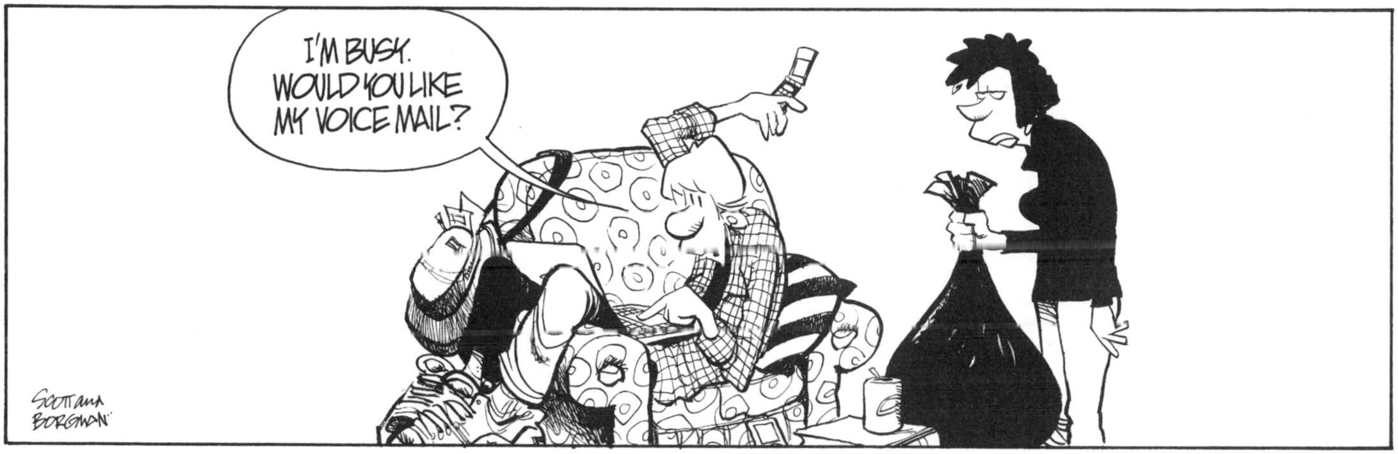
I'M BUSY. WOULD YOU LIKE MY VOICE MAIL?

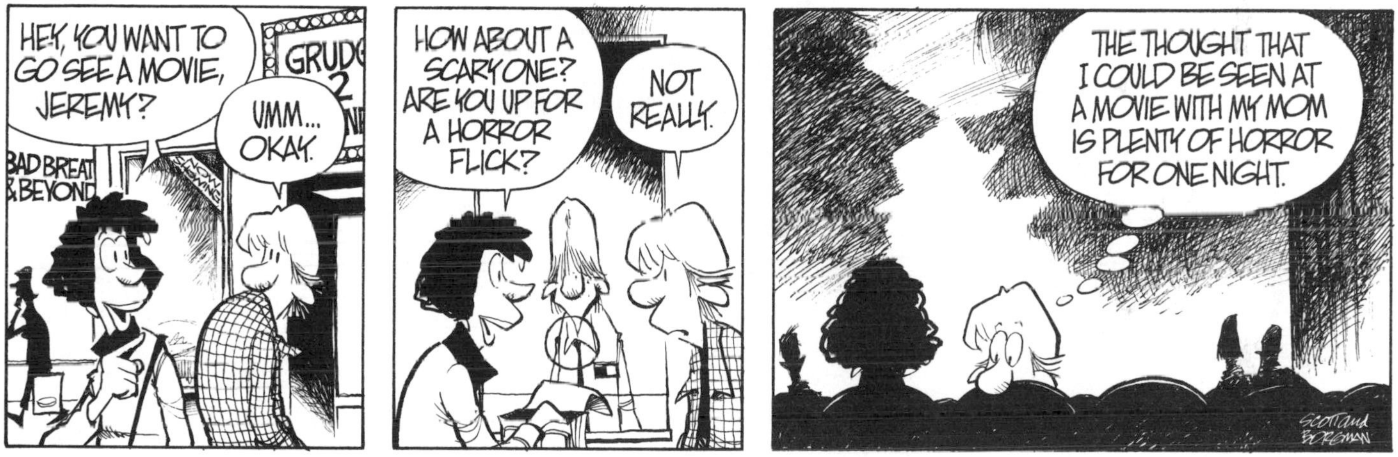
HEY, YOU WANT TO GO SEE A MOVIE, JEREMY?
UMM... OKAY.
BAD BREAT
& BEYOND
GRUDG
2
HOW ABOUT A SCARY ONE? ARE YOU UP FOR A HORROR FLICK?
NOT REALLY.
THE THOUGHT THAT I COULD BE SEEN AT A MOVIE WITH MY MOM IS PLENTY OF HORROR FOR ONE NIGHT.

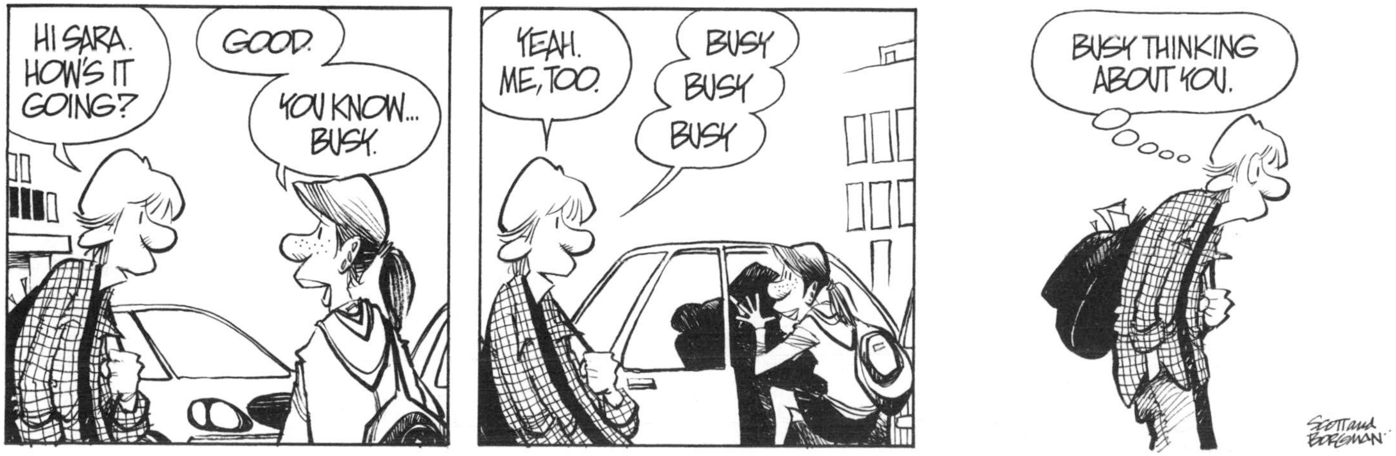
HI SARA. HOW'S IT GOING?
GOOD.
YOU KNOW... BUSY.
YEAH. ME, TOO.
BUSY
BUSY
BUSY
BUSY THINKING ABOUT YOU.

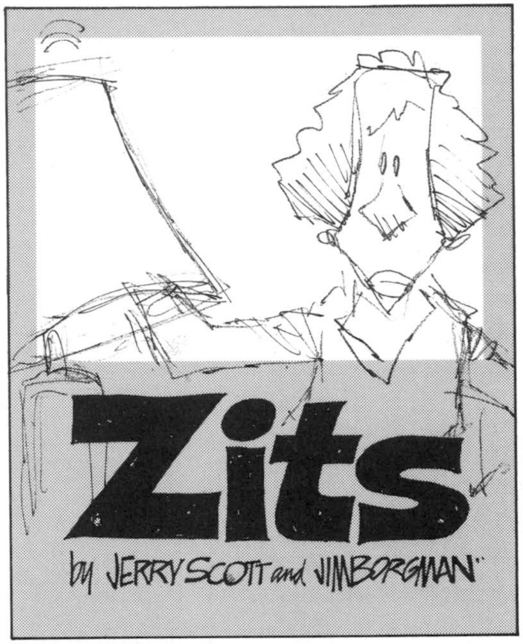
Zits
by JERRY SCOTT and JIM BORGMAN

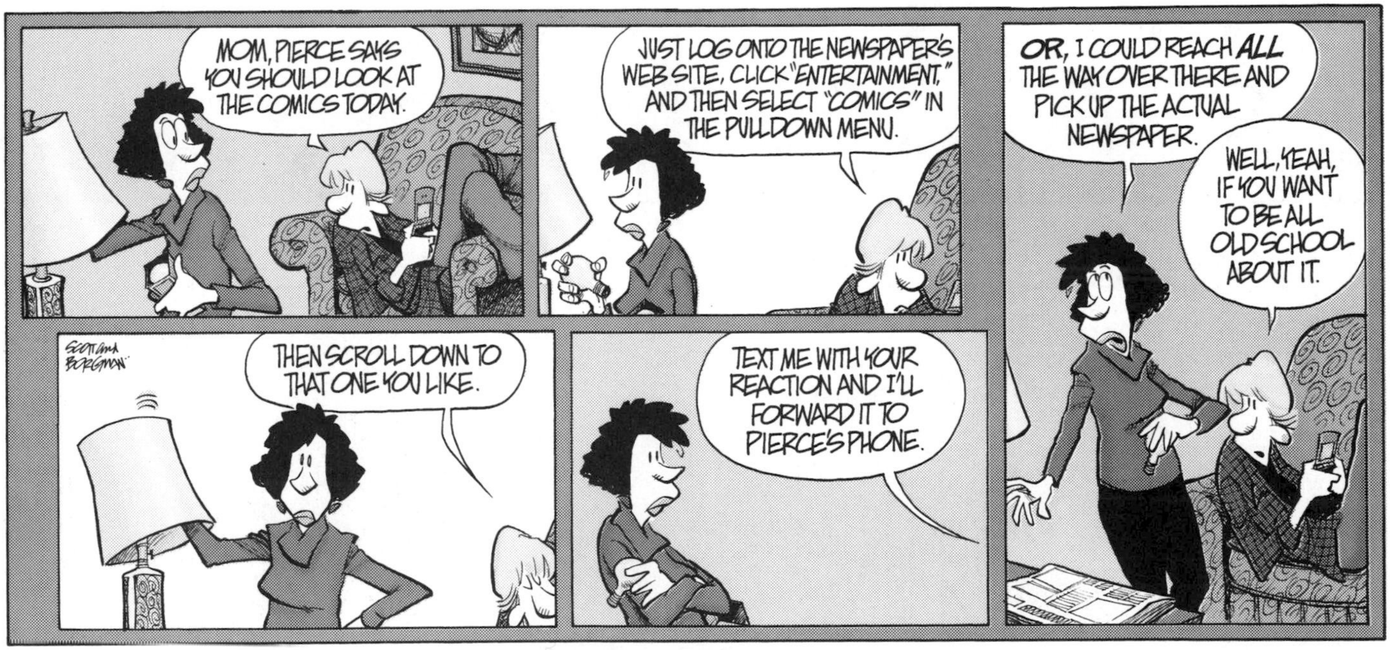
MOM, PIERCE SAYS YOU SHOULD LOOK AT THE COMICS TODAY.
JUST LOG ONTO THE NEWSPAPER'S WEB SITE, CLICK "ENTERTAINMENT," AND THEN SELECT "COMICS" IN THE PULLDOWN MENU.
SCOTT and BORGMAN
THEN SCROLL DOWN TO THAT ONE YOU LIKE.
TEXT ME WITH YOUR REACTION AND I'LL FORWARD IT TO PIERCE'S PHONE.
OR, I COULD REACH ALL THE WAY OVER THERE AND PICK UP THE ACTUAL NEWSPAPER.
WELL, YEAH, IF YOU WANT TO BE ALL OLD SCHOOL ABOUT IT.

Zits
by JERRY SCOTT and JIM BORGMAN

GO AWAY! DINNER IS IN FIFTEEN MINUTES!
I JUST WANT A TASTE.
SCOTT and BORGMAN

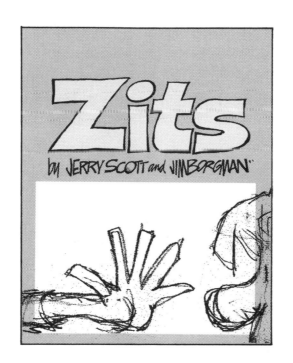

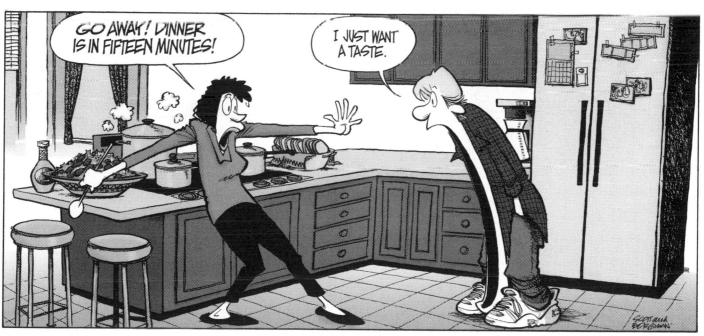

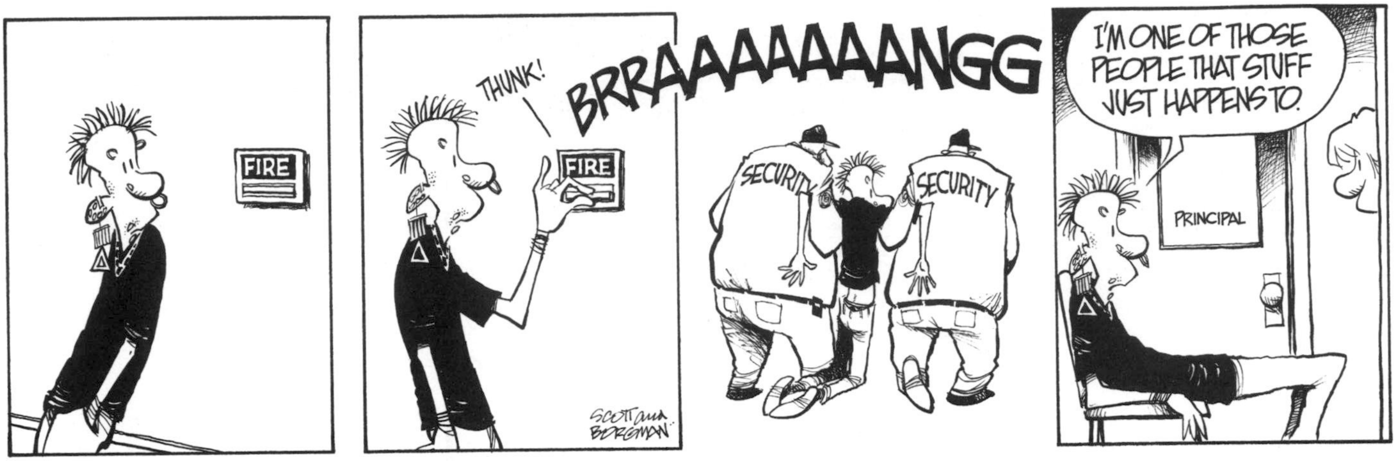
FIRE
THUNK!
FIRE
BRRAAAAAAAANGG
SECURITY
SECURITY
I'M ONE OF THOSE PEOPLE THAT STUFF JUST HAPPENS TO.
PRINCIPAL

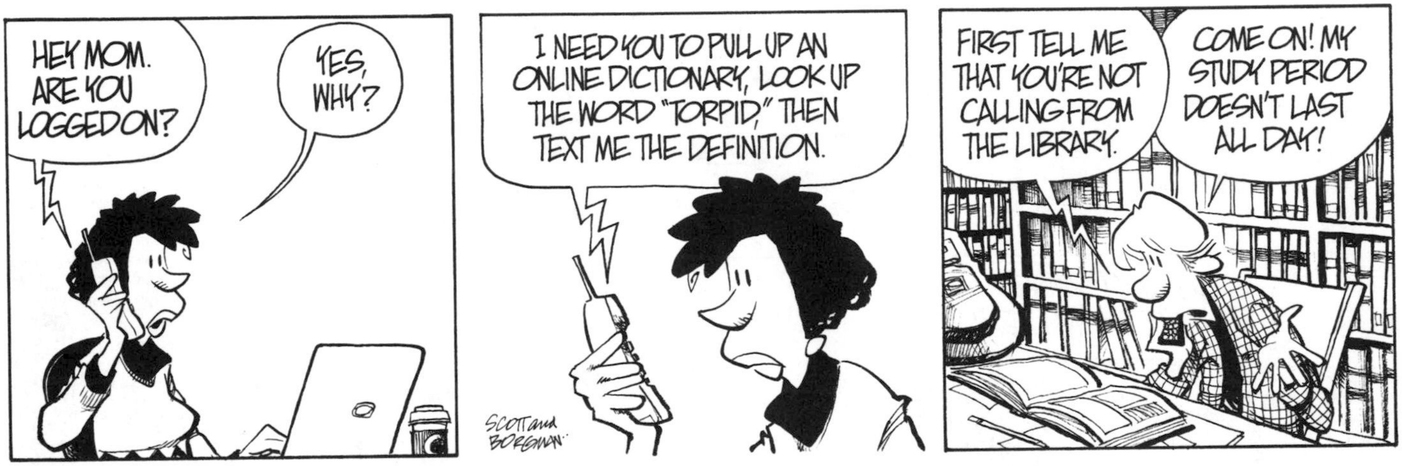
HEY MOM. ARE YOU LOGGED ON?
YES, WHY?
I NEED YOU TO PULL UP AN ONLINE DICTIONARY, LOOK UP THE WORD "TORPID," THEN TEXT ME THE DEFINITION.
FIRST TELL ME THAT YOU'RE NOT CALLING FROM THE LIBRARY.
COME ON! MY STUDY PERIOD DOESN'T LAST ALL DAY!

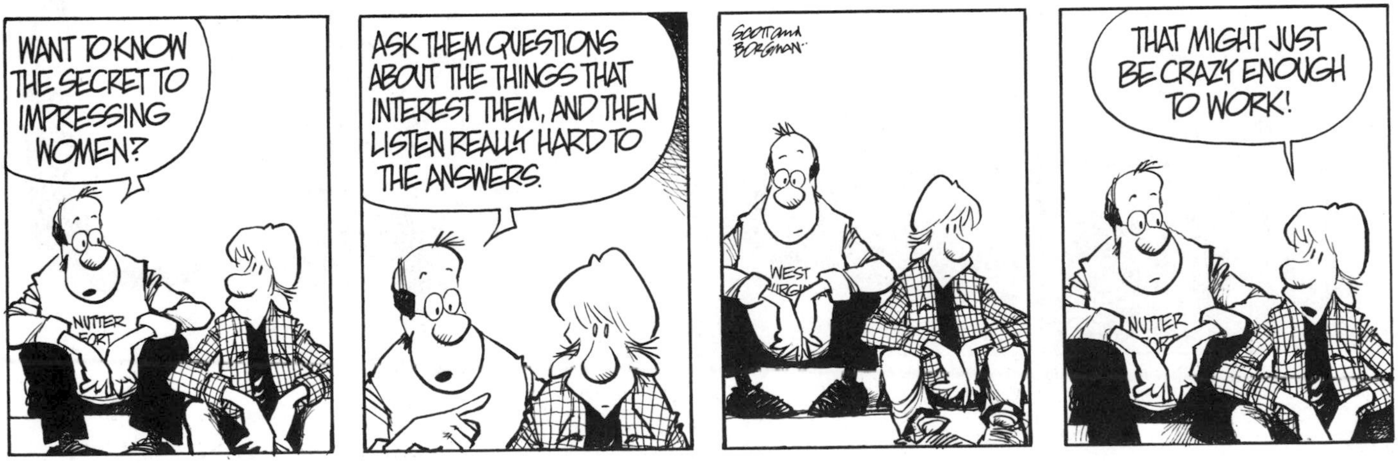
WANT TO KNOW THE SECRET TO IMPRESSING WOMEN?
ASK THEM QUESTIONS ABOUT THE THINGS THAT INTEREST THEM, AND THEN LISTEN REALLY HARD TO THE ANSWERS.
THAT MIGHT JUST BE CRAZY ENOUGH TO WORK!

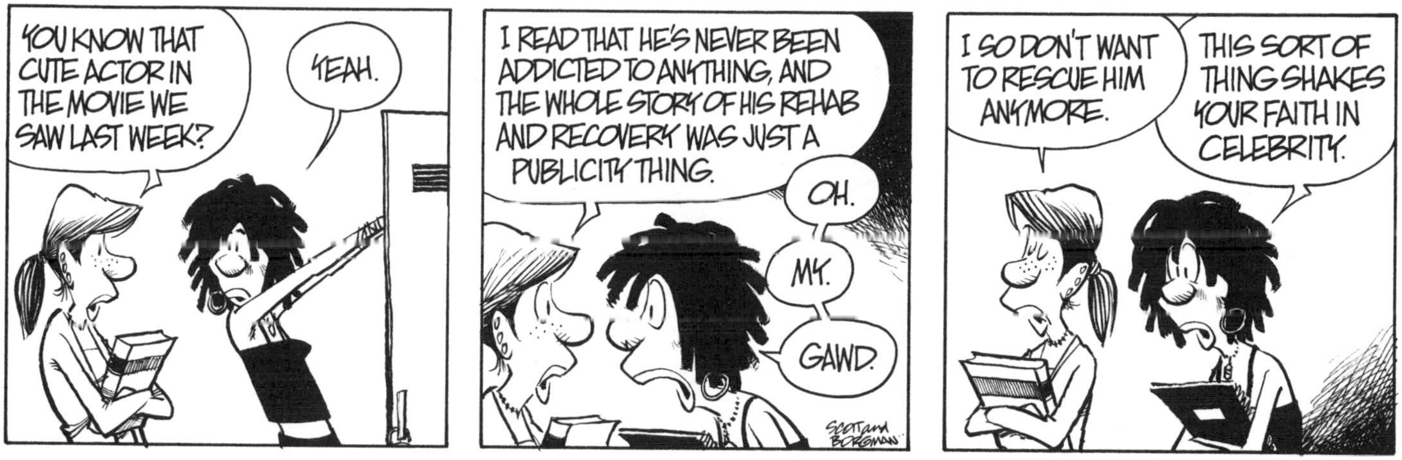
YOU KNOW THAT CUTE ACTOR IN THE MOVIE WE SAW LAST WEEK?
YEAH.
I READ THAT HE'S NEVER BEEN ADDICTED TO ANYTHING, AND THE WHOLE STORY OF HIS REHAB AND RECOVERY WAS JUST A PUBLICITY THING.
OH.
MY.
GAWD.
SCOTT and BORGMAN
I SO DON'T WANT TO RESCUE HIM ANYMORE.
THIS SORT OF THING SHAKES YOUR FAITH IN CELEBRITY.

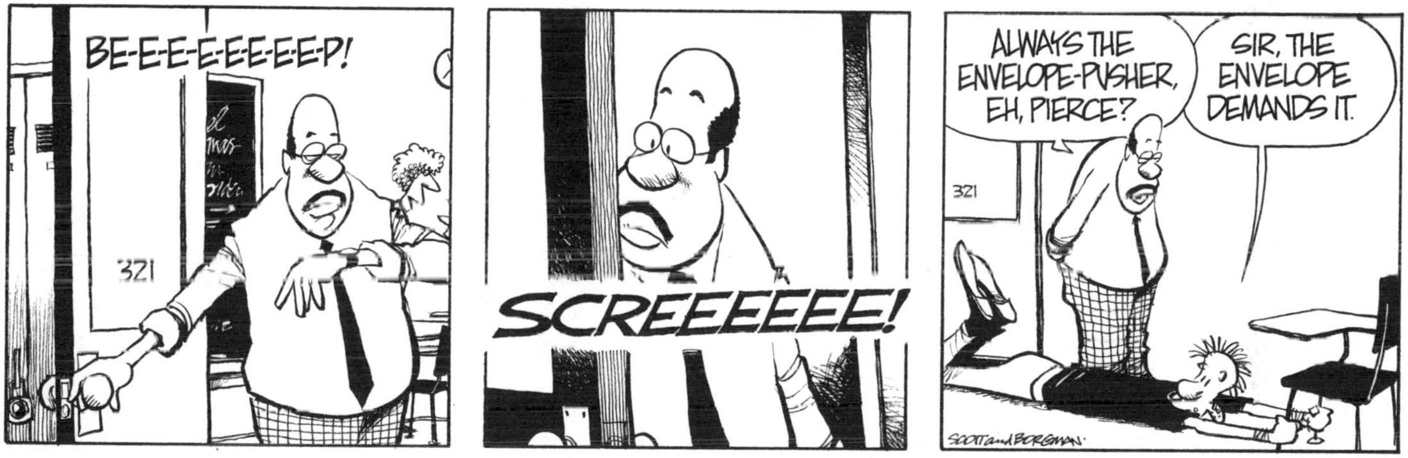
BE-E-E-E-E-E-E-E-P!
321
SCREEEEEEE!
ALWAYS THE ENVELOPE-PUSHER, EH, PIERCE?
SIR, THE ENVELOPE DEMANDS IT.
321
SCOTT and BORGMAN

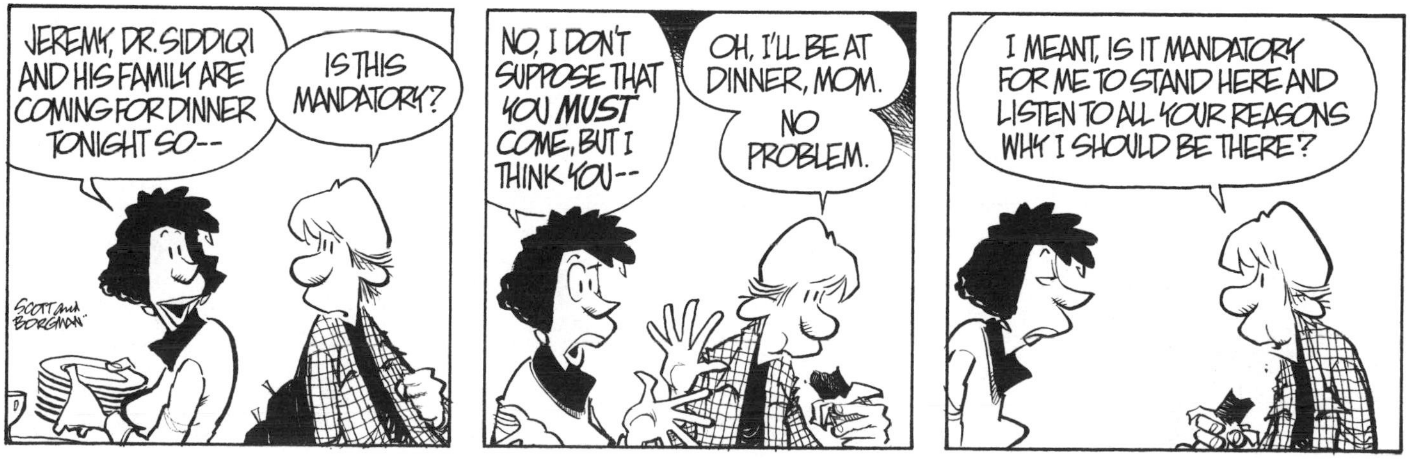
JEREMY, DR. SIDDIQI AND HIS FAMILY ARE COMING FOR DINNER TONIGHT SO--
IS THIS MANDATORY?
SCOTT and BORGMAN
NO, I DON'T SUPPOSE THAT YOU MUST COME, BUT I THINK YOU--
OH, I'LL BE AT DINNER, MOM.
NO PROBLEM.
I MEANT, IS IT MANDATORY FOR ME TO STAND HERE AND LISTEN TO ALL YOUR REASONS WHY I SHOULD BE THERE?

Zits
by JERRY SCOTT and JIM BORGMAN
RING
RING!

MOM
555-8623
RING! RING! RING!
MOM
555-8623
RING! RING! RING!
MOM
555-8623
RING! RING! RING! RING!
MOM
555-8623
JEREMY! I'VE BEEN TRYING TO CALL YOU FOR AN HOUR!
WHY DIDN'T YOU PICK UP?
I'D BLAME CALLER I.D.

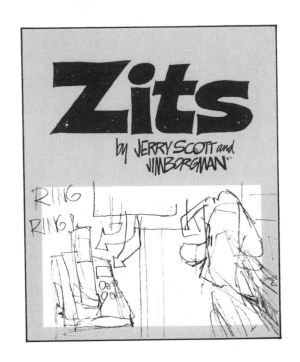

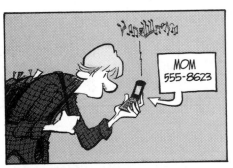

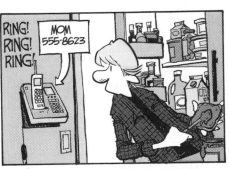

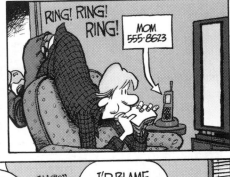

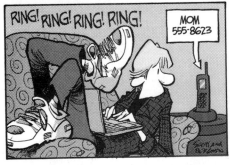

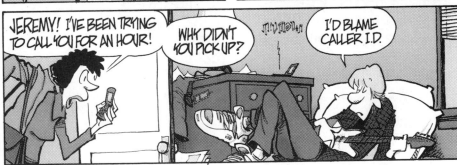

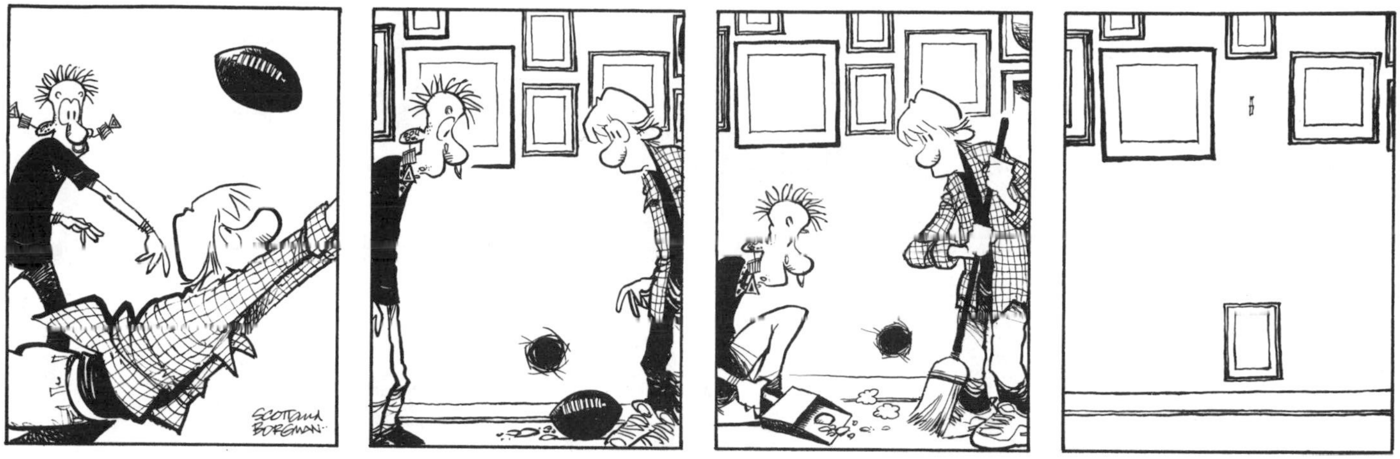

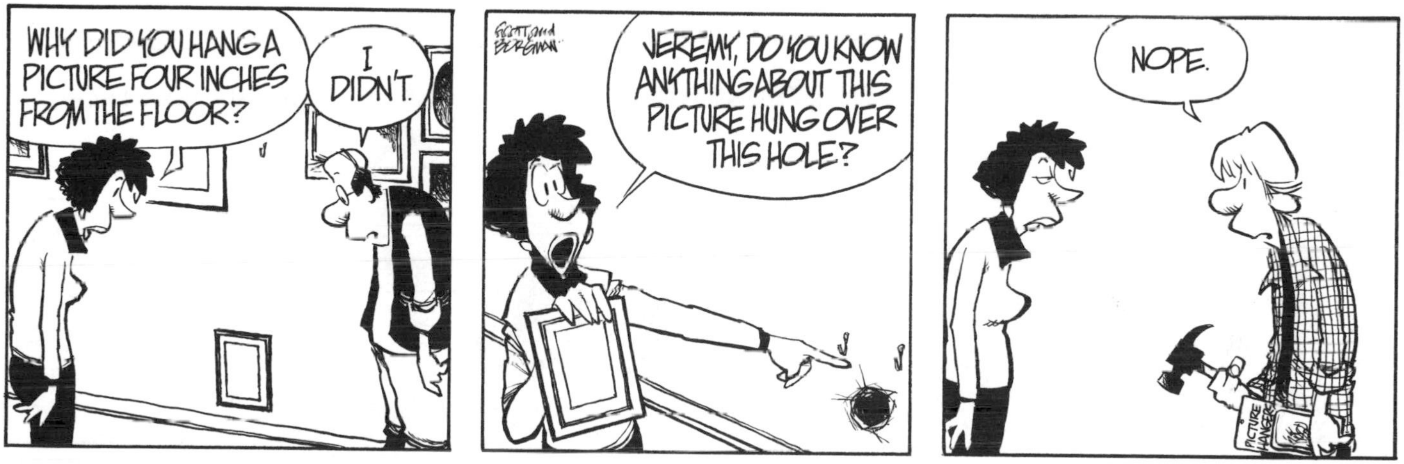
WHY DID YOU HANG A PICTURE FOUR INCHES FROM THE FLOOR?
I DIDN'T.
JEREMY, DO YOU KNOW ANYTHING ABOUT THIS PICTURE HUNG OVER THIS HOLE?
NOPE.
PICTURE HANGERS

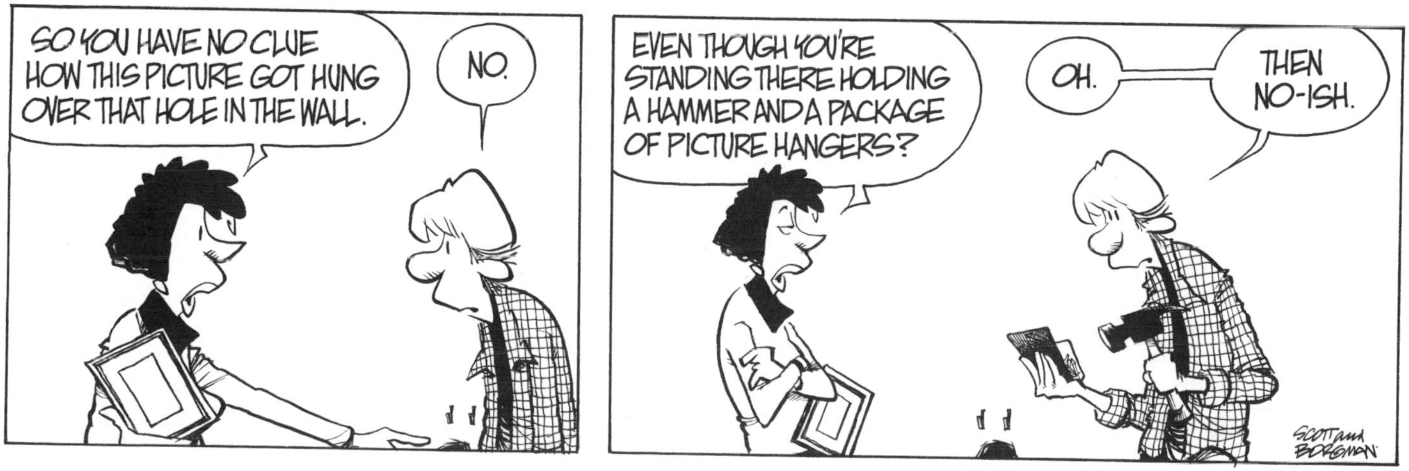
SO YOU HAVE NO CLUE HOW THIS PICTURE GOT HUNG OVER THAT HOLE IN THE WALL.
NO.
EVEN THOUGH YOU'RE STANDING THERE HOLDING A HAMMER AND A PACKAGE OF PICTURE HANGERS?
OH.
THEN NO-ISH.

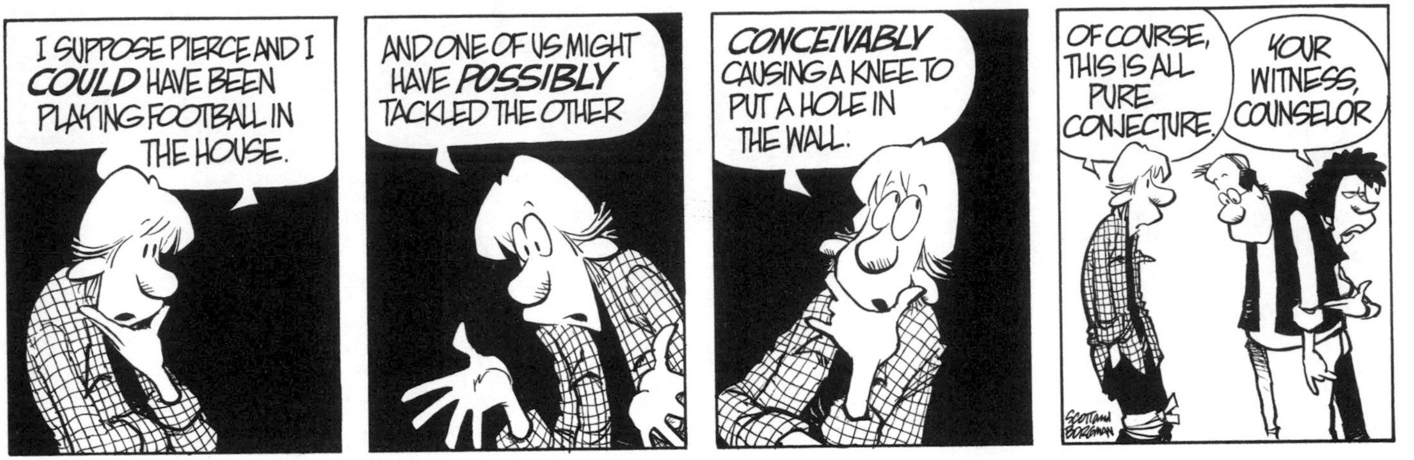
I SUPPOSE PIERCE AND I **COULD** HAVE BEEN PLAYING FOOTBALL IN THE HOUSE.
AND ONE OF US MIGHT HAVE **POSSIBLY** TACKLED THE OTHER
CONCEIVABLY CAUSING A KNEE TO PUT A HOLE IN THE WALL.
OF COURSE, THIS IS ALL PURE CONJECTURE.
YOUR WITNESS, COUNSELOR

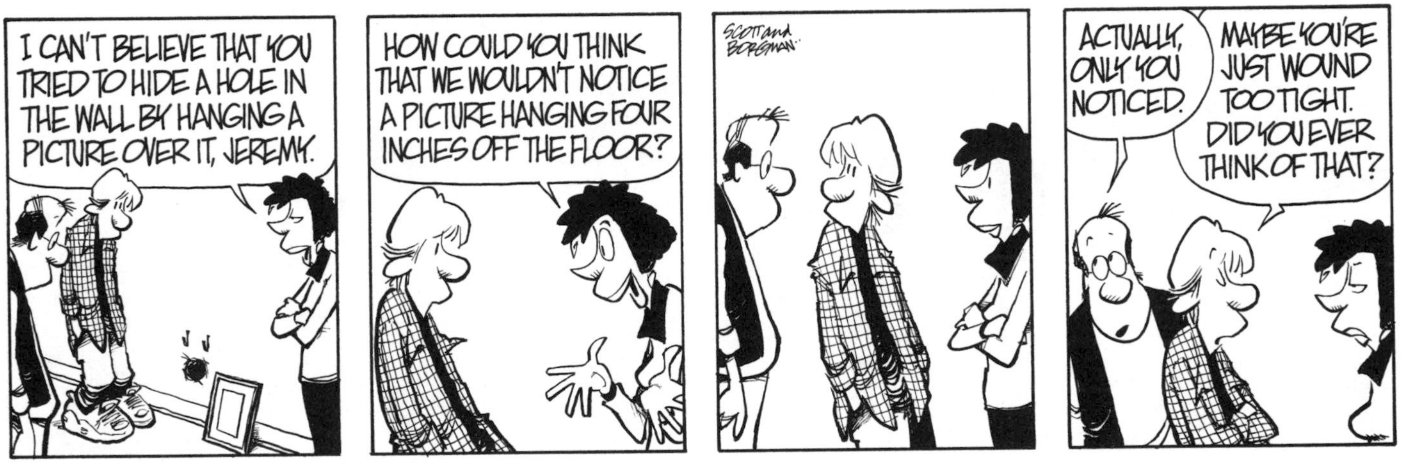
I CAN'T BELIEVE THAT YOU TRIED TO HIDE A HOLE IN THE WALL BY HANGING A PICTURE OVER IT, JEREMY.
HOW COULD YOU THINK THAT WE WOULDN'T NOTICE A PICTURE HANGING FOUR INCHES OFF THE FLOOR?
ACTUALLY, ONLY YOU NOTICED.
MAYBE YOU'RE JUST WOUND TOO TIGHT. DID YOU EVER THINK OF THAT?

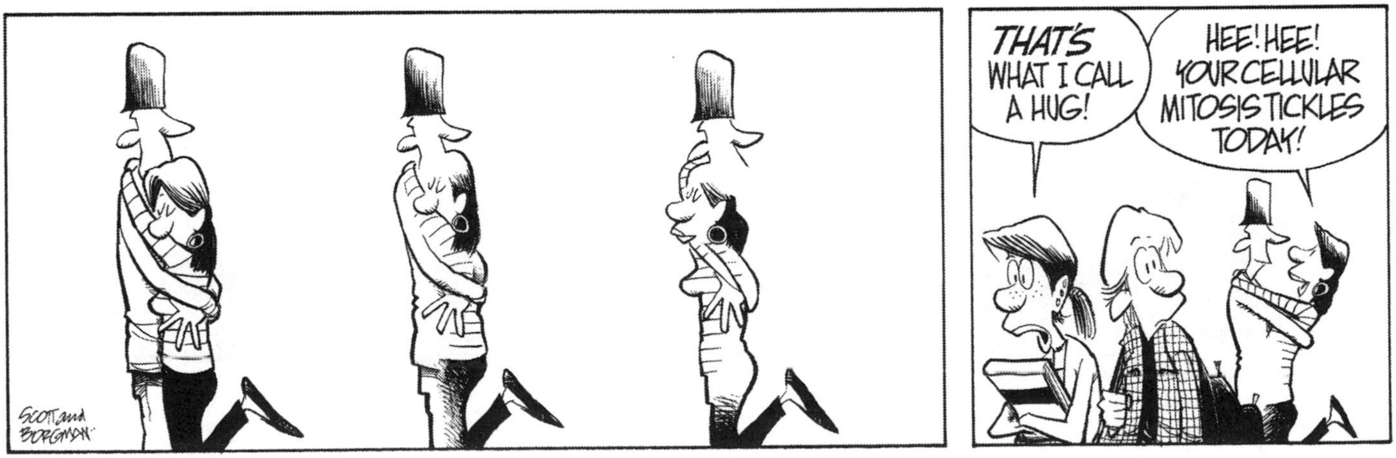
THAT'S WHAT I CALL A HUG!
HEE! HEE! YOUR CELLULAR MITOSIS TICKLES TODAY!

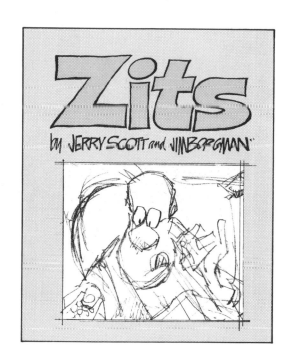

Zits

by JERRY SCOTT and JIM BORGMAN

BOOP! BIP! BIP! BEEP! BIP! BEEP! BOOP!

CLICK!

FOOM!

SCOTT and BORGMAN

IN THIS WORLD THERE ARE MULTI-TASKERS AND MONO-TASKERS.

YOU, DAD, ARE A MONO-TASKER.

OW

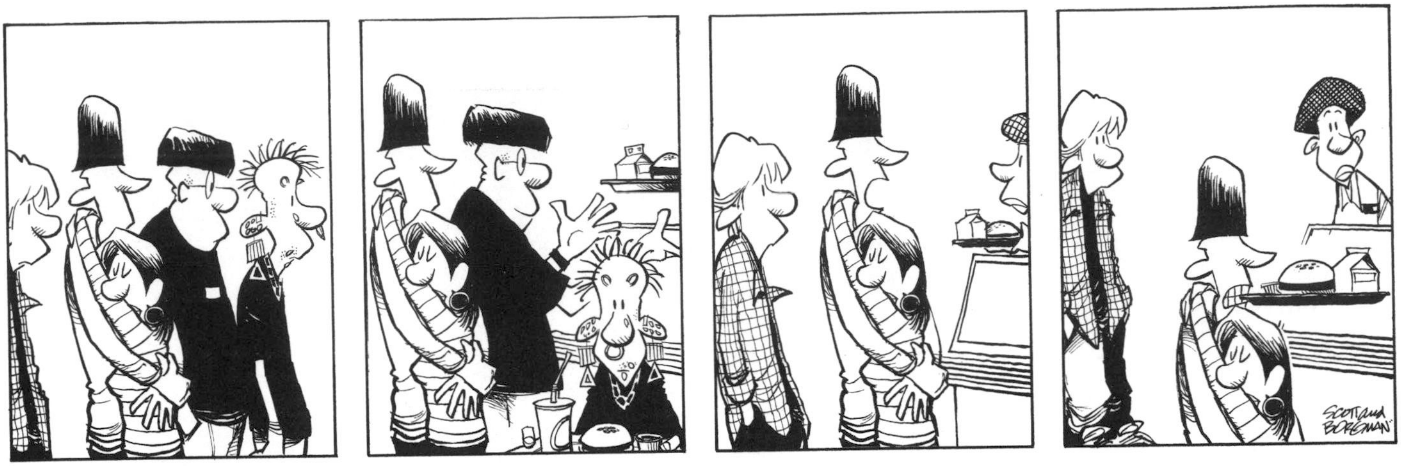

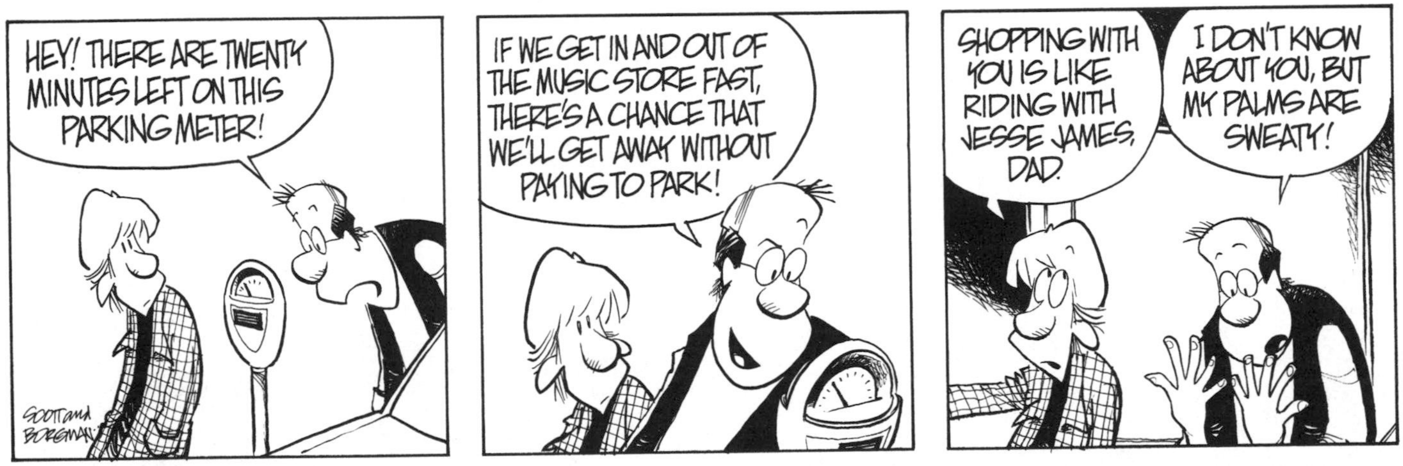
HEY! THERE ARE TWENTY MINUTES LEFT ON THIS PARKING METER!
IF WE GET IN AND OUT OF THE MUSIC STORE FAST, THERE'S A CHANCE THAT WE'LL GET AWAY WITHOUT PAYING TO PARK!
SHOPPING WITH YOU IS LIKE RIDING WITH JESSE JAMES, DAD.
I DON'T KNOW ABOUT YOU, BUT MY PALMS ARE SWEATY!

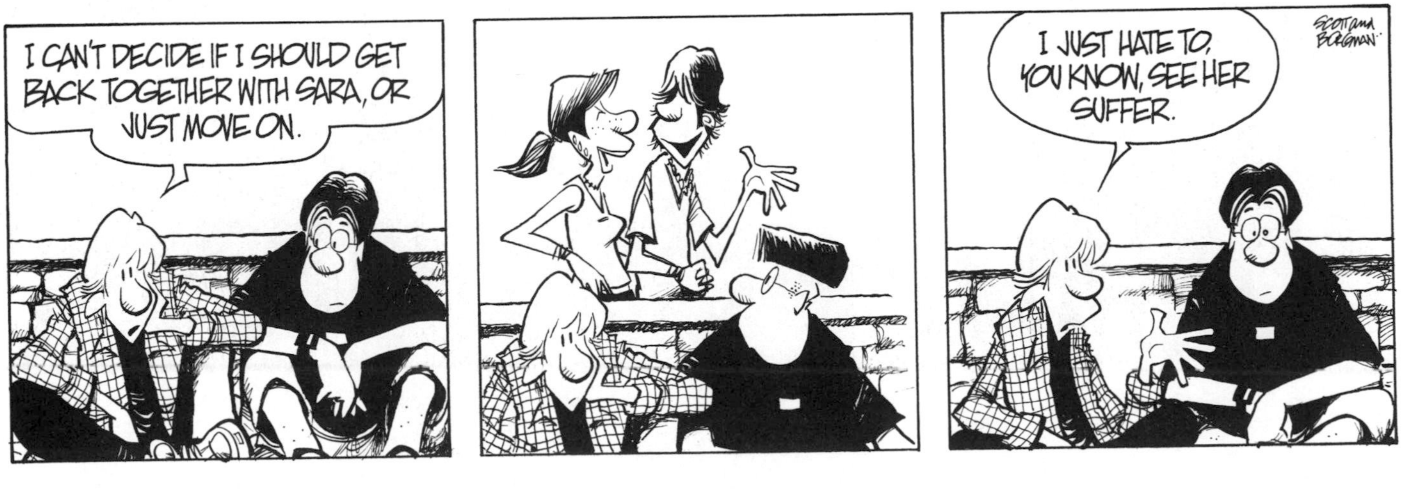
I CAN'T DECIDE IF I SHOULD GET BACK TOGETHER WITH SARA, OR JUST MOVE ON.
I JUST HATE TO, YOU KNOW, SEE HER SUFFER.

Zits
by JERRY SCOTT and JIM BORGMAN

SO, YOUR BEDROOM IS NOW YOUR CLOSET, AND YOUR CLOSET IS NOW YOUR BEDROOM...
I FINALLY GOT MY PRIORITIES STRAIGHT!
SCOTT and BORGMAN

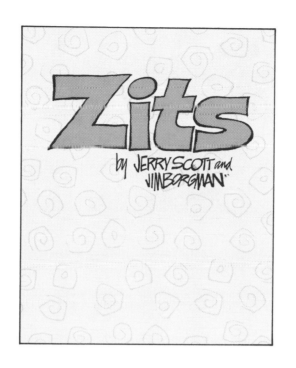

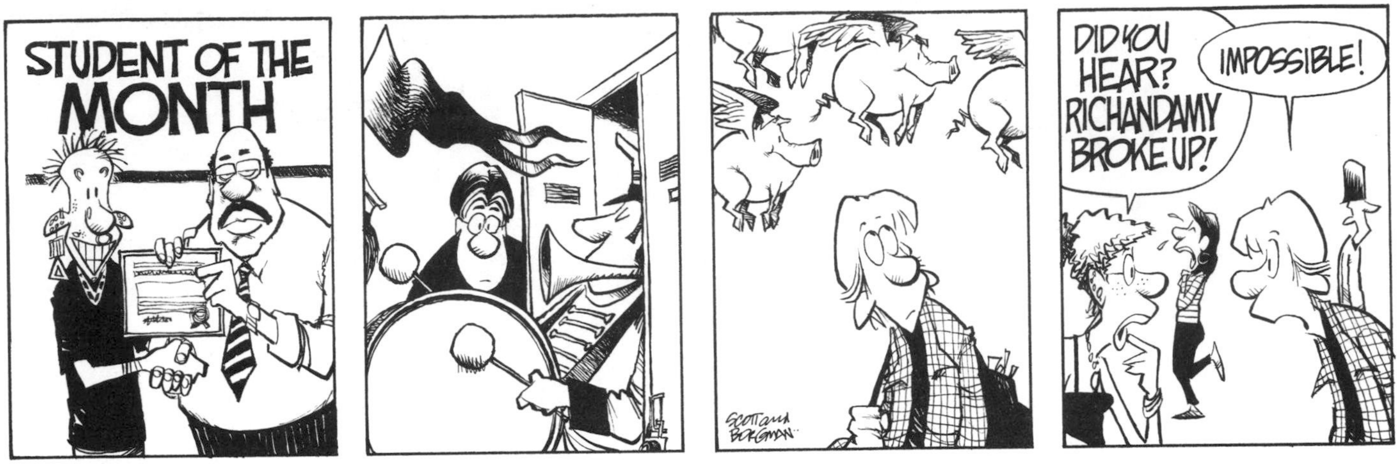

STUDENT OF THE MONTH
SCOTT and BORGMAN
DID YOU HEAR? RICHANDAMY BROKE UP!
IMPOSSIBLE!

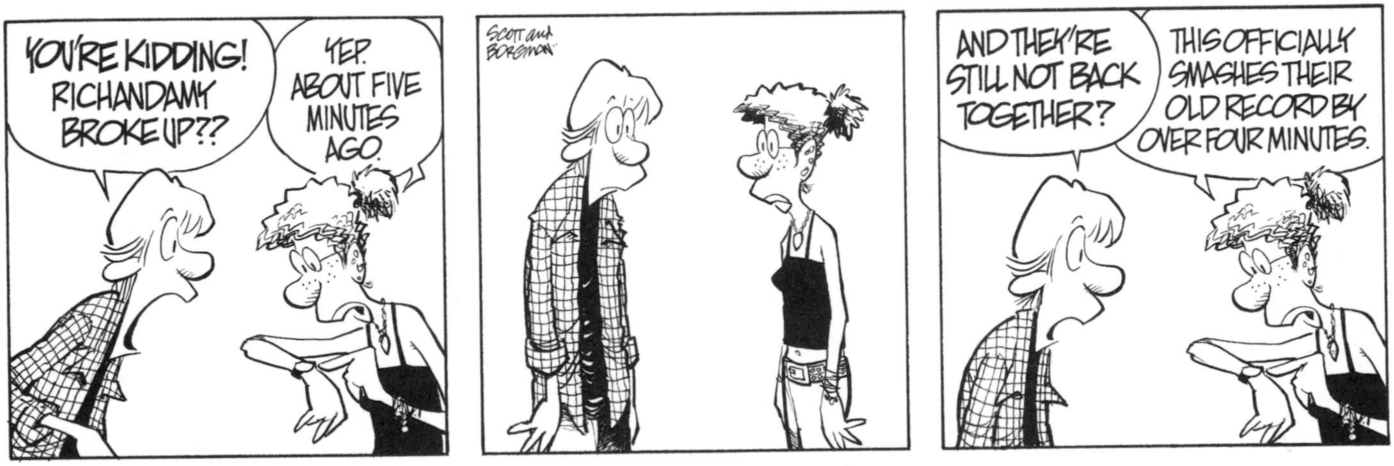

YOU'RE KIDDING! RICHANDAMY BROKE UP??
YEP. ABOUT FIVE MINUTES AGO.
SCOTT and BORGMAN
AND THEY'RE STILL NOT BACK TOGETHER?
THIS OFFICIALLY SMASHES THEIR OLD RECORD BY OVER FOUR MINUTES.

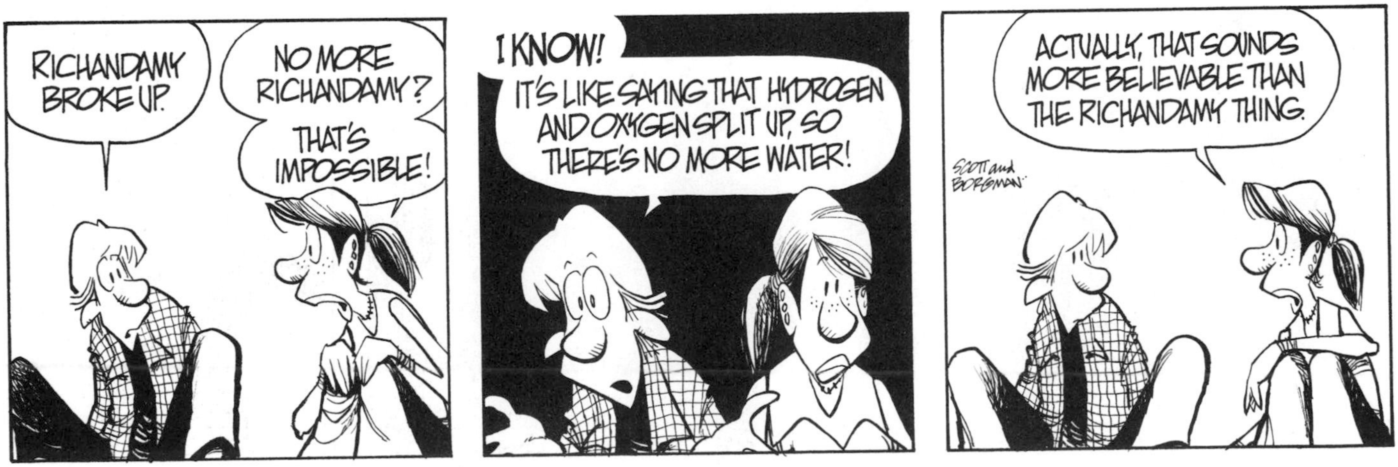

RICHANDAMY BROKE UP.
NO MORE RICHANDAMY?
THAT'S IMPOSSIBLE!
I KNOW!
IT'S LIKE SAYING THAT HYDROGEN AND OXYGEN SPLIT UP, SO THERE'S NO MORE WATER!
SCOTT and BORGMAN
ACTUALLY, THAT SOUNDS MORE BELIEVABLE THAN THE RICHANDAMY THING.

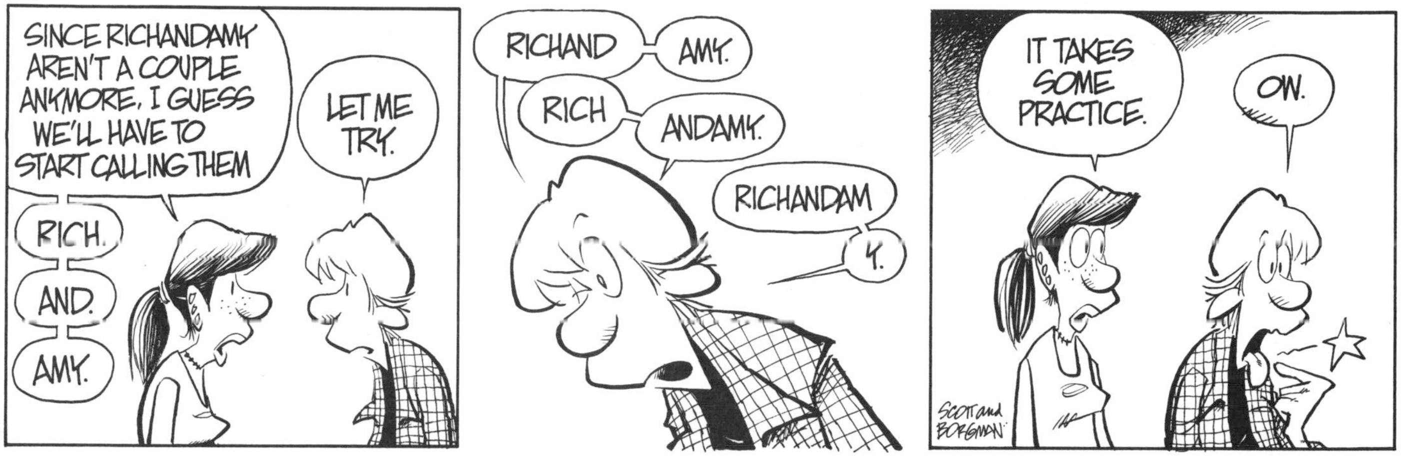
SINCE RICHANDAMY AREN'T A COUPLE ANYMORE, I GUESS WE'LL HAVE TO START CALLING THEM
RICH.
AND.
AMY.
LET ME TRY.
RICHAND
AMY.
RICH
ANDAMY.
RICHANDAM
Y.
IT TAKES SOME PRACTICE.
OW.
SCOTT and BORGMAN

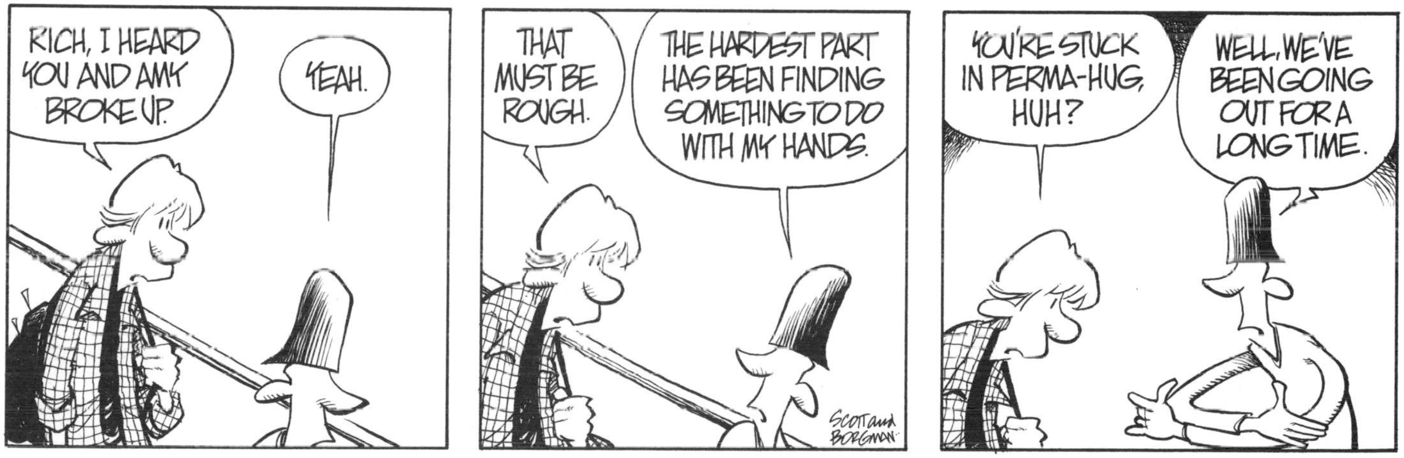
RICH, I HEARD YOU AND AMY BROKE UP.
YEAH.
THAT MUST BE ROUGH.
THE HARDEST PART HAS BEEN FINDING SOMETHING TO DO WITH MY HANDS.
SCOTT and BORGMAN
YOU'RE STUCK IN PERMA-HUG, HUH?
WELL, WE'VE BEEN GOING OUT FOR A LONG TIME.

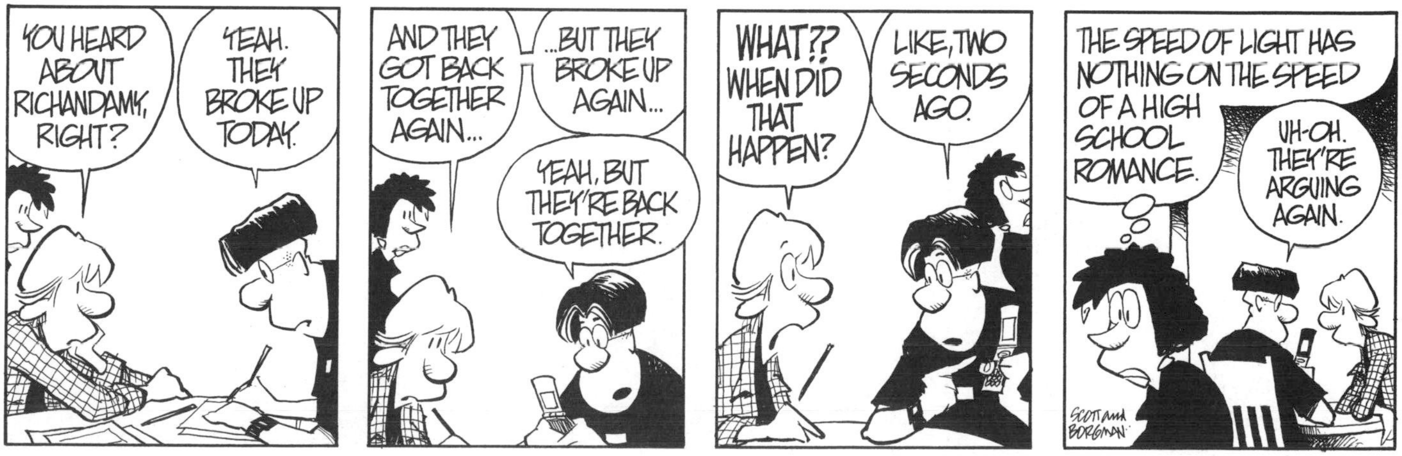
YOU HEARD ABOUT RICHANDAMY, RIGHT?
YEAH. THEY BROKE UP TODAY.
AND THEY GOT BACK TOGETHER AGAIN...
...BUT THEY BROKE UP AGAIN...
YEAH, BUT THEY'RE BACK TOGETHER.
WHAT?? WHEN DID THAT HAPPEN?
LIKE, TWO SECONDS AGO.
THE SPEED OF LIGHT HAS NOTHING ON THE SPEED OF A HIGH SCHOOL ROMANCE.
UH-OH. THEY'RE ARGUING AGAIN.
SCOTT and BORGMAN

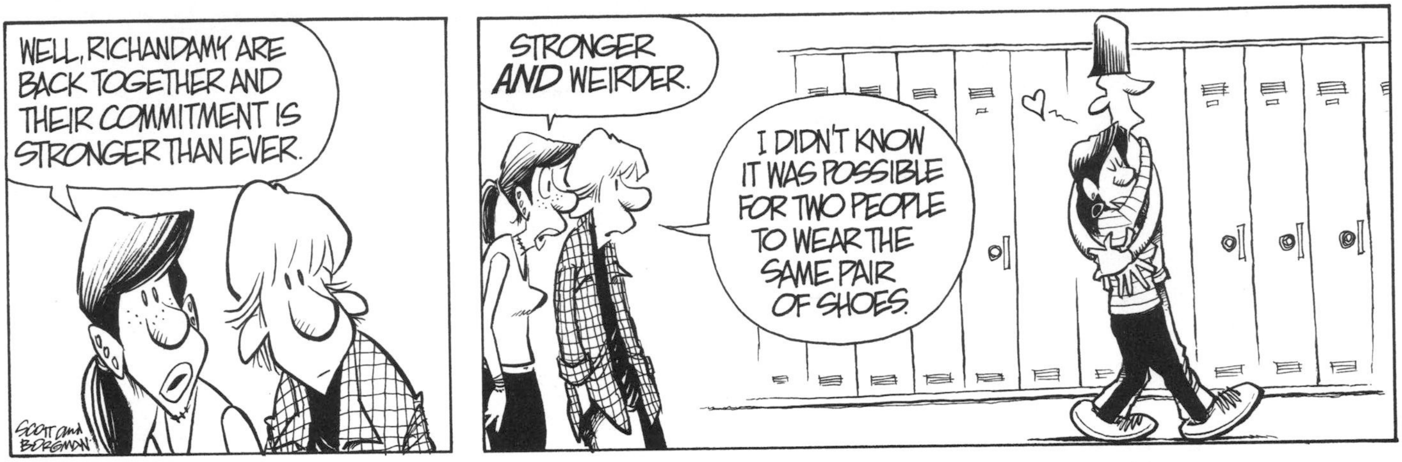
WELL, RICHANDAMY ARE BACK TOGETHER AND THEIR COMMITMENT IS STRONGER THAN EVER.
STRONGER AND WEIRDER.
I DIDN'T KNOW IT WAS POSSIBLE FOR TWO PEOPLE TO WEAR THE SAME PAIR OF SHOES.
SCOTT and BORGMAN

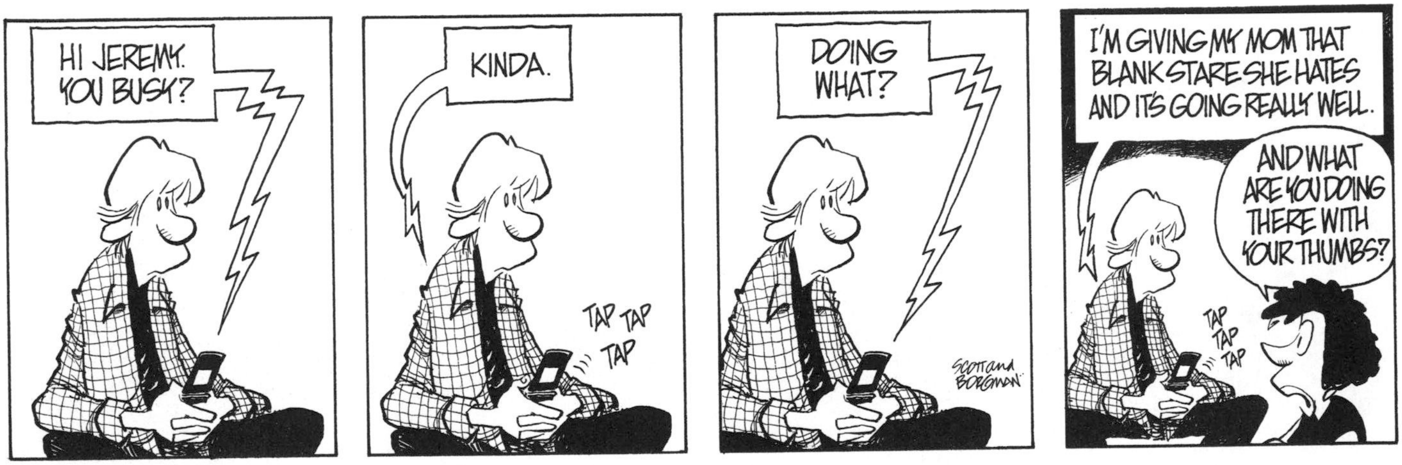
HI JEREMY. YOU BUSY?
KINDA.
TAP TAP TAP
DOING WHAT?
SCOTT and BORGMAN
I'M GIVING MY MOM THAT BLANK STARE SHE HATES AND IT'S GOING REALLY WELL.
AND WHAT ARE YOU DOING THERE WITH YOUR THUMBS?
TAP TAP TAP

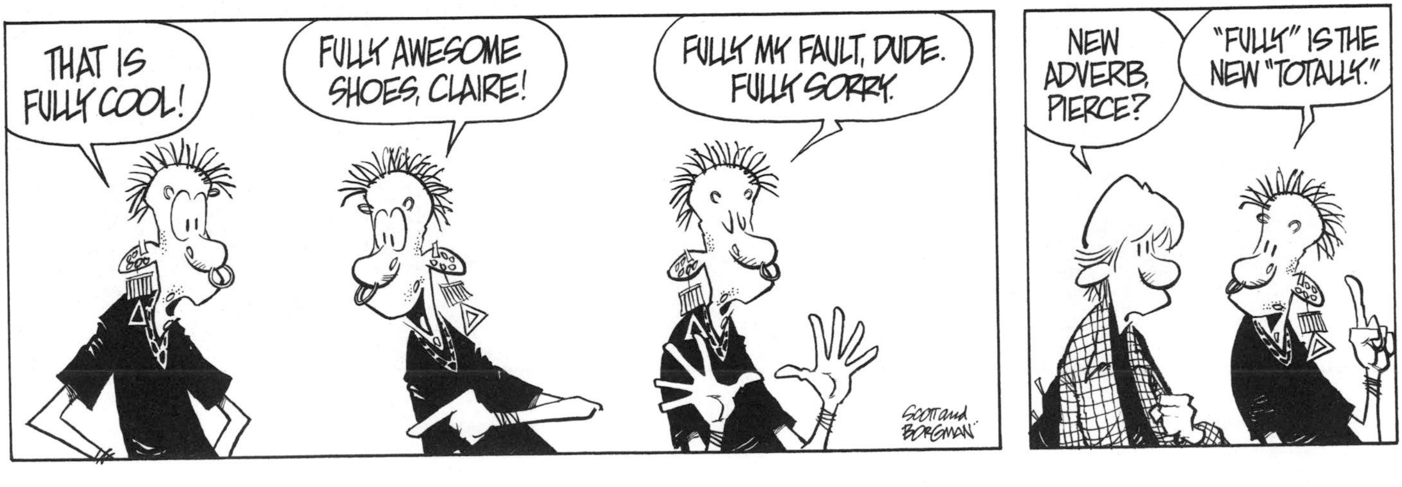
THAT IS FULLY COOL!
FULLY AWESOME SHOES, CLAIRE!
FULLY MY FAULT, DUDE. FULLY SORRY.
SCOTT and BORGMAN
NEW ADVERB, PIERCE?
"FULLY" IS THE NEW "TOTALLY."

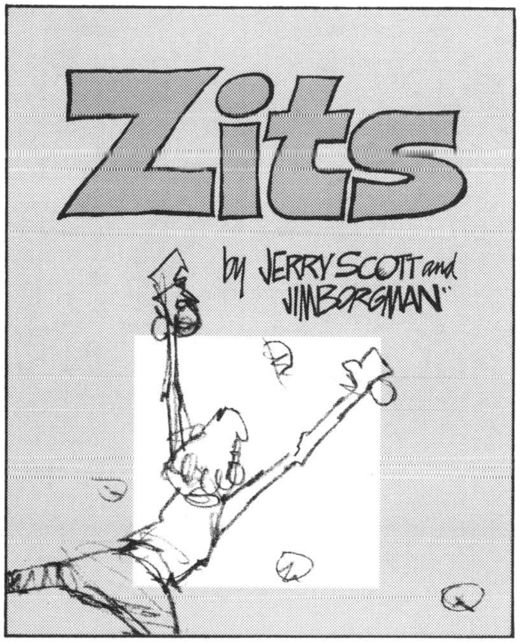
Zits
by JERRY SCOTT and
JIM BORGMAN

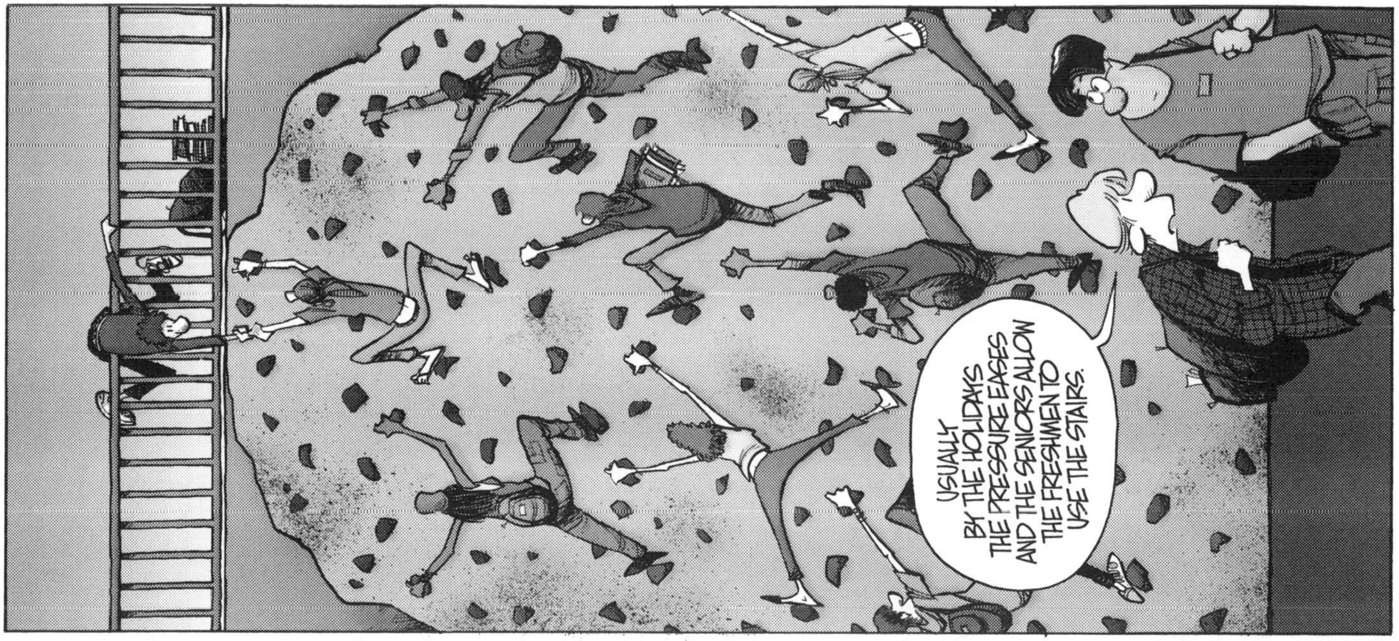
USUALLY BY THE HOLIDAYS THE PRESSURE EASES AND THE SENIORS ALLOW THE FRESHMEN TO USE THE STAIRS.

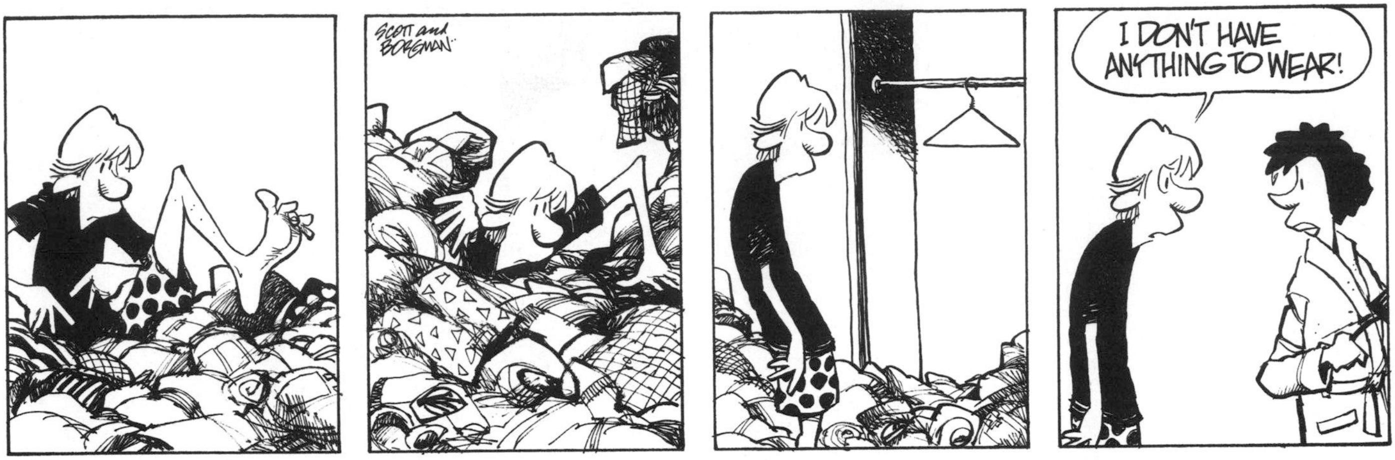
SCOTT and BORGMAN
I DON'T HAVE ANYTHING TO WEAR!

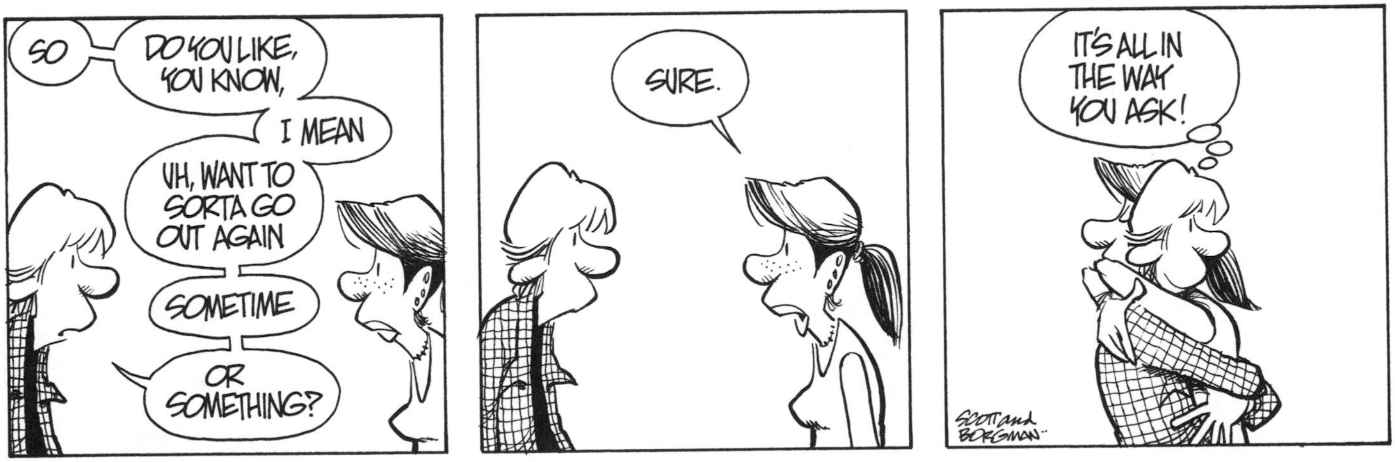
SO
DO YOU LIKE, YOU KNOW,
I MEAN
UH, WANT TO SORTA GO OUT AGAIN
SOMETIME
OR SOMETHING?
SURE.
IT'S ALL IN THE WAY YOU ASK!
SCOTT and BORGMAN

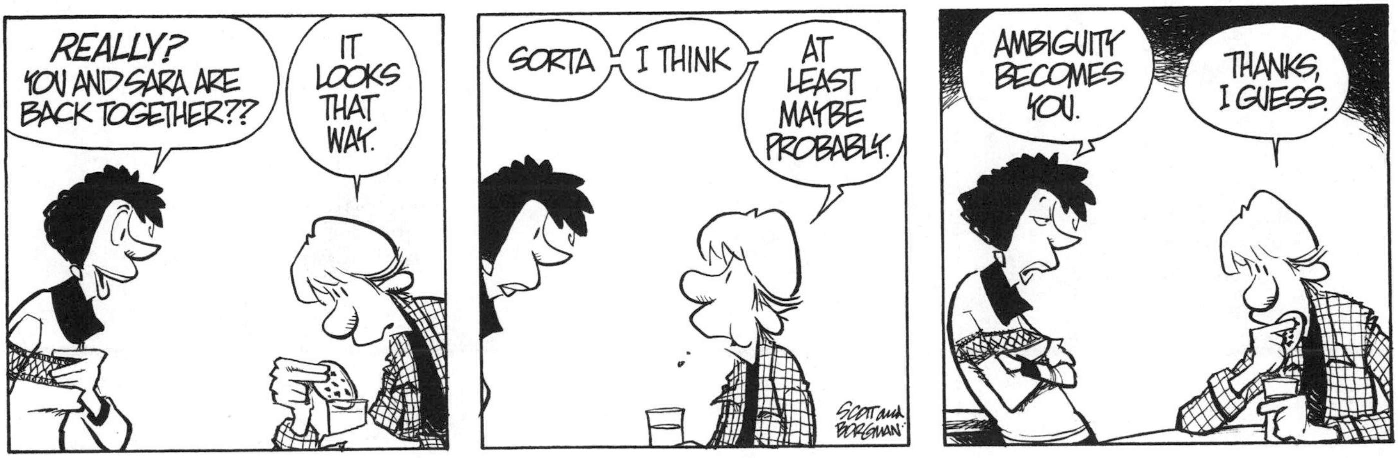
REALLY? YOU AND SARA ARE BACK TOGETHER??
IT LOOKS THAT WAY.
SORTA
I THINK
AT LEAST MAYBE PROBABLY.
SCOTT and BORGMAN
AMBIGUITY BECOMES YOU.
THANKS, I GUESS.

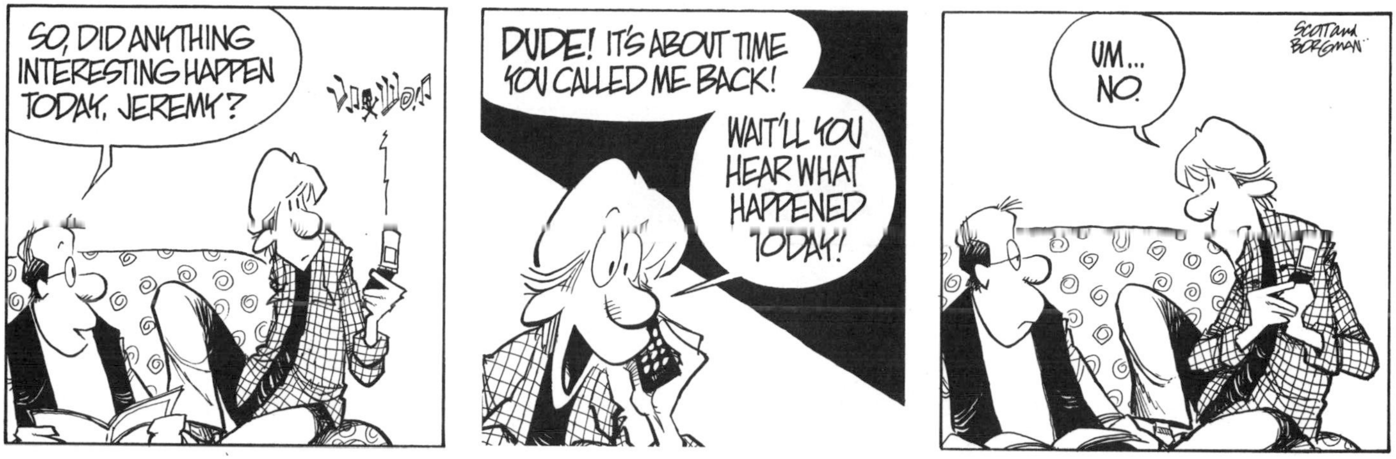
SO, DID ANYTHING INTERESTING HAPPEN TODAY, JEREMY?
DUDE! IT'S ABOUT TIME YOU CALLED ME BACK!
WAIT'LL YOU HEAR WHAT HAPPENED TODAY!
UM... NO.

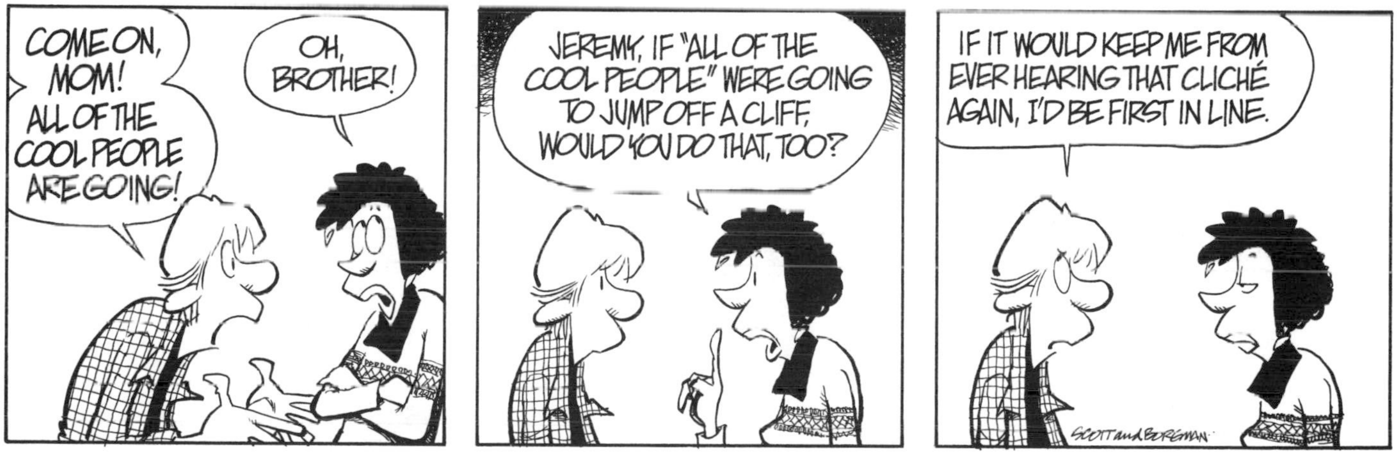
COME ON, MOM! ALL OF THE COOL PEOPLE ARE GOING!
OH, BROTHER!
JEREMY, IF "ALL OF THE COOL PEOPLE" WERE GOING TO JUMP OFF A CLIFF, WOULD YOU DO THAT, TOO?
IF IT WOULD KEEP ME FROM EVER HEARING THAT CLICHÉ AGAIN, I'D BE FIRST IN LINE.

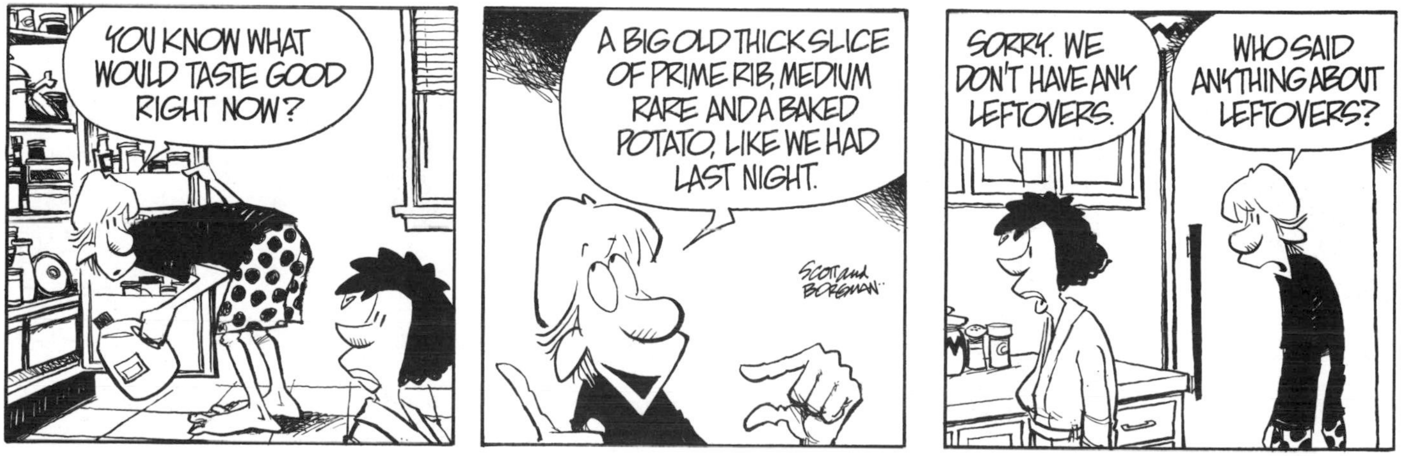
YOU KNOW WHAT WOULD TASTE GOOD RIGHT NOW?
A BIG OLD THICK SLICE OF PRIME RIB, MEDIUM RARE AND A BAKED POTATO, LIKE WE HAD LAST NIGHT.
SORRY. WE DON'T HAVE ANY LEFTOVERS.
WHO SAID ANYTHING ABOUT LEFTOVERS?

JERRY SCOTT and JIM BORGMAN
Zits

SCOTT and BORGMAN
n
10
ADOLESCENCE CAN BE A FRUSTRATING EQUATION
MY LIFE IS ONE BIG ALGEBRA PROBLEM.

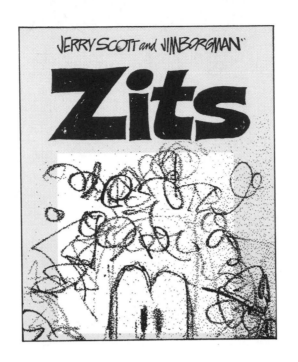

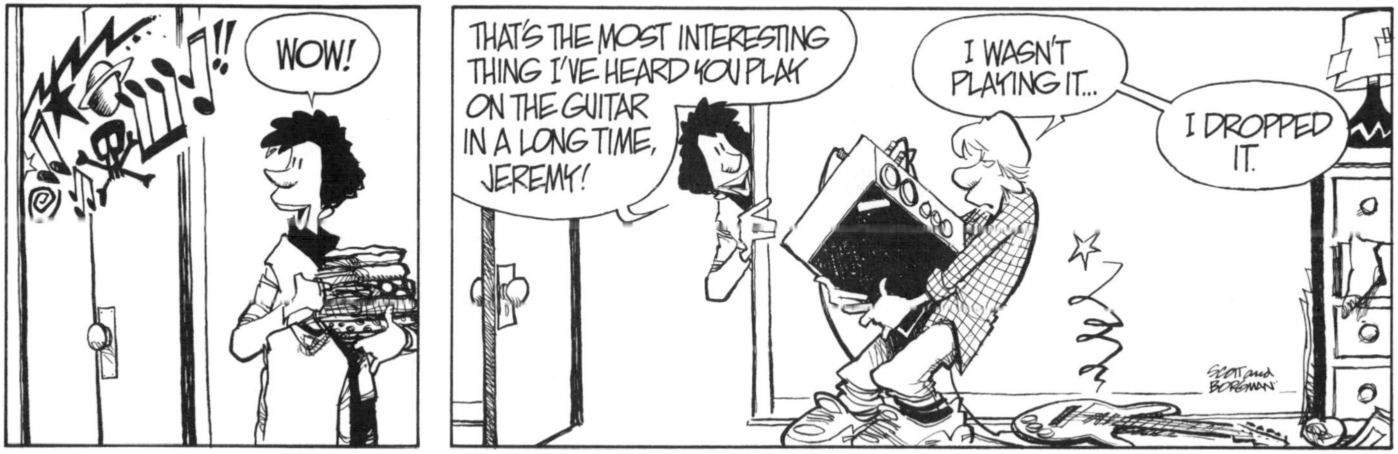
WOW!
THAT'S THE MOST INTERESTING THING I'VE HEARD YOU PLAY ON THE GUITAR IN A LONG TIME, JEREMY!
I WASN'T PLAYING IT...
I DROPPED IT.
SCOTT and BORGMAN

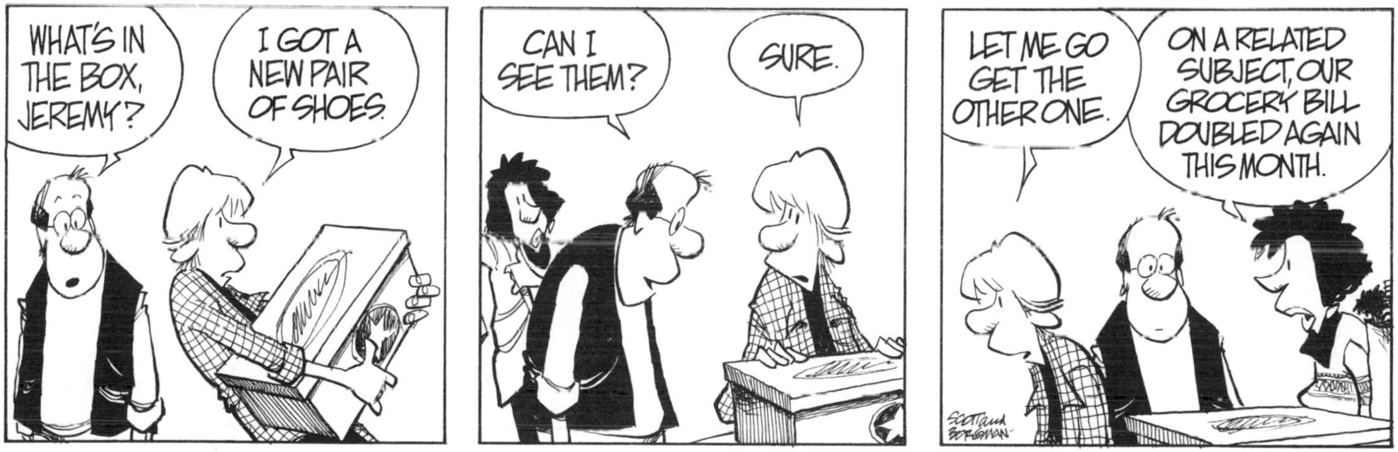
WHAT'S IN THE BOX, JEREMY?
I GOT A NEW PAIR OF SHOES.
CAN I SEE THEM?
SURE.
LET ME GO GET THE OTHER ONE.
ON A RELATED SUBJECT, OUR GROCERY BILL DOUBLED AGAIN THIS MONTH.
SCOTT and BORGMAN

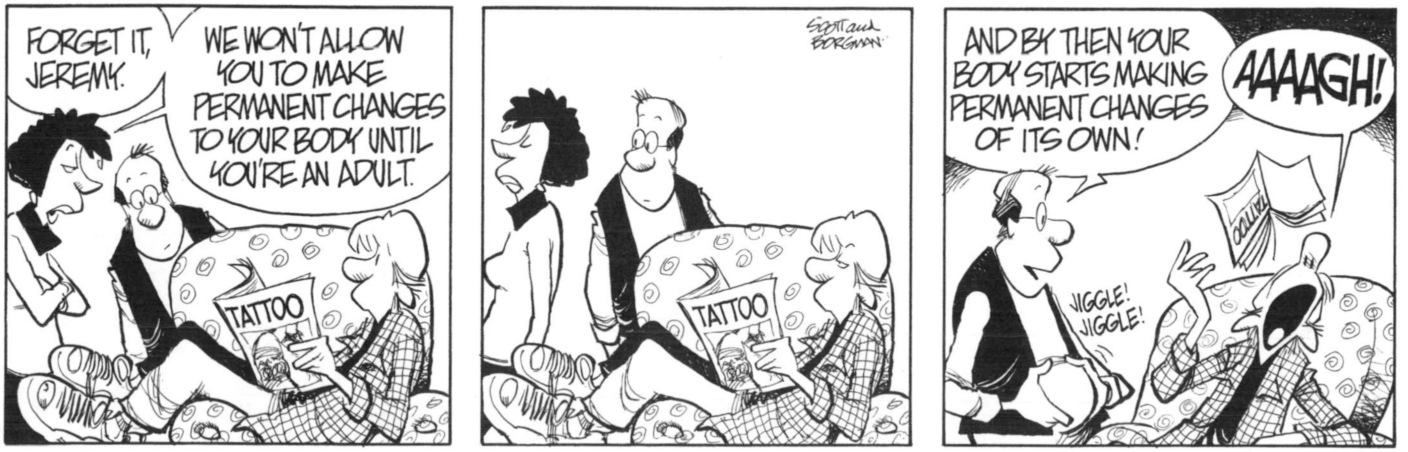
FORGET IT, JEREMY.
WE WON'T ALLOW YOU TO MAKE PERMANENT CHANGES TO YOUR BODY UNTIL YOU'RE AN ADULT.
TATTOO
SCOTT and BORGMAN
TATTOO
AND BY THEN YOUR BODY STARTS MAKING PERMANENT CHANGES OF ITS OWN!
AAAAGH!
JIGGLE! JIGGLE!

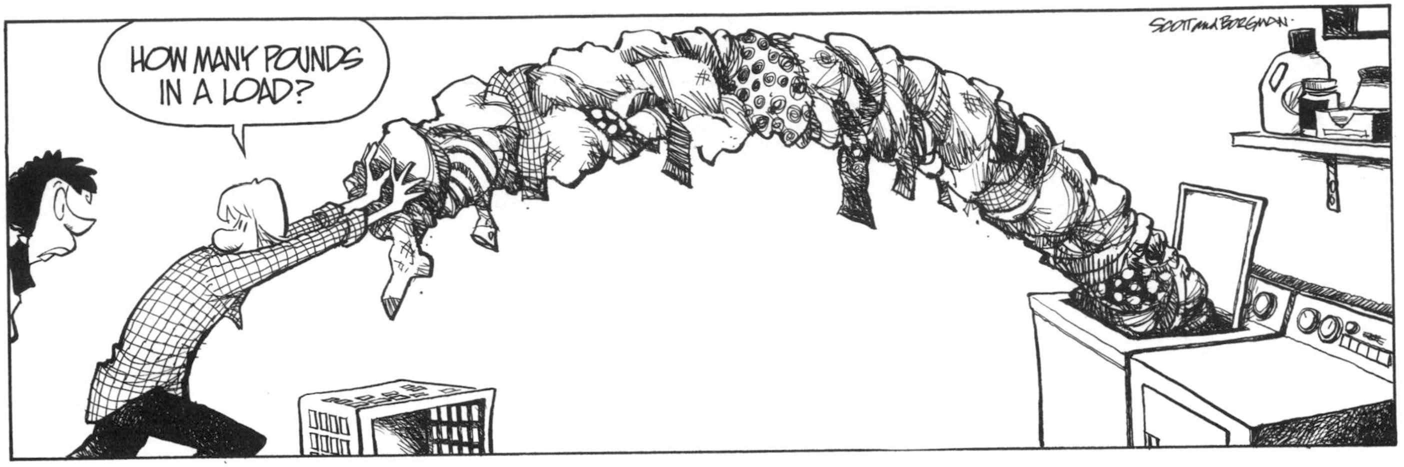
SCOTT and BORGMAN
HOW MANY POUNDS IN A LOAD?

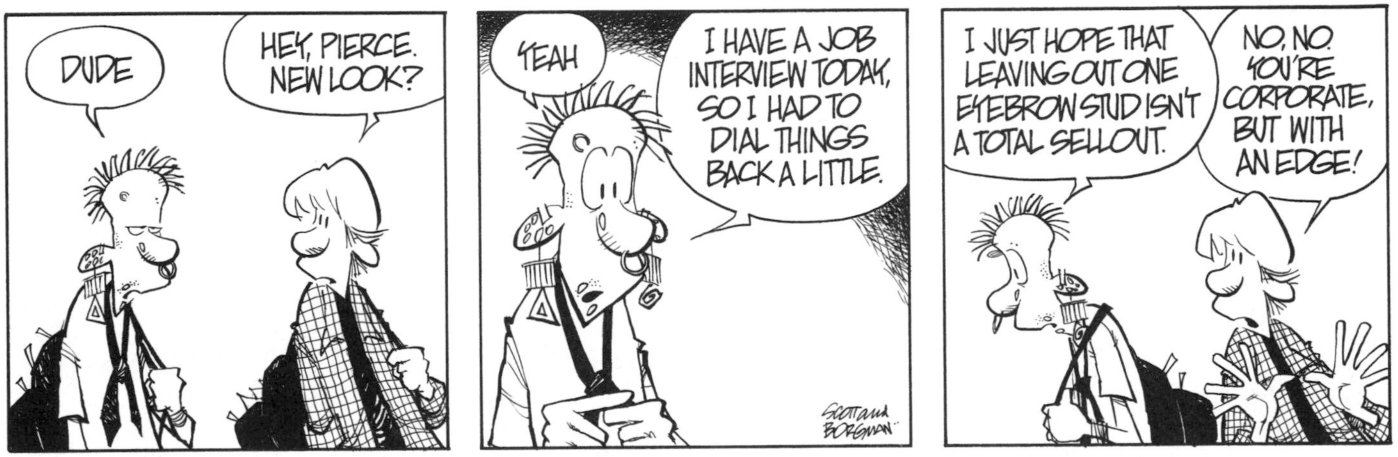
DUDE
HEY, PIERCE. NEW LOOK?
YEAH
I HAVE A JOB INTERVIEW TODAY, SO I HAD TO DIAL THINGS BACK A LITTLE.
SCOTT and BORGMAN
I JUST HOPE THAT LEAVING OUT ONE EYEBROW STUD ISN'T A TOTAL SELLOUT.
NO, NO. YOU'RE CORPORATE, BUT WITH AN EDGE!

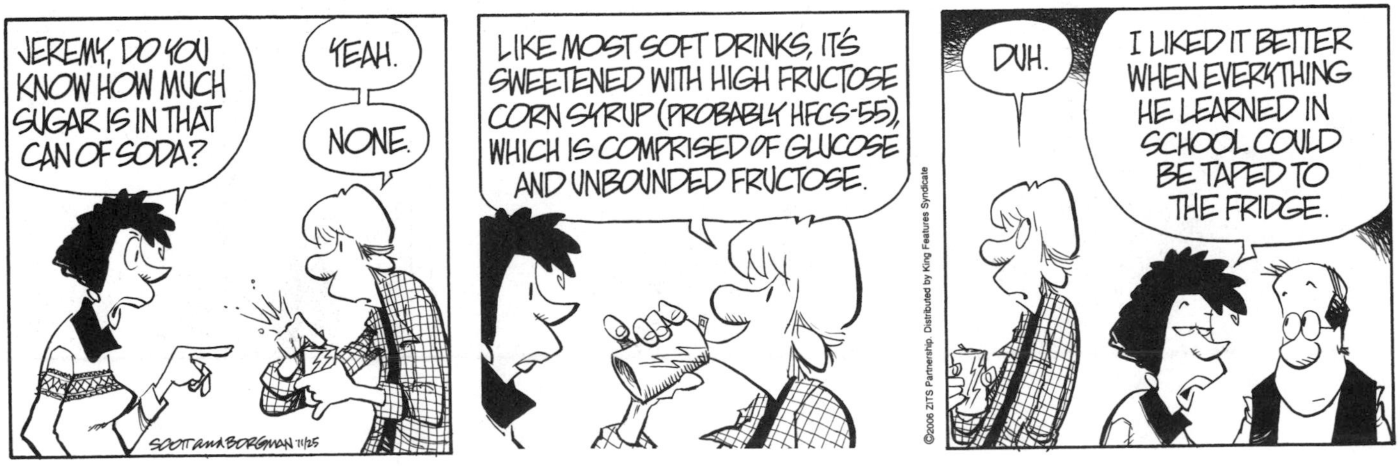
JEREMY, DO YOU KNOW HOW MUCH SUGAR IS IN THAT CAN OF SODA?
YEAH.
NONE.
SCOTT and BORGMAN 11/25
LIKE MOST SOFT DRINKS, IT'S SWEETENED WITH HIGH FRUCTOSE CORN SYRUP (PROBABLY HFCS-55), WHICH IS COMPRISED OF GLUCOSE AND UNBOUNDED FRUCTOSE.
DUH.
I LIKED IT BETTER WHEN EVERYTHING HE LEARNED IN SCHOOL COULD BE TAPED TO THE FRIDGE.

Zits
by JERRY SCOTT and JIM BORGMAN

HERE'S YOUR KEY.
HAD ENOUGH PRACTICE DRIVING IN AND OUT OF THE DRIVEWAY FOR ONE DAY, HUH?
NO
YOU'RE OUT OF GAS.
SCOTT and BORGMAN